TECHNOLOGY-MEDIATED LEARNING ENVIRONMENTS FOR YOUNG ENGLISH LEARNERS

CONNECTIONS IN AND OUT OF SCHOOL

EDITED BY

L. LEANN PARKER

UNIVERSITY OF CALIFORNIA, BERKELEY

Lawrence Erlbaum Associates
Taylor & Francis Group

New York   London

Lawrence Erlbaum Associates
Taylor & Francis Group
270 Madison Avenue
New York, NY 10016

Lawrence Erlbaum Associates
Taylor & Francis Group
2 Park Square
Milton Park, Abingdon
Oxon OX14 4RN

Library of Congress Cataloging-in-Publication Data

Parker, Leann.
  Technology-mediated learning environments for young English learners : connections in and out of school / L. Leann Parker.
     p. cm.
  Includes bibliographical references and index.
  ISBN 978-0-8058-6233-1
  1. English language--Computer-assisted instruction for foreign speakers. 2. English language--Study and teaching--Foreign speakers. 3. English language--Study and teaching--Technological innovations. 4. Information technology. 5. Educational technology. I. Title.

PE1128.3P37 2008
428.0285--dc22

2007016035

Visit the Taylor & Francis Web site at
http://www.taylorandfrancis.com

and the Routledge Mental Health Web site at
http://www.routledgementalhealth.com

For

T

Contents

Preface

Many of the increasing number of immigrant children from diverse linguistic and cultural backgrounds struggle to learn English well enough to succeed in schools in the United States. Their challenge is not only to learn English as a new language, but also to learn through the medium of English. They must develop the oral and reading skills necessary to learn new content and challenging concepts in various subject areas, to learn from oral instruction as well as textbooks, to gather information, to analyze and solve problems, and to express what they have learned in ways that are appropriate for the subject area as well as for the audience. Developing such language and literacy skills can take several years for children to be able to compete academically with their grade level peers who already have the advantage of English as a first language.

The challenge for educators is how to help children accomplish this task as effectively as possible. In the midst of the digital age, we are quick to turn to new technologies to seek possible solutions to such thorny educational issues. With a wide variety of language learning software available for computers, resources on the Internet, and electronic devices such as small mobile computers, game consoles, bilingual dictionaries, and electronic translation tools, it would appear that electronic and digital technologies offer much potential for helping children learn a second language. But, can these new technologies assist children from diverse backgrounds, especially children in the elementary grades, who are struggling to succeed in school and, if so, how and what factors are important to consider?

This book brings together a number of researchers to consider these little-explored questions. The chapters were originally prepared as a set of working papers for a project sponsored by the William and Flora Hewlett Foundation. For this book, other authors were asked to reflect on the chapters and provide additional perspectives. The chapters and reflections encourage readers to consider a range of social and cultural factors in utilizing technology as a tool to help elementary school-age children from diverse linguistic and cultural backgrounds develop their English and reading skills.

The authors examine key issues, significant research, and promising programs and strategies to address such questions by considering the role of technology in learning environments designed to enhance second language skills. In particular, they examine various dimensions of learning environments that affect the capacity of new technologies to fulfill their educational potential for young English learners. Among the themes woven throughout the chapters and reflections are the needs and perspectives of bilingual learners; the possibilities for specific technologies to support the development of second language and literacy skills in and out of school; new literacies of the Internet for multilingual learners in a globalized world; and design considerations for creating and assessing language learning environments. A contribution is the authors' efforts to consider ways that technology used outside of school can benefit English language development in school. The themes are integrated with implications for teaching, research, and bridging school and nonschool settings as contexts for developing second language skills that are important for school success. The authors who contributed to this volume have shown themselves to be passionate about providing educational opportunities to all students and about exploring ways to address the difficult issues facing young English learners and their educators in the 21st century digital world.

Acknowledgments

As with every edited volume, this one relies on the expertise and cooperation of the authors. The book is rich with their perceptive analyses and ideas, and I appreciate the authors' contributions, advice and support, and the substantial time and effort they spent in preparing and honing their thought-provoking chapters and reflections. My thanks also go to the William and Flora Hewlett Foundation for its support for the project which was the genesis of this book.

Any publication effort also owes much to others along the way for inspiration, insights, and suggestions. There are many, too numerous to mention, who have shared their time with me over the years and whose ideas have greatly influenced my thinking during this project. However, I would especially like to acknowledge Lily Wong Fillmore, professor emerita at the University of California at Berkeley, whose continuing concern for the well-being of young English learners has been a constant source of inspiration to me; Charles Underwood, executive director of the University–Community Links program, for our rich discussions about technology and learning, and his insights about uses of technology in informal after-school activities for children; and Joan Bissell, director of Teacher Education and Public School Programs at the California State University Chancellor's Office, who encouraged me to undertake this project in the first place. I am also grateful to Naomi Silverman, Erica Kica, and Joy Tatusko at Lawrence Erlbaum Associates and anonymous reviewers for their advice on shaping the book; their suggestions were invaluable. Last, but by no means least, my very special thanks go to Vince de'Armond for his technology expertise, counsel, and moral support throughout the preparation of this book.

—*L. Leann Parker*
Berkeley, California

1

Introduction

Technology-Mediated Learning Environments for Young English Learners

L. LEANN PARKER

University of California, Berkeley

"What do you suppose is the use of a child without any meaning?"

(The Red Queen, in Lewis Carroll's
***Through the Looking Glass,* 1986, p. 272)**

This book weaves together several themes related to its central focus on elementary school-age children in the United States from diverse cultures and language backgrounds[1] who are learning English. Among these themes are the importance of language skills, especially reading, for learning content and for school success; learning English and learning *through* English; ways that new electronic technologies can support children's English learning; and contexts for learning English in and out of school. Yet, the book is fundamentally about meaning and how children learn to make meaning in a new language and in new contexts, making the Red Queen's query about the use of a child without any meaning particularly apt. In short, the book is about how children from various language backgrounds learn to understand and make meaning in, and with, a new language, as well as to make meaning about themselves, and about the role of technology in the process. It is also about learning environments and how activities, technology and other tools, as well as to society affect language learning. The purpose of the present chapter is to introduce the central issues and concerns that led to the book, provide a theoretical framework for the discussions, and offer an overview of the chapters and reflections.

A continuing and pressing concern among educators in the United States is how to prepare children from diverse cultural and language backgrounds for later success in higher learning, careers, and society in general (e.g., see news reports such as Zehr, 2005). A wide range of factors has been found to affect English learners' academic success. Among these factors are: families' limited financial resources; academically and financially challenged schools; differences between home and school cultures; lack of understanding of the

American educational system; parents with limited educational attainment; negative perspectives that mainstream gate-keepers hold about families from diverse cultures and linguistic backgrounds; differences between educators' perceptions about, and uses of, literacy for learning in school; students' perceptions and uses of literacy outside of school; and students' limited knowledge of English (e.g., see Au, 1998; García, 2002; Jiménez, 2003; and Valdés, 1998 for more discussion). An important factor for many children is their struggle to learn English. It is the last factor that is the focus of this book.

Children from families with a primary language and cultural heritage different from that of the mainstream society in which they have come to live must learn the functional language needed to play games with their peers outside of school and to negotiate settings such as a grocery store or a doctor's office, but they must also learn the special oral and literate skills needed for academic achievement in school. The latter is often an obstacle to school success for many children who have to learn simultaneously the school culture, understand and participate in instructional activities, comprehend what they read in textbooks, and communicate in school-appropriate ways in class activities and on tests—all through a new language. In the process, they must make sense of themselves in these settings as bilinguals and as learners.

Although all immigrant students face these kinds of challenges no matter what age they enter U.S. schools, this book focuses on children at the elementary school level. It is at the primary grades when initial literacy skills are taught to all children, monolingual English speakers and newcomers alike, and when children make the transition from learning basic literacy skills to using language and literacy for learning new content. Some children succeed in this context; others do not. Many children from low-income families, particularly English learners, begin to fall behind around the fourth grade (Cummins, 2001; Jiménez, 2003) and continue to do poorly in school (see Durán, this volume). Because the elementary school years are important foundational years for learning, they are also important for examining questions of language learning and technology.

The challenge for English learners at school is to learn *academic language* or *academic English* (e.g., see Scarcella, 2003). Academic language requires oral and literacy skills to learn new and complex concepts through both oral instruction and written subject matter textbooks, understand various genres of written language (such as stories, poems, myths, essays, and explanations of factual information for different subject areas), and explain orally and in writing what one has understood or discovered. It is a version of English that has been influenced by extended written texts in which sentences are typically longer and syntactically more complex than in the informal language found in children's games on the playground, text-messaging with peers, or in daily activities such as riding a bus, grocery shopping, or interacting socially. Fluency in academic English involves more than knowledge of basic

English syntax, common vocabulary, and formulaic expressions needed for informal social situations. For literacy especially, it also involves facility with a wide range of rich vocabulary (August, 2003; August & Shanahan, 2006) that sometimes uses specific meanings (as in mathematics) and other times employs connotations, nuances, or figurative perspectives that may change depending on the subject area or genre. Fluency in academic English involves facility with the richness of the language for literature, science, and historical discussions and the accepted ways that professionals discuss concepts that are embodied in those disciplines. It involves oral language skills as well as reading and writing skills that are closely connected to critical thinking skills. This fluency evolves gradually throughout the school years for all students as they mature and experience different kinds of texts and uses of language in learning subject matter content, but it is a special challenge for children who are new to U.S. schools.

Immigrant children's limited knowledge of English reading and speaking skills has been of particular concern to educators in the United States, not only because these skills are crucial for learning in school, but also because of the amount of time it takes to learn English. It is not surprising that it takes most students their entire K–12 career or more to master this variety of English, because success in school involves progressively expanding and deepening one's knowledge of new content and the language forms—oral and written—in which concepts and instruction are embedded. The particular challenge for young English learners is to learn it quickly enough to keep up academically with their school peers who have the advantage of having English as their primary language. However, it takes several years for children to acquire the academic English skills necessary for school success in comparison with their native English speaking peers, which suggests that it is difficult to provide sufficient instructional support during the school day to help these learners acquire English more quickly (Hakuta, Butler, & Witt, 2000; Valdés, 1998).

These concerns raise the question of whether there are particular strategies or tools to expedite the English learning process both in and out of school so that English learners can flourish in school. Language educators have looked to electronic technologies for some time as a way to enhance second language development (see Chapelle, 2001; Salaberry, 2001; and chapters by Zhao and Lai and by Parker, this volume, for discussions). Although these efforts have typically focused on older learners (high school and college-level) who are already literate and have developed more sophisticated academic language skills than children in the elementary grades have achieved, there is a dazzling array of electronic and digital technologies that might be helpful for younger children. Thus, the central question examined in this book is: What is the potential of new technologies to assist younger children, especially those in the elementary grades who are struggling in school to develop their oral English and reading skills?

The purpose of the central chapters of the book is to address this question by framing major perspectives and themes, discussing significant research findings, highlighting important design considerations for technology-mediated English learning environments in and out of school, and providing illustrations of promising strategies and programmatic efforts. Through the reflections, additional voices expand on the themes raised in the central chapters and add new perspectives on the issues. An overview of each chapter and reflection is provided later.

A Sociocultural Framework for Second Language and Reading Development and Technology

A sociocultural perspective permeates the chapters and reflections, as they each highlight the importance of the contexts, activities, and interactions in which second language learning occurs and the way that physical and symbolic tools such as digital technologies and language itself facilitate, and are influenced by, language and reading development.

Sociocultural theories emphasize that learning in general is a social enterprise accomplished through interaction with others around tasks and activities. More specifically, learning is mediated by physical and symbolic tools, and influenced by their history, place, participants, political factors, and power relationships (Cole, 1999). Among the most significant influences on current theory and research about the role of society and culture on learning has been the work of Russian psychologists Lev Vygotsky (1962, 1978), and Alexander Luria (1928; cited in Cole 1999) during the 1920s and 1930s. Vygotsky and Luria believed that physical tools like hammers and symbolic or psychological tools like language and literacy, along with humans' activities and interactions with the physical world and with each other, mediate cognitive and linguistic development and learning. In their view, artifacts (physical objects) and symbols in one's culture not only influence the way people interact with the world, but also shape the way people think about the world. The result is that cognitive development and learning are intricately tied to each other (Cole, 1999; Wertsch, 1985). This perspective also emphasizes the historical dimension of contexts and physical and symbolic tools, which are transformed as cultures pass them on to succeeding generations. In turn, other generations continue to use and change these contexts and tools to meet their often-changing needs (Lantolf, 2000). Thus, tools evolve as they mediate how humans learn, think, and communicate. From this conception of learning, Western researchers have developed a richer understanding of the role of the social influences on learning (Minick, Stone, & Forman, 1993).

Activity theory, also referred to as *cultural historical activity theory,* following the work of Leontiev (1978; cited in Lantolf, 2000; also see Brown & Cole, 2002), provides an overall framework for sociocultural research on learning. From this perspective, activity involves doing something that is motivated by some need or goal that results in actions (operations) in particular times and places with appropriate tools. Activities are characterized and shaped by the settings, roles and relationships, goals of the participants, and by the specific uses of physical and symbolic tools, especially language. Because activities are socially, culturally, and historically framed, they may require special behaviors based on individuals' roles and social relations and may mean different things to different participants. Externally it may appear that participants are engaged in the same task, but internally they may be engaged in different activities; further, the overall activity may morph into a different kind of activity as the goals, relationships, and physical and symbolic tools change (Lantolf, 2000). Meaning—the interpretation of what is occurring through activity—is constructed by the participants both individually and collectively.

Learning how to use physical and symbolic tools and interpret contexts is shaped by communities of practice and by activities that are themselves motivated by goals and needs of participants and situated in a specific time, location, set of social relations, and use of tools (Brown & Cole, 2002; Brown, Collins, & Duguid, 1989; Lantolf, 2000; Lave & Wenger, 1991; Scribner & Cole, 1981). Vygotsky (1962, 1978) suggested that people learn through scaffolding from others who are already more experienced, a process that he called the *zone of proximal development* (ZPD). The ZPD refers to the difference between what one can do or learn in collaboration with others and what one can do alone, and the process by which one can move from one to the other (Lantolf, 2000; Vygotsky, 1978). It has also been interpreted as experts transmitting knowledge to novices through practice, which in time comes to constitute a community of practice (e.g., see Lantolf, 2000; Lave & Wenger, 1991). This ecology of collaborative opportunities or affordances supports cognitive as well as linguistic development (Van Lier, 2000). Some have observed that the effectiveness of ZPD varies according to the expertise of the expert, the nature of tasks, participants' goals, and developmental levels of learners (Ohta, 2000).

Interaction serves as a way by which learners can control their own mental processes and function independently. In other words, learners (novices) do not imitate the skills of experts, but rather adapt and, to some extent, reconstruct or transform what experts model for them. As participants in groups, learners' skills and knowledge are co-constructed through group dynamics and interaction (Lantolf, 2000). However, what is learned can be strongly influenced by power relationships, resulting in either failure to learn or in privileged opportunities to learn. Anthropological work showing how children in different cultures become competent adults reflects this sociocultural framework (e.g., see Schieffelin & Ochs, 1986).

Like Vygotsky, Bakhtin also believed that social processes are paramount in both learning in general and learning language in particular (see Purcell-Gates, Jacobson, & Degener, 2004; Zuengler & Miller, 2006, for discussions). For Bakhtin, oral language and literacy are based on shared meanings of words among speakers and listeners or readers and writers, but words and sentences can have different meanings in different contexts. He used the concept of dialogism to link interaction and context. From his perspective, language is not neutral but inherently ideological and political. Learning the language of the community involves "appropriating" words and ways of speaking in particular situations from other people in the community, and it transforms their roles and understandings in the process (Rogoff, 1995; Zuengler & Miller, 2006).

Another emphasis of sociocultural theory has been called critical theory. Although the social nature of learning is central, critical theory focuses on power relations among the participants. Proponents of critical theory are especially concerned about the ways that power relationships can inhibit access to learning and other resources by marginalized groups in society. By valuing some identities and not others, power relationships can affect how learners see themselves as learners and members of that society (Zuengler & Miller, 2006). For Freire (1970), the role of education and literacy was to help marginalized groups of people to question the power relationships in their world.

From a sociocultural perspective, language and nonverbal communication involve a social process. Its forms, meanings, and conventions are shaped over time by their use in particular contexts (Gee, 2001; Kramsch, 2000; Orellana, 2004). Language is an aggregation of genres and semiotic devices (such as oral and written language) associated with particular contexts (like classrooms and the playground), social institutions (like school and home) and practices (like games and lessons), rather than an abstract and decontextualized system (Gee, 2004; Minick, Stone, & Forman, 1993). Gee (2004) argues that language, genres, and their appropriateness in specific contexts are acquired through socialization into *Discourses* (with a capital D), or cultural models of ways of communicating through oral or written language, interpreting, valuing, and interacting, and as such are *identity kits* for participants as they move through various contexts and activities.

Not only are there Discourse forms used by communities for their day-to-day lives, but there are also Discourse forms and registers for academic disciplines. Scientists, for example, have specific ways of using language, communicating, reporting, working, analyzing, interpreting, and valuing that are different from that of poets or business managers. Learning the knowledge of these fields requires learning something of their accepted discourses, beliefs, and rhetorical styles (Lemke, 2000). School language is a form of academic language, in that it involves uses of language for such purposes as inquiry, explanation, and taking standardized tests. As has already been discussed, school learning requires more than basic aspects of grammar and general ways of speaking and reading; it requires learning and to some extent adopting the registers appropriate to the culture of school and appropriate to different subject areas (Lemke, 2000).

Sociocultural theory also suggests that thinking and speaking are interrelated rather than separate, such that one's privately developed thoughts can only be revealed through language and, conversely, that language is evidence of thought (Lantolf, 2000). It is through this interrelationship of thought and language that *inner speech* to oneself helps regulate an individual's actions and thinking that, in turn, is internalized into higher or more complex thinking. In this view, rather than imitating others or memorizing linguistic forms abstracted from specific context, children acquire their native language and literacy skills (as well as other forms of knowledge) from the way the language is used by competent adults and older children in the context of the community. From a Bakhtian perspective, they appropriate the speech patterns and uses of language from adults and other peers through engagement in meaningful social activities, in which linguistic forms and gestures are tools used to influence meaning and the behavior of others and oneself (Kramsch, 2000; Minick, Stone, & Forman, 1993; Van Lier, 2000). In this way, children learn to participate as competent members of the community.

Learning a second or third language is thus not simply a matter of mapping new labels and meanings onto the learners' primary language. Rather, it requires reconfiguring the ways symbols are used and what they mean according to how they are used and what they mean by fluent speakers of the language in specific meaningful contexts (Kramsch, 2000). The interrelation among linguistic, cognitive, and social factors and strategies affects what children learn about their second language (García, 2002). Second language development is also affected by the learner's culture, self-concept or identity, attitudes, and goals in relation to the new language and group (Norton & Toohey, 2001), and it has been suggested that learners construct somewhat different identities when speaking different languages or dialects to become more like native speakers (Lemke, 2000). Social and cultural factors are powerful forces on second language learning and cognitive development. García (2002), for example, suggests that it is important for school cultures to build on immigrant children's home culture and language in order to enhance their cognitive development and their academic language abilities in both English and their primary language.

Literacy development is also affected by context, shared meanings and practices, and interaction. As Purcell-Gates, Jacobson, and Degener (2004) explain, the same written words take on different meanings when read in different contexts. Researchers with this perspective focus on *multiliteracies* that emphasize cultural and language diversity and various modes of communications (Schultz & Hull, 2002). Literacy is situated in social and cultural practices, power relationships, and discourses (Street, 1984). It varies by domain, conventions, and practices set and valued by social institutions, and by history and can change over time (Barton & Hamilton, 2000, cited in Purcell-Gates, Jacobson, & Degener, 2004). Ways of thinking, believing, and behaving in these contexts affect the way groups use literacy and how they interpret the meaning of texts (Gee, 2004; Gee, 1996, cited in Schultz & Hull, 2002; Heath, 1983; Lam, 2004; Purcell-Gates, Jacobson, & Degener, 2004; Scribner & Cole, 1985; Street, 1984). The kind of literacy required for participating in school activities is but one of many forms of literacy.

Electronic technologies constitute another set of tools for communicating, learning, thinking, and creation of identity. Like other tools, electronic technologies are shaped by the ways they are used in specific sociocultural settings and by specific groups (Jonassen & Land, 2000). For education, it is important to understand what students can learn with technology as well as from it (Jonassen, Carr, & Yueh, 1998; Labbo & Reinking, 1999). Researchers working from a sociocultural perspective have tended to focus on the contexts and activities of learning created through technologies (as in educational software products); on uses of technology to support instructional activities; on learners' uses of various electronic tools such as e-mail and the Internet for collaboration, communication, information gathering, and creation and presentation of ideas and understandings of what one has learned; and on the implications of these technologies on society and education.

In particular, sociocultural research has focused on how technology can support the development of literacy skills, complex and critical thinking, and problem-solving through communities of practice. Technology provides "mind tools" for constructing and representing knowledge, as well as for communicating and collaborating (see Gee, 2003; Jonassen, 2000; Jonassen & Land, 2000; Jonassen et al., 1998). Sociocultural research has also investigated learners' perspectives about the technology and how that impacts literacy (e.g., see Anderson-Inman & Horney, 1998).

The social implications of using technology for learning have been another emphasis of sociocultural research. For example, some research has emphasized the importance of bringing children's culture into the contexts and activities mediated by technology (e.g., see Lee, 2003; Pinkard, 1999; Selfe & Hawisher, 2004). A major focus of discussion has been the larger societal issues of technology. It has included, for example, explorations of the globalization of new technologies and the importance of English as the predominant language for information on the Internet (Warschauer, 2004), and concerns about access to technology for underserved linguistically and culturally different children and families—the "digital divide" (Selfe & Hawisher, 2004; Warschauer, 2002). This societal focus has led to discussions of how technology has influenced culture, especially in the United States. The technology culture values speed, informality, debate, multitasking, efficient communication, and sense of agency for authorship, control, and creativity (see Kern, 2006). It is a culture in which many children, especially those from affluent mainstream affluent families, are becoming digital natives (Prensky, 2001).

Yet another line of emphasis has focused on ways that technology, particularly the Internet, affects the kind of literacy skills that students will need (Coiro, 2003; Leu, Kinzer, Coiro, & Cammack, 2004; Warschauer, 2004). For example, in addition to decoding and comprehension skills, new literacies of the Internet include the ability to comprehend nonlinear text (or hypertext[2]) that allows readers to pursue information other than what may be intended by the author; multimedia texts that involve text, graphics, and sound that may require good listening and visual comprehension skills as well as good reading skills; and interactive texts that allow readers to add to or react to text as part of the reading experience (Coiro, 2003).

Before closing this section, it should be noted that there has been a continuing debate in the fields of literacy and second language learning about the importance of sociocultural as opposed to cognitive theories of second language learning and literacy development (see Pearson, 2004; Purcell-Gates, Jacobson, & Degener, 2004; and Zuengler & Miller, 2006, for discussions).[3] Although the goal for Vygotsky (1962, 1978) was to understand how sociocultural contexts and tools (including language) result in cognitive development, the debates in both fields have had important implications for research and pedagogy. For example, in contrast to research that focuses on social and interactional factors in language learning, cognitive-oriented research tends to separate acquisition from use and, often using metaphors of information processing, to focus on how learners acquire specific grammatical forms of the new language. Some researchers have emphasized the importance of both theories and have advocated balancing the two theoretical approaches both in second language research and in reading research (Pearson, 2004; Purcell-Gates, Jacobson, & Degener, 2004; Zuengler & Miller, 2006); however, the theories stem from fundamentally different perspectives, and their separate points of origin raise issues about the possibility of aligning them (Zuengler & Miller, 2006). Although the chapters in this volume have a strong sociocultural stance, there are echoes of cognitive perspectives in some chapters, especially in the descriptions of specific technological tools and educational software used to teach second language and reading skills. Uses of technology for education (e.g., to have children practice pronunciation or common vocabulary words) have often been informed by a cognitive theoretical perspective. This debate raises interesting theoretical questions for the future. Although this book does not address the issue of either reconciling or settling these theoretical questions, the questions nonetheless hover behind the perspectives on second language and literacy development this book presents.

Overview of the Chapters and Reflections

To analyze the potential of technology for second language development, the contributors to this book take different tacts to examine issues of context, activity, language, identity, history, power, and electronic technologies. Their central focus is on how these factors affect children with linguistic and cultural backgrounds different from that represented by mainstream schools and children. Together, the chapters and reflections weave together themes relating to English learners and their linguistic and cultural heritage, the development of oral language and reading skills, considerations for instructional design of learning environments, new literacies engendered by digital technologies, the implications of a globalized society brought about by new technologies, and the implications for research and teaching. Summaries cannot do justice to the richness of the chapters and reflections; the following discussion briefly touches on some of their highlights.

The central issue for chapters 2, 3, and 4, and the related reflections is literacy for young English learners and sociocultural issues around technology and academic success. The chapters and reflections begin with a focus on literacy development for Latino children, then move to an examination of issues involved in assessing and creating effective learning environments for literacy and academic achievement, and then a discussion of principles for enhancing the education of multilingual children in a globalized world.

Chapter 2, "Technology and Literacy Development of Latino Youth," by Richard Durán, examines the role of technology for young English learners by emphasizing learners' circumstances and the importance of meaningful activities to build vocabulary development and literacy skills needed for academic learning. He focuses on Latino children, who are part of the largest and fastest growing group of students in U.S. schools. Latino children tend to come from low-income homes where Spanish is spoken natively, do less well in school than their mainstream peers, and have limited access to technology at home. The issue for Durán is how computer-based activities that respect Latino children's cultural and linguistic needs can be used to support their literacy development. Drawing on a cultural psychology perspective, he discusses the importance of children developing a strong sense of their identity as learners, readers, and speakers of English and having access to settings and activities that help them construct meaning for new subject matter concepts and the associated ways of talking about them in English. Durán sees technology playing an important role in developing literacy skills for Latino children when utilized in ways that help children make sense of written English. Using several in-depth examples, he analyzes how specific kinds of technology-mediated instructional strategies and informal activities can be crucial to helping elementary school-aged children develop the kinds of literacy, higher order thinking, and communication skills they need to be more successful in school.

Robert Rueda then considers Durán's chapter in the reflection for chapter 2, "Literacy and English Learners: Where Does Technology Fit?" He emphasizes that having a facility with technology is "a requirement" for anyone who hopes to participate effectively in the current world, including children from diverse groups, but cautions that some of the same differentials of access, instruction, and achievement across groups that characterize schooling in general may be replicated in the uses of technology in schools. He reminds us, too, that groups labeled "Latinos" or "English learners" are not homogenous, and that technology and literacy are not neutral but influenced by social, cultural, educational, and historical contexts. To make technology an effective tool for literacy development and to design appropriate learning environments, Rueda argues that it is important to consider children's prior experience with the technologies in other settings and to consider our expectations for how children will use these tools later.

Chapter 3, "Technology, Literacy, and Young Second Language Learners: Designing Educational Futures," by Jim Cummins, examines how technologies can promote academic success for low-income English learners by supporting reading comprehension and academic literacy. Cummins emphasizes the importance of academic literacy rather than the development of conversational fluency, which most bilingual children develop rather quickly in naturalistic conversational settings with peers or through direct instruction and the development of discrete language skills such as phonology, grammar, and spelling. From his perspective, technology-based interventions that support reading comprehension, especially vocabulary development and extensive reading in both English and in children's primary language, are a good investment, especially when technology is used in activities that involve constructivist and experiential approaches to transmit information and support higher order thinking skills. Cummins emphasizes that such technology interventions may be especially effective when classroom instruction allows children to invest themselves in the activities and talk with native English speakers about what they are creating. He elaborates on these themes by outlining specific principles for creating and evaluating technology-mediated learning environments designed to teach academic English. He uses these criteria to assess the potential of several different exemplary activities and programs. His design principles suggest that educational software that promotes literacy and content knowledge through collaborative inquiry and knowledge-building and that technology tools that enable children to develop and present their own creations are particularly well-suited to facilitating academic literacy development for young English learners.

In her reflection, "Rules of Engagement for Achieving Educational Futures," Olga Vásquez extends Cummins' vision of how technology can support academic literacy to serve nonmainstream English learners. Echoing Castek and colleagues (this volume), Vásquez focuses on the larger political context of education and envisions a world that is "culturally diverse, multilingual, and democratic" fostered through "collaboration, creativity, technological versatility, and a global and critical perspective." She extends Cummins' design considerations for developing and assessing technology-based programs by proposing four rules of engagement for creating second language learning contexts that reflect a globally and technologically connected world but yet provide links among home, school, and community. Vásquez culminates her reflection with a rich, in-depth example of the impact of an innovative after-school program called *La Clase Mágica*, which she developed with sociocultural principles in mind.

Building on the theory that language and literacy are socially constructed processes and influenced by larger societal contexts, chapter 4, "Developing New Literacies Among Multilingual Learners in the Elementary Grades," by Jill Castek, Donald J. Leu, Jr., Julie Coiro, Mileidis Gort, Laurie A. Henry, and Clarisse O. Lima, focuses on the implications of new literacies for online reading comprehension. Viewing multilingualism as an important national asset for creating citizens for a global society, the authors advocate building on the language and cultural resources that multilingual children bring. Observing that literacy is transformed as technologies advance and change, they discuss how new literacies are essential to participating in a global society and merit attention from the educational community. The authors also argue that language and literacy are global in nature and are affected by new technologies that enable people to interact immediately with others in different parts of the world. The authors go on to lay out a set of integrated principles grounded in research for developing these new kinds of literacy skills, and then use them to analyze technology-based programmatic models, including several out of school technology-based projects, online international pen pal projects, and collaborative inquiry projects that can be done either in or out of school.

In her reflection, "Integrating Language, Culture, and Technology to Achieve New Literacies for All," Bridget Dalton considers several dimensions of technology-mediated learning environments: design principles that focus on a broad range of learners; the needs of bilingual learners; research to inform design of digital learning environments; and the importance of influencing publishers, Web site designers, and schools to take into account the needs of a bilingual learners when they create or purchase educational software tools. Her focus on design principles for educational software emphasizes multiple ways of representing concepts, learners expressing their learning, and engaging learners by meeting a broad range of needs. Based on experience and findings from her and her colleagues' research on what works with technology, Dalton offers suggestions for harnessing new technology-mediated learning environments to support English literacy by taking into account bilingual and struggling learners as well as monolinguals and adept learners.

The next two chapters and their related reflections shift the focus from literacy to the potential of electronic technologies to develop second language competence. With chapter 5, "Technology and Second Language Learning: Promises and Problems," Yong Zhao and Chun Lai discuss the role of technology in developing primarily oral second language skills. These authors observe that much of the research in second language learning and technology has investigated adult foreign language learners rather than children, the development of specific linguistic skills rather than the learning process as a whole, and the role of individual technologies rather than how different technologies might complement each other in comprehensive second language learning environments. Reviewing research evidence, Zhao and Lai analyze the potential of specific technologies to provide essential contextual conditions that research has identified as essential for acquiring new linguistic forms and the knowledge of how to use them appropriately in specific settings. However, their purpose is broader. They ask readers to rethink the use of technology inside and outside the classroom, in terms of ecologies of learning and to consider taking advantage of "older" as well as newer digital technologies that may be found in children's homes. Offering recommendations for policy research and practice, they expand on these themes by describing their vision of how a comprehensive and coherent technology-mediated environment might foster authentic second language learning by bridging instruction in school with support outside of school.

Gary Cziko expands on Zhao and Lai's discussion of technologies in his reflection, "Technology and Second Language Learning: Current Resources, Tools and Techniques," by commenting on various technology resources, tools, and techniques that may assist teachers in individualizing second language learning. Cziko's perspective of language and language learning resonates with a sociocultural theoretical perspective, as he sees language as a tool for acquiring knowledge and skills, for social interaction, and for controlling the environment. He also sees language learning as purposeful and children as learners who follow their own interests and goals for learning. Describing a wide array of technological tools with specific suggestions for younger learners, he shows how such tools can provide access to authentic uses of the new language (input) as well as interaction and feedback, and support language learner autonomy. By using these kinds of tools, Cziko suggests that learners will not only learn how to use the technologies (an important consideration to others in this volume), but at the same time will learn the English language skills to fulfill their goals and interests.

In chapter 6, "Technology in Support of Young English Learners in and out of School." I also examine the potential of technologies to develop second language abilities, focusing on those used for second language learning among children. In addition to discussing a number of technological tools from television to the Internet and videogame consoles, I pay particular attention to the characteristics that virtual language learning environments found in language-teaching software programs offer elementary school-age children. These products typically introduce and provide practice on specific vocabulary and grammatical patterns, albeit often in engaging and multimedia ways, rather than emulating the kinds of naturalistic contexts in which children learn a new language, in part because of the current limitations of technology such as speech recognition. The broader issue in this chapter is the extent to which these tools and educational software products can help children from diverse backgrounds develop the English language and literacy they need for school. A major portion of the chapter is devoted to discussing the importance of individual and sociocultural factors such as use of technology as a mediating tool in instruction; the role of teachers; children's face-to-face talk about computers or educational software; cultural relevance of technology tools and educational software; the multiple complexities of access in and out of school; and individual learners' perspectives. The chapter concludes with a discussion of implications of these findings for both in-school and out-of-school settings, design and development, and research.

In her reflection, "ELLs and Technology: Transforming Teaching and Learning," Carla Meskill considers the role of technology in the constellation of factors that affect teaching language and literacy skills to English language learners (ELLs). Advancing a sociocultural and ecological perspective of second language learning, she explains that language learning comes not from the educational software program on the computer screen, but from the talk among children about what they are doing, guided by the instructional goals and ancillary literacy activities in conjunction with the computer. In this way technology can serve as a prompt for face-to-face authentic interaction and provide opportunities to understand English through multimedia means. It can also provide publishing tools by which English learners can express themselves in a supportive environment and at the same time demonstrate what they have learned. As the key to creating such language development environments is the teacher, it is not surprising that Meskill also suggests technology as a tool for teacher professional development.

The final chapter turns our attention once again to the English language learners (ELLs) themselves and the special resources and needs they bring. In chapter 7, "Technology Opening Opportunities for ELL Students: Attending to the Linguistic Character of these Students," Eugene E. García is concerned with how traditional schooling typically excludes the histories, experiences, and especially language skills of students from diverse cultural and linguistic backgrounds, even though these factors provide important cognitive and social foundations for learning, for acquiring a second language, and for succeeding in school. For such reasons, García argues that it is essential that bilingual students not be excluded from new technological tools. He argues that advanced technologies offer powerful tools for enhancing educational experiences for bilingual students by building on primary language and culture, by offering them complex inquiry and problem-solving activities in various subject areas that foster critical thinking and cognitive development, by helping them learn appropriate uses of language for different subject areas, and by enabling them to enrich their primary language. To illustrate how technologies might accomplish these goals, he suggests computer-supported collaborative learning (CSCL), a model that has been successfully used for building science concept and language skills. He shows how various tools in these online environments provide rich visual contexts that structure and scaffold learners' understanding of both science concepts and academic language associated with the topic. An important advantage of new technologies for García is that by offering a wide variety of tools in the students' primary language (e.g., multilingual and multimedia glossaries), computer-supported collaborative learning can help bilingual children build academic language skills in their primary language as well as in English.

To conclude the book, the Afterword, "Reflections on Technology for Young English Learners," briefly highlights some of the key themes and conclusions running through the various chapters and reflections. Throughout the discussion is the notion that strategically organized learning environments are crucial for technologies to make a difference in the English development of children from diverse circumstances.

Acknowledgment

The author would like to thank Charles Underwood for suggestions on an earlier version of this chapter.

Notes

1. In this chapter, I refer to young English learners in various ways. What we call children from diverse cultures and linguistic groups is problematic. Authors in this book and elsewhere have used various terminology such as English learners, English language learners (ELLs), minority language children, children of color, bilingual children, immigrant children, children from culturally and linguistically different backgrounds, children from economically disadvantaged homes, children from low-income families. The variation in terminology reflects something of the heterogeneity among children who are not "mainstream" but who nonetheless share common circumstances. There is much diversity among children from diverse backgrounds, as Robert Rueda aptly points out in his reflection in this volume, and any analyses need to take these differences as well as commonalities into account. These issues are not the focus of this book, but I raise them here as a reminder that it is an area deserving continued dialogue.

2. Hypertext is a way of constructing nonlinear digital text, where links permit the text to branch to topics through hyperlinks or cross-references to other documents by which the computer loads the relevant document or information (see Wikipedia, http://www.wikipedia.com and http://www.thefreedictionary.com for more information).

3. It should also be noted that the field of second language acquisition is not dominated by a single theory. In addition to sociocultural and cognitive theories, for example, there are interactionist theories that focus on discourse; systemic-functional linguistics theories that focus on registers and genres in computer-mediated communication, and semiotic theories that address issues of meaning through multimedia modes of expression (Kern, 2006).

References

Anderson-Inman, L., & Horney, M. A. (1998). Transforming text for at-risk readers. In D. Reinking, M. C. McKenna, L. D. Labbo, & R. D. Kieffer (Eds.), *Handbook of technology and literacy: Transformations in a post-typographic world* (pp. 15–44). Mahwah, NJ: Erlbaum.

Au, K. (1998). Social constructivism and the school literacy learning of students of diverse backgrounds. *Journal of Literacy Research, 30*(2), 297–319.

August, D. (2003). *Supporting the development of English literacy in English language learners: Key issues and promising practices.* Baltimore, MD: Center for Research on the Education of Students Placed At Risk (CRESPAR)/Johns Hopkins University.

August, D., & T. Shanahan (2006). Executive summary: *Developing literacy in second-language learners: Report of the National Literacy Panel on Language-Minority Children and Youth.* Mahwah, NJ: Erlbaum. Retrieved from the Center for Applied Linguistics website, May 22, 2006, http://www.cal.org/natl-lit-panel/reports/Executive_Summary.pdf.

Brown, K., & Cole, M. (2002). Cultural historical activity theory and the expansion of opportunities for learning after school. In G. Wells & G. Claxton (Eds.), *Learning for life in the twenty-first century: Sociocultural perspectives on the future of education* (pp. 225–238). Oxford, UK: Blackwell. Retrieved July 31, 2006 from http://129.171.53.1/blantonw/dClhse/publications/tech/cole-chat-exp.html.

Brown, J. S., Collins, A., & Duguid, P. (1989). Situated cognition and the culture of learning. *Educational Researcher, 18,* 32–42.

Carroll, L., & Tenniel, J. (1986). *Alice in wonderland and Through the looking glass.* Grosset & Dunlap.

Chapelle, C. A. (2001). *Computer applications in second language acquisition: Foundations for teaching, testing, and research.* Cambridge, UK: Cambridge University Press.

Coiro, J. (2003). Reading comprehension on the Internet: Expanding our understanding of reading comprehension to encompass new literacies. *The Reading Teacher, 56,* 446–453. Also available from Reading Online at http://www.readingonline.org/electronic/elec_index.asp?HREF=rt/2-03_column/index.html.

Cole, M. (1999). Cultural psychology: Some general principles and a concrete example. In Y. Engestrom, R. Miettinen & R.-L. Punamaki (Eds.), *Perspectives on activity theory* (pp. 87–106). Cambridge, UK: Cambridge University Press.

Cummins, J. (2001, September/October). Magic bullets and the fourth grade slump: Solutions from technology? *NABE News, 25,* 4–6.

Freire, P. (1970). *Pedagogy of the oppressed* (M. B. Ramos, Trans.). New York: Seabury Press.

García, E. E. (2002). Bilingualism and schooling in the United States. *International Journal of the Sociology of Language, 155/156,* 1–92.

Gee, J. P. (2001). Reading as situated language: A sociocognitive perspective. *Journal of Adolescent & Adult Literacy, 44*(8), 714–725.

Gee, J. P. (2003). *What video games have to teach us about learning and literacy.* New York: Palgrave MacMillan.

Gee, J. P. (2004). Reading as situated language: A sociocognitive perspective. In R. B. Ruddell & N. J. Unrau (Eds.), *Theoretical models and processes of reading* (5th ed.; pp. 116–132). Newark, DE: International Reading Association.

Hakuta, K., Butler, Y., & Witt, D. (2000). How long does it take English learners to attain proficiency? *University of California Linguistic Minority Research Institute Policy Report 2000–1.* Retrieved February 5, 2003, from http://lmri.ucsb. edu/publications/policyreports.php#00_hakuta.

Heath, S. B. (1983). *Ways with words.* New York: Cambridge University Press.

Jiménez, R. T. (2003). The interaction of language, literacy, and identity in the lives of Latina/o students. In R. L. McCormack & J. R. Paratore (Eds.), *After early intervention, then what? Teaching struggling readers in grades 3 and beyond* (pp. 25–38). Newark, DE: International Reading Association.

Jonassen, D. H. (2000). Revisiting activity theory as a framework for designing student-centered learning environments. In D. H. Jonassen & S. M. Land (Eds.), *Theoretical foundations of learning environments* (pp. 89–121). Mahwah, NJ: Erlbaum.

Jonassen, D., Carr, C., & Yueh, H.-P. (1998). Computers as mindtools for engaging learners in critical thinking. *TechTrends, 43*(2), 24–32.

Jonassen, D. H., & Land, S. M. (2000). Preface. In D. H. Jonassen & S. M. Land (Eds.), *Theoretical foundations of learning environments* (pp. iii–ix). Mahwah, NJ: Erlbaum.

Kern, R. (2006). Perspectives on technology in learning and teaching languages. *TESOL Quarterly, 40*(1), 183–210.

Kramsch, C. (2000). Social discursive constructions of self in L2 learning. In J. P. Lantoff (Ed.), *Sociocultural theory and second language learning* (pp. 133–153). Oxford, UK: Oxford University Press.

Labbo, L. D., & Reinking, D. (1999, October/November/December). Negotiating the multiple realities of technology in literacy research and instruction. *Reading Research Quarterly, 34*(4), 478–492.

Lam, W. S. E. (2004). Second language socialization in a bilingual chat room: Global and local considerations. *Language Learning & Technology, 8*(3), 44–65.

Lantolf, J. P. (2000). Introducing sociocultural theory. In J. P. Lantoff (Ed.), *Sociocultural theory and second language learning* (pp. 1–26). Oxford, UK: Oxford University Press.

Lave, J., & Wenger, E. (1991). *Situated learning: Legitimate peripheral participation.* Cambridge, UK: Cambridge University Press.

Lee, C. D. (2003). Toward a framework for culturally responsive design in multimedia computer environments: Cultural modeling as a case. *Mind, Culture, and Activity, 10*(1), 42–61.

Lemke, J. L. (2000, March 17–19). *Learning academic language identities: Multiple timescales in the social ecology of education.* Paper presented at the Language Socialization, Language Acquisition: Ecological Perspectives Conference, University of California, Berkeley. Retrieved September 28, 2006, from http://www-personal.umich.edu/~jaylemke/ecosoc.htm.

Leu, D. J., Kinzer, C. K., Coiro, J., & Cammack, D. (2004). Toward a theory of new literacies emerging from the Internet and other information and communication technologies. In R. B. Ruddell & N. Unrau (Eds.), *Theoretical models and processes of reading* (5th ed.; pp. 1568–1611). Newark, DE: International Reading Association.

Minick, N., Stone, C. A., & Forman, E. A. (1993). Introduction: Integration of individual, social, and institutional processes in accounts of children's learning and development. In E. A. Forman, N. Minick & C. A. Stone (Eds.), *Contexts for learning: Sociocultural dynamics in children's development* (pp. 3–16). Oxford, UK: Oxford University Press.

Norton, B., & Toohey, K. (2001). Changing perspectives on good language learners. *TESOL Quarterly,* 35(2), 307–322.

Ohta, A. S. (2000). Rethinking interaction in SLA: Developmentally appropriate assistance in the zone of proximal development and the acquisition of L2 grammar. In J. P. Lantoff (Ed.), *Sociocultural theory and second language learning* (pp. 51–78). Oxford, UK: Oxford University Press.

Orellana, M. F. (2004). *Latino children as family translators: Links to literacy.* Retrieved June 4, 2004, from http://www.gseis.ucla.edu/faculty/orellana/Translations. html.

Pearson, P. D. (2004). The reading wars. *Educational Policy,* 18(1), 216–252.

Pinkard, N. (1999). *Learning to read in culturally responsive computer environments.* Center for the Improvement of Early Reading Achievement. Retrieved October 23, 2003, from http://www.ciera.org/library/reports/inquiry-1/1-004/1-004. html.

Prensky, M. (2001). Digital natives, digital immigrants. *On the Horizon (NCB University Press),* 9(5). Also available online, as of September 5, 2006, at http://simschoolresources.edreform.net/download/267/Prensky%20-%20Digital%20Natives,%20Digital%20Immigrants%20-%20Part1.pdf.

Purcell-Gates, V., Jacobson, E., & Degener, S. (2004). *Print literacy development: Uniting cognitive and social practice theories.* Cambridge, MA: Harvard University Press.

Rogoff, B. (1995). Observing sociocultural activity on three planes: Participatory appropriation, guided participation and apprenticeship. In J. V. Wertsch, P. Del Rio & A. Alvarez (Eds.), *Sociocultural studies of mind* (pp. 139–164). Cambridge, UK: Cambridge University Press.

Salaberry, M. R. (2001). The use of technology for second language learning and teaching: A retrospective. *Modern Language Journal,* 85(i), 30–56.

Scarcella, R. (2003). *Academic English: A conceptual framework: A technical report of the Linguistic Minority Research Institute.* Santa Barbara, CA: University of California.

Schieffelin, B. B., & Ochs, E. (Eds.). (1986). *Language socialization across cultures (Studies in the social and cultural foundations of language).* Cambridge, UK: Cambridge University Press.

Schultz, K., & Hull, G. (2002). Locating literacy theory in out-of-school contexts. In G. Hull & K. Schultz (Eds.), *School's Out! Bridging out-of-school literacies with classroom practice* (pp. 11–31). New York,: Teachers College Press.

Scribner, S., & Cole, M. (1981). *The psychology of literacy.* Cambridge, MA: Harvard University Press.

Selfe, C. L., & Hawisher, G. E. (2004). Conclusion: Stories from the United States in the information age. In C. L. Selfe & G. Hawisher (Eds.), *Literate lives in the information age: Narratives of literacy from the United States (pp. 211–234).* Mahwah, NJ: Erlbaum.

Street, B. (1984). *Literacy in theory and practice.* Cambridge, UK: Cambridge University Press.

Valdés, G. (1998). The world outside and inside schools: Language and immigrant children. *Educational Researcher,* 27(6), 4–18.

Van Lier, L. (2000). From input to affordance: social-interactive learning from an ecological perspective. In J. P. Lantoff (Ed.), *Sociocultural theory and second language learning* (pp. 245–259). Oxford, UK: Oxford University Press.

Vygotsky, L. S. (1962). *Thought and language* (E. Hanfmann & G. Vakar, Trans.). Cambridge, MA: MIT Press.

Vygotsky, L. S. (1978). *Mind in society.* Cambridge, MA: Harvard University Press.

Warschauer, M. (2002). Reconceptualizing the digital divide. *First Monday, 7*(7).

Warschauer, M. (2004). *Technology and social inclusion: Rethinking the digital divide.* Cambridge, MA: MIT Press.

Wertsch, J. V. (1985). *Vygotsky and the social formation of mind.* Cambridge, MA: Harvard University Press.

Zehr, M. A. (2005, March 23). Federal data show gains on language: But most states miss English-learner goals. *Education Week,* pp. 1, 25.

Zuengler, J., & Miller, E. R. (2006). Cognitive and sociocultural perspectives: Two parallel SLA worlds? *TESOL Quarterly, 40*(1), 35–58.

2
Technology and Literacy Development of Latino Youth

RICHARD P. DURÁN

University of California, Santa Barbara

Although much is made of the importance of basic reading and writing skills as a foundation for literacy development of elementary age youth, there is great advantage to viewing literacy in a more complex "multilayered manner" involving cultural, social, and linguistic factors when considering the fuller range of literacy-learning opportunities that might serve Latino[1] youth, especially those from non-English language backgrounds in our schools and communities. Ample evidence exists that Latino youth, and in particular youth from low-income backgrounds and youth who have yet to develop strong English proficiency[2] for use in school settings show lower academic achievement in schools and lower educational attainment.[3] As cited in the following section, there is strong evidence that a gap in English reading skills for purposes of school performance emerges early on in the schooling of Latino children relative to the academic reading skills of non-Latino nonminority children.

Many educators and researchers propose that the "problems" of "low reading achievement" among Latino youth arise from the "failure" of these children to acquire basic decoding skills required to recognize words and their isolated meaning (Swanson et al., 2004). This chapter does not dispute the fact that research, particularly in the psycholinguistic tradition, has consistently shown that basic decoding skills are essential for acquisition of reading fluency. Nor does this chapter disagree with the claim that the automatization of these skills is an important and essential end in the education of all children (*op. cit.*). However, the notion of "literacy" as a desired end is broader and not well captured by sole attention to development of fluency in basic language and reading/writing skills at the single word level. Attention is needed beyond understanding at the word level. In addition, attention is needed for developing skills related to understanding the meaning of sentences, connected sentences, texts as a whole, and most importantly the relationship of written language to the situations that call for the use of language and information conveyed by written language. "Situations" and their demands must themselves be "read." As Gee (2003) proposes, literacy must be examined in a fuller manner, attentive to the range of meaning-making capabilities of humans and the many symbol systems that humans have devised to make sense of the world and that guide their interactions with others and the environment.

Highly decontextualized strategies to teach word decoding and recognition in instructional programs such as *Open Court* or as presented in electronic form in software such as *Reader Rabbit* can be effective in helping children, including second language learner children, rapidly acquire the most basic elements of word decoding; that, however, is not enough and not reflective of the sense-making with language that can motivate children to acquire deeper critical thinking skills, modes of reflection, and capabilities to communicate.

Broader notions of literacy are especially important when we consider how information and communications technology (ICT) has infused so much of everyday culture in the form of computers and multimedia interactive displays of information, the Internet, personal digital assistants, cell phones/cameras and other digital devices used for learning, communication, life enhancement, and entertainment.[4,5] Given the many ways in which young learners are becoming exposed to and familiar with these technologies, there is value in better understanding ways in which some these technologies might be harnessed to create literacy-learning opportunities for Latino youth. This chapter pays close attention to these broader opportunities for literacy development with special concern for Latino youth in activity settings extending beyond classrooms to community and home settings. Although some of the examples of ways in which ICT can support literacy development are very appropriate for schools and classrooms, and for training and acquisition of discrete English language processing and vocabulary skills, others can only be realized in community and home settings that allow youth a fuller, more flexible control of their social and cultural identity, and learning and communication opportunities, than can be implemented traditional classrooms.

It is quite a challenge to attempt to reconcile notions of basic literacy skill development with broader notions of literacy development tied to sense-making and how this linkage itself can be understood in terms of technological interventions. Following Gee (2003), however, it might be imagined that such a linkage might be possible via the use of complex game and simulation software that embeds acquisition of basic word recognition and decoding skills within complex meaning-making scenarios. Although a viable theory of how this reconciliation can be framed is not readily at hand, as will be shown in the following section, there are examples and demonstrations of English learning activities that have the capability of "blending" basic skill acquisition in English at the word and connected sentence level with exercise of higher order thinking and sense-making skills—see especially the discussion of research by Bauer and O'Hara later in this chapter.

Yet another challenge in understanding ways that ICT can promote learning of reading and writing skills is better understanding of how oral competence in English or a primary language can support acquisition of reading and writing skills in both languages. Although there is clear evidence from the psycholinguistic research literature that oral skills (and in particular phonological skills) are intimately related to recognition of graphemes in writing as carriers of word meaning and that fluency and automaticity in this recognition are essential to development of reading, there is also ethnographic evidence that oral language practices are culturally and socially much more complex and essential to the development of literacy skills. Analytic and empirical studies of literacy done in the tradition of cultural psychology (e.g., Scribner & Cole, 1981) and sociolinguistics (e.g., Cook-Gumperz & Gumperz, 1981; Heath, 1983) show complex interlinkages between oral and written language practices and sense-making activities that are part of the socialized lives of community members. Reading and writing in real-life settings are about sense-making, expression of self-identity, and social participation in cultural practices. We read and write in real-life settings to accomplish personally and socially important objectives. When such objectives are missing, there is a deep risk that learning will not occur. How might ICT facilitate the acquisition of both basic and more complex literacy skills among Latinos? This is the central question explored in this chapter.

In this context, the goals of this chapter are four-fold. One goal is to lay out some basic facts and patterns regarding what we know about Latinos' demographic characteristics and achievement in reading and writing when viewed from the perspective of national education statistics, and about Latinos' access to certain forms of technology, principally access to computers in school and home settings. A second goal is to develop more fully a partial account of how computer-based activities can support literacy development of Latino youth while showing cultural and linguistic responsivity to the background and interests of youth. A third goal is to overview significant examples of projects and practices that suggest some worthwhile ways in which this can be accomplished. A final goal is to discuss further work and research that can further this end.

Demographic Factors and the Reading Test Score Gap

Demographic Characteristics

There are a number of important demographic, linguistic, social, and cultural characteristics of Latino youth that raise both challenges, and, as we shall propose, opportunities for English literacy development. These factors are very much intertwined. The most fundamental fact is that during 2005 Hispanics[6] became the largest minority group in the United States, representing 13% of the U.S. population (Bureau of the Census, 2000).

Latino youth who are immigrants to the United States or whose parents are immigrants to the United States are more likely to reside in low-income households than U.S. residents as a whole, have parents who have less than

12 years of formal education and who work as laborers or service employees, and who reside in homes where Spanish is the primary household language (Llagas & Snyder, 2003).

Census Bureau CPS data indicate that in 1999 about 72% of all children and young adults aged from 5–24 years from non-English language households ($N = 13.729K$) in the United States were from Latino backgrounds where Spanish is spoken at home ($N = 9.195K$; Wirt et al., 2003, Table 4.2). The same survey data source indicated that 36% of these Hispanic children aged 5–24 years judged that they spoke English with difficulty (*op. cit.*).

Census data for the period 1990–2000 shows a dramatic rate of growth in the number of English language learners (ELL) youth in the age range of 5–17 years of age (NCELA, retrieved December 19, 2004). The total size of the 5–17 years of age population grew by 17% from 45,342,448 to 53,096,003 during this period—a growth rate of 17%. In contrast, the number of ELL youth in this same age range grew from 2,388,243 to 3,493,118—a growth rate of 46%. The growth rate for ELL students from Spanish-speaking households was the most dramatic. The numbers of these youth grew from 1,636,874 to 2,584,684—a growth rate of 57%.

The main points arising from the foregoing are that the number of Latino youth are growing rapidly in the U.S. population, that such youth are more likely to come from low-income households compared to other youth and from households where Spanish is the primary language. These facts set the stage for understanding better many of the challenges schools and society at large face in assisting the literacy development of Latino youth.

Literacy Exposure of Latino Children in Early Childhood NCES survey data for the period 1991–1999 (Table 2.1) indicate that 3- to 5-year-old Hispanic children are less likely to have certain home and community literacy experiences that are allied with readiness for schooling (Llagas & Snyder, 2003) than White, non-Hispanic children of the same age range. Specifically:

> In 1999, 61% of Hispanic children had been read to three or more times in the past week [Compared to nearly 90% of White non-Hispanic children.], 40% were told a story by a family member in the past week [Compared to more than 50% of White non-Hispanic children.], and 25% had visited a library within the past month [Compared to nearly 40% of White non-Hispanic children] … However, The percent of Hispanic 3- to 5-year-olds being read to rose from 53% in 1991 to 62% in 1993, but there has been no change since. (*op. cit.*, p. 25)

Data such as these suggest that even before school starts, preschool-aged Latino children are not getting exposed to the same language experiences as White, non-Hispanic children and that, accordingly, they are likely entering schooling with different resources and expectations about the nature of literacy

Table 2.1 Percent of 3- to 5-Year-Olds Not Yet Enrolled in Kindergarten Who Participated in Various Home Literacy Activities with a Family Member, by Race/Ethnicity: Selected Years 1991 to 1999

Activity/Year	Total	White, Non-Hispanic	Black, Non-Hispanic	Hispanic
Read to[1]				
1991	72 (0.6)	79 (0.7)	58 (2.1)	53 (2.0)
1993	78 (0.6)	83 (0.7)	65 (2.3)	62 (2.4)
1995	84 (0.6)	89 (0.7)	74 (2.0)	60 (2.0)
1996	83 (0.7)	88 (1.1)	72 (3.5)	61 (2.7)
1999	81 (0.7)	89 (0.7)	71 (2.7)	61 (2.1)
Told a story[2]				
1991	39 (0.7)	40 (0.8)	35 (2.0)	37 (2.0)
1993	43 (0.9)	44 (1.0)	39 (2.7)	38 (2.2)
1995	50 (0.9)	53 (1.1)	43 (2.3)	42 (2.0)
1996	55 (0.9)	60 (1.7)	42 (3.9)	47 (2.8)
1999	50 (1.1)	53 (1.2)	45 (2.7)	40 (2.3)
Visited a library[3]				
1991	35 (0.7)	40 (0.8)	25 (1.8)	23 (1.7)
1993	38 (1.0)	42 (1.3)	29 (2.6)	27 (1.6)
1995	39 (0.8)	43 (1.1)	33 (2.2)	27 (1.8)
1996	37 (0.9)	36 (1.7)	24 (3.4)	24 (2.4)
1999	36 (0.9)	39 (1.3)	35 (2.6)	25 (1.6)

[1] Refers to being read to at least three times in the past week.
[2] Refers to being told a story at least once in the past week.
[3] Refers to visiting a library at least once in the past month.
Note: Standard errors are in parentheses.
Source: From the U.S. Department of Education, National Center for Education Statistics, National Household Education Survey (NHES), 1991 (Early Childhood Education Component), 1993 (School Readiness Component), 1995 (Early Childhood Program Participation Component), 1996 (Parent and Family Involvement in Education Component), and 1999 (Parent Interview Component), restricted-use data.

and its relationship to schooling. There is little doubt that the limited formal schooling background of some Latino parents, their limited access to institutions building on schooled literacy, and limited socioeconomic resources are related to these differences. More to the point, however, is the reality that Latino youth from low-income backgrounds are less likely to encounter fewer literacy practices at home and in the community, such as being read or told stories and visiting libraries. Such literacy practices socialize children for school and schools' models of early literacy and for using language as a tool for learning in formal school classrooms. Rogoff (2003) puts it nicely, commenting "In middle class European American families, children learn to participate in school-like conversations before they enter school. They learn to "talk like a book" before they learn to read" (p. 302).

Although there is the strong likelihood that the early childhood literacy experiences of low-income Latino children are not as well-matched with the literacy expectations of schools for White, non-Hispanic, middle-class children, it is important to not assume a deficit model orientation. Such an orientation might lead to the conclusion that Latino children, altogether, have not learned valuable components of literacy in their home, natal, and community experiences that can contribute to schooling preparation under the best environmental circumstances. Indeed, understanding better how these existing forms of background and community literacy can connect to enhanced literacy development becomes a central issue explored in later sections of this chapter.

Reading Test Score Gap Emerges before the Start of School and Grows   What do we know about the reading achievement of Latino youth? Results from the Early Childhood Longitudinal Survey of Kindergarteners (1998–1999) up through the third grade (2001–2002) revealed that Hispanic children showed lower levels of literacy acquisition based on English language arts/reading test scores in comparison to non-Latino White children and Asian children. This gap emerged in kindergarten (Rathburn & West, 2004). Hispanic third-graders who knew enough English to be tested in English, like their White non-Hispanic counterparts, showed near-perfect mastery rates for fundamental reading skills that included "ending sounds," and recognition of "sight words."[7] Regardless of ethnicity during the first grade, very few students showed more complex reading capabilities; nonetheless a small gap between Hispanic and White non-Hispanic students on more complex reading skills appeared favoring White non-Hispanic students. This gap grew dramatically by the third grade and was evident for higher-level reading skills related to recognition of "words in context," capacity to make "literal inferences," "deriving meaning" from texts, and "interpreting [meaning] beyond text." The relevant data are shown in Table 2.2.

A most interesting finding of the ECLS-K study data just cited is that the reading achievement gap in reading tests scores between Latino and non-Hispanic students at the third grade-level still occurs after controlling for the incidence of family "risk factors" and their association with low test scores. The authors of the study created a risk factor index based on: (1) living below the federal poverty level; (2) primary home language was not English; (3) mother's highest education was less than a high school diploma/GED; and (4) living in a single-parent household. Although incidence of these factors had a significant statistical effect on reading scores of all students, including Hispanic students, a statistically significant difference remained in reading

Table 2.2 Percentage of Fall 1998 First-time Kindergartners Demonstrating Specific Reading Knowledge and Skills in the Spring of First and Third Grade, by Grade Level and Race/Ethnicity: Spring 2000 and Spring 2002

Selected Child, Family, and School Characteristics	Reading Knowledge and Skills											
	Ending Sounds		Sight Words		Words in Literal Deriving						Interpret beyond Text	
					Context		Inference		Meaning			
	First Grade	Third Grade	First Grade	Third Grade	First Grade	Third Grade	First Grade	Third Grade	First Grade	Third Grade	First Grade	Third Grade
Total	93	100	77	99	46	95	16	78	4	46	3	29
Child's race/ethnicity												
White, non-Hispanic	95	100	81	99	50	97	18	84	5	53	3	34
Black, non-Hispanic	88	100	66	98	33	90	8	63	1	27	1	15
Hispanic	92	100	74	99	40	93	11	74	2	39	2	23
Asian/Pacific Islander	95	100	83	99	57	98	24	82	6	48	4	31
Other, non-Hispanic	87	100	67	97	35	90	11	67	4	35	2	21

Note: Estimates reflect the sample of children assessed in English in all assessment years. The ECLS-K assessment was not administered in 2001, when most of the children were in second grade. Although most of the children in the sample were in third grade in the spring of 2002, 10% were in second grade, and about 1% were enrolled in other grades.

Source: From the U.S. Department of Education, National Center for Education Statistics, Early Childhood Longitudinal Study, Kindergarten Class of 1998–99 (ECLS-K), Longitudinal Kindergarten-First Grade Public-Use Data File and Third Grade Restricted-Use Data File, Fall 1998, Spring 1999, Spring 2000, and Spring 2002.

scores between Latino and White non-Hispanic students, in favor of the latter students, in three areas of higher order reading skills: "literal inference," "deriving meaning," and "interpreting beyond text."

Moving up in grade span, fourth- and eighth-grade data from the National Assessment of Educational Progress (NAEP) survey indicates that the gap in reading achievement test scores between Latino and White non-Latino students continues after Grade 3, persisting at the fourth- and eighth-grade levels. Although 39% of White non-Hispanic fourth- and eighth-graders were found to perform at or above the proficient level in reading in 2003, only 14% of Hispanics at each of these grades performed at or above the proficient level on the NAEP reading test. The results of the NAEP reading assessment for 2003 also indicated that the gap did not change significantly from 1992 to 2003 at either grade (Plisko, 2003), indicative of the difficulty of schools' implementation of curriculum and teacher preparation changes ameliorating this gap.

Although one may be critical of reading tests as adequately valid indicators of higher-level reading and literacy skills because they are capable of only sampling authentic reading skills in a limited manner, the results just described—taken at face value—suggest that the literacy "gap" encountered by Latinos who are sufficiently proficient in English to be tested in English is not arising primarily because of a gap in acquisition of the most basic reading skills associated with word decoding in English, though there is no doubt that these skills are essential to reading development. The results reported here suggest the importance of drawing attention to ways that ICT might be used to help Latinos acquire higher-level reading and literacy skills and not just the most basic reading skills.

As noted, the data just reported did not address the English reading skill development of Hispanic students who were evaluated as not knowing enough English to have their reading skills in English assessed in that language. It is obvious that the basic English reading skills of these students would be very low in comparison to their Hispanic counterparts who knew enough English to be tested in that language, not to speak of their monolingual non-Hispanic English speaking peers. Reading test score data from the 2003 NAEP assessment is consistent with this inference, though the available data is for LEP students as a whole and not disaggregated by Hispanic ethnicity. As shown earlier in Table 2.3, in 2003 72% of fourth-grade LEP students tested in English performed at the "Below Basic" level in reading in comparison to 34% of non-LEP students (Wirt et al., 2003).[8] This same gap exists at the eighth-grade level and is greater. Data mentioned earlier in Table 2.4 shows that, in 2003, 71% of LEP eighth-grade students scored at the "Below Basic" level in comparison to 24% of non-LEP students.

Psycholinguistic research on acquisition of literacy skills in a second language strongly suggests that children's acquisition of reading skills in a second language, as well as in a first, or primary language, requires rapid and

Table 2.3 National/Reading Composite/Grade 4/2003, 2002, 2000, and 1998 Students Classified by Schools as Limited English Proficient (LEP; Results from This Sample Cannot Be Generalized to the Total Population of Such Students) [*LEP*]. Percentage of Students at or above Each Achievement Level (with Standard Errors in Parentheses)

	Year	N	Average Scale Score	Below Basic	At or Above Basic	At or Above Proficient	At Advanced
Yes	2003	11834	186(0.8)	72%(1.1)	28%(1.1)	7%(0.6)	1%(0.1)
	2002	6924	183(2.1)	76%(2.1)	24%(2.1)	5%(0.8)	#(0.1)
	2000	287	167(5.2)	82%(3.8)	18%(3.8)	3%(1.6)	#(***)
	1998	279	174(5.2)	79%(3.7)	21%(3.7)	6%(1.9)	1%(***)
No	2003	175051	221(0.3)	34%(0.3)	66%(0.3)	33%(0.3)	8%(0.1)
	2002	133563	221(0.3)	33%(0.4)	67%(0.4)	33%(0.4)	8%(0.2)
	2000	7787	216(1.1)	38%(1.2)	62%(1.2)	31%(1.1)	7%(0.6)
	1998	7533	217(1.0)	39%(1.1)	61%(1.1)	30%(1.0)	7%(0.5)

Percentage rounds to zero.
(***) Standard error estimates cannot be accurately determined.
Note: The NAEP Reading scale ranges from 0 to 500. Observed differences are not necessarily statistically significant.
Sources: From the U.S. Department of Education, Institute of Education Sciences, National Center for Education Statistics, National Assessment of Educational Progress (NAEP), 2003, 2002, 2000, and 1998 Reading Assessments.

automatic decoding of syllabic word components, and then whole words represented in writing (Snow et al., 1998). Given this persistent finding across multiple first language populations, there is much merit to the idea that computer software can be applied to the learning of basic reading skills in a second language. It is argued here, however, that in order to make such learning activities most effective requires embedding such activities emphasizing basic skills acquisition within fuller sense-making activities—see Bauer and O'Hara, this chapter, for ways to create such bridges.

Latino Access to Computers and the Internet   In considering the potential of computers to support the acquisition of literacy skills among Latinos, it is important to examine their access to technology. When we examine relevant data, we see rapid change occurring for the better, but the fundamental question remains: Are computers used to their full potential for development of literacy and problem-solving skills?

U.S. Latino students show the same access to computer technology in schools as students from other backgrounds, though noticeably less access in home contexts (Durán, 2002; Llagas & Snyder, 2003). Access in homes, however, is rapidly increasing. In 1998, 25.5% of Hispanic homes possessed computers as compared to 46.6% of White, non-Hispanic households. By 2001, 40%

Table 2.4 National/Reading Composite/Grade 8/2003, 2002, 2000, and 1998 Students Classified by Schools as Limited English Proficient (LEP; Results from This Sample Cannot Be Generalized to the Total Population of Such Students) [*LEP*]. Percentage of Students at or above Each Achievement Level (With Standard Errors in Parentheses)

	Year	N	Average Scale Score	Below Basic	At or Above Basic	At or Above Proficient	At Advanced
Yes	2003	5637	222(1.5)	71%(1.6)	29%(1.6)	5%(0.6)	#(***)
	2002	3609	224(1.4)	71%(2.1)	29%(2.1)	4%(0.7)	#(0.1)
	1998	338	218(2.5)	76%(4.9)	24%(4.9)	3%(1.0)	#(***)
No	2003	148656	265(0.3)	24%(0.3)	76%(0.3)	34%(0.3)	3%(0.1)
	2002	111567	266(0.4)	22%(0.5)	78%(0.5)	34%(0.5)	3%(0.2)
	1998	10855	264(0.7)	26%(0.8)	74%(0.8)	33%(1.1)	3%(0.3)

\# Percentage rounds to zero.

(***) Standard error estimates cannot be accurately determined.

Note: The NAEP Reading scale ranges from 0 to 500. Observed differences are not necessarily statistically significant.

Source: From the U.S. Department of Education, Institute of Education Sciences, National Center for Education Statistics, National Assessment of Educational Progress (NAEP), 2003, 2002, 2000, and 1998 Reading Assessments.

of Hispanic households had computers as compared to 61.6% of White, non-Hispanic households (Tomatzky et al., 2002). Limited access to computers and use of computers is particularly marked relative to White, non-Hispanic youth in the households of Latino children as they first prepare to enter school. NCES data on kindergartners in Spring 1999 indicated that 30% of Hispanic children had access to computers and use of computers at home in contrast to 62% of White, non-Hispanic children (Table 2.4; Rathburn, West, & Hausken, 2003). Only 3% of Hispanic children had access to and use of the Internet at home, in contrast to 8% of White, non-Hispanic children. The rates of access showed improvement 1 year later. An estimated 39% of Hispanic children by the end of the first grade had access to and use of a computer at home as compared to 74% of White, non-Hispanic children (*op. cit.*).

The gap in access to computers and the Internet between low-income and ethnic/racial minorities and White nonminority persons has been coined as the "digital divide." Fairlie (2004) reported that for Mexican-Americans this gap in access, and also lower rates of use of computers and the Internet at home, can largely be accounted for by racial differences in education, income and occupation between Mexican–Americans and White, non-Latinos. However, Fairlie also finds evidence that Latinos' use of technology can be hindered by familiarity with English, given the widespread availability of useful information only in English on the Internet for information of local relevance to families.

Some argue that the so-called "digital divide" in computer and Internet access and use is too simplistic a notion. Warschauer (2003), for example, on the basis of international as well as U.S. studies of technology access, argues that the digital divide notion has been coupled with a belief that the divide can be simply ameliorated by improving ownership rates to computers and access to the Internet in home and/or community settings. From this perspective, the divide is underspecified and not sensitive to the sociocultural dimensions of communication and learning in everyday life. The underlying problem is that in order for computer technology to reach its potential, community members need to want technology to meet important ends relevant to survival and life enhancement, and further that community members need support systems to help them learn to use technology. Warschauer's argument is important because it calls attention to the wide span of knowledge needed to use technology and its fundamental links to social practice and social resources for using technology. The argument is also useful for broaching the topic of what we mean by "literacy" in the first place and why it will be helpful to link communicative purpose and social context to exploring ways that technology can assist the literacy development of Latino youth.

Literacy from a Cultural Psychology Perspective[9]

Traditionally, educators have tended to view literacy in terms of the basic capacity to read and write language with varying attention to the social and cultural functions of literacy and to notions of literacy that are of a broader nature pertaining to ways of knowing, understanding, and acting as a person in the world in the most fundamental sense. From a cultural psychology perspective (Cole, 1996), however, literacy is a much more complex phenomenon and includes all forms of symbolic mediation acquired through social and cultural experience. We know the world through symbolic mediation. When we perceive objects and events, and understand language, we do so in terms of symbolic representations. Objects are not just "blobs" we perceive in our environment, they are "things" like "chairs," "apples," "houses," etc. that are learned through social experience and that point to meaningful properties of things. The same can be said for events. We interpret events as "ordering at McDonalds," "making a phone call," or "classroom reading time," rather than anomalous arrangements of people and movements. These examples themselves suggest the role and power of language as a symbolic mediator in their foregoing descriptions. Language itself has meaning, indeed many layers of meaning. Its sounds and physical expression in writing point not to anomalous stimuli, but are processed to have relevance to interpreting concrete experiences or other forms of conceptual information that also serve as mediators.

Cultural Psychology researchers also interpret mediators in terms of tools— artifacts that enable new meaning making. The term *technology* is itself a reference to artifacts that enable meaning-making through activity and language.

For example, technologies like pens and typewriters are artifacts that enable written language. Likewise, as discussed in the following section, electronic artifacts like computers and word-processing software are technological artifacts that mediate communication, meaning-making, and learning. As new electronic technologies are introduced, with proper configuration and functional utility, they can become new tools for learning and communication.

Importantly from this perspective, we need to understand how human capacity to acquire and use language is embedded in knowledge of everyday contexts and practices associated with competent functioning in contexts—these forms of knowledge themselves constitute fundamental forms of literacy. As put forth by Freire (1985) from a critical pedagogy perspective, our literate knowledge is also about reading and writing the world as we experience it and learn new possibilities for its social and collaborative construction. Our very personhood and agency in the world is realized in this way. This is not to denigrate the importance of acquiring competency in basic reading and writing skills as components of literacy. The intent is rather to situate learning of basic skills in a more comprehensive orientation to literacy that foregrounds the importance of sense-making of situations and purpose in all human activity. The new question arises: How might information communications technology become a tool for learning language by using it for meaningful communication and learning?

The Broader Realm of Information Communications Technology

Before returning to an analysis of social and cultural context and why this is fundamental to understanding the opportunities for literacy development of Latino youth, it will be helpful to consider what we mean by ICT. Many tend to think of ICT as restricted to personal computers, associated software and hardware, and the Internet as a well-bounded realm of electronic artifacts. The truth is different and not readily appreciated by investigators of ways that technology mediates communication and learning. In reality, we would be better served by stepping back and examining how digital electronics in the form of microprocessors are incorporated into a wide range of everyday electronic artifacts and how they become interfaced with human activity. In simplistic, but useful, terms a microprocessor is a miniature central processing unit that constitutes the simplest embodiment of a computer.

Microprocessors are ubiquitous in everyday electronic devices, for example, watches, cell phones, electronic components of televisions, CD players, cameras, etc. Indeed, it is getting hard to find everyday electronic devices that don't incorporate such devices. Norman (1998), indeed, argues that the most effective everyday artifacts that employ microprocessors and electronics do so without requiring knowledge of overly technical means of interaction with humans. Effective electronic appliances are user-friendly and combine form and function so that human users concentrate on what they are trying to accomplish with technology, rather than on special codes and steps removed from function needed to input information into devices in order to accomplish ends. Indeed, already there are microprocessor devices embedded in appliances such as refrigerators, home appliances, cellular telephones, personal digital appliances, and so on, and in the foreseeable future these appliances will automatically communicate via the Internet or telecommunications network to other devices or information services to customize their function based on the needs of their human users (Gershenfeld, Krokorian, & Cohen, 2004). Consider, for example, how our cellular telephones give users access to recordings of phone calls left as messages or messages sent as e-mail via the Internet.

The point to all this with regard to literacy development of Latino youth is that we should be ready to attend to ways that a variety of microprocessor appliances, not just personal computers, enhance communications and learning among youth. From a cultural psychology perspective it is important to understand that literacy as *mediated action* is more than reading and writing. It is embodied in the tools and artifacts that make communication and learning possible, and in the very actions that constitute communication and learning (see Wertsch, 1998, on *mediated action*). Literate practices are sense-making practices for communicating and learning. As Wertsch points out, there is a deep relationship between the material (and here, electronic) tools that underlie making sense of things, communicating, and learning. We perceive and see our world through electronic media that shape our sense-making, a point also brought out in the chapter by Castek et al. in this volume. If we want to fully understand the new literacies enabled by electronic media, we need to be alert to how microprocessor-based appliances might enhance communication and learning.

Example Projects Informing Potential Design Principles and Issues for Literacy Development of Latino Youth

We now turn to examples of literacy learning strategies and projects involving Latino and other youth that illustrate a range of literacy skills that can be stimulated by ICT. Attention is first given to two examples of computer-based strategies that illustrate ways in which English reading skills at the word and problem-solving statement level can be stimulated and connected to learning English. These examples integrate learning of English with learning of academic subject matter content. The English reading skills taught in these two first examples amply show concern for mastery of English important to classroom learning. Importantly, these examples of ICT use could be implemented both within school contexts and after-school contexts.

Second, attention is given to examples of projects that stimulate acquisition and use of higher order thinking and communication skills found to show the greatest gap in academic reading skills between Latino and White, non-Latino students in major national educational achievement surveys. Recall that these skill areas involve higher order processing of text meaning and application of what is understood to making new meaning in new contexts. These are skills important to educational success, successful completion of high school, and preparation for higher education. To these concerns, however, attention is focused on how participants enact these skills as components of complex practices constituting membership in a community of practice embodied in an activity setting (Lave & Wenger, 1991). These communities of practice and the opportunities they create for language learning may be structured to occur in classrooms as part of project-based learning strategies. However, they also illustrate the importance of youth extending their knowledge of literacy and acquisition of literacy beyond the boundaries of the school to increase their literacy competence.

The role of ICT varies across the two sets of strategies and projects described depending on the nature of a project and the goals and practices of participants. It is fair to state, that in every project cited here, ICT is not an end in itself; rather, ICT serves as a medium for communication and language learning through participating in meaningful action, making sense of solving situations, and achieving communicative ends in activities.

Learning English Vocabulary in Science via Hypermedia

O'Hara and Pritchard (in preparation) describe a pilot study showing positive impacts of using a hypermedia authoring system on English as Second Language middle school students' acquisition of biology vocabulary and concepts. This project is consistent with a Cultural Psychology perspective in that it demonstrated how students can use their background knowledge and sense-making capabilities to acquire and communicate knowledge about the meaning of new words and their associated concepts in authentic science learning contexts. Working in pairs, English as a second language (ESL) students were taught to use PowerPoint software to create hyperlinked presentations for other students that conveyed the meaning of English language terms used in the study of biology. In particular, the authors examined ESL students' learning about vertebrates and invertebrate animals in words, sentences, images, and sounds constructed by students for display on interconnected PowerPoint slides.

The following are three examples of the hyperlinked presentations developed by students for target biology terms (O'Hara, personal communication, December 1, 2004):

Students created a slide for *cold-blooded*. On the slide they put an explanation of cold-blooded in their own words (the temperature of cold-blooded animals changes when the temperature outside changes) they also included a picture of a snake as an example of a cold-blooded animal. They also included a scanned drawing that they had created showing a snake with the sun above and a thermometer at certain level, then the same animal in the snow with the thermometer at a lower level.

Students created a slide for *classification*: They wrote an explanation of classification in their own words. They then had all the six animal classes and a picture of six animals one for each class. Using the Power-Point animation they had each animal fly into the slide and land under its appropriate class to represent classification. They also included a verbal recording of the word "classification."

Students created a slide for *vertebrate*. On the slide they put a picture of an animal with an arrow pointing to the back bone and the word backbone. They provided an explanation in English and in Spanish (vertebrates are animals with a backbone). They also recorded the word vertebrate and included the sound bite with their slide. When the students had created their final report including all the target words they hyperlinked each word to its appropriate slide.

Using a pre-post assessment design, O'Hara and Pritchard (in preparation) report improvements in 14 ESL students' vocabulary knowledge using both quantitative and qualitative procedures. One procedure involved assessing frequency of knowledge of the particular vocabulary terms that were target terms for instruction. On a pretest, students showed incorrect or no knowledge for 100% of target vocabulary terms on a specialized "index card assessment" that allowed them to define in words or drawings what target vocabulary terms meant. In contrast, students showed complete understanding or partial understanding of 69% of target vocabulary terms on a post-test using the same format following development of hyperlinked target word projects. Qualitative interviews of students during and after hyperlink target word projects revealed that some students found it easier to talk about target vocabulary following projects than to demonstrate this knowledge using the "index card format." Other interview data found evidence that students judged that use of multiple representations of word meaning strengthened their memory for word meaning.

Although the methodology for establishing evidence of gains in ESL students' vocabulary development in this pilot study did not involve a comparison group design and other refinements for a defensible evaluation of gains, the findings are provocative on theoretical grounds and merit replication in a methodologically stronger study.

An important quality of this work is that it views learning of new knowledge as a constructive communicative act (Jonassen, 2002). ESL students are asked to learn new terms by actively constructing interactive PowerPoint slides that allow others to explore the meaning of terms based on the ESL students' own learning. In other words to know the meaning of a new vocabulary term is to be able to demonstrate this understanding via a multimedia presentation exhibiting this understanding. Students' reports that multiple representations of target vocabulary information aid the acquisition of words are consistent with cognitive theory and findings regarding learning in multimedia settings (Kozma et al., 1996; Mayer, 2001).

This work is also of special interest, in part, because it illustrates the importance of developing prerequisite technology skills in order to enable enhanced learning of English. In effect, students learned how to use PowerPoint software as a thinking and learning tool attuned to the learning activities at hand. Students first had to learn how to use PowerPoint software and how to have PowerPoint slides contain imported graphic images and hyperlink tags that would allow persons to navigate among PowerPoint slides with related content. As part of this process, students had to learn how to access and download images for slides from the Internet or other multimedia sources such as CDs. Secondly, as a prerequisite for learning new words via PowerPoint projects, students first had to learn how to create PowerPoint presentations showing that they understood the meaning of familiar English words. For example, students were asked to embed or link pictures of objects referred to by familiar terms as a way of showing they understood the meaning of words. The foregoing demonstrates that it is possible to explore ways to use commonly available ICT software, such as PowerPoint, as powerful tools for improving students' English literacy skills when learning and communication activities are designed appropriately.

BELLA: Blended English Language Learning and Assessment[10]

Bauer and Kim (2004) are investigating implementation of a prototype computerized learning system to simultaneously assess and instruct subject matter vocabulary among English language learner (ELL) students. The prototype system is a small-scale, pilot project that uses a series of animated storybooks presented via a computer to simultaneously assess students' knowledge of target English vocabulary terms in mathematics, while helping master underlying math concepts. The technique involves having children "play" the role of selected characters in an animation. These characters are asked to solve problems pertaining to target vocabulary and concepts presented in English.

The version of the prototype aimed at third- to fifth-grade ESL students targets vocabulary and concepts that sample National Council of Teachers of Mathematics (NCTM) geometry standards for Grades 3–5 and Teachers of English to Speakers of Other Languages Organization (TESOL) standards for English competence for Grades 4–8. Geometry standards for Grades 3–5 include, among other standards, students' development of vocabulary to describe the attributes of geometric shapes and the ability to recognize classes of geometric shapes such as triangles and pyramids. TESOL standards require, for example, the ability to use English for the purpose of defining, comparing, and classifying objects according to characteristics such as number, shape, color, and size. Problems presented to students differ in complexity in terms of the mathematical demands and in terms of demands on English proficiency. The BELLA system assesses students' capacity on each of these dimensions and "scaffolds" children's learning (Wood, Bruner, &

Ross, 1976) by placing students at an appropriate "challenge-level" whereby they can gain experience and mastery in solving easier problems before being presented more complex problems, vocabulary, and academic language or mastery by the system.

As an example of a low-demand problem on both the dimensions of concepts and English vocabulary, students participate in an animated story scenario showing a treadmill with simulated two-dimensional unlabeled graphic figures that are instances of either quadrilateral or triangle shapes. They are given the simple English problem "Select a triangle." Using a keyboard with specially designated keys, students then have their story character "pick-up" each shape passing on the treadmill and "place" it into a box labeled either "quadrilaterals" or "triangles." Their resulting performance is scored and used in developing a profile of their academic language proficiency in math and knowledge of the underlying math concept.

As an example of a high-demand problem involving both more complex math concepts and academic English competence, students participate in a related story animation where their story character is presented with 5 types of two-dimensional geometric shapes passing on the treadmill, an empty box, and a complex English problem statement such as:

> Dell Publishing says these shapes need to be stacked in the box in the order I tell you, so pay attention. Dell Publishing needs 5 shapes. Put an equilateral triangle on the bottom of the box, then a trapezoid on top of it, followed by 2 rectangles that are longer in one dimension than in the other dimension, and finally a square. (Bauer & Kim, 2004)

BELLA is a prototype system. It is not a completed system, but rather it is a research test-bed used at present to explore the feasibility and effectiveness of a variety of scaffolding strategies to simultaneously assess and guide students' learning of math vocabulary and concepts. Additional scaffolding strategies for supporting students' learning that are being investigated include altering the ways that vocabulary and problem information are presented and supplementing the basic use of animations. Attention, for example, is being given to the effect of presenting problems in either written or spoken form, using graphic organizers to represent relationships among concepts in diagrams, and using interaction with teachers or students to stimulate thinking and learning while solving problems.

BELLA illustrates ways in which ICT animations and other forms of computer-mediated language and problem representations can be used in an innovative manner to connect learning of academic English literacy with content subject matter learning. BELLA involves ELL students' active sense-making and ownership of their own learning. This active and interactive mode is not as well reflected by a traditional pencil and paper worksheet, or more static, single-shot verbal question posing and answer evaluation by a teacher.

Next, we examine projects illustrating interesting possibilities for how sense-making in technology-mediated after-school settings involving Latino youth (and parents) can stimulate acquisition of complex literacy skills. These examples include several programs in the University–Community (UC) Links network in California:

The UC Links Network: Youths Learning and Applying Literacy Skills in After-school Computer Clubs[11]

The University–Community (UC) Links Network is an international network of after-school computer clubs founded on the notion that after-school activities involving collaborations between universities, community agencies, families, and other agencies—including schools—can provide youth with unique opportunities to develop literacy and problem-solving skills through technology-mediated activities (http://www.uclinks.org).[12] The UC Links computer clubs vary in the age of youth they serve, but are concentrated in the 6–10 years age range. A number of UC Links sites implement a Fifth Dimension (http://www.uclinks.org) cultural model featuring an imaginary entity known as a "wizard" that oversees the well-being and practices of a site. Examples fitting this model and primarily serving Latino children and their mythical entities include "Las Redes Club," UCLA (entity, "El Maga"), "La Clase Mágica," UC San Diego (entity, "El Maga"), and "Club Proteo," UCSB (entity "Proteo"). The function of the "entity" is to oversee the activities of the clubs and to reinforce the element of play and creativity in the activity of a site. The entity performs these functions by e-mail correspondence with the participants.

A good number of the children attending these sites are from low-income and immigrant Latino households where Spanish is the primary home language. The sites all have a coordinator and use university undergraduates as facilitators of children's learning and as informal mentors. The undergraduates provide expertise in computer and content/conceptual knowledge regarding how to play games and use software. They also provide support for children's literacy practices at site and serve as models for the proficient use of English.

Children attending the sites play software games and use other forms of software such as desktop publishing programs enhancing children's acquisition of cognitive and linguistic skills. As children demonstrate expertise in games and software, they progress through rooms in a special maze. As they become accomplished experts in the games in a given maze room, they are allowed to enter new maze rooms featuring new computer games and software. The games and software used by children are accompanied by "task cards" or "adventure cards" offering children scaffolded guidance on developing increased expertise on games and software. Undergraduates assist children in using these cards and provide children with additional prompts, hints, and cues, aiding children in developing increasing levels of independent competencies in playing games and using software. A number of games, such as *Word Muncher,* specifically focus on helping children acquire vocabulary content knowledge and other linguistic knowledge of English.

In addition, children play other software games helping them acquire mathematical, logical, scientific, and historical–social science concepts and skills. Through these games they are exposed to related uses of English to communicate game problems and goals, and to receive feedback on performance. It is also common for sites to engage children in writing and communications activities with adult support and feedback. For example, children write the mythical club entity about their club activities and other experiences and, in turn, the entity will write children back. At La Clase Mágica, children in collaboration with parents have published newsletters containing articles and stories developed by participants (Vásquez & Durán, 2000). *El Maga* at La Clase Mágica and at Las Redes corresponds via e-mail with children. Indeed, at Las Redes children are in daily correspondence with *El Maga*. Thus, the club entity can become part of a language-learning and literacy support system for English learners.

Club Proteo

At Club Proteo, Proteo has children periodically write to him or her in English via e-mail about their interests, club experiences, and other matters such as plans for a site field trip to a local institution. Proteo responds to children, often with humorous anecdotes and invitations to maintain a dialogue. In this role, Proteo serves as an electronic "buddy" who shares interests with children, cares about their well-being, and encourages English writing on the part of children through the medium of computers. Although not necessarily overtly noticed by children, Proteo evaluates the English syntactic structure, diction, and genre competence of children who write. Proteo's replies sometimes offer corrections to children's writing by "correct" use of language that then is available for children to model, with the assistance of undergraduate student helpers to children when they next write.

Support for literacy learning via e-mail also occurs through pen-pal activities across UC Links sites. Most recently for example, children at Club Proteo have been in e-mail contact with fellow UC Links participants at a Fifth Dimension site in Ausberg, Germany about the cultural celebration of Halloween and *Día de los Muertos*. With the assistance of undergraduate students, Club Proteo children drafted and revised e-mail letters to the Ausberg children that included digitized photos and drawings on Halloween and *Día de los Muertos* activities. Club Proteo children have received correspondence from the Ausberg site regarding cultural celebrations there such as *Kartoffel Fest*. Undergraduates' field notes about the sorts of writing assistance given Club Proteo children along with children's e-mail letters are examined by project staff to guide the design of letter-writing activities for children. (Obviously, these notes and children's letters could be analyzed more systematically as part of an evaluation effort provided requisite resources were available.)

Club Proteo has also featured learning field trips to local institutions that help children appreciate forms of literacy and problem solving, many involving use of computers that are required by institutions in performing their function. Institutions have included businesses such as banks, car dealerships, radio and television stations, a local airport, fire stations, and university classrooms, research laboratories, library, and other university facilities and "treasure hunt" searches concerning local community businesses (Arteaga et al., 2003; Vásquez & Durán, 2000). A number of these activities have been embedded in KWLQ inquiry exercises[13] requiring children to explore the Internet for information relevant to a site and to prepare "research questions" in advance that will be answered by knowledge uncovered during a field trip.

The significance of field trips to children's enhanced understanding of their cultural and social environments needs to be better understood and has much potential given the social experiences and background of children as immigrants from low-income families and parents often with limited formal education and proficiency in English. Everyday knowledge of literacy practices in institutions and connections to functions of institutions such as a bank may be understood in a limited fashion or accessed in a limited fashion because of the social situation of immigrant families. For example, children may be aware that a bank stores money and can be used for buying money orders to pay bills, but children may not be aware that they can establish personal savings accounts and checking accounts when they are old enough. Through a bank field trip, Club Proteo children were to question bank officers and staff about the work they do at a bank, the services they provide clients, how access to bank facilities such as safety deposit boxes and bank card machines operates and how ICT technology supports bank operation in a hands-on manner, allowing children to see how clients interact with bank staff, but also through a behind-the-counter personal inspection of bank facilities.

An important point here is that field trips help children see English and their primary language in action. Consistent with the "new literacies" orientation, they see language and its acquisition as avenues for development of self-identity and competency as community members. Through field trips they experience in the concrete how competence in a language enables activities and practices that realize desired ends, albeit the social ideological dimensions of this literacy need further interrogation (Gee, 1996; n.d.). Children's exposure to the meaning and use of language terms such as *loan, savings account,* and *safety deposit box* in a bank setting were concrete. They experienced the meanings and uses of these terms and how they are embedded in banking communications, as modeled by bank employees and clients, in grammatical and sociolinguistic forms expected of persons interacting in a competent fashion within a bank as community institution. Most importantly, by design, children as an additional component of the field trip, were given the opportunity to ask bank officers and staff questions about bank practices and concepts—for example, "How much money do you have in the safe?" In so doing, children had to use English language terms referring to banking and to embed these terms in English sentences that made sense to bank officers and staff. The replies of these officers and staff to children's questions exposed children to appropriate English usage responsive to children's queries—for example, "We are not allowed to tell clients how much currency we store in the vault." Through the replies, children could gain a better awareness and understanding of how their use of English in questions was echoed back in the language and associated meanings of the bank personnel, and further the children could add follow-on questions allowing them additional use of English and to hear additional replies from personnel.

Club Proteo children have also undertaken field trips to local radio and television stations, and a campus newspaper office to learn how these institutions function, including how they use computer technology and other ICT technology to broadcast and publish. These experiences have exposed children to complex forms of literacy that involve multimedia, planning of the content of communication such as "news," and the ways in which knowledge of audience is connected to the "voice" and identity of persons serving as broadcasters and reporters. One might hypothesize that such educational software designed along the lines of such field trips might be helpful to English learners who are unable to take actual field trips.

Traditional pre-post assessment evaluation studies of the effects of UC Links and Fifth Dimension projects of outcomes on Latino and other children exist and have shown positive effects on children's cognitive and linguistic developments, gains in standardized test scores, and aspirations across a range of UC Links sites (Underwood et al., 2002) and Fifth Dimension sites (Cole & the Distributed Literacy Consortium, 2006; Mayer et al., 1999). With regard to Club Proteo, statistically significant gains in children's knowledge of how to solve verbal math problems (Mayer et al., 1997) and marginally significant evidence of growth in writing skills (Arteaga et al., 2003) have been found. It remains to be seen whether traditional pre-post comparison group evaluation studies will be tractable with regard to showing effects of complex activities such as field trips. It is quite possible that qualitative, ethnographic case study methods may prove the best evaluation tools for evaluating outcomes of these complex activities.

Digital Story Development in DUSTY[14]

Glynda Hull (2003) and her team's work on digital story development now is incorporated into the UC Links system as part of her team's DUSTY project in Oakland, California. The project concept deserves special attention because of its conception of literacy, service to inner-city youth from diverse cultural and linguistic backgrounds, and grounding in after-school community settings. DUSTY now serves primarily middle and high school students but has rich experience and success with younger children. Relying primarily on Apple Computer iLink software, the project supports participants' development and electronic publication of multimedia projects concerning community histories and expressions of social identity. The work of DUSTY is attuned to ways in which multimedia literacies enable youth to represent their experiences and perspectives in creative projects using sound, graphic and photographic images, and videoclips, as well as in written words.

This work explores how creation of narratives or stories about self and community create rich opportunities for adolescent youth to express their appreciation of culture and language and their role in the making and experiencing of identity in everyday life (Hull & Zacher, 2004). After-school settings are ideal for such purposes in that they allow youth flexibility in asserting their interests and expressive capabilities that are not easily made part of school and classroom activities. The digital story compositions of youth are powerful and gripping renditions of youth's experiences and their sense-making about the world around them. They are often "proleptic" in nature (Cole, 1996), that is, the digital stories talk about future selves envisioned by the authors as they analyze the social, cultural, and economic opportunities or lack of opportunities before them. This aspect of DUSTY is of special significance given the fact that many of the youths served by DUSTY are low achievers in school and reside in community settings that are rife with the negative impacts of poverty and high crime rates.

The community settings served by DUSTY are also home to many immigrant families and English learners. Immigrants in this setting can experience "subtractive bilingualism" in an English-speaking context: social devaluation of persons who speak a non-English primary language by considering them as less capable and inferior. Case-study research from DUSTY has found that the effects of subtractive bilingualism can be reversed when youths are given the opportunity to demonstrate the richness of culture, meaning, and identity that can be conveyed by speakers of multiple languages (Katz, 2004).

The Parents, Children, and Computers Project

The Parents and Children's Computer Project is now entering its seventh year and is also now part of the UC Links system. The PCCP serves low-income Latino immigrant families and school children in the community of Isla Vista and Goleta near the University of California, Santa Barbara (UCSB) campus. The PCCP supports parents' computer literacy acquisition via the Spanish language, and supports parents' and children's Internet learning and digital publication in Spanish and English (Durán et al., 2004). Evaluation research has found that parents show statistically significant gains in pre-post assessments of knowledge in a range of computer skills (Durán et al., 2000).

With assistance from project staff that included UCSB graduate and undergraduate students, and community members active in professional publishing, parents and children have collaborated on complex desktop publishing projects. Desktop publications range from elaborate spiral-bound collections of stories and narratives accompanied by graphics, to two- to four-page color newsletters consisting of brief essays, poems, and stories. The involvement of community members such as a publisher of a community bilingual newspaper and university faculty members who publish a literary journal, fictional, and autobiographical works has been particularly effective. Parents and children have come to see the importance of producing written work that must take into account audience and purpose, and the essential importance of editing and revising written work to meet community standards for clear and structurally correct language. Adults and children in the PCCP came to a better appreciation of writing as a dialectic process requiring collaboration with others and feedback from "language experts" in order to publish high-quality work. This appreciation was substantially different from the perception that errors in spelling and grammatical form were reflective of personal inadequacies. As one faculty participant put it: "The Chancellor of UCSB or any important public person never releases a memorandum or letter without asking assistants for editorial help. Everyone needs help and by studying the help that is given, one learns how to improve his or her writing."

The authorship and publications of materials at the PCCP follows a writing process model. The participants first complete initial drafts of pieces. These pieces are then revised by participants with successive drafts undergoing improvements in grammar, diction, and rhetorical organization. Revisions are guided by project staff and UCSB undergraduate and graduate student participants, as well as by participants themselves. Parents and children react to each other's pieces as part of the authorship and revision process. Through the writing process approach, PCCP participants learn new language skills through "language experts" and have an opportunity to develop desktop publications that are then shared with local community members beyond the PCCP participants. Cummins (this volume) characterizes products such as the written desktop publications of parents and children just described as "identity texts." This is a useful characterization in that the notion of "identity text" connotes that the written products project the self-identity and understandings of the authors as members of a literate community who might value and make use of the information and cultural understandings conveyed by published pieces.

Principles and Directions for Research Stimulated by ICT Demonstrations Summarized

The examples of literacy-learning strategies and programs cited in this chapter are demonstrations that show promise for Latino and other students, many of whom are ELL students. Collectively, they raise the importance of better understanding how Latino and ELL youths' literacy acquisition can be stimulated by implementing computerized learning tasks that are embedded in meaning-making activities. The cultural psychology and new literacies approach adopted in this chapter places a premium on better understanding of how individuals acquire and exercise literacy competencies as part of activities and practices that are centered on social communication in one form or another. The approach described here is different from, but complementary to, approaches to language learning investigated in the field of "computer assisted language learning" (CALL; see Warschauer, 1996, for an overview and http://edvista.com/claire/call.html for resources). Warschauer (1996) offers a particularly helpful insight cautioning against the belief that CALL as a method of instruction will necessarily facilitate language learning. Quoting Garrett (1991), he states: "the use of the computer does not constitute a method." Rather, it is a "medium in which a variety of methods, approaches, and pedagogical philosophies may be implemented" (p. 75). Warschauer adds that the effectiveness of CALL cannot reside in the medium itself but only in how it is put to use.

A synthesis of effective teaching practices for Latino youth (and ELLs in general) by Waxman and Tellez (2002) suggests some of the ways that ICT might be combined with pedagogical approaches that resonate well with the example methods and programs cited in this paper and the advice offered by Warschauer. These approaches are described by Waxman and Tellez as: Collaborative Learning Communities; Providing Multiple Representations; Building on Prior Knowledge; Instructional Conversations; Culturally Responsive Instruction, and Cognitively Guided Language Instruction.

The academic vocabulary and concept development strategies embodied in the O'Hara and Pritchard work on language learning and concept learning in biology and by Bauer in the BELLA project on simultaneous learning of math language and math concepts, illustrate in particular how multiple representations of linguistic and conceptual information can utilize ICT as a tool to facilitate learning. ICT is used to help students acquire new English academic vocabulary by connecting the meanings of vocabulary terms to instances of terms presented visually as figures and diagrams via hypermedia links or actions in an animated environment. Students' language use and problem-solving performance is cognitively guided via feedback from other classroom members or by ICT software.

In the case of the O'Hara and Pritchard work, students are required to engage in instructional conversations—that is, verbal interaction in small groups leading to the development of small-group multimedia projects created via PowerPoint on a computer. The projects demonstrate that students have acquired the meaning of target vocabulary terms. In effect, this work shows that "knowing the meaning of a vocabulary term is effectively showing others how they can know it as well"—a form of "generative learning" (Wittrock, 1989). As students converse with each other (and with oversight by a teacher who can guide students), they cognitively construct and guide their understanding of vocabulary terms. As part of this self-guidance and teacher guidance, they generate and receive feedback on how to best demonstrate their understanding of vocabulary terms in hypermedia projects. In order for students to use hypermedia media projects to learn new academic vocabulary and concepts, students first need to build on prior knowledge of existing vocabulary in order to learn how to author hyperlinked documents in PowerPoint. Once the skills for creating PowerPoint-hyperlinked documents are acquired, students in turn use this prior knowledge to construct/demonstrate knowledge of new vocabulary terms acquired through biology lessons.

Like O'Hara and Pritchard's work, Bauer's BELLA project uses multiple representations of language and related concepts targeted for learning via ICT. Targeted mathematics vocabulary and academic language tied to presenting and solving math problems are embedded in scenarios enacted in a fictive warehouse animation where animation characters (including the learner) are asked to solve mathematics problems. The animations involve fictive characters interacting with each other as they pursue problem solving. The resulting instructional conversation (i.e., language interaction) between the characters uses English language structures appropriate to teaching and learning mathematics and English at the same time. In addition to learning the meanings of new English terms for mathematical objects and relationships, students need to master elements of "mathematics register"—how people competent in mathematics talk about mathematics and how they use this knowledge to show mathematical knowledge and to learn new mathematical knowledge. The BELLA project also demonstrates how an ICT system can cognitively diagnose and cognitively guide an ELL student's English capability and mastery of math concepts. The system "scores" students' mastery of English usage based on criteria drawn from TESOL English-learning standards and mathematics-learning standards. The system determines what prior knowledge of both English and math students bring to easier versus more difficult problem-solving tasks. It then cognitively guides students to new problem tasks that can help students progress in their language and math learning.

These aforementioned demonstration projects beg for systematic research in order to more fully understand their potential and limitations as techniques to stimulate literacy learning and subject matter learning. Both projects are focused on specific language learning and subject matter knowledge objectives, though it will be important to conduct research on further specification of learning objectives and the effectiveness, functioning, and generalizability of the instructional components of each project. Qualitative research using "cognitive lab" methods ought to be pursued. These methods involve interviewing learners about how they go about the problem solving and decision making required of participants. The results of interviews could be used to develop a better diagnostic understanding of what students do when they encounter impasses in language and problem-solving performance. This knowledge, in turn, could be used to test-out alterations in project components that could ameliorate impasses, quite possibly by use of computer-aided interventions. Under appropriate circumstances, research on the effectiveness, functioning, and generalizability of the O'Hara and Pritchard and Bauer techniques (and others like them) could involve randomized experiments or quasiexperimental designs involving treatment and comparison groups offered different configurations of techniques or a standard curriculum in a target subject matter curriculum.

The second set of demonstration projects described in this chapter focused on improving literacy learning of Latino and ELL students. This set of projects is substantially different from the first set. The second set cited practices of UC Links-based projects implementing a Fifth-Dimension cultural model (e.g., as found in La Clase Mágica, Las Redes Club, and Club Proteo), DUSTY (a digital story production after-school activity), and the Parents, Children, and Computers Project (a joint parent and child computer literacy and learning project). These projects all involved literacy learning opportunities arising in informal after-school and out-of-classroom learning settings. However, they too resonate with Waxman's and Tellez' (2002) account of effective teaching practices for ELL and Latino youth that integrate ICT with effective practices. The main difference between this second set of projects and the first set of strategy projects is that the second set projects engage participants more directly and intensively in the creative construction and maintenance of cultural and social practices at their respective sites. In contrast, the first set of strategy projects by O'Hara and Pritchard, and Bauer are driven by predetermined practices helping students achieving prespecified curriculum learning objectives via use of ICT.

Children, youth, and adults participating in UC Links Fifth Dimension Sites, DUSTY, and the PCCP are all in collaborative learning communities that show high attention to background knowledge and sensitive culturally relevant modes of interaction among participants. Participants in all three types of projects form a microculture in their setting that includes much attention to academic language and literacy learning mediated by technology while at the same time drawing on members' folk knowledge and informal ways of communicating as central resources for participation in site activities and practices. As participants converse informally they are also engaged in instructionally relevant conversation. The topics of their conversation do at times focus very deliberately on solving problems of formal literacy tied to the goals of a site. These microcultures are collaborative in nature and allow participants to take on "ownership" of participation in their practices. At UC Links Fifth Dimension sites, children develop enthusiasm for formal literacy tasks such as learning new words or composing letters on a computer because they are sense-making activities and because these activities are made to be enjoyable and rewarding to children. As they pursue tasks, children receive cognitive guidance on the appropriateness of their performances, including mastery of reading and writing from more capable peers and adult site participants.

Youth participating in DUSTY engage in similar practices in their literacy-learning activities, and their development of digital stories demonstrates in particular their creative attention to "identity" expression enabled through multimedia story compositions. Participants in DUSTY form collaborative learning communities, build on prior knowledge, learn and communicate by using multiple representations of knowledge via ICT, focus on culturally relevant communication, and engage actively in interactions with other participants in the development of digital stories. The digital story development of DUSTY youth allow them to appropriate new forms of literacy enabled by ICT that then are harnessed to foster expression of self-identity and sense-making of community experiences that can be shared with others.

Likewise participants in the PCCP exercise effective teaching and learning practices enabled by ICT of the sort mentioned by Waxman and Tellez (2002). Participants form a community of intergenerational learners that use technology to communicate complex cultural understandings, life experiences and goals through desktop publications and electronic explorations of knowledge via the Internet. PCCP settings draw on culturally and socially familiar knowledge of the Latino participants and ways of interacting. Adults and children learn literacy practices from each other. In addition, as the participants collaborate to develop electronic publications they receive expert guidance on reading and writing from a coordinator, and graduate and undergraduate students who model expertise in fluent language use and who help parents and children revise their language. In addition, the parent and children participants receive literacy-learning guidance from experts in the community who publish professionally using ICT, and who help them understand the standards for literacy in public communication and the role of the editing process in public communication.

Research can contribute much to our understanding of how the foregoing second set of demonstration projects lead to evidence of literacy acquisition. However, unlike the first set of strategies projects described in this chapter, investigation of these projects will benefit from a different epistemological stance on what counts as evidence of effectiveness, understanding of process, and generalizability as a function of the maturity of projects. In their early stages (and in some cases, "forever"), these projects are like "living design experiments." They undergo constant evolution as their participants and managers negotiate goals and adopt and change practices. The participants monitor and evaluate outcomes in an informal day-to-day manner that in turn informs changes in the goals and practices of projects. Qualitative research studies of these projects can nonetheless uncover valuable information on how these projects aid literacy development by examining the linguistic and literacy practices they support, the content of products created by project participants, and the habits of mind and communication enabled by project activities. The latter issue is about whether the participants learn new communicative and learning skills that show evidence of redeployment or transfer to new situations within the project context or outside the project context. For example, it would be valuable to investigate whether the skills and practices learned in out-of-school project contexts can become tools for communication and learning in regular classroom contexts. It would also be valuable to use qualitative methods to investigate in detail the kinds of linguistic challenges faced by Latino project participants and how the provision of assistance by project staff helps improve the literacy performance of students.

In those circumstances where there are stable program practices, it is possible to apply empiricist methods for research involving experimental and quasiexperimental designs to explore the effectiveness, functional processes, and generalizability of effects of these projects on literacy acquisition of Latino and other ELL students. Indeed, evaluation studies of the impact of Fifth Dimension projects on learning of verbal, cognitive, and mathematical skills using quasiexperimental comparison group methods have been successful and shown statistical evidence of program effectiveness (Mayer et al., 1999).

Although the discussion of principles for program design and research has focused on the particular projects and strategies described in this chapter, it seems that the same principles and similar directions for research would emerge for a broader range of strategies and projects. This is a reasonable and testable hypothesis that can help guide exploration of the field of intervention program research on improving Latino youths' acquisition of literacy skills.

Notes

1. The term Latino in this chapter is used to refer to persons from a Latin American heritage. By default, Latino will refer to persons residing in the United States, although the term is applicable more generally to persons of Latin American origin.
2. The term English proficiency in this chapter refers to fluency and knowledge of spoken and written English. There is no "one" form of English in reality and there is widespread variation in how English is spoken and written in the United States, as well as around the world. However, the term in the field of education is often characterized as referring to either English as required at school or by formal community institutions as opposed to English spoken for conversational, informal purposes in everyday settings.
3. A valuable synthesis on the status of Latino education has been provided by the National Center for Education Statistics (NCES; Llagas & Snyder, 2003) and it along with other NCES reports are important resources for this chapter because they allow for inferences to be made about the entire population of Latinos in the United States.

4. The term information and communications technology or "ICT" is used to refer to electronically powered devices and related media that store and process information.

5. I am not aware of major research studies that have investigated the propagation and use of personal electronic artifacts in the U.S. population.

6. In this chapter, the term Hispanic is used interchangeably with the term Latino. Usage of Latino is preferred by the author. However, the term Hispanic is used when the source material cited utilized this term.

7. The definitions of reading skills used in the ECLS-K report (Rathbun & West, 2004) were as follows: "In addition to an overall reading achievement score at each time point, the reading assessments contained eight proficiency levels. This report focuses on the six highest proficiency levels that reflect a progression of knowledge and skills at the third grade level, including (from easiest to most difficult): (1) understanding the letter–sound relationship at the end of words (identifying the letter that represents the sound at the end of a word); (2) recognizing words by sight (reading simple words aloud); (3) understanding words in context (listening comprehension and reading simple text passages); (4) making inferences using cues that were directly stated with key words in text (literal inference); (5) identifying clues used to make inferences (deriving meaning); and (6) demonstrating understanding of author's craft and making connections between a problem in the narrative and similar life problems (interpreting beyond text)."

8. According to NAEP, fourth-grade students performing at the Basic level should demonstrate an understanding of the overall meaning of what they read. When reading text appropriate for fourth-graders, they should be able to make relatively obvious connections between the text and their own experiences, and extend the ideas in the text by making simple inferences. For example, when reading literary text, they should be able to tell what the story is generally about—providing details to support their understanding—and be able to connect aspects of the stories to their own experiences. When reading informational text, Basic-level fourth-graders should be able to tell what the selection is generally about or identify the purpose for reading it, provide details to support their understanding, and connect ideas from the text to their background knowledge and experiences.

9. A cultural psychology perspective shares many commonalties with a "New Literacies" perspective. See Castek et al. (this volume) for a characterization of this latter perspective.

10. More information on the theoretical rationale for the design of BELLA can be found in Bauer, Williamson, Mislevy, and Behrens, 2004.

11. Additional, valuable coverage of the UC Links network can be found in the chapter by Castek et al. The present account is intended to be a stand-alone account from the perspective of an implementer, and highlights the cultural components of participation, and implementation of field trips and their value to literacy learning as part of site activities.

12. The UC Links network is a rapidly expanding international network of after-school computer clubs. Attention is given here to mentioning only three sites that serve primarily Latino students because of the intensive collaboration among the Principal Investigators, but there are others that deserve attention in

a more extended treatment of the Clubs. Additional sites serving many Latino participants are located in Riverside, Whittier CA, Miami, and Denver among other locales.

13. K-W-L stands for "What do we know, what do we want to know, and what have we learned?" The K-W-L approach is fairly widely used among teachers. K-W-L is a process to find out what students already know (K), what they want to know (W) and what they have learned (L). K-W-L can be very effective at the beginning of the session thinking about the course in general, and it is effective at the beginning of a unit as well.

   As portrayed by the Johns Hopkins Center for Talented Youth (retrieved December 19, 2004, from http://www.jhu.edu/gifted/teaching/strategies/brainstorm/kwl.htm), "The 'K' can be an interactive process in which students convey what they already know; this will provide you with information to decide how to proceed with the course or unit. The 'W' is a chance to brainstorm what students want to cover during the course or unit. Have students complete the statement "I want to know _____." The 'L' is reviewed at the end of the course or unit and should cover the list of what the students wanted to know. To this technique we add 'Q' as a final and recursive step. The 'Q' activity asks students what more do they now want to learn about their chosen topic."

14. The DUSTY project is also described by Castek et al. in this volume. The present account highlights a case study of self-identity construction and language maintenance from the point of view of a participant in the project.

References

Arteaga, G., Durán, R., & Moore, T. (2003). Evaluating children's writing development at Club Proteo. *UC Links Newsletter* 2 (1).

Bauer, M., & Kim, H. (2004, July). *BELLA: Blended English language learning and assessment.* Presentation at ETS-Rutgers meeting, Educational Testing Service, Princeton, New Jersey.

Bauer, M., Williamson, D., Mislevy, R., & Behrens, J. (November 2004). *Using evidence-centered design to develop advanced simulation-based assessment and training.* Paper presented at the 2004 E-Learn Conference, Washington DC.

Bureau of the Census. (2000). *Statistical abstract of the United States: 2000.* Washington, DC: U.S. Department of Commerce.

Cole, M. (1996). *Cultural psychology: A once and future discipline.* Cambridge MA: Harvard University Press.

Cole, M., & the Distributed Literacy Consortium. (2006). *The Fifth Dimension: An after-school program built on diversity.* New York: Russell Sage.

Cook-Gumperz, J., & Gumperz, J. (1981). From oral to written culture: The transition to literacy. In M. Farr Whiteman (Ed.) *Writing: The nature, development, and teaching of written communication. Volume 1 Variation in writing: Functional and linguistic differences* (pp. 89–109). Hillsdale, NJ: Erlbaum.

Durán, R. P. (2002). Technology, education, and at risk students. In Stringfield, S. & Land, D. (Eds.) *Educating At Risk Students.* National Society for the Study of Education. Chicago: University of Chicago Press. pp. 210–230.

Durán, R. P., Durán, J., Perry-Romero, D., & Sánchez, E. (2001). Latino immigrant parents and children learning and publishing together in an after-school setting. *Journal of Education for Students Placed At-Risk,* 95–113.

Durán, R. P., Durán, J., Ramírez, R., & Perry-Romero, D. (2004). *The immigrant parents' computer literacy project: A strategies guide for implementation.* Center for Research on Education, Diversity, and Excellence, UC Santa Cruz.

Fairlie. R. W. (2004). Race and the digital divide, *Contributions to Economic Analysis & Policy,* 3(1), 15.

Freire, P. (1985). *The politics of education: Culture, power and liberation.* (D. Macedo, Trans.). London: Macmillan.

Garrett, N. (1991). Technology in the service of language learning: Trends and issues. *Modern Language Journal,* 75(1), 74–101.

Gee, J. P. (n.d.). The new literacy studies and the "social turn." Retrieved September 6, 2004, http://www.schools.ash.org.au/litweb/page300.html.

Gee, J. P. (1996). *Social linguistics and literacies: Ideology in Discourses* (2nd ed.). London: Taylor & Francis.

Gee, J. P. (2003). *What Video Games Have to Teach Us About Learning and Literacy.* New York: Palgrave/Macmillan.

Gershenfeld, N., Krokorian, R., & Cohen, D. (2004, October). The Internet of things. *Scientific American,* 76–81.

Heath, S. B. (1983). *Ways with words: Language, life, and work in communities and classrooms.* New York: Cambridge University Press.

Hull, G. (2003, November). Youth culture and digital media: New literacies for new times. *Research in the Teaching of English* 38(2), 229–233.

Hull, G., & Zacher, J. (2004). What is after-school worth? Developing literacies and identities out-of-school. *Voices in Urban Education,* Winter/Spring, 3, 36–44.

Jonassen, D. H. (2002). Engaging and supporting problem solving in online learning. *Quarterly Review of Distance Education,* 3(1), 1–13.

Katz, M. (February 2004). *Performing agentive identities through multimedia composing: A case study of Selina.* Paper presented at The Annual Meeting of the National Council of Teachers of English, Assembly for Research, Berkeley, CA.

Kozma, R.B., Russell, J., Jones, T., & Marx, N. (1996). The use of multiple, linked representations to facilitate science understanding. In S. Vosniadou, E. DeCorte, R. Glaser, & H. Mandl (Eds.), *International perspectives on the design of technology-supported learning environments* (pp. 41–60). Mahwah, NJ: Erlbaum.

Lave, J., & Wenger, E. (1991). *Situated learning.* New York: Cambridge University Press.

Llagas, C., & Snyder, T. (2003). *Status and Trends in the Education of Hispanics. NCES 2003–2008,* Washington, DC: National Center for Education Statistics.

Mayer, R.E. (2001). *Multimedia learning.* New York: Cambridge University Press.

Mayer, R., Blanton, B., Durán, R., & Schustak, M. (1999). *Final Report to the Andrew W. Mellon Foundation, Using new information technologies in the creation of sustainable afterschool literacy: Evaluation of cognitive outcomes.* Santa Barbara, CA: University of California, Santa Barbara.

Mayer, R., Qulici, J., Moreno, R., Durán, R., Woodbridge, S., Simon, R., et al. (1997). Cognitive consequences of participation in a "Fifth Dimension" after-school computer club. *Journal of Educational Computing Research,* 16(4), 352–369.

NCELA (National Clearinghouse on English Language Acquisition). (2004). *English language learners & the U.S. Census 1990–2000.* Retrieved December 19, 2004, from www.ncela.gwu.edu.

Norman, D. A. (1998). *The invisible computer: Why good products can fail, the Personal Computer is so complex, and information appliances are the answer.* Cambridge, MA: MIT Press.

O'Hara, S., & Pritchard, R. (in preparation). *Hypermedia authoring as a vehicle for vocabulary development in a middle school ESL classroom.*

Plisko, V. (2003). *The Release of the National Assessment of Educational Progress (NAEP) The nation's report card: Reading and mathematics 2003*, Washington DC: National Center for Education Statistics.

Rathburn, A., & West, J. (2004). *From kindergarten through third grade: Children's beginning school experiences.* Washington DC: National Center for Education Statistics.

Rathburn, A., West, J., & Hausken, E. (2003). *Young children's access to computers in the home and at school in 1999 and 2000.* NCES 2003–036. Washington DC: National Center for Education Statistics.

Rogoff, B. (2003). *The Cultural Nature of Human Development.* Oxford: Oxford University Press.

Scribner, S., & Cole, M. (1981). Unpackaging literacy. In M. Farr Whiteman (Ed.), *Writing: The nature, development, and teaching of written communication. Volume 1 Variation in writing: Functional and linguistic differences.* (pp. 71–87). Hillsdale, NJ: Erlbaum.

Snow, C., Burns, M., & Griffin, P. (Eds.). (1998). *Preventing reading difficulties in young children.* Washington, DC: National Research Council.

Swanson, H. L., Saez, L., Gerber, M., & Leafstedt, J. (2004). Literacy and cognitive functioning in bilingual and non-bilingual children at or not at risk for reading disabilities. *Journal of Educational Psychology, 96*, 3–18.

Tomatzky, L., Macias, E., & Jones, S. (2002). *Latinos and Information Technology: The Promises and Challenges.* Claremont, CA: Tomas Rivera Policy Institute.

Underwood, C., Welsh, M., Emmons, C., Lerner, D., & Sturak, T. (2002). *University–Community Links to higher learning program impact report.* Oakland, CA: University of California, Office of the President, Educational Outreach Department, UC Links Statewide Office.

Vásquez, O. (2003). *La Clase Mágica. Imagining optimal possibilities in a bilingual community of learners.* Mahwah, NJ: Erlbaum.

Vásquez, O., & Durán, R. (2000) *La Clase Mágica* and El Club Proteo: Multiple literacies in new community contexts. In G. Gallego & S. Hollingsworth (Eds.), *Challenging a single standard: Perspectives on multiple literacies.* New York: Cambridge University Press.

Warschauer, M. (1996). Computer-assisted language learning: An introduction. In S. Fotos (Ed.), *Multimedia language teaching* (pp. 3–20). Tokyo: Logos International.

Waxman, H., & Tellez, K, (2002). *Research synthesis on effective teaching practices for English language learners.* Philadelphia, PA: Mid-Atlantic Laboratory for Student Success. (ERIC Document Reproduction Service No. ED474821)

Wertsch, J. (1998). *Mind as action.* New York: Oxford University Press.

Wirt, J., Choy, S., Rooney, P., Provasnik, S., Sen, A. and Tobin, R. (2004). *The condition of education 2004* (NCES 2004-077). Washington, DC: National Center for Education Statistics.

Wittrock, M. (1989). Generative processes of comprehension. *Educational Psychologist, 24*, 325–344.

Wood, D., Bruner, J., & Ross, G. (1976). The role of tutoring in problem solving. *Journal of Child Psychology and Psychiatry, 17*, 89–100.

REFLECTION

Literacy and English Learners
Where Does Technology Fit?

ROBERT RUEDA

University of Southern California

There are two important considerations (or "givens," in more colloquial terms) that are useful to point out in framing the discussion of technology, literacy, and English learners. One is that the mastery of technology is not an option, but rather a requirement for those who hope to be productive and participatory citizens as Castek and her colleagues (this volume) discuss. It is true that some technology is designed to be transparent to the user while helping accomplish tasks such as telling time more accurately, microwaving a frozen dinner, or conversing on a cellular phone. However, other uses of technology require a much more proactive approach on the part of the user. These uses are much more dependent on user knowledge, sophistication, and creativity for maximum effect such as designing a PowerPoint presentation or publishing a newsletter.

A second consideration is that the discussion of technology in instructional settings is situated in a historical context in which there are systematic and long-standing differences in achievement as well as a wide variety of school-related (and beyond) differences across ethnic, racial, language, and socioeconomic (SES) groups in the United States (Noguera, 2001). As other authors such as Durán (this volume) explore this point more in detail, this point will not be elaborated here. Yet both of these points are important factors that belie the significance and promise of technology.

Because the focus of this discussion is English learners, it is important to lay out some general assumptions that concern the education of these students that may or may not be shared by all readers. First is that all children in the United States should be provided maximum opportunity to become proficient speakers and literate users of the English language. Second, English learners should be held to the same expectations and have the same opportunities for achievement in academic content areas as other students. Finally, in an increasingly global economic and political world, proficiency in languages other than English and an understanding of different cultures are valuable in their own right, and represent a worthwhile goal for schools.

What Is Unique about English Learners?

Given the focus on English Learners, it is worthwhile to consider what is unique about this group of students with respect to technology and literacy. How are issues related to technology and literacy different for this group than for the population of students in general? Other chapters in this volume provide important background data on the demographic characteristics of this population in terms of factors such as numbers and achievement levels, and these data will not be reiterated here (see also Genesee, Lindholm-Leary, Saunders, & Christian, 2005, for a recent review). What are other important factors to consider in addition to demographic profiles?

Although the term *English Learners* is typically used with reference to issue of language-related issues, in truth there are a constellation of interrelated sociocultural variables (including language status or proficiency) that need to be considered jointly. For example, factors such as such as ethnicity, SES, language use patterns, culture, and immigration status do not occur in isolation. Although the issue of intragroup variability is discussed shortly, it is often the case that these constellations of factors co-occur in systematic ways. For example, a recently immigrated non-English proficient individual in search of employment opportunities is likely to have less education and fewer economic resources than another individual who does not share these characteristics. At the same time, although these factors may be interrelated, they should not be assumed to be interchangeable. For example, constituting a sample in a study on the basis of ethnic or racial identity should not automatically lead to assumptions about cultural beliefs and practices, for example, as is often done in the literature.

Equally important, individuality should not be lost in the convenience of group labels. The group of students often referred to as "Latinos," or English Learners, for example, includes those who are recent immigrants as well as those who have been in the United States for decades; those who speak no English to those who speak no Spanish; those who are very low SES to those who are at the highest levels of SES; those who have a significant amount of school-relevant background knowledge and those who do not. As one example, a recent study examined motivational variables related to language acquisition of recent immigrant secondary students in comparison to "generation 1.5" peers, that is, students who were born in the United States but whose parents were immigrants. Even within this population of English Learners that is rarely differentiated in the literature, the results indicated that first generation ELs reported higher levels of effort, desire, attitudes, and motivation to learn English, whereas generation 1.5 ELs reported higher levels of U. S. acculturation and identity, and more competence with English (del Carmen García, 2006).

Not only does this variability characterize individuals, but it characterizes communities as well. Latino communities can vary on a host of variables that may have implications for students' acquisition of literacy and use of technology. In short, any analysis of the needs of Latino students with respect to technology, language, and literacy needs to be situated within a specific context and community and grounded with specific students in mind. Dimensions of importance to examine might include cultural beliefs and cultural practices, including those revolving around literacy and technology; first and/or second language proficiency and language use patterns; access to technology; and access to models who use technology in a variety of ways. As a final complicating factor, the dynamic nature of development means that the relationships among the components of literacy are not static and that they may change due to the learner's age, levels of second language oral proficiency, underlying cognitive abilities, and previous learning.

Why the Focus on Technology?

In general, there are two principal areas that advocates of technology focus on with respect to English Learners. One concerns the increasing role that technology plays in negotiating the demands of everyday life and keeping up with an increasingly technological society. This aspect of technology use focuses on questions related to access, social and cultural capital around technology resources and use, and related political and social justice issues. Generally this concern is embodied under the label "digital divide" (Warschauer, 2002, 2003). It is of concern to the larger society because of the need for a stable, productive, and educated workforce, as well as a population that can fulfill important civic duties and engage in political and other arenas. Recent data indicate that this digital divide is not disappearing (DeBell & Chapman, 2006).

A second and equally important reason related to the push for equal access to the use of technology is the promise of technology's role in facilitating the delivery of instruction in more effective and novel ways with a population that has not achieved at desired levels. That is, technology is seen as having promise for increasing the amount and/or nature of learning, making it more effective, quicker, or otherwise enhanced and thus impact achievement differences. In some ways, the first concern is a civil rights issue, whereas the second is an instructional issue, although these two issues are likely intertwined in complex ways. For example, lower access to technology resources may co-occur with poor instructional resources such as credentialed and highly qualified teachers (Warschauer, Knobel, & Stone, 2004). However, given my own areas of expertise, as well as the focus of the Durán's chapter, I will concentrate on the second instruction-related aspect.

The Role of Technology in Language and Literacy for English Learners

An important consideration in examining the role of technology to improve academic performance and instructional options for English Learners is to examine for a moment what we mean by literacy and the role it plays in academic success. It is clear that research demonstrates the key role of early reading in later academic success for all students. However, it is necessary to distinguish "reading" and "literacy." Reading, for purposes of discussion, can be described as the individual psychological processes underlying the decoding of text. Literacy, on the other hand, is much broader, and also includes the social, affective, motivational, and cultural (and even political) practices that characterize interactions with text (Rueda & McIntyre, 2002). Teaching a child to decode words is both necessary and worthy and lends itself to measurable objectives, but if that child does not value reading, does not engage in literate practices outside of school, and in general is not able to value and use literacy as a tool to solve important life problems, academic "success" has been only partially achieved even though short-term objective gains may have been demonstrated. Any use of technology to support academic achievement thus has to take into account the social and cultural context and the larger educational context, and also must look at gains beyond those that are convenient or easy to measure. Like all cultural tools that we inherit from those who have preceded us, technology and literacy are not neutral, but always are "fit" in to a specific context. With English learners, it is important to consider the range and nature of contexts in which literacy and technology were experienced prior to efforts to intervene in order to appropriately scaffold later use. Likewise, it is important to consider how literacy and technology are expected to be used afterwards so that instruction and activities provide adequate preparation. Low-level remedial activities, even though they may be mediated through computers, will not facilitate higher level problem solving and other complex applications and uses. In other words, instruction and the introduction of technology needs to take into account the "before" and the "after" – that is, what role does technology and literacy play in the lives of students now, and how would we like them to use it later?

In addition, the integration of technology into literacy instruction cannot be considered apart from the already existing debates in the area of literacy and language acquisition. What is the role of basic skills vs. higher order processes? What is the role of second language? What transfers from the first to the second language? What role do social and cultural processes play? What role does motivation play in this process? Fortunately, there is significantly more information on these questions than even a decade ago. A recent comprehensive and exhaustive review of research (August & Shanahan, 2006) has considered many of these questions in detail, focusing specifically on the acquisition of literacy. For example, although the benefits of key basic components of literacy are critical (phonemic awareness, decoding, oral reading fluency, reading comprehension, vocabulary, and writing) are critical, second language proficiency is an important mediator of progress and requires attention in instruction. Importantly, those students who are literate in their first language are likely to be advantaged in the acquisition of English literacy, and students instructed in both their native language and English perform, on average, better on English reading measures than language-minority students instructed only in English. This report also suggested that individual differences contribute significantly to English literacy development.

However, the quality of the existing research base is not always as good as it could be, and significant questions and gaps remain. As one example, there is surprisingly little evidence for the impact of sociocultural variables on literacy achievement or development (Goldenberg, Rueda, & August, 2006) for example, but this is more a function of the lack of studies that have asked this question rather than evidence that such factors are unimportant. Overall, the descriptive research base on cultural and social factors is rich and suggests that attention should be focused on these factors, and technology initiatives need to be embedded with these concerns in mind.

As noted earlier, one general argument for the use of technology is that it affords an opportunity to help scaffold instruction in ways that might not be possible otherwise. Thus, technology has the potential to provide useful means of mediating instruction, in the Vygotskian sense (Cole & Engeström, 1993). That is, technology can help scaffold and mediate learning by altering critical features of the learning tasks under consideration. More accurately, technology can be used strategically to mediate or "remediate" more effectively the use of existing cultural tools such as language and literacy (González, Moll, & Amanti, 2005). Just as a pole vaulter's act of jumping is transformed by the use of a pole (Wertsch, 1998), technology can help transform the nature of learning and literacy tasks in order to make them more accessible and to boost performance above what would be otherwise possible, as illustrated by the examples in Durán's chapter. This is a double-edged sword however, in the sense that technology can harm or help learning outcomes. One potential danger is that technology can be used to replicate already-existing patterns of impoverished instructional practices (Warschauer, Knobel, & Stone, 2004) that characterize the educational experience of many English Learners. Technology imposed on impoverished learning tasks and environments should not be expected to yield outcomes different that those that already exist. There have been too many cases where computers have been used simply to automate individual worksheet exercises or to copy handwritten essays into electronic form with no overarching learning goals. Alternatively, and on a more positive note, technology can be used in creative and enriching ways such as those documented by Durán. In essence, technology needs to be used strategically, creatively, and in enriching ways, taking into account the multidimensional and dynamic of language and literacy acquisition (August & Shanahan, 2006) in order for potential benefits to be realized.

Conclusion

Given the preceding comments, what are the considerations for the use of technology? It is clear that the use of technology to improve literacy and overall academic outcomes for English Learners must be tied to current theory and research, drawing on current notions of learning and the creation of instructional environments rather than being used in non-strategic ways that replicate problematic patterns of the past. A great deal is now known about learning, motivation, second language acquisition, and instruction and technology should not ignore but embed and draw on this existing body of knowledge. A great deal of technology use in the past has been used in an atheoretical way, with the assumption that technology by itself would produce learning effects. Yet current learning and motivation theories point to the importance of factors such as the need for challenging learning tasks, drawing connections to prior knowledge, active engagement with learning materials, effective use of strategies, appropriate motivational beliefs in areas such as self-efficacy, appropriate learning goals, etc.

In addition, it is necessary to address technology concerns with the joint purposes of both access and instructional enhancement in mind, but the two purposes should not be confounded. In particular, it is important to remember that access alone does not guarantee improved instruction nor positive learning outcomes. As with first-language learning, becoming literate in a second language depends to a great extent on the quality of the instructional environment that is provided to second-language learners, including what is taught, the instructional methods and routines that are used, the intensity or thoroughness of instruction, how well and appropriately learning is monitored, and teacher preparation and development. As the Durán chapter illustrates, good models do exist and should be built on.

References

August, D. & Shanahan, T. (Eds.). (2006). *Developing literacy in second-language learners: Report of the National Literacy Panel on Language-Minority Children and Youth.* Mahwah, NJ: Erlbaum.

Cole, M., & Engeström, Y. (1993). A cultural–historical approach to distributed cognition. In G. Salomon (Ed.), *Distributed cognitions: psychological and educational considerations* (pp. 1–46). New York: Cambridge University.

DeBell, M., & Chapman, C. (2006). Computer and Internet Use by Students in 2003 (NCES 2006–065). Washington, DC: U.S. Department of Education, National Center for Education Statistics.

del Carmen García, M. (2006). Motivation, language learning beliefs, self-efficacy, and acculturation patterns among two groups of English Learners. Unpublished doctoral dissertation, University of Southern California.

Genesee, F., Lindholm-Leary, K., Saunders, W., & Christian, D. (2005). English language learners in U.S. Schools: An overview of research findings. *Journal of Education for Students Placed at Risk,* 10(4), 363–385.

Goldenberg, C, Rueda, R.S., & August, D. (2006). Sociocultural influences on the literacy attainment of language-minority children and youth. In D. August & T. Shanahan (Eds.), *Developing literacy in second-language learners: Report of the National Literacy Panel on Language-Minority Children and Youth.* (pp. 269–318). Mahwah, NJ: Erlbaum.

González, N., Moll, L.C., & Amanti, C. (2005). *Funds of knowledge: Theorizing practices in households, communities, and classrooms.* Mahwah, NJ: Erlbaum.

Noguera, P. (2001). Racial politics and the elusive quest for excellence and equity in education. *Education and Urban Society,* 34(1), 18–41.

Rueda, R., & McIntyre, E. (2002). Toward universal literacy. In S. Stringfield & D. Land (Eds.), *Educating at risk students: One Hundred-first Yearbook of the National Society for the Study of Education* (pp. 189–209). Chicago, IL: The University of Chicago Press.

Warschauer, M. (2002). Reconceptualizing the digital divide. *First Monday,* 7(7).

Warschauer, M. (2003). *Technology and social inclusion: Rethinking the digital divide.* Cambridge, MA: MIT Press.

Warschauer, M., Knobel, M., & Stone, L. (2004). Technology and equity in schooling: Deconstructing the digital divide. *Educational Policy,* 18(4), 562–588.

Wertsch, J.V. (1998). *Mind as action.* New York: Oxford University Press.

3

Technology, Literacy, and Young Second Language Learners
Designing Educational Futures

JIM CUMMINS

The University of Toronto

This chapter addresses the following question: *To what extent can technological interventions be designed to improve the academic performance of elementary-age students who are learning English as an additional language?* The major focus of this chapter is on the literacy development of Latino/a students in the United States. The bulk of the English language learners (ELL) in the United States come from Latino/a backgrounds and many live in impoverished and socially marginalized conditions. Because there is significant overlap among the categories of home language, socioeconomic status (SES) and cultural/racial background, the chapter addresses each of these categories in discussing access to, and use of, digital technologies in schools.

Clearly, throughout human history, technological tools have been crucial to survival and the evolution of human intelligence. Writing and communication tools associated with literacy (sticks, pencils, the printing press, typewriters, computers), for example, have enabled ever-more sophisticated forms of human interaction and collaboration. The focus of the chapter is on recently developed *digital* technologies that have transformed modes of oral and literate communication during the past 30 years.

Debates on the efficacy of educational investment in digital technologies have evoked polarized responses to the question of whether technology represents an effective and cost-effective enhancement of learning (e.g., Armstrong & Casement, 1998; European Commission, 2003; Oppenheimer, 2003). In this chapter, the focus shifts from this somewhat simplistic advocacy/opposition paradigm to a more modest, and complex, question: *Under what conditions can digital technologies promote particular kinds of learning in particular educational and socioeconomic contexts?* Thus, questions regarding the efficacy of technological investment in education must be focused on specific contexts rather than being posed in a general way.

Investment in educational technology in schools has been motivated by two major goals:

- To promote the development of the kinds of literacy (and numeracy) skills required to function effectively in the global economy and society of the 21st century (henceforth, *21st-century literacy skills*);
- To improve traditional learning outcomes for all students, but particularly for socioeconomically marginalized students who experience disproportionate underachievement.

The bulk of research evidence at this point in relation to these two goals is descriptive. As discussed in more detail later in this chapter, the research suggests that students in affluent schools are well on their way to developing 21st-century literacy skills both as a result of extensive access to appropriate technologies at home and at school and pedagogies in school that use these technologies as tools for collaborative inquiry.

The research provides a much less optimistic picture for low-income and minority students. These students have considerably less access than their affluent peers to appropriate technologies both at home and at school and they are much more likely to engage in technology-supported drill and practice activities at school than technology-supported collaborative inquiry activities. There is also no evidence that greater technology access has resulted in any measurable increase in traditional literacy achievement, although small-scale research studies suggest that the potential for benefits does exist.

Thus, for socioeconomically marginalized students, the recent investment in educational technology is currently achieving neither of the goals just outlined. These students appear much less likely to develop strong 21st-century literacy skills in comparison to their affluent peers and the potential benefits of technology-supported learning for the development of traditional literacy skills remains unrealized.

The chapter argues that reversal of these trends for socioeconomically marginalized students requires a sustained challenge to the *pedagogical divide* that separates affluent and less affluent schools. Case studies show clearly that less affluent and English language learning (ELL) students are very much capable of using technological resources for collaborative critical inquiry when they are given opportunities in school or out-of-school contexts to do so. However, the accountability mandates of adequate yearly progress (AYP) and high-stakes testing associated with the No Child Left Behind (NCLB) legislation have resulted in a pedagogical focus on teaching to the test in many less affluent schools and a perception that imaginative inquiry-focused teaching is "off-task." Consequently, the potential power of technology is only rarely and minimally harnessed in these school contexts.

In order to foreground the centrality of pedagogical issues related to technology use, the next section discusses three broad pedagogical orientations—

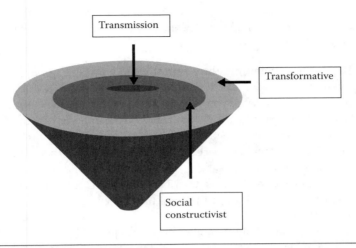

Figure 3.1 Nested pedagogical orientations

transmission, social constructivist, and *transformative*—that have significant consequences for how computers and other new technologies will be used to support learning.

Pedagogical Orientations for Computer-Supported Learning

The representation of these three pedagogical orientations in Figure 3.1 is intended to highlight the fact that, ideally, they co-exist in a complementary rather than an oppositional relationship to each other (Skourtou, Kourtis-Kazoullis, & Cummins, 2006). The orientations are nested within each other rather than being distinct and isolated from each other. Transmission-oriented pedagogy is represented in the inner circle with the narrowest focus. The goal is to transmit information and skills articulated in the curriculum directly to students. Social constructivist pedagogy, occupying the middle pedagogical space, incorporates the curriculum focus of transmitting information and skills, but broadens it to include the development among students of higher order thinking abilities based on teachers and students co-constructing knowledge and understanding. The focus is on experiential learning, collaborative inquiry, and knowledge building. Finally, transformative approaches to pedagogy broaden the focus still further by emphasizing the relevance not only of experiential learning and collaborative inquiry but also of enabling students to gain insight into how knowledge intersects with power. Transformative pedagogy uses collaborative critical inquiry to enable students to analyze and understand the social realities of their own lives and of their communities. Students discuss, and frequently act on, ways in which these realities might be transformed through various forms of social action. The goal is to promote critical literacy among students with a focus on social realities relevant to issues of equity and justice. For example, in discussing a historical text, students might pursue the following lines of inquiry (Chascas & Cummins, 2005):

- The text is written from the perspective of ... (people, group, country, etc.)
- People in the text whose perspectives are not discussed include ...
- Why was this text written? What audience did the author(s) have in mind? What response does the author hope readers will have to the text?
- How does the language used by the author help him/her influence the readers' response?
- How are males and females described in the text? Are there any differences or inequalities in the roles that males and females play in the text?
- How are members of different cultural groups described in the text? Are there inequalities in the roles that members of different cultural groups play in the text?
- Would people with different life experiences see the issues in the same way? For example, would the issues be perceived in a similar way by people of different income levels (poor people as compared to rich people), different genders (females as compared to males), or different cultures?
- What evidence is provided in the text for the views that are expressed? Is this evidence valid or convincing? If yes, why? If no, why not?
- Could people in the text have acted differently than how they did? What alternative actions could they have taken? How would these alternatives have affected events in the story or history?

The rationale for nesting these orientations within each other is to highlight the fact that features of traditional/transmission pedagogy are relevant to all kinds of learning. Both in classrooms that are clearly traditionally oriented as well as in communities of critical inquiry among students and teachers, structured guidelines and explicit instruction can play an important role in effective teaching/learning. Transmission of information and skills become problematic only when they constitute the predominant or even exclusive focus of instruction. Similarly, a transformative orientation builds on and expands social constructivist approaches in order to pursue a wider variety of pedagogical goals and a broader educational vision.

The different instructional emphases of the three pedagogical orientations can be illustrated in relation to a concrete technology-supported classroom example. Bracey (2000) described a project where her students, many of them ELL, worked with scientists from the National Aeronautics and Space Administration (NASA):

In one NASA project I did with my 4th- and 5th-graders called Marsville, we connected with other classrooms online to design a Marsville City. (www.challengercenter.org/tr/tr_prpro_set.htm). Marsville was a project-based activity where students created a prototype habitat for Mars. The children came together to learn and build their city and make their own living spaces using a variety of interdisciplinary skills. In the process, they learned creative problem-solving, cooperative learning and data analysis. We studied the systems needed to survive on Mars. We did not just read about it, we did it! It was exciting to see how such a project engaged my immigrant students who were still learning English, and motivated their reading and science learning. (Bracey, 2000, pp. 4–5)

This example clearly reflects a social constructivist orientation insofar as it involves collaborative inquiry and cognitive challenge intended to develop higher order thinking skills. It also is likely to be much more highly motivating for students than simply learning about Mars or human habitats from a textbook, as they might within a transmission-oriented classroom. It is worth noting also that the active, hands-on, cooperative activities appeared to be cognitively engaging and motivating for the ELL students who were learning through a second language. These students were learning both scientific content and second language structures and functions simultaneously.

Within a transformative pedagogical orientation, the Marsville project described by Bracey (2000) might be followed up or integrated with a project that examines the problems of human habitats *on earth* and the causes of these problems. Students might design a habitat on earth that addresses or avoids current urban problems such as homelessness, violence, poverty, and pollution. This would require that students research and analyze sources of inequity in income and causes of pollution and violence and discuss how these problems can be resolved.

It is clear that technology has very different potential for supporting learning within each of these pedagogical orientations. Within a transmission orientation, technology is likely to play a minimal role because all the information that students are expected to learn is already contained in the textbook. As the cognitive challenge and learning expectations expand within social constructivist and transformative orientations, the information resources and communication and presentation tools afforded by various forms of digital technology increase in significance.

Obviously, these three broad orientations incorporate considerable variation in emphasis and implementation. For example, it is possible to acknowledge the importance of clearly and explicitly transmitting information and skills without endorsing one-size-fits-all scripted instructional approaches that reduce students to passive roles within the teaching–learning process. Similarly, social constructivist and transformative approaches may vary considerably and merge into each other even in the same lesson or curriculum unit. Thus, the nested orientations should be viewed as a continuum of pedagogical emphasis rather than as discrete categories.

These pedagogical orientations are crucial to understanding the pattern of research on the effects of computers and other digital technologies on student learning. The evidence reviewed later in this chapter suggests that technology is likely to have far greater impact on student learning when it is harnessed to social constructivist or transformative orientations to pedagogy than when it is employed to reinforce transmission of a prescribed curriculum with the focus on the internalization of information and skills. However, this impact may not be picked up by experimental or quasi-experimental research designs because typical standardized tests are minimally sensitive to the kinds of learning promoted by social constructivist and transformative orientations (e.g., building a Web page, analyzing bias in news coverage, etc.). These learning outcomes can be identified by ethnographic and case study research but qualitative forms of research are often dismissed or ignored by policymakers. An additional reason why convincing research evidence for the impact of technology on achievement is lacking is that the power of technology is very much under-utilized when it is harnessed only to transmission-oriented pedagogy and thus large effects are unlikely to be observed. These points are elaborated in subsequent sections.

Access To and Use of Technology in Affluent and Less Affluent Schools

Surveys carried out during the late 1990s and early 2000s have consistently shown a significant gap in both home and school access to new technologies across income and ethnic/racial groups, as Durán's and Parker's chapters (this volume) also discuss. For example, DeBell and Chapman (2003) report that, in 2001, 5- to 17-year-olds whose families lived in poverty were less likely to use the Internet at home than 5- to 17-year-olds whose families were not in poverty (47% compared with 82%). With respect to disparities in home access to computers between ethnic/racial groups, Wilhelm, Carmen, and Reynolds (2002) report the following statistics:

> In 2001, 83% of non-Hispanic White children lived in households with computers, compared to only 46% of Black children and 47% of Hispanic children. ... There are similar gaps in access to the Internet at home. Based on data collected in 2001, 50% of non-Hispanic White children were able to connect to the Internet at home, compared to only 25% of Black children and 20% of Hispanic children. (p. 4)

Within schools, overall access to computers has increased rapidly but the digital divide still persists. According to Parsad and Jones (2005):

- Schools with the highest poverty concentration in 2003 had 5.1 students for each instructional computer with Internet access whereas schools with the lowest poverty concentration had 4.2 students to each instructional computer with Internet access;
- Schools with high minority enrollment (at least 50%) had 5.1 students per instructional computer with Internet access compared to 4.1 students in schools with low minority enrolment (less than 6%);
- High poverty schools and those with high minority enrollment were less likely to have a school Web site than more affluent schools and those with low minority enrolment (72% vs. 96% for highest vs. lowest poverty categories, and 80% vs. 94% for highest vs. lowest minority enrolment categories).

The persistence of the digital divide reflected in these trends is reinforced by data showing significant differences in the ways technology is used in affluent as compared to less affluent schools. A survey carried out by the periodical *Education Week* (Manzo, 2001) reported that for low achievers and for students in poor urban schools, technology is typically introduced as a remedial tool involving skills-based software whereas teachers of more advanced students tend to use a variety of more sophisticated programs. Warschauer, Knobel, and Stone (2004) similarly review a number of studies showing an emphasis on remedial or vocational uses of new technology by low socioeconomic status (SES) or Black and Hispanic students and more academic uses of technology by higher-SES or White and Asian students.

Warschauer and colleagues' (2004) study of eight low- and high-SES California high schools compared the availability of, access to, and use of information and communication technologies (ICT) within these schools. Although student-to-computer ratios in the schools were similar, significant differences emerged between schools in the effectiveness with which computers were used. The low-SES schools were affected by uneven human support networks and irregular home access to computers by students. In addition, pedagogical options were constrained by the intense pressure teachers experienced to raise test scores, particularly among the many English learners in these schools. High-SES schools, by contrast, had considerably fewer English learners and were able to integrate technology more effectively into classroom instruction.

Warschauer and colleagues identified "performativity" as a predominant pattern of computer use in the schools they studied. This construct "refers to situations in which teachers are going through the motions or ticking off checklists of skills without paying due attention to larger issues of knowledge construction and purposeful learning" (pp. 574–576). Performativity is illustrated in activities such as learning basic computer skills or how to use a particular program such as PowerPoint as an end in itself. Performativity was evident in both high- and low-SES schools, but it seemed to have a special impact on students in low-SES schools insofar as teachers often focused on basic computer skills because they assumed (often incorrectly) that students didn't have home access to computers. Warschauer and colleagues suggest that the instructional focus on enabling students to acquire fluent skills in particular software applications acts as a distraction from more powerful applications of technology for knowledge generation and inquiry, a distraction that low-SES students can ill-afford. They conclude that rather than reducing educational inequities, the introduction of information and communication technologies in the eight schools they investigated served to *amplify* existing forms of inequality.

In summary, although significant differences across socioeconomic groups in access to digital technologies both at home and at school still exist, these quantitative disparities have been reduced in recent years. However, the digital divide has been replaced by a *pedagogical divide* in the way new technologies are used to support instruction, and a corresponding *cognitive divide* in the way students use the new technologies as they engage in different forms of learning. Students in low-SES schools experience transmission-oriented pedagogy focused predominantly on skills acquisition whereas social constructivist orientations, associated with considerably more powerful uses of technology, are employed in higher SES schools. As suggested by Warschauer and his colleagues, technology may actually have exacerbated this inequitable access to learning opportunities by amplifying the impact of inquiry-oriented pedagogy in high-SES schools while reinforcing transmission approaches in low-SES schools.

The next section examines the empirical evidence on the extent to which information and communication technologies (ICT) are effective in supporting language and literacy learning among the general student population and more specifically among Latino/a and other English learners.

Effectiveness of ICT IN Supporting Student Learning
Minimal Evidence for Large-scale Impact as Measured by Standardized Tests

If technology infusion by itself were effective in advancing student achievement (as many policymakers have naively assumed), then we would expect to see some overall gains in standardized test scores that could be attributed to greater technology access in schools. Contrary to these expectations, there is minimal evidence of any overall enhancement of academic learning among school-age learners despite massive ICT expenditure in both North American and European schools during the past decade (Angrist & Lavy 2002; Bennett, 2002; Cuban, 2001; Fuchs & Woessmann, 2004; Goolsbee & Guryan, 2002). For example, national achievement scores have remained flat in the United States for most of the past 30 years, impervious to multiple reform initiatives as well as dramatically increased technology spending. This apparent lack of impact is not surprising when digital technologies are viewed as simply one component in a complex ecology of learning and teaching. As Cuban (2001) has pointed out "the most serious problems afflicting urban and rural poor schools—inequitable funding, extraordinary health and social needs growing out of poverty, crumbling facilities, unqualified teachers—have little to do with a lack of technology" (pp. 188–189).

Two recent studies illustrate the failure to demonstrate academic gains on standardized tests associated with technology use. An analysis of large-scale data from countries in the Organization for Economic Cooperation and Development (OECD) carried out by Fuchs and Woessmann (2004) suggested that access to computers might even exert a negative impact on achievement. The study involved a sample of more than 100,000 15-year-old students in 31 countries. The authors report that when family background and school characteristics are controlled, "the mere availability of computers at home is negatively related to student performance in math and reading and the availability of computers at school is unrelated to student performance" (2004, p. 17). Some uses of computers at home, however, did show a positive association with achievement. These uses included accessing e-mails and Web pages, and having educational software at home.

In the United States, Warschauer (2006) conducted a multisite case study that examined literacy practices in ten culturally and linguistically diverse K–12 schools in California and Maine in which all the students in at least one classroom were provided with laptop computers. The introduction of laptops appeared to increase students' engagement with literacy in a variety of ways. Teachers, students, and parents all reported that students spent more time on task, worked more independently, enjoyed learning more, and took part in a greater variety of learning activities at school and at home than they had prior to receiving laptops. They incorporated multimedia into their assignments and in many cases demonstrated highly creative work (e.g., they probed literature more deeply by composing music to it). However, these enhancements of students' literacy experience and engagement were not reflected in reading, writing, or language arts test scores that remained flat. Warschauer attributes the discrepancy between measured outcomes and the expanded literacy activities in which students engaged to several factors including the newness of the laptop program at the schools and the fact that standardized tests are not sensitive to the kinds of literacy processes that laptops enhanced (e.g., ease of searching for information, revision of writing, incorporation of multimedia, etc.).

Some Evidence of Impact in Small-scale Studies

Although there is as yet little evidence that access to and use of computers will increase overall test scores among the general student population, meta-analyses of small-scale studies suggest that, under certain conditions, ICT can promote academic learning among both school age and adult samples. Typically in these studies, the outcome measures are designed to assess specific instructional objectives and thus are more sensitive than standardized tests to the learning that takes place. Fletcher's (2003) review of research on the effects of technology-assisted instruction, for example, showed effect sizes ranging from .39 to 1.05 depending on the extent of individualization or "intelligent tutoring" incorporated into the program. These effect sizes are the equivalent of raising percentiles ranks from the 50th percentile to the 65th percentile (effect size of .39) and from the 50th percentile to the 85th percentile (effect size 1.05). He concludes: "This review of technology-based instruction suggests that it will most probably lower costs and increase effectiveness for many applications" (2003, p. 97).

Willis (2003) summarizes a range of meta-analyses of computers in schools that conclude that computers can positively impact learning: "The 15 or so meta-analyses of computers in schools are cited over and over in the literature to support increased use of technology in education" (p. 18). He argues cogently, however, that it doesn't make sense to even try to answer a general question about effectiveness of computers in education because there are so many specific contextual variables and so many ways that computers can be used in education that the general question is meaningless: "No single example is sufficiently typical enough to allow us to generalize from the research study to other examples of that type" (p. 22).

Willis' (2003) point about the centrality of context is relevant to the interpretation of two meta-analyses of the impact of computer use on reading carried out by the National Reading Panel (NRP, 2000) and Blok, Oostdam, Otter, and Overmaat (2002). The NRP focused on 21 experimental studies published between 1986 and 1996. They concluded that: "All the studies in the analysis report positive results" (NRP, 2000, p. 6–2). These results spanned a range of decoding and comprehension skills. With respect to instructional applications they suggest that the ability of the computer to transform speech to print and the use of hypertext hold promise. However, the NRP authors go on to lament the fact that so little research has been carried out on the impact of computers on reading (a point also addressed by Kamil, Intrator, & Kim, 2000). Furthermore, they claim to have uncovered "few examples of truly new uses for computer technology to date. ... For now, the computer seems to be used as technology to either present or augment traditional instructional practices" (2000, p. 6–2). The failure of the NRP to uncover "truly new uses for computer technology" is hardly surprising in view of their refusal to consider any qualitative research on reading (or technology). The projects described throughout this book showcase multiple innovative and powerful uses of computers. However, these projects usually do not lend themselves to experimental and quasi-experimental research designs and so were not reviewed by the NRP. Leu, Ataya and Coiro (2002) have also highlighted the limitations of the NRP findings in relation to technology and the fact that we do have a much more extensive research basis for policy and practice than acknowledged by the NRP (see also Castek et al. this volume).

A second meta-analysis of the impact of computers on reading development carried out by Blok and colleagues reviewed 42 studies of beginning reading published between 1982 and 2000. Only six of these studies overlapped with those in the NRP review. The selection of studies in the two reviews differed partly because Blok and colleagues focused on reading subskills related to decoding and fluency, excluding studies whose primary focus was vocabulary and reading comprehension. The NRP included such studies in its database and also did not restrict the focus to the beginning reading phase.

Blok and colleagues found an overall effect size of $d = 0.2$ indicating a positive but minimal effect. They note that the effect size rises to $d = 0.5$ when only studies involving beginning reading in English are considered. They consider the possibility that this difference is due to the less regular sound–symbol relationship in English as compared to many other languages. However, they warn against concluding that students do profit from computer-assisted instruction programs when English is the language of instruction. They point out that the effect size estimate is based on comparison with untrained control groups. In other words, the data may reflect the fact that any intervention might exert an effect regardless of whether it is technology-based. Furthermore, they note that research on phonological awareness training reviewed by Foster et al. (1994) suggests that teacher-based training is more effective than computer-based training. Blok and colleagues conclude that if this pattern "withstood further scrutiny and if it could be generalized to other CAI [Computer Assisted Instruction] program types, there is little reason for teachers of beginning reading to convert to computer-assisted reading instruction" (2002, p. 123).

The issue of cost-effectiveness is also raised by Wenglinsky (1998) with reference to mathematics instruction. He argues that computer-assisted instruction is not cost-effective insofar as tutoring produces greater gains for less money. In the case of early reading instruction, the reality is that a large majority of students (ELL and native English-speakers) acquire relatively fluent decoding skills in English when they receive appropriate instruction (e.g., Geva, 2000; Kwan & Willows, 1998). Although there may be cost-effective benefits associated with particular computer software for students who have specific reading or learning disabilities, for most students expensive technological supports are neither necessary nor cost-effective. Many low-SES and Latino/a students experience difficulties, however, in sustaining growth in literacy development beyond the primary years. As I argue in the following section, certain kinds of technology-based interventions show promise in reversing this trend and supporting sustained literacy development. For the most part, these technology supports involve the standard suite of software applications that are available on most modern computers (e.g., word processors, presentation and image/ video manipulation software, Internet access, Web-page design, etc.). Thus, no additional hardware or software cost is involved beyond the cost of the basic infrastructure.

The next section focuses on research, albeit minimal, that has examined the impact of technology on the literacy development of ELL students.

ICT, Literacy, and ELL Students

None of the literature reviews of experimental and quasi-experimental research just summarized includes any study focused directly on ELL students. Similarly, no study focused on Latino/a students whether ELL or non-ELL. The lack of research linking ICT, literacy and ELL students can be appreciated in relation to the virtual absence of any discussion of empirical research in Butler-Pascoe and Wiburg's (2003) book *Technology and Teaching English Language Learners.* The book is an excellent review of various software resources available on the market and their relationship to the broader literature on second language learning; however, very little research related to the various software resources is discussed.

A useful survey of technology applications with ELL students was prepared by the North Central Regional Educational Laboratory and contains considerable detail about how various school systems are using technology to support language learning (Svedkauskaite & Reza-Hernández, n.d.). However, there is minimal focus on research in the document, presumably because the research itself is minimal. This conclusion is supported by LeLoup and Ponterio's (2003) review of the research in second language acquisition and technology that reported that most of the research has been carried out with college-level participants and "[v]ery little research in this area has been done at the K–12 level, but this is where most language instruction takes place in the United States" (p. 1).

Similarly, August and Associates' (2003) review entitled *Supporting the Development of English Literacy in English Language Learners* could identify very few research studies that focused on the impact of ICT on ELL students. One of the few studies that did focus on ELL students was reported by Meskill and Mossop (2000). These authors carried out a survey of technology use by more than 800 ESL teachers and observed extensively in two classrooms over a 2-year period. Their survey and observation data (considered in more detail in a later section) suggested increased motivation and excitement for learning as a result of technology use.

The apparent paucity of research might lead one to conclude (erroneously, I believe) that there is very little scientific basis for planning technology-supported interventions for ELL students. On the contrary, I would argue that the available research (much of it in case study form—see, e.g., Castek and colleagues, this volume) does provide a basis for making coherent claims regarding the potential impact of certain technologically supported interventions. Traditional experimental and quasi-experimental research designs for investigating ICT and education are limited on at least two counts. First, applications to policy and practice are usually problematic because, as Willis (2003) has argued, the multiple contexts and complexity of interacting variables make it largely futile to search for broad generalizations regarding the impact of ICT on learning. Second, as Castek and colleagues (this volume) have argued, technologies and literacies are continuously changing and the emergence of new technologies requires and evokes the development of new literacies. This conception of *literacy as deixis* limits the relevance of traditional forms of research that have typically focused on specific *technologies* rather than on underlying pedagogical principles. The problem is compounded by the fact that inevitably, by the time traditional research is published and digested by policymakers, the technologies under investigation have been superseded by newer technologies.

By contrast, a well-documented case study of a particular project or intervention can provide considerable information and insight that is relevant for both policy and pedagogy. For example, a case study of a particular technology-supported intervention can demonstrate or suggest:

- that this kind of intervention *can* be implemented (because it *was* implemented);
- the conditions that need to be in place for successful implementation;
- the forms of cognitive engagement and affective response that the intervention evokes on the part of participating students.

Case studies can also contribute to hypothesis testing and theory development by refuting certain assumptions or hypotheses that may be influencing policy. For example, the assumption (reflected in the practice of many school districts) that low-SES and culturally diverse students are not as capable of benefiting from higher order technology-supported academic work compared to high-SES students can be called into question by case studies of technology-supported inquiry demonstrating higher order knowledge generation by low-SES students.

In summary, the apparent lack of evidence for large-scale impact of technology in education reflects a variety of factors including the lack of sensitivity of standardized tests to the learning processes involved in social constructivist and transformative pedagogical approaches and the uneven implementation of technology-supported learning in many schools serving low-income students. As pointed out by Willis (2003), these contextual variables render questions about the general or overall impact of technology on learning largely meaningless. The lack of obvious overall impact has increased the credibility of critics who challenge the general assumption that investment in ICT will improve educational outcomes. Critics have highlighted the diversion of scarce resources by cash-strapped schools from other areas of the curriculum and pointed to the failure of virtually every technological innovation introduced to schools during the past century to improve learning in any significant way (Armstrong & Casement, 1998; Cuban, 1986, 2001; Healy, 1998; Oppenheimer, 1997, 2003). The lack of demonstrable impact on standardized test scores, however, should not obscure the findings of case studies and ethnographic research (e.g., Warschauer, 2006; Warschauer, Grant, Del Real, & Rousseau, 2004) that highlight the expanded range of literacy practices that technology can promote when it is liberated from rigid and narrowly focused varieties of transmission pedagogy.

The remainder of this chapter focuses on understanding the potential of ICT to increase academic achievement among ELL and low-SES Latino/a students. The goal is to articulate a set of design principles that can be applied to creating technological tools and evaluating technology-supported interventions aimed at promoting Latino/a students' literacy development. A first step in this process is to clarify exactly what aspects of literacy development are most problematic for low-income Latino/a students. If we know where the literacy development process breaks down, then we can design technology-supported interventions that are focused directly on the problems that students are experiencing. To this end, the next section examines the nature of academic development and the conditions that promote optimal learning.

Academic Language Development Among Low-Income ELL Students

In order to understand patterns of academic development among ELL students, we must distinguish between three very different aspects of proficiency in a language: (a) conversational fluency, (b) discrete language skills, and (c) academic language proficiency. The rationale for making these distinctions is that each dimension of proficiency follows very different developmental paths among both ELL and non-ELL students and each responds differently to particular kinds of instructional practices in school.

Conversational Fluency   This dimension of language proficiency represents the ability to carry on a conversation in familiar face-to-face situations. The vast majority of native speakers of English have developed conversational fluency when they enter school at age 5. This fluency involves use of high frequency words and simple grammatical constructions. Certainly, conversational fluency evolves in complexity according to sociolinguistic context and the language registers required in particular situations (e.g., a job interview). However, for present purposes, it is sufficient to note that ELL students generally develop peer-appropriate fluency in conversational aspects of English within a year or two of intensive exposure to the language either in school or in the environment.

In elementary school contexts where English is the language of the environment, there is little rationale for providing computer-assisted support for the acquisition of English conversational skills in school. These skills are generally picked up rapidly through social interaction in and out of the classroom.

Discrete Language Skills These skills involve the learning of rule-governed aspects of language (including phonology, grammar, and spelling) where acquisition of the general case permits generalization to other instances governed by that particular rule. Becker describes this process with respect to decoding as follows: "… one can teach a set of sounds, blending skills, and rapid pronunciation skills, so that the student can read any regular-sound word composed from the sounds taught" (1977, p. 533). Research suggests that a combination of rich literacy experiences and explicit instruction appears to yield the most positive outcomes in teaching decoding and other discrete language skills (e.g., Cunningham, 1990; Hatcher et al., 1994). Students exposed to a literacy-rich environment in the home generally acquire initial literacy-related skills, such as phonemic awareness and letter-sound correspondences, with minimal difficulty in the early grades of schooling (e.g., Neuman, 1999).

ELL students can learn these specific language skills concurrently with their development of basic vocabulary and conversational fluency. However, little direct transference is observed to other aspects of oral language proficiency such as linguistic concepts, vocabulary, sentence memory, and word memory (Geva, 2000; Kwan & Willows, 1998). Similar findings are reported by Verhoeven (2000) for minority language students in the Dutch context and by Lambert and Tucker (1972) for English-speaking students in French immersion programs.

As reported by Blok et al. (2002), there is some evidence that computer-supported instruction can enhance the acquisition of these discrete language skills in contexts where English is the target language of instruction. However, the evidence is not particularly strong, especially given the fact that the vast majority of students (including ELL students—e.g., Geva, 2000) do acquire phonological awareness and decoding skills with relative ease given appropriate (noncomputer-supported) instruction.

Academic Language Proficiency This dimension of proficiency includes knowledge of the less frequent vocabulary of English as well as the ability to interpret and produce increasingly complex written language. As students progress through the grades, they encounter far more low frequency words (primarily from Greek and Latin sources), complex syntax (e.g., passives), and abstract expressions that are virtually never heard in everyday conversation. Students are required to understand linguistically and conceptually demanding texts in the content areas (e.g., literature, social studies, science, mathematics) and to use this language in an accurate and coherent way in their own writing.

Acquiring academic language is challenging for all students. For example, schools spend at least 12 years trying to extend the conversational language that native-speaking children bring to school into these more complex academic language spheres. It is hardly surprising, therefore, that research has repeatedly shown that ELL students, on average, require *at least* 5 years of exposure to academic English to catch up to native-speaker norms (Cummins, 1981; Hakuta, Butler & Witt, 1999; Klesmer, 1994).

In addition to the complexity of the academic language they are attempting to acquire, ELL students must catch up to a moving target. Every year, native-speakers are making large gains in their reading and writing abilities and in their knowledge of vocabulary. In order to catch up to grade norms within 6 years, ELL students must make 15 months' gain in every 10-month school year. By contrast, the typical native-speaking student is expected to make 10 months' gain in a 10-month school year (Collier & Thomas, 1999).

All three aspects of language proficiency are important. However, policy-makers and the media frequently confuse them. Many ELL students who have acquired conversational fluency and decoding skills in English are still a long way from grade-level performance in academic language proficiency. Students who can "read" English fluently may have only a very limited understanding of the words they can decode.

There is considerable evidence that the major challenge for ELL students (and the major potential for technology-supported learning) resides in developing reading comprehension and academic language proficiency to grade-appropriate levels rather than in acquiring the subskills of beginning reading (Geva, 2000). Low-income and ELL students seem to be particularly susceptible to what has been termed "the fourth grade slump" (see Chall, Jacobs, & Baldwin, 1990; Chall & Snow, 1988; RAND Reading Study Group, 2002). Chall and Snow (1988) reported that "[e]xperienced teachers of low-income children have long reported a fourth-grade 'slump,' when their students' reading achievement slows down and reading problems increase" (p. 1). Chall and colleagues note:

> Whereas the major hurdles prior to grade 4 are learning to recognize in print the thousands of words whose meanings are already known and reading these fluently in connected texts with comprehension, the hurdle of grade 4 and beyond is coping with increasingly complex language and thought. (1990, p. 45)

The importance of vocabulary knowledge for reading has been frequently articulated (e.g., Corson, 1997). Nation and Coady (1988), for example, in reviewing research on the relationship between vocabulary and reading point out that "vocabulary difficulty has consistently been found to be the most significant predictor of overall readability." Once the effect of vocabulary difficulty (usually estimated by word frequency and/or familiarity and word length) is taken into account, other linguistic variables, such as sentence structure, account for little incremental variance in the readability of a text. They summarize their review as follows: "In general the research leaves us in little doubt about the importance of vocabulary knowledge for reading, and the value of reading as a means of increasing vocabulary" (p. 108).

The implication here for technology-supported instruction for English learners is that vocabulary acquisition is a potentially fertile focus for technology interventions designed to promote reading comprehension and academic language development. Although direct instruction of vocabulary has a place in supporting its development, this instruction is likely to be most effective when integrated into an authentic context that is relevant to students' learning goals. If low-frequency (nonconversational) vocabulary is found predominantly in written text, then logically, extensive reading of text must be promoted as a crucial component of both vocabulary acquisition and reading comprehension development.

Academic Language Development: Pedagogical Implications

There is considerable evidence for the importance of extensive reading in building up academic language proficiency in both the first and second language (L1 and L2; e.g., Elley, 1991; Guthrie, 2004; Krashen, 2004; Postlethwaite & Ross, 1992). Guthrie (2004), for example, highlights the centrality of literacy *engagement* for reading achievement. Drawing on 1998 NAEP data from the United States and the international comparisons of the 2002 Programme for International Student Assessment [PISA] he notes that students

> … whose family background was characterized by low income and low education, but who were highly engaged readers, substantially outscored students who came from backgrounds with higher education and higher income, but who themselves were less engaged readers. Based on a massive sample, this finding suggests the stunning conclusion that engaged reading can overcome traditional barriers to reading achievement, including gender, parental education, and income. (p. 5)

Guthrie notes that the term *engagement* incorporates notions of *time on task* (reading extensively), *affect* (enthusiasm and enjoyment of literacy), *depth of cognitive processing* (strategies to deepen comprehension), and *active pursuit of literacy activities* (amount and diversity of literacy practices in and out of school). He notes that engaged readers are active and energized in reading and use their minds with an emphasis on either cognitive strategies or conceptual knowledge. Furthermore, he notes that engaged reading is often socially interactive insofar as engaged students are capable of discussion or sharing with friends despite the fact that much of their reading may be solitary. Guthrie's emphasis on the development of strategies to deepen comprehension draws on extensive research highlighting the effectiveness of strategy instruction in reading achievement (Postlethwaite & Ross, 1992; Pressley, Duke, & Boling, 2004).

Guthrie's account of the centrality of literacy engagement is consistent with the Academic Expertise framework articulated by Cummins (2001). This framework argues for the importance of both cognitive engagement and identity investment in any conception of teaching for deep understanding. Teacher–student interactions, and other interactions within the learning community, create an interpersonal space within which knowledge is generated and identities are negotiated. Learning will be optimized when these interactions maximize both cognitive engagement and identity investment (Cummins, 2001; Cummins, Brown, & Sayers, 2007). Thus, the Academic Expertise framework makes explicit the fact that classroom instruction always positions students in particular ways that reflect the implicit (or sometimes explicit) image of the student in the teacher's mind. How students are positioned either expands or constricts their opportunities for identity investment and engagement in cognitively challenging tasks. Although the construct of identity investment has not received much attention in the cognitive psychology or educational reform research literature, it has emerged as a significant explanatory construct in the educational anthropology and second language learning literature (e.g., Fordham, 1990; Norton, 2000).

The framework attempts to express in a very concrete way the kinds of instructional emphases and language interactions required to build students' academic expertise. Optimal instruction will include a *Focus on Meaning*, a *Focus on Language*, and a *Focus on Use*. The focus on meaning entails the development of critical literacy rather than surface-level processing of text. The focus on language involves promoting not just explicit knowledge of how the linguistic code operates but also critical awareness of how language operates within society. If students are to participate effectively within a democratic society they should be able to "read" how language is used to achieve social goals: to elucidate issues, to persuade, to deceive, to include, to exclude, and so on. The focus on use component argues that optimal instruction will enable students to generate knowledge, create literature and art, and act on social realities.

Thus far the analysis of patterns of academic language development among low-SES and ELL students suggests that technology-supported interventions might be most profitably directed at sustaining vocabulary growth and reading comprehension beyond the primary years of schooling. Attempts to synthesize the research literature on academic language development and draw out pedagogical implications (e.g., Cummins, 2001; Guthrie, 2004) have highlighted the importance of literacy engagement, cognitive challenge, and identity investment. What do we know about learning itself that might contribute to the design of appropriate technology-supported learning environments? This issue is considered in the next section.

How People Learn: Criteria for Effective Learning Environments

Technological tools attempt to create electronic environments that will effectively support students' learning. This immediately raises the issue of what we know about how people learn. A scientific basis for answering this question is provided in the volume written by Bransford, Brown, and Cocking (2000) entitled *How People Learn* and published by the National Research Council. This volume synthesized the research evidence regarding how learning occurs and the optimal conditions to foster learning. A follow-up volume edited by Donovan and Bransford (2005) examined the application of these learning principles to the teaching of History, Mathematics, and Science. The relevance of these principles for developing technological supports for Latino/a and other English learners is that they constitute design principles for instructional effectiveness whether the instructional environment is face-to-face or electronic. If these design principles are not identifiable in technological supports or computer programs for English learners then these electronic environments are not congruent with the scientific evidence.

Bransford and his colleagues emphasize three conditions for effective learning: engaging prior understandings, integrating factual knowledge with conceptual frameworks, and taking active control over the learning process.

Engaging Prior Understandings

Donovan and Bransford (2005, p. 4) point out that *"new understandings are constructed on a foundation of existing understandings and experiences"* (emphasis in the original). Prior knowledge, skills, beliefs, and concepts significantly influence what learners notice about their environment and how they organize and interpret it. This principle implies that both classroom instruction and electronic learning environments should explicitly activate students' prior knowledge and build relevant background knowledge as necessary.

Integrating Factual Knowledge with Conceptual Frameworks

Bransford and colleagues (2000) point out that to develop competence in an area of inquiry "knowledge of a large set of disconnected facts is not sufficient" (p. 16). Students must be provided with opportunities to learn with understanding because "[d]eep understanding of subject matter transforms factual information into usable knowledge" (p. 16). This focus on deeper understanding clearly suggests an inquiry-oriented pedagogical approach rather than a transmission approach.

Taking Active Control over the Learning Process

Donovan and Bransford (2005) point out that "a 'metacognitive' or self-monitoring approach can help students develop the ability to take control of their own learning, consciously define learning goals, and monitor their progress in achieving them" (p. 10). When students take ownership of the learning process and invest their identities in the outcomes of learning, the resulting understanding will be deeper than when learning is passive.

Bransford and colleagues (2000) also emphasize the importance of support within the community of learners. Learning takes place in a social context and a supportive learning community encourages dialogue, apprenticeship, and mentoring. Learning is not simply a cognitive process that takes place inside the heads of individual students; it also involves socialization into particular communities of practice. Within these learning communities novices are enabled to participate in the practices of the community from the very beginning of their involvement. Lave and Wenger (1991) describe this process as *legitimate peripheral participation*. The learning community can include the classroom, the school, the family and broader community, and virtual communities enabled through electronic communication.

In the present context, these principles imply that in planning any technology-supported intervention, policymakers and administrators must consider the extent to which technology-supported interventions promote deep rather than superficial understanding, activate or ignore students' prior knowledge, and evoke active rather than passive learning. As just outlined, in low-SES classroom contexts, technology implementation is frequently "on the wrong side of the track" as far as these principles of learning are concerned. Thus, these principles can serve as criteria for judging the consistency of any software program or technology-supported intervention with what we know about how people learn.

Design Criteria for Technology-Supported Learning and Teaching

The articulation of design criteria for technology-supported interventions for ELL students draws on Wood's (2001) analysis of 16 computer programs that showed promise or claimed to support children's vocabulary development. Based on the research literature, Wood identified five criteria for evaluating the nature of the vocabulary instruction in software products:

Criterion 1: Does it relate the new to the known?
Criterion 2: Does it promote active, in-depth processing of new words?
Criterion 3: Does it provide multiple exposures to new words?
Criterion 4: Does it teach students to be strategic readers?
Criterion 5: Does it promote additional reading?

These five criteria are clearly consistent with the principles of learning proposed by Bransford and his colleagues (2000) and with the analysis of literacy development and academic language learning articulated by Guthrie (2004) and Cummins (2001). Wood's analysis revealed that many software products that made no explicit claims about fostering vocabulary learning reflected the five criteria better than many that made explicit claims. Programs designed explicitly to teach vocabulary often simply presented drill and practice routines rather than helping students to develop a deeper understanding of a word.

The common themes highlighted in these accounts can be synthesized into the following six design principles expressed as questions:

- Does the technology-supported intervention (TSI) provide cognitive challenge and opportunities for deep processing of meaning?
- Does the TSI relate instruction to prior knowledge and experiences derived from students' homes and communities?
- Does the TSI promote active collaborative inquiry?
- Does the TSI promote extensive engaged reading and writing across the curriculum?
- Does the TSI help students develop strategies for effective reading, writing and learning?
- Does the TSI promote identity investment on the part of students?

Following the procedure adopted by Wood (2001), these design criteria, derived directly from the research on academic language development, are applied to case studies of technology-supported learning involving ELL students.

Applying the Design Criteria to the Evaluation of Technology-Supported Interventions Involving ELL Students

As noted in the first part of this chapter, there are virtually no experimental or quasi-experimental research studies focused on the impact of technology on Latino/a students' literacy development (e.g., August & Associates, 2003). The available research consists of surveys and case studies, examples of which are outlined in the following section (see also Castek and colleagues, this volume). The six design principles just articulated are used to interpret this research.

Prior to considering the available research, it is useful to distinguish two broad categories of technology-mediated interventions relevant to literacy development:

- Interventions that make use of software specifically designed to teach or support the development of reading, writing, or content knowledge
- Interventions that make use of the standard suite of software found on most modern computers (e.g., word-processing, presentation software, Internet access, spreadsheets, databases, etc.).

Among the former are programs such as *Inspiration/Kidspiration*, *Knowledge Forum*® (Bereiter & Scardamalia, 2003), the *Thinking Reader* (Rose & Dalton, 2002), and *e-Lective Language Learning* (Cummins, Ardeshiri, & Cohen, in press; Chascas & Cummins, 2005). *Inspiration* and *Knowledge Forum*®

both support the process of knowledge building. *Knowledge Forum*® has been used successfully with ELL (Inuit) students in the Canadian Eastern Arctic (McAuley, 1998, 2001, 2003) and its collaborative inquiry-based environment results in students reading and writing more extensively than in regular instruction and also being willing to read more difficult texts in pursuit of their research and theory generation (Bereiter & Scardamalia, 2003). Donsky (2006) has recently illustrated how *Knowledge Forum*® can be harnessed as a potent tool for critical antiracist education.

Thinking Reader and *e-Lective Language Learning* provide scaffolds to support comprehension of electronic text and expansion of students' knowledge of academic language. A major difference between them is that *Thinking Reader* builds scaffolds into specific texts that are already embedded in the program whereas *e-Lective* permits any text in electronic form to be imported into the program. This allows considerably more flexibility in what can be read but at some cost to the type of scaffolds that can be used. For example, scaffolds must be generic rather than focused on the content of the specific texts incorporated within the program.

The second category of technology-supported interventions offers significant promise for enhancing the academic development of ELL students even though the technological tools they utilize were not developed or designed specifically for this purpose. Many of the common functionalities available on computers can be viewed as *mindtools* (Jonassen, 1996, 1999; Jonassen, Carr, & Yueh, 1998). Jonassen introduced the concept of *mindtools* to highlight ways in which computer applications can be used for knowledge construction and critical thinking. Jonassen and colleagues argue that technologies should not support learning by attempting to instruct the learners, but rather should be used as knowledge construction tools that students learn *with*, not *from*. In this way, learners function as designers, and the computers function as mindtools for interpreting and organizing their personal knowledge.

> Mindtools are computer applications that, when used by learners to represent what they know, necessarily engage them in critical thinking about the content they are studying. (1998, p. 24)

Jonassen (1999) elaborates a framework for assessing the extent to which computer applications are being used as mindtools to generate knowledge and promote critical thinking. He specifies *engagement* (active to passive), *generativity* (focus on creation rather than presentation), and *control* (residing in the student as compared to the teacher or machine) as key dimensions. Knowledge generation and critical thinking require that the instructional emphasis be on student control, active engagement, and creation. This emphasis is clearly consistent with the six design principles articulated in the present chapter.

Examples of technology-supported interventions that reflect this social constructivist orientation are reviewed in the subsequent sections.

The Meskill and Mossop Study

As just noted, Meskill and Mossop (2000) carried out a survey of nearly 800 ESL teachers. They also carried out observations of student technology use over a 2-year period in two classrooms in which technology was being extensively used. They report that almost half (49%) of the surveyed teachers used technologies as part of their second language and literacy instruction. The study highlighted the role of the computer as a motivator for students to engage in learning tasks (with the exception of self-study drills) and the fact that use of the computer was associated with a growth of student status. ELL students who had received extensive hands-on computer experience became experts in their classes and school and were called on frequently by adults and peers for assistance in setting up hardware and software and troubleshooting problems.

Two types of software were extensively used by the two teachers involved in the extended case study: enhanced text processing tools and content-rich simulations. These are described as follows:

> Use of the former in the elementary context consisted of children creating their own stories with the software Once Upon a Time (1995)—a multimedia product that allows children to hear and use semantically grouped vocabulary items and manipulate accompanying illustrations to build stories. Use of the content-rich simulations such as MECC's Oregon Trail series and the Sim-series published by Maxis was frequent in both classrooms. Teachers pointed to the generative aspects of these software genres, for example, the amount and quality of literacy opportunities, the content richness and relevance, and the degree to which the software could be exploited for opportunities to practice the language and literacy needed for school. (Meskill & Mossop, 2000, p. 588)

The teachers reported that students were "especially responsive when they were able to create products of their learning to share with others" (p. 588). Meskill and Mossop note that "tremendous enthusiasm for learning with e-texts pervaded the class sessions observed and interviews with students" (p. 588). They elaborate on this description as follows:

> Because of the public nature of e-text activity, children could share their minute-by-minute successes with teachers and peers. ... Their finished work, whether a word processed, desktop-published document, an animated story, a multimedia presentation, or a fully functioning city of their own design, was consistently a source of great pride and, among peers and family members, admiration. [One] ESOL teacher reported that her children had designed and had had a hand in producing a two-page, illustrated supplement to the local newspaper. That supplement presented aspects of the students' home culture and their adjustment to life in the United States. (p. 589)

This description reinforces the potential of technology-supported instruction to increase both cognitive engagement and identity investment in learning. ELL students in this study were enabled to participate in classroom instruction to the full extent of their intelligence and imagination. This contrasts with many traditional classroom contexts where ELL students are unable to follow grade-level curriculum and participate in learning for several years after starting to learn English.

The Meskill and Mossop (2000) study provides sufficient information on the e-text and simulation activities observed in the focal classrooms to apply most of the design criteria just outlined:

- Does the technology-supported intervention (TSI) provide cognitive challenge and opportunities for deep processing of meaning? *Yes.*
- Does the TSI relate instruction to prior knowledge and experiences derived from students' homes and communities? *Insufficient detail provided.*
- Does the TSI promote active collaborative inquiry? *Yes.*
- Does the TSI promote extensive engaged reading and writing across the curriculum? *Yes.*
- Does the TSI help students develop strategies for effective reading, writing and learning? *Yes.*
- Does the TSI promote identity investment? *Yes.*

The Dual Language Showcase (Chow & Cummins, 2003)

This project can be viewed at http://thornwood.peelschools.org/Dual/. The research consisted of a case study involving ELL students from a broad range of linguistic backgrounds. Grades 1 and 2 students created stories initially in English (the language of school instruction); they illustrated these stories and then worked with various resource people (parents, older students literate in L1, some teachers who spoke a variety of students' languages) to translate these stories into their home languages. The stories were then word processed (or scanned in the case of some languages where fonts were not available) and the illustrations scanned into the computer. The Dual Language Web site was then created, enabling students' dual-language texts to be shared with relatives or friends in their countries of origin who had Internet access. This project illustrates the fact that even very young ELL students can create, publish, and disseminate their literature and art (see also Ada & Campoy, 2003 for an early literacy curriculum based on authoring stories and other texts).

The term *identity texts* (Cummins, 2004; Skourtou, Kourtis-Kazoullis, & Cummins, 2006) has been used to describe the literacy practices and products exemplified in the Dual Language Showcase. Students invest their identities in creating texts (written, spoken, visual, musical, or combinations in multimodal form) that then hold a mirror up to them in which their identities are reflected back in a positive light. When students share identity texts with multiple audiences (peers, teachers, parents, grandparents, sister classes, the media, etc.) they are likely to receive positive feedback and affirmation of self in interaction with these audiences. This in turn will promote both cognitive engagement and identity investment in literacy practices.

The Dual Language Showcase has been extended in the context of a project entitled *From Literacy to Multiliteracies* (Early et al., 2002). This project has reported a variety of case studies focusing on the creation of identity texts by linguistically diverse students at both elementary and secondary levels (see www.multiliteracies.ca). Technology enters the process in various ways from word processing of texts, to scanning of illustrations and uploading students' work to web pages. Numerous dual language stories have been created by ELL students and the research has documented similar processes of affirmation of identity and increases in status that were reported by Meskill and Mossop (2000). In all these cases, technology facilitated the creation of students' books, increased the audience for these books and provided encouragement for sustained engagement in literacy practices (Cummins et al., 2005).

The design criteria just articulated can be applied to these projects in the following manner:

- Does the technology-supported intervention (TSI) provide cognitive challenge and opportunities for deep processing of meaning? *Yes.*
- Does the TSI relate instruction to prior knowledge and experiences derived from students' homes and communities? *Yes.*
- Does the TSI promote active collaborative inquiry? *Yes.*
- Does the TSI promote extensive engaged reading and writing across the curriculum? *Yes.*
- Does the TSI help students develop strategies for effective reading, writing and learning? *Yes for writing.*
- Does the TSI promote identity investment? *Yes.*

Project FRESA (Cummins, Brown, & Sayers, 2007; Singer & Perez, n.d.)

There are many accounts and case studies that focus on the creative use of technology to enhance the quality and quantity of students' literacy practices and engagement (e.g., Cummins, Brown, & Sayers, 2007; Cummins & Sayers, 1995; Skourtou, Kourtis-Kazoullis, & Cummins, 2006; WestEd Eisenhower Regional Consortium, 1996). One outstanding example is Project FRESA initiated by a grade 3 and a grade 5 teacher in Oxnard, California, an area that specializes in growing strawberries. Details about the project can be found at http://equity4.clmer.csulb.edu/netshare/cti/%20FOR%20PSRTEC%20WEBSITE/Amada%20and%20Michelle/. A detailed portrait is included in Cummins, Brown, & Sayers, (2007), from which this brief account is abstracted.

Using an educational process based on dialogue and problem-posing, and employing computers as a communication and research tool, third- and fifth-grade students from farm-working families investigated their parents' work in the fields and shared the results of their investigation. The students used both English and Spanish in carrying out the project and published their work online in both languages. The online publication took the form of a multimedia, cross-curricular anthology about the relationship of the strawberry crops, which surround their school and sustain the local community and economy, to their lives.

Students' work included in the web site includes poems, drawings, and graphs based on their interviews with family members, and research carried out on the Web. They also e-mailed the Governor of California and contacted representatives of agribusiness who control the strawberry growing operation and set the conditions of work. Students also engaged in sister class exchanges with students in Puerto Rico and India and they corresponded with students and workers in Paraguay and Chile who had worked picking strawberries.

In short, this project is an excellent example of transformative pedagogy. Students engaged in collaborative critical inquiry into issues that concerned their lives and the living and working conditions of their families. They used technology as a tool to generate new knowledge through dialogue and web-based research, and they published and disseminated their findings also by means of technology. During the entire project the two teachers (Amada Irma Perez and Michelle Singer) were careful to integrate the academic work that students were doing related to strawberries to the California content standards in geography, language arts, math, and science.

This project can readily be described in the context of the Academic Expertise framework (Cummins, 2001). In particular, the role of identity investment is evident. Similarly, the sister class connections and the availability of the web site provided a fertile environment for the production and dissemination of identity texts.

The design criteria can be applied as follows:

- Does the technology-supported intervention (TSI) provide cognitive challenge and opportunities for deep processing of meaning? *Yes.*
- Does the TSI relate instruction to prior knowledge and experiences derived from students' homes and communities? *Yes.*
- Does the TSI promote active collaborative inquiry? *Yes.*
- Does the TSI promote extensive engaged reading and writing across the curriculum? *Yes.*
- Does the TSI help students develop strategies for effective reading, writing and learning? *Yes.*
- Does the TSI promote identity investment? *Yes.*

A question that arises in relation to projects such as Project FRESA that include sister class collaborations is in what ways are these projects different from "pen pal" exchanges that connect classes through e-mail. The difference lies in both the substantive nature of the collaborative inquiry and the extent to which students actively engaged in extensive reading and writing in pursuit of this inquiry. Many pen pal exchanges are unmotivated by substantive inquiry and consequently remain at a very superficial level of cultural exchange that quickly dissipates. The utility of the six design principles can be seen in the fact that many technology-mediated pen pal exchanges would generate negative answers to all six questions.

The DiaLogos Project (Kourtis-Kazoullis, 2002; Skourtou, Kourtis-Kazoullis, & Cummins, 2006)

DiaLogos was an Internet-based sister class project that was carried out over 2 school years between elementary school classes (4th, 5th, and 6th grades) in Canada and Greece. Students in the Greek elementary schools attended English lessons for three 1-hour periods per week. The DiaLogos students attended regular English classes twice a week and engaged in the DiaLogos project once a week. A number of the students in Toronto were of Greek heritage and were learning Greek in community-run classes.

A wide variety of cognitively challenging projects were carried out collaboratively by the students over the course of the 2 years. The potential for literacy development in this kind of exchange can be illustrated with reference to just one of these projects.

Evgenios Trivizas, a well-known Greek writer of children's stories was asked for permission to use one of his stories for DiaLogos in order to foster sister class collaboration through creative writing. Trivizas provided the introduction to a story that he had just begun but had not completed. This introduction was translated into English and was circulated in Greek and English to all the schools via e-mail with directions to the teachers and students on how it could be used. The students were to continue the story in any way they wanted and were to decide on joint endings with students in their sister classes.

Each class in Greece was divided into smaller groups of two or three students who jointly worked on the activity. Eighty different stories were written. Fifty-nine stories were written by the students in Greece (35 stories in Greek and 24 in English) and 21 stories were posted on the bulletin board from students in Canada (nine in Greek and 12 in English).

What is particularly significant about this project in the present context is the degree of cognitive engagement and identity investment that was evident on the part of the students. Although the activity was begun in the first year of DiaLogos' implementation, editing of the texts went on throughout the 2 years. The students often went back to the texts on the Web site adding information and making changes. Kourtis-Kazoullis (2002) points out that this was the first time most of the Greek students had shown this kind of sustained interest in one particular text. As just noted, this kind of collaboration and engagement with literacy does not happen in typical "pen pal" projects. For sister class collaboration to contribute to students' literacy development, students need to feel ownership of both the process and products of the collaboration. The motivation must be intrinsic rather than just extrinsic. Constructs such as *identity investment* and *identity text* attempt to capture essential features of this engagement with literacy.

The design criteria can be applied to the DiaLogos project as follows:

- Does the technology-supported intervention (TSI) provide cognitive challenge and opportunities for deep processing of meaning? *Yes.*
- Does the TSI relate instruction to prior knowledge and experiences derived from students' homes and communities? *Yes.*
- Does the TSI promote active collaborative inquiry? *Yes.*
- Does the TSI promote extensive engaged reading and writing across the curriculum? *Yes.*
- Does the TSI help students develop strategies for effective reading, writing and learning? *Yes.*
- Does the TSI promote identity investment? *Yes.*

Options for Pedagogically Powerful Applications of Technology Among ELL Students

The following list is intended to show the range of powerful applications of technology in schools with large numbers of ELL and low-SES students. The list is illustrative rather than exhaustive and most of the suggestions have been implemented in various projects at one time or another. All of these projects reflect either a social constructivist or transformative orientation to pedagogy. They are also consistent with the principles for learning and literacy development that have been discussed in previous sections.

- *From kindergarten on, students bring in words (in L1, L2, or L3) to class to explore with peers and teacher and they incorporate these words into technology-supported bilingual/multilingual dictionaries.* These words can be discussed in the class and entered into Google image searches to find images that depict the meanings. Students can also look up the words in electronic dictionaries and create their own multimedia glossaries (print, image, audio). This kind of functionality reflects the Focus on Language component of the Academic Expertise framework and has been implemented successfully in various contexts (Cummins, Brown, & Sayers, 2007).
- *Students write creatively in L1 and L2 and amplify these identity texts through technology (as in the Dual Language Showcase).* Audio can also be integrated into the texts that appear on the web. For example,

students can read their stories (in L1 and/or L2) and enable the sound to be turned on or off by those who visit the web page. If the student is not fully literate in his or her L1 (or L2), a parent, teacher, or peer might read the story in that language.

- *Students create movies, audio CDs, and/or web pages to communicate the outcomes of their projects aimed at generating new knowledge, creating literature and art, and acting on social realities.* Durán and Durán (2001) and Hull and Schultz (2001, 2002) have described how low-SES minority students created various kinds of multimedia resources on substantive topics of relevance to their lives in the context of after-school technology-mediated initiatives. Bilingual/ELL students can utilize both their languages in creating these identity texts. Currently, it seems to be more feasible to engage in this kind of project with low-SES and ELL students in after-school contexts; however, the powerful learning that appears to characterize these projects highlights the lack of powerful learning associated with technology in the schools attended by these students.

- *Newly arrived students write in L1 and work with peers, teachers, older students, community volunteers, and technology (Google or Babel Fish translations) to create bilingual identity texts.* For example, a newly arrived student in Grade 5 might write a story or a personal account of some aspect of his/her experience in Spanish. Students and/or the teacher can then cut and paste this text into Google or Babel Fish for automatic translation into English. The resulting translation will likely be somewhat garbled but sufficiently comprehensible to give the teacher (and other students) the gist of what the new arrival is trying to communicate. A group of students can then be assigned to work with the newly arrived student to edit the English version of the text and to "teach the computer proper English." Then the dual language text can be entered into the class or school Web site as a bilingual identity text. Thus the newly arrived student very quickly attains the status of a published bilingual author.

- *Students engage in technology-mediated sister class exchanges using L1 and L2 to create literature and art and/or to explore issues of social relevance to them and their communities (e.g., Social History of Our Community, Voices of our Elders, Working Conditions of Farm Workers [as in Project FRESA] etc.).* These sister class exchanges can provide powerful motivation for students to engage in language learning and/or language maintenance activities. As just noted, the *DiaLogos* project (Kourtis-Kazoullis, 2002; Skourtou, Kourtis-Kazoullis, & Cummins, 2006) linked students in Greece and Canada and enabled students to engage in extensive collaborative writing as well as a variety of other collaborative inquiry activities.

All of these different genres of technology-mediated projects can take place in school or in out-of-school contexts and be aligned to content standards across the curriculum (as in the Project FRESA case). It is interesting that many of the case studies that have reported innovative applications of computer technologies among Latino/a students in the United States have taken place in out-of-school contexts (see Durán, this volume; Castek and colleagues, this volume, and Parker, this volume). This is because, as noted previously, transmission pedagogies currently dominate classroom practice for low-SES students and this pedagogical orientation leaves little room for innovative technology applications. Out-of-school contexts are less subject to these constraints and have therefore been fertile ground for exploration of technology-supported social constructivist and transformative projects.

However, it is important also to problematize the relationship between technology and social constructivist and transformative pedagogical orientations. Technology itself will not transform a classroom into a more inquiry-based environment regardless of good intentions. Feldman, Conold, and Coulter's (2000) report on technology-mediated networking projects designed to promote the learning of science and math found that students engaged in little online discussion and made minimal use of data they collected for analysis of authentic scientific problems. The initial orientation of these projects (such as the *National Geographic Society Kids Network;* http://www.ngsednet.org/community/about.cfm?community_id=94) was inquiry-based and attempted to enable students to "discover" science by constructing their own knowledge. Feldman and colleagues express the initial vision and somewhat disappointing outcomes as follows:

> Early advocates for network science hoped that the use of the network would help classrooms break this pattern by providing both authentic questions for students' investigations (ones for which the teachers did not know the answers) and real audiences for students' thinking and work. ... Unfortunately, we still see few instances of these sorts of dialogue occurring among network science classrooms. (2000, p. 77)

They suggest that, in retrospect, it was naïve to expect this constructive dialogue to happen online if it is not already happening in the classroom:

> Furthermore, it is not that we necessarily want such discussions to occur online: rather, we want them to take place somewhere. Our contention is that the classroom is the best place for discussions to occur and the place where they are easiest to initiate and sustain. (2000, p. 98)

From the point of view of the present analysis, we might hypothesize that the network science projects failed to meet expectations at least partly because there may have been little identity investment on the part of students in these projects. This interpretation is speculative but consistent with the account provided by Feldman and colleagues (2000).

In short, it is insufficient to create a curriculum based on student inquiry and knowledge construction if this curriculum does not directly address issues related to why this knowledge is relevant to students' lives and why they should care about building this kind of knowledge. Students' pre-existing knowledge needs to be considered not just in the narrow sense of specific subject-matter knowledge but more broadly in terms of their lives and identities. For students to take ownership of the knowledge construction process and invest their identities therein requires concrete outcomes (*identity texts*) that affirm students' identities. Technology has a powerful role to play in this entire process.

Conclusion

Most governments in industrialized countries, supported by business interests and parents, have placed a high priority on introducing ICT into their schools. The assumption appears to be that ICT is an integral part of the new economy of the 21st century and therefore it should be an integral part of the school systems that are supposed to prepare students for this new economy. There has been considerable discussion in some contexts regarding the wisdom of this direction. For example, in North America, critics have argued that there is little evidence that ICT has resulted in significant improvement in students' overall school achievement and they point to the diversion of scarce resources from other subject matter, such as the arts and literature. However, these criticisms have had little impact and the introduction of ICT in schools gains momentum with every passing year.

Despite the increase in access to ICT in schools, there is still no consensus as to *how* computers should be used to support learning in general or academic language learning among ELL students in particular. One reason for this lack of consensus is that there is minimal research that specifically addresses the impact of computers on the achievement of ELL and Latino/a students. A number of reasons for this absence of definitive research have been suggested. For example, the wide range of contexts and the complexity of interacting variables make it difficult to generalize about the impact of technology on the basis of research studies carried out in particular contexts (Willis, 2003).

Despite the paucity of research, there is suggestive evidence from case studies that ICT *can* play a significant and positive educational role, but only if the pedagogical possibilities of ICT are clearly understood. ICT is minimally useful as a pedagogical tool when it is used only within a transmission-oriented and skills-based curriculum. Within this curricular orientation, applications of specific computer software programs are likely to be cost-effective only for student populations with special needs (e.g., reading disabled, blind students, etc.; Healy, 1998).

The underlying pedagogical orientation represents a major reason why few computer programs have demonstrated significant utility in promoting academic language learning among ELL students. The vast majority of computer programs for English language learning operate from didactic transmission-oriented assumptions. These programs are also of limited use within school contexts because they do not teach the language that students need to gain access to the curriculum through a second language. When technology-supported transmission-oriented pedagogy is expanded into social constructivist and transformative oriented pedagogy, greater gains in both learning and second language learning are likely to be realized (Bereiter & Scardamalia, 2003; Jonassen, 1999).

Case study research demonstrates clearly that less affluent and ELL students are very much capable of using technological resources for collaborative critical inquiry when they are given opportunities in school or out-of-school contexts to do so. The Web sites, electronic books, and research reports that students in these projects have produced represent a portfolio that cannot be adequately assessed by standardized tests, any more than a visual or recording artist's talent can be assessed by a standardized test.

Therefore, in evaluating technology-supported instruction the questions we must ask include the following:

- To what extent did the technology-supported intervention provide cognitive challenge and opportunities for deep processing of meaning?
- To what extent did the technology-supported intervention relate instruction to prior knowledge and experiences derived from students' homes and communities?
- To what extent did the technology-supported intervention promote active collaborative inquiry?
- To what extent did the technology-supported intervention promote extensive engaged reading and writing across the curriculum?
- To what extent did the technology-supported intervention help students develop strategies for effective reading, writing, and learning?
- To what extent did the technology-supported intervention promote significant identity investment on the part of students?

An important research challenge for the future is to assess the adequacy of these design principles. They have been proposed in the present chapter on the basis of the empirical research on learning in general and academic language learning in particular. However, these design principles have not been adequately evaluated in technology-supported environments. Among the relevant research questions to consider are the following:

- Do technology-supported interventions that include these components promote the academic achievement of English learners more adequately than technology-supported interventions that are modeled on other sets of design principles?

• How adequate are these design principles? How should each of them be operationalized for purposes of quantitative research? Should some be omitted and others added?

The research orientation proposed here would shift the core question from the impact or effectiveness of technology *per se* to students' achievement to the relative contributions of different pedagogical components on achievement when these components are realized in electronic environments.

Both quantitative and qualitative research approaches are appropriate to investigate the issues. Experimental or quasi-experimental studies are clearly appropriate to evaluate the impact of specific software programs or broader technology-supported interventions. However, case studies and action research are likely to yield more insight into the potential of technology-supported interventions for specific groups of learners and the instructional conditions that must be in place for this impact to occur. Collaborative action research involving school-based educators and university-based researchers is likely to be of particular value. Teachers can attempt to expand English learners' academic engagement using a variety of technological tools to demonstrate what these students *can* achieve intellectually and imaginatively. The extent to which there is impact on standardized test scores can be assessed by tracking the achievement of students who are engaged in these projects in relation to appropriate comparison groups. However, equally important is the evidence of achievement revealed in portfolios of student work.

In short, a variety of research approaches should be pursued. The credibility of conclusions or recommendations is heightened when there is congruence between the findings emerging from very different forms of research.

Acknowledgments

I would like to thank Sandy McAuley, The University of Prince Edward Island, and Leann Parker, University of California, Berkeley, for very constructive feedback on an earlier version of this chapter.

References

Ada, A. F., & Campoy, I. (2003). *Authors in the classroom: A transformative educational process*. Boston: Allyn & Bacon.

Angrist, J., & Lavy, V., New evidence on classroom computers and pupil learning. *Economic Journal, 112*, 735–765.

Armstrong, A., & Casement, C. (1998). *The child and the machine: Why computers may put our children's education at risk*. Toronto: Key Porter Books.

August, D., & Associates. (2003, February). *Supporting the development of English literacy in English language learners: Key issues and promising practices*. Report No. 61. Baltimore, MD: CRESPAR.

Becker, W. C. (1977). Teaching reading and language to the disadvantaged: What we have learned from field research. *Harvard Educational Review, 47,* 518–543.

Bennett, F. (2002). The future of computer technology in K–12 education. *Phi Delta Kappan,* 83(8), 621–625.

Bereiter, C., & Scardamalia, M. (2003, November). Technology and literacies: From print literacy to dialogic literacy. Paper presented at the OISE/UT Literacy Conference.

Blok, H., Oostdam, R., Otter, M. E., & Overmaat, M. (2002). Computer-assisted instruction in support of beginning reading instruction: A review. *Review of Educational Research,* 72(1). 101–130.

Bracey, B. (2000, Spring). A different divide: Teachers and other professionals. *Edutopia,* 4–5.

Bransford, J. D., Brown, A. L., & Cocking, R. R. (2000). *How people learn: Brain, mind, experience, and school.* Washington, DC: National Academy Press.

Butler-Pascoe, M. E., & Wiburg, K. M. (2003). *Technology and teaching English language learners.* Boston: Allyn & Bacon.

Chall, J. S., Jacobs, V., & Baldwin, L. (1990). *The reading crisis: Why poor children fall behind.* Cambridge, MA: Harvard University Press.

Chall, J. S., & Snow, C. E. (1988). School influences on the reading development of low-income children. *The Harvard Education Letter,* 4(1), 1–4.

Chascas, S. & Cummins, J. (2005). *The e-Lective Language Learning Program* [computer program]. Retrieved November 23, 2006, from www.e-Lective.net.

Chow, P., & Cummins, J. (2003). Valuing multilingual and multicultural approaches to learning. In S. R. Schecter & J. Cummins (Eds.), *Multilingual education in practice: Using diversity as a resource* (pp. 32–61). Portsmouth, NH: Heinemann.

Collier, V. P., & Thomas, W. P. (1999). Making U.S. schools effective for English language learners, Part 1. *TESOL Matters,* (9)4 (August/September), pp. 1, 6.

Corson, D. (1997). The learning and use of academic English words. *Language Learning,* 47(4), 671–718.

Cuban, L. (1986). *Teachers and machines: The classroom use of technology since 1920.* New York: Teachers College Press.

Cuban, L (2001). *Oversold and underused: Computers in the classroom.* Cambridge MA: Harvard University Press.

Cummins, J. (1981). Age on arrival and immigrant second language learning in Canada: A reassessment. *Applied Linguistics,* 1, 132–149.

Cummins, J. (2001). *Negotiating identities: Education for empowerment in a diverse society* (2nd ed.). Los Angeles: California Association for Bilingual Education.

Cummins, J. (2004). Multiliteracies pedagogy and the role of identity texts. In K. Leithwood, P. McAdie, N. Bascia, & A. Rodigue (Eds.), *Teaching for deep understanding: Towards the Ontario curriculum that we need* (pp. 68–74). Toronto: Ontario Institute for Studies in Education of the University of Toronto and the Elementary Federation of Teachers of Ontario.

Cummins, J., Ardeshiri, M., & Cohen, S. (in press). Computer supported scaffolding of literacy development. *Pedagogies.*

Cummins, J., Brown, K., & Sayers, D. (2007). *Literacy, technology, and diversity: Teaching for success in changing times.* Boston: Allyn & Bacon.

Cummins, J., & Sayers, D. (1995). *Brave new schools: Challenging cultural illiteracy through global learning networks.* New York: St. Martin's Press.

Cunningham, A. (1990). Explicit versus implicit instruction in phonemic awareness. *Journal of Experimental Child Psychology,* 50, 429–444.

DeBell, M., & Chapman, C. (2003). Computer and Internet use by children and adolescents in 2001 (NCES 2004–014). U.S. Department of Education. Washington, DC: National Center for Education Statistics.

Donovan, M. S., & Bransford, J. D. (Eds.). (2005). *How students learn: History, mathematics, and science in the classroom*. Washington, DC: The National Academy Press.

Donsky, D. (2006). *Critical pathways towards antiracism in an elementary knowledge building classroom*. Unpublished doctoral dissertation, The University of Toronto.

Durán, R., & Durán, J. (2001). Latino immigrant parents and children learning and publishing together in an after-school setting. *Journal of Education for Students Placed at Risk*, 6(1/2), 95–113.

Early, M., Cummins, J., & Willinsky, J. (2002). *From literacy to multiliteracies: Designing learning environments for knowledge generation within the new economy*. University of British Columbia, research proposal submitted to the Social Sciences and Humanities Research Council.

Elley, W. B. (1991). Acquiring literacy in a second language: The effect of book-based programs. *Language Learning*, 41, 375–411.

European Commission (2003). *A world of learning at your fingertips: Pilot projects under the eLearning Initiative*. Retrieved August 20, 2004, from http://europa. eu.int/comm/education/programmes/elearning/projects_en.html.

Feldman, A., Konold, C., & Coulter, B. (2000). *Network science a decade later: The Internet and classroom learning*. Mahwah, NJ: Erlbaum.

Fletcher, J. D. (2003). Evidence for learning from technology-assisted instruction. In H. F. O'Neill, Jr., & R. S. Pérez (Eds.), *Technology applications in education: A learning view* (pp. 79–99). Mahwah, NJ: Erlbaum.

Fordham, S. (1990). Racelessness as a factor in Black students' school success: Pragmatic strategy or Pyrrhic victory? In N. M. Hidalgo, C. L. McDowell, & E. V. Siddle (Eds.), *Facing racism in education* (Reprint series No. 21 ed., pp. 232–262). Cambridge, MA: Harvard Educational Review.

Foster, K. C., Erickson, G. C., Foster, D. F., Brinkman, D., & Torgesen, J. K. (1994). Computer administered instruction in phonological awareness: Evaluation of the DaisyQuest program. *The Journal of Research and Development in Education*, 27, 126–137.

Fuchs, T., & Woessmann, L. (2004). *Computers and students learning: Bivariate and multivariate evidence on the availability and use of computers at home and at school*. CESIFO Working Paper, No. 1321. Retrieved April 22, 2005, from www.cesifo-group.de/.

Geva, E. (2000). Issues in the assessment of reading disabilities in L2 children—beliefs and research evidence. *Dyslexia*, 6, 13–28.

Goolsbee, A., & Guryan, J. (2002). *The impact of Internet subsidies in public schools*. Chicago: National Bureau of Economic Research.

Guthrie, J. T. (2004). Teaching for literacy engagement. *Journal of Literacy Research*, 36, 1–30.

Hakuta, K., Butler, Y. G., & Witt, D. (2000) *How long does it take English learners to attain proficiency?* Santa Barbara, CA: University of California Linguistic Minority Research Institute.

Hatcher, P., Hulme, C., & Ellis, A. (1994). Ameliorating early reading failure by integrating the teaching of reading and phonological skills: The phonological linkage hypothesis. *Child Development*, 65, 41–57.

Healy, J. M. (1998). *Failure to connect: How computers affect our children's minds—and what we can do about it.* New York: Simon & Schuster.

Hull, G., & Schultz, K. (2001). Literacy and learning out of school: A review of theory and research. *Review of Educational Research, 71*(4), 575–612.

Hull, G. & Schultz, K. (Eds.). (2002). *School's out! Bridging out-of-school literacies with classroom practice.* New York: Teachers College Press.

Jonassen, D. H. (1996). *Computers in the classroom: Mindtools for critical thinking.* Englewood Cliffs, NJ: Prentice-Hall.

Jonassen, D. H. (1999). *Computers as mindtools for schools: Engaging critical thinking* (2nd ed.). Englewood Cliffs, NJ: Prentice-Hall.

Jonassen, D. H., Carr, C., & Yueh, H-P. (1998). Computers as mindtools for engaging learners in critical thinking. *TechTrends, 43*(2), 24–32.

Kamil, M. L., Intrator, S. M., & Kim, H. S. (2000). The effects of other technologies on literacy and literacy learning. In M. L. Kamil, P. B. Mosenthal, P. D. Pearson, & R. Barr (Eds.), *Handbook of reading research* (Vol. III; pp. 771–788). Mahwah, NJ: Erlbaum.

Klesmer, H. (1994). Assessment and teacher perceptions of ESL student achievement. *English Quarterly, 26*(3), 8–11.

Kourtis-Kazoullis, V. (2002). *DiaLogos: bilingualism and the teaching of second language learning on the Internet.* Unpublished doctoral dissertation, University of the Aegean, Primary Education Department, Rhodes, Greece.

Krashen, S. D. (2004). *The power of reading: Insights from the research* (2nd ed.). Portsmouth, NH: Heinemann.

Kwan, A. B., & Willows, D. M. (1998, December). *Impact of early phonics instruction on children learning English as a second language.* Paper presented at the National Reading Conference, Austin, TX.

Lambert, W. E., & Tucker, G. R. (1972). *Bilingual education of children: The St. Lambert experiment.* Rowley, MA: Newbury House.

Lave, J., & Wenger, E. (1991). *Situated learning: Legitimate peripheral participation.* Cambridge, UK: Cambridge University Press.

LeLoup, J. W., & Ponterio, R. (2003, December). *Second language acquisition and technology: A review of the research. CAL Digest.* Washington, DC: Center for Applied Linguistics.

Leu, D. J., Ataya, R., & Coiro, J. (2002, December). *Assessing assessment strategies among the 50 states: Evaluating the literacies of our past or our future?* Paper presented at the National Reading Conference. Miami, FL.

Manzo, K. K. (2001, May). Academic record. In *Technology Counts 2001. Education Week on the Web.* Retrieved April 15, 2002, from http://www.edweek.org/reports/tc01article.cfm?slug=35academic.h20.

McAuley, A. (1998). Virtual teaching on the tundra. *Technos, 7*(3), 11–14.

McAuley, A. (2001). Creating a community of learners: Computer support in the Eastern Arctic. *Education Canada, 40*(4), 8–11.

McAuley, A. (2003). *Illiniqatigiit: Implementing a knowledge building environment in the Eastern Arctic.* Unpublished doctoral dissertation, The University of Toronto.

Meskill, C., & Mossop, J. (2000). Electronic texts in ESOL classrooms. *TESOL Quarterly, 34*, 585–592.

Nation, P., & Coady, J. (1988). Vocabulary and reading. In R. Carter & M. McCarthy (Eds.), *Vocabulary and language teaching* (pp. 97–110). London: Longman.

National Assessment of Educational Progress (2001). *The nation's report card: Fourth grade reading 2000.* Washington, DC: National Educational Goals Panel.

National Reading Panel. (2000). *Teaching children to read: An evidence-based assessment of the scientific research literature on reading and its implications for reading instruction.* Washington, DC: NICHD.

Neuman, S. B. (1999). Books make a difference: A study of access to literacy. *Reading Research Quarterly,* 34(3), 286–311.

Norton, B. (2000). *Identity and language learning: Gender, ethnicity and educational change.* London: Longman.

Oppenheimer, T. (1997). The computer delusion. *The Atlantic Monthly,* 280(1), 45–62.

Oppenheimer, T. (2003). *The flickering mind: The false promise of technology in the classroom, and how learning can be saved.* New York: Syndetic Solutions Inc.

Parsad, B., and Jones, J. (2005). *Internet access in U.S. public schools and classrooms: 1994–2003.* Washington, DC: National Center for Educational Statistics. Retrieved April 24, 2005, from http://nces.ed.gov/pubsearch/pubsinfo.asp?pubid=2005015.

Postlethwaite, T. N., & Ross, K. N. (1992). *Effective schools in reading: Implications for educational planners. An exploratory study.* The Hague: The International Association for the Evaluation of Educational Achievement.

Pressley, M., Duke, N. K., & Boling, E. C. (2004). The educational science and scientifically based instruction we need: Lessons from reading research and policymaking. [Electronic Version]. *Harvard Educational Review,* 74(1).

RAND Reading Study Group. (2002). *Reading for understanding: toward an R&D program in reading comprehension.* Santa Monica: RAND Corporation.

Rose, D. H., & Dalton, B. (2002). Using technology to individualize reading instruction. In C. C. Block, L. B. Gambrell, & M. Pressley (Eds.) *Improving comprehension instruction: Rethinking research, theory, and classroom practice* (pp. 257–274). San Francisco: Jossey Bass Publishers.

Singer, M. & Pérez, A. I. (n.d.). *Project FRESA reflections.* Unpublished manuscript.

Skourtou, E., Kourtis-Kazoullis, V., & Cummins, J. (2006). Designing virtual learning environments for academic language development. In J. Weiss, J. Nolan, J. Hunsinger, & P. Trifonas (Eds.), *The international handbook of virtual learning environments* (pp. 441–467). Dordrecht: Springer.

Svedkauskaite, A. & Reza-Hernández, L. (n.d.). *Critical issue: Using technology to support Limited-English-Proficient (LEP) students' learning experiences.* North Central Regional Educational Laboratory. Retrieved August 6, 2004, from http://www.ncrel.org/sdrs/areas/issues/methods/technlgy/te900.htm.

Verhoeven, L. (2000). Components in early second language reading and spelling. *Scientific Studies of Reading,* 4(4), 313–330.

Warschauer, M. (2006). *Laptops and literacy: Learning in the wireless classroom.* New York: Teachers College Press.

Warschauer, M., Grant, D., Del Real, G., & Rousseau, M. (2004). Promoting academic literacy with technology: Successful laptop programs in K–12 schools. *System,* 32, 525–537.

Warschauer, M., Knobel, M., & Stone, L. (2004). Technology and equity in schooling: Deconstructing the digital divide. *Educational Policy,* 18(4), 562–588.

WestEd Eisenhower Regional Consortium. (1996). *Tales from the electronic frontier: First-hand experiences of teachers and students using the Internet in K–12 math and science.* San Francisco: Author.

Wenglinsky, H. (1998). *Does it compute? The relationship between educational technology and student achievement in mathematics* (Policy Information Report). Princeton, New Jersey: Educational Testing Service.

Wilhelm, T., Carmen, D., & Reynolds, M. (2002, June). *Connecting kids to technology: Challenges and opportunities. Kids Count Snapshot. The Anne E. Casey Foundation.* Retrieved August 23, 2004, from http://www.aecf.org/publications/data/snapshot_june2002.pdf.

Willis, J. (2003). Instructional technologies in schools: Are we there yet? *Computers in the Schools*, 20(1/2), 11–33.

Wood, J. (2001). Can software support children's vocabulary development? *Language Learning & Technology*, 5(1), 166–201.

REFLECTION

Rules of Engagement for Achieving Educational Futures

OLGA A. VÁSQUEZ

University of California, San Diego

A Reflection on Jim Cummins' Vision

Reflecting on Jim Cummins' vision of educational futures from outside the ideological structure of the educational system, I am reminded that very few educational innovations have successfully gained widespread acceptance or have lasted any significant length of time (Healey & DeStefano, 1997). "In education, everything has been tried with very meager (sic) results" Tedesco (1998, p. 80) said, and what has been tried with diverse populations has been ineffective in bringing about substantive change in achievement patterns (Springfield, Datnow, & Ross, 1998). In sum, the "real core of schools"—that is, the process of teaching and learning—has been intractably resistant to change, as Elmore (1990) and others point out. But Cummins knows this, and states it in his wonderfully crafted vision of a technology intervention design for elementary school-age learners of English.

Cummins' vision, however, captures only part, the "how-to" of the real change that must take place in education. In effect, the changes that must be made in order to adequately serve nonmainstream students who experience the core of schooling as inaccessible and meaningless amount to nothing less than a shift from an industrial model of education to a knowledge and information model. This new model marks a shift from preparing citizens and workers, particularly people of color, for an outdated, hierarchical, routinized, and predictable social world to preparing them for a world that is in constant flux at every level of our social experience. Skills borne out of the "education of the future" that I propose here are far from the discrete, reified, and knowable skills promoted by conventional education. Instead, they are conditionally based on the flows of change brought about by new advances in knowledge and information. A new vision of our world—one that is culturally diverse, multilingual, and democratic—must be engendered by a learning context that is grounded on integrative collaboration (John-Steiner, 1997), flexibility, creativity, technological versatility, and a global and critical perspective; a far cry from the rule-bound, monocultural, and individual-based character of today's education.

Cummins' design principles and basic criteria for assessing the potential effectiveness of technology-supported instruction for English learners comprise only the first of four rules of engagement[1]—to borrow a military term in these times of war—that I believe are necessary to overcome the forces that inhibit the provision of a high-quality education for second language learners. I propose we think beyond the assessment of program effectiveness that Cummins lays out and examine the goals of the entire decision-making process. As educators, to push the military analogy further, we must decide when, where, how, and against whom/what do we mobilize the force of our educational expertise and resources. My reflection below presents a seemingly modest approach that builds on Cummins' vision. I dare to reflect on possibilities knowing well that my proposed rules of engagement may make Cummins' vision even harder to implement. I am suggesting, here, a theory of action that catapults education into the future; ironically, a theory of education that hails back to the beginning of the 20th century when Lev Vygotsky proposed an interventionist approach to education (Moll, 1990).

The second rule of engagement suggests pedagogical interventions that explicitly delineate the kind of learner, worker, citizen, and world relevant to an age of globalization that education is aiming towards—that is, flexible, creative, and autonomous learners and workers of a technologically connected world with a global reach. I am suggesting here an education that not only focuses on science and mathematics or skills related to advance services that fuel globalization: research and development, engineering, law, and finance. In essence, I am suggesting an education of the future that considers the skills that language minority youth possess as intellectual resources highly valued in today's globalized world—for example, the versatility to navigate across a variety of distinct cultural contexts, fluency in more than one language, and a collaborative nature. The development of such a learner requires the learning ecology to foster performance beyond an individual's capacities—that is, to operate within Vygotsky's zone of proximal development (Vygotsky, 1978).

The third rule of engagement calls for considering the broader context as an important mechanism for bringing about effective change in the individual as well as the society. That is, the social milieu that is important to child development (Rogoff, 1994; Wells, 2000; Wertsch, 1985) must be taken into consideration in planning a technological intervention. Education can no longer stand apart from its constituent communities, but rather must form part of a cross-system collaborative effort that links to the ecological contexts that learners traverse as a matter of daily life. Linking relevant cultural systems (i.e., the family, community, and educational systems) and multiple institutional contexts (i.e., the individual schools, research units, funding organizations, and various learning sites such as the classroom, after-school learning settings, and staff meetings) into an elaborate cross-system collaborative provides a socializing system for the developing learner, citizen, and worker. It also supports the mission and development of each of the integral components, creating change across the system. Structurally, the relations of exchange formed by such a system create the pathways from which accumulated knowledge generated at each point of contact is circulated throughout the system (Vásquez, 2003). Thus, each part of this multilevel system contributes to the formation of new visions of learners and the institutions that serve them.

The fourth and last rule of engagement is to reinforce a dynamically dialogic learning environment where learners use language to learn language, literacy, and, following Vygotsky's adherents, a new consciousness (Leontiev & Luria, 1968; Wells, 2000). We must move away from a focus on the individual and the idea that instructional tools, such as books and technology, have the power to transform learning in and of themselves. Rather than produce the ideal conditions for a high-quality learning environment in today's classroom this convention reinforces silence, isolation, and narcissism (Vásquez, 2005). What I am proposing instead is a view of technology as a symbolic tool that fosters communication—in Cummins' terms, a tool for "collaborative inquiry"—rather than an independent tool with an instrumental function.

In Vygotskian interpretation, the computer is a language tool: "the medium for both collective sharing and for transmission [and, I would add, construction] of new forms of consciousness across generations and circumstances" (Bruner, 1984, p. 95). Currently, a new consciousness of how the world works has more currency outside of school where youths are using information technology in socially innovative ways—for example, establishing communication networks, gaming, friendships, and romancing. Jonassen's notion of "mindtools" (see Cummins, this volume) is useful to consider technology as part of the social body that constructs knowledge:

> Technologies should not support learning by attempting to instruct the learners, but rather should be used as knowledge construction tools that students learn *with*, not *from*. In this way, learners function as designers, and the computers function as mindtools for interpreting and organizing their personal knowledge. (Cummins, this volume, p. 82)

> Mindtools are computer applications that, when used by learners to represent what they know, necessarily engage them in critical thinking about the content they are studying. (Jonassen, Carr, & Yueh, 1998, quoted in Cummins, this volume, p. 82)

Together these four rules of engagement—that is, an assessment framework of program effectiveness, new visions of learner and world, a cross-system collaborative effort, and a dialogic learning environment—allow us to exercise our educational expertise and resources to fulfill not only the needs of the learner, but also the needs of the educational system to prepare learners and citizens for the new social conditions that surround us. Our pedagogical visions must be strategic, system-based, and future-oriented to meet the demands of a diverse, multilingual, globalized world.

This is a lofty goal, indeed, and Cummins is correct in stating that the changes he proposes, and by extension the ones I add above, are more easily accomplished outside the classroom where one can imagine optimal possibilities and tweak the system accordingly (Vásquez, 2003). The flexibility of these out-of-school, informal programs makes them ideal contexts for testing the viability of innovative technology-supported learning environments, for exploring nonstandard sources of knowledge, and for creating a new vision of education. After-school enrichment activities, for example, have been shown to have a long-term social and academic benefit for participants (Miller, 2003).

Cummins provides examples of successful technology interventions that bridge the digital, cognitive, and pedagogical divide, albeit outside of school. I would like to offer another example, one whose ideals over its 17-year history have generated local success in serving language minority youth in San Diego County: a computer-based social action project that exemplifies Cummins' design principles and basic criteria for effective learning as well as incorporates the additional three rules of engagement I presented above (for details, see Vásquez, 2003).

La Clase Mágica, as this after-school program is called, is an innovation of "The Fifth Dimension" model developed by Michael Cole and colleagues at the Laboratory of Comparative Human Cognition, University of California, San Diego (UCSD; Cole, 1996). Its bilingual, bicultural framework and its focus on the academic achievement of minority youth and their representation in higher education made it possible for The Fifth Dimension/*La Clase Mágica* combination to serve as a proactive strategy to support the academic achievement of underserved youth after the dismantling of affirmative action. Our collective efforts in San Diego County gave rise to UC Links, a highly successful network of 26 after-school programs that represents community-university partnerships dedicated to maintaining the flow of underserved youth into higher learning. For more than 10 years now, UC Links has sustained a strong presence as a provider of quality after-school learning in sites throughout California.

As one of the founding programs in the UC Links community, *La Clase Mágica* continues to flourish as a consortium of six after-school sites situated in community institutions and linked to UCSD and Palomar Community College through two undergraduate courses and an extensive research agenda. Annually, it serves approximately 300 children ranging in age from 3 to 16, 60–80 UCSD undergraduates, and 10–15 Palomar Community College students. The project is composed of a research and implementation team involving a university staff and a staff of 7–10 community women who coordinate the activities at the community sites. The implementation part of the project is supported by a nonprofit organization called The Center for Academic and Social Advancement (CASA) that grew out of the community activities at the initial site, a small Catholic mission located in the Mexican-origin sector of Solana Beach, California. Today, CASA supports the daily operations of the computer clubs located in two schools, two community centers, an American Indian Reservation, and the small Catholic mission where it shares space with a Head Start program. A cross-system collaborative effort of 21 institutional units—including funding agencies, educational institutions, and community agencies—supports the financial, intellectual, and material resources that *La Clase Mágica* requires for its sustainability.

Undergraduate students enrolled in the UCSD practicum course on child development and a Multicultural Studies course at Palomar College are trained to engage their younger partners in robust, theoretically informed interactions that support active engagement in their learning and development. The *amigas/os,* as the undergraduate students are called, help the children progress through a series of computer-based educational games and collaborative activities specifically selected to emphasize language, literacy, and problem-solving skills. For example, children in *La Clase Mágica* engage in dialogically rich learning activities guided by their *amigas/os* using such educational software as *Storybook Weaver* (http://www.swexpress.com/home. nsf) and *Math Blaster* (http://www.associatedcontent.com). Field-developed materials, adult–child interactions, and an electronic support system create a bilingual, bicultural ecological system that fosters active learning, bilingualism, and expert–novice collaboration. Computer-based resources are key to both attracting the children's active participation and giving children access to quality learning materials and resources that they would otherwise not have at home or at school. Child participants, under the guidance of their undergraduate pals or the community staff, use the Internet to complete homework assignments, to communicate regularly with a magical entity via electronic written communication, and to play computer-based educational games, all the while practicing numerous academic skills such as reading, writing, and problem-solving (Vásquez & Durán, 2000).

Yet, although the technology is considered crucial to attracting and maintaining the child's active participation, the collaboration between the undergraduate pals and the child participants is the major factor behind their motivation, engagement, and visions of self. As Susana, now 25, one of 20 former child participants interviewed for an extensive sustainability study, reported, the project had a major impact on her life:

> Being in *La Clase Mágica* helped me with reading and writing. Up to then, I had a hard time because in my classes everything was in English and I didn't understand anything. Slowly, though, I learned thanks to

> *La Clase Mágica* because I could also use Spanish there. *La Clase Mágica* influenced me greatly with my present interest in technology, that I now work repairing computers. I have five PCs, two laptops, and two PDAs, and everything I do is related to the world of technology. Learning to use a computer and the Internet helped me decide what I wanted to do in life. In relation to *El Maga* [the electronic entity], *La Clase Mágica* opened my eyes to a different world. I didn't know I could talk to beings in another world, which helped my imagination fly into fantasy and develop a curiosity for learning. (Martínez & Vásquez, 2006)

The design of the intervention is neither localized nor unidirectional, but rather is founded on a community of learners' ideals (Rogoff, 1994). Everyone has a special role in the workings of the project, and everyone learns and develops. The effect that *La Clase Mágica* has had on the undergraduates and the community adults clearly demonstrates this assertion. Many participants, young and old have pursued higher education as a result of their participation in *La Clase Mágica*. For example, a community college undergraduate student who participated in the collaboration between UCSD and the community college in 2001 has joined the research staff as an undergraduate assistant, illustrating the efficacy of the education pipeline set up by the system of collaboration created by *La Clase Mágica*. According to the preliminary results of a year-long sustainability study conducted during the 2005–2006 academic year, all but one of the undergraduates who participated as research assistants had pursued advanced degrees. Three quarters of them reported that *La Clase Mágica* had played an influential role in the choice of research tools—that is, ethnographic and qualitative methods—they used in their graduate work. Graduate students who participated in the project as research assistants also reported that *La Clase Mágica* had a strong influence on the research topics they pursued. The community adults, too, report benefits from their involvement in the computer-based activity. Isabel, an emergent speaker of English who has served as site coordinator for several years, had this to say about the impact *La Clase Mágica* has had on her:

> Before I did not even know how to turn on a computer. *La Clase Mágica* encouraged me to take a course on computation, and nowadays I use computers almost everyday. I also look for almost any information that I need on the Internet. Thanks to the Internet, I am also aware about a lot more things that are going on. (Martínez & Vásquez, 2006)

As can be seen from the preliminary findings of the sustainability study, Cummins' pedagogical framework is a fait accompli at *La Clase Mágica*. *La Clase Mágica* incorporates the two design principles of "scientifically credible" learning environments—effective environments and the promotion of literacy—and all four conditions for effective learning borrowed from Bransford and colleagues: (a) learning with deep understanding, (b) building on pre-existing knowledge, (c) promoting active learning, and (d) support within a community of learners. Cummins' design principles of effective environments, in fact, resonate perfectly with Vygotsky's (Cole, 1996; Vygotsky, 1978) notion of cultural and cognitive development on which the project is based (see Vásquez, 2003). We create the culture of *La Clase Mágica* by socially structuring "… the kinds of tasks that the growing child faces and the kinds of tools, both mental and physical, that the young child is provided to master those tasks …" (Vygotsky, quoted in Luria, 1979). In short, what this means is that the particular cultural framework of *La Clase Mágica* and the embedded cross-age interactional practice, intellectual tools, and electronic activities that we emphasize aim at a specific kind of learning and development, one that prepares participants for an information-based world. Our technology-based curriculum, our bilingual format, and our collaborative engagement aligns perfectly with an education of the future. This notion of culture allows us to think about how we can create new socially structured ways to think and act within a technologically based world.

La Clase Mágica is an effective learning environment whose underlying goals and objectives assume a particular kind of learner for a particular kind of life he or she will live. In other words, it envisages a world that reaches beyond the local community with the aid of information and communication technology and an individual who is able to find herself or himself through the complexities of a diverse global society. Theoretically, this perspective allows us to think about how we can strategically tweak the system of artifacts that make up the after-school program to encourage the development of active, bilingual learners who are fully prepared to enter into a technologically based, globally extended society. Furthermore, we are able to design innovative environments where cognitive development and identity investment are crucial parts of learning and where learners can reap new visions of self. For example, Tomás cited *La Clase Mágica*'s influence on him to study computer science at college:

> *La Clase Mágica* helped me to learn everything about computers. I used to teach adults in my community about the use of computers, which I think was very helpful for them and also for me. That encouraged me to apply for a computer science program at the university. I finally changed my mind and I ended up studying business but, the fact that I started in computer science has definitely much to do with my experience in *La Clase Mágica*. (Martínez & Vásquez, 2006)

The pursuit of higher education is one of the goals that we work into in the adult–child interactions and the curricular materials we design. Our findings show that the 20 former participants who had completed a series of 70 activities and who had advanced to the level of wizard assistant when they were children had either attended college or were planning to attend. Of those who were college age, all had received a minimum of a 2-year college education, and those former participants who are still in high school reported that they plan to attend college.

The project's aim to improve the social conditions of language minority youth and their families also filtered down to the child participants and is visible in life choices they make as young adults. Alex Carter, for example, who joined the project at age 7 and who is now 19, highlights the values he picked up at *La Clase Mágica* to help out his community: "I think that the influence of *La Clase Mágica* is very important for constructing a social conscience about the Latino community and its social needs" (Martínez & Vásquez, 2006).

Bransford's (cited in Cummins, this volume) criteria for effective learning are also aligned with the sociocultural framework of *La Clase Mágica*. This is particularly seen from perspective of Vygotsky's (1978) notion of the zone of proximal development that adults in *La Clase Mágica* are trained to create for child learners. According to Vygotsky (1978), the zone of proximal development is the:

> … distance between the actual level of development as determined by independent problem solving and the level of potential development as determined through problem solving under adult guidance or in collaboration with more capable peers. (p. 86)

Adults, many of whom are undergraduate students, prompt children's progress by using their home language and culture, giving them possible clues to solve problems, holding their progress in memory, and urging them to try harder. Through theoretically informed interactional practices, they create zones of proximal development that support active learning with deep understanding, and build on the ideal of a community of learners. The zone of proximal development incorporates the fourth rule of engagement: it creates a dynamically dialogic learning environment.

The zone of proximal development provides the framework to conceptualize the point of intervention in which the values just cited and the sense of self as active learners can be scaffolded by the adults who work with the children. As more capable peers, the undergraduates engage their child collaborators in dynamically charged interactions, opening up the opportunity for them to invest their identity as capable and able doers and thinkers while they develop cognitively and socially. Claudia Leal, 17, who participated in the project when she was 9, attributes her strong sense of self to her participation in *La Clase Mágica*: "The best of the program is the confidence it gives you to express yourself in public and in front of the others" (Martínez & Vásquez, 2006).

Our evaluation studies in 2005 and 2006 confirm our assertions that *La Clase Mágica* has a tremendous potential to bridge the pedagogical, cognitive, and digital divide that exists between language minority youth and more well-off mainstream youth. Every age group we studied over these last two years showed higher performance on both field-developed assessment measures and standardized tests than nonparticipants. Although our numbers are small and our evaluation classifies under Cummins' case study designation, elementary school-aged participants outperformed the control group on reading readiness skills in the first year of intervention and five years later on the state-administered test, which was given up to three years after they had left the program. The participants, considered "at risk" by their kindergarten teachers, not only showed superiority on language and math scores on the California STAR test, but they were also rated higher by their fifth-grade teachers in leadership, bilingual language arts, problem-solving, and computer literacy skills (Vásquez, 2006). Preschool children in a *La Clase Mágica*–Head Start combination activity also demonstrated incredible gains in 7 out of the 12 developmental domains of the Desired Results Profile after having started statistically lower than their slightly higher-income peers in a migrant education program (Pastor-Relaño & Vásquez, in preparation).

Although these findings do not tell us whether our rules of engagement could or would work in the classroom, they do show us that an effective learning environment outside of school can affect the academic achievement of participants. In other words, the skills learned in the after-school program transfer to the classroom. We have learned that the bilingual–bicultural activities that we arrange for the child participants give them ample opportunities to maintain their native language, in this case Spanish, and to acquire a second language, English, with the same or higher level of proficiency as their control group (Vásquez, 1993, 2003).

There is still much we have to learn about transporting educational activities like *La Clase Mágica* to the classroom. Its flexible nature, its dynamism, and its multidimensionality runs counter to conventional educational practice that demands stability, control, and linearity. We have learned that *La Clase Mágica* is no match for the dominance of the school culture (Vásquez, 2005). Just being on school grounds changes the dynamics and the content goals of the project. For example, when *La Clase Mágica* operated in the classroom during the teacher's preparation period, the norms of the school culture weighed heavily on the children's spontaneity and verbal expression. The same was true in another school where *La Clase Mágica* was held in a separate classroom. In both these cases, its rich dialogic environment, its goals and objectives, and its innovative use of the technology, that I argue is necessary to foster new ways of doing and thinking, were negatively affected. The school culture influenced the social and intellectual tenor of the activities of *La Clase Mágica* rather than the other way (Vásquez, 2005). Although the participants fared well in the state standardized tests as compared to nonparticipants, we believe that they would have performed even greater if *La Clase Mágica* would have been able to operate in its optimal form. However, both cases reconfirmed the value of collaboration between in-school and out-of-school teaching and learning and also the reticence of the culture of learning in American schools (Gallego & Cole, 2001). They also demonstrated that it is in the space between in-school and out-of-school teaching and learning that we have the best opportunity to have an impact on the achievement of English learners.

Acknowledgment

I would like to acknowledge Lee Charles Pooler for his insightful comments on the significance of the military notion of "rules of engagement."

Note

1. Wikipedia (2006) definition of rules of engagement:
   In military or police operations, the **rules of engagement** (**ROE**) determine when, where and how force shall be used. Such rules are both general and specific, and there have been large variations between cultures throughout history. The rules may be made public, as in a martial law or curfew situation, but are typically only fully known to the force that intends to use them.

References

Bruner, J. (1984). Vygotsky's Zone of proximal development: The hidden agenda. In B. Rogoff & J. Wertsch (Eds.), *Children in the zone of proximal development* (pp. 93–97). San Francisco, CA: Jossey Bass.

Cole, M. (1996). *Cultural psychology: A once and future discipline.* Cambridge, MA: Harvard University Press.

Elmore, R. (1990). *Restructuring schools: The next generation of educational reform.* San Francisco: Jossey-Bass.

Gallego, M. A., Cole, M., & The Laboratory of Comparative Human Cognition (LCHC). (2001). Classroom cultures and cultures in the classroom. In V. Richardson (Ed.), *Handbook of research on teaching* (4th ed; pp. 951–997). Washington, DC: American Educational Research Association.

Healey, F. H., & De Stefano, J. (1997). *Education reform support: A framework for scaling up school reform.* Unpublished document. Advancing Basic Education and Literacy Project. US Agency for International Development (USAID).

John-Steiner, V. (1997). *Notebooks of the mind: Explorations of thinking.* New York: Oxford University Press.

Leontiev, A. N., & Luria, A.R. (1968). The psychological ideas of L. S. Vygotsky. In B. B. Wolman (Ed.), *Historical roots of contemporary psychology* (pp. 338–367). New York: Harper & Row.

Luria, A.R. (1979). *Vygotsky, in the making of mind.* Cambridge, MA: Harvard University Press.

Martínez, M., & Vásquez, O. A. (2006). *Sustainability: La Clase Mágica beyond its boundaries.* Unpublished manuscript.

Miller, B. M. (2003, May). *Critical hours: After school programs and educational success.* Brooklyn, MA: Nellie Mae Education Foundation.

Moll, L. (Ed.). (1990). *Vygotsky and education: Instructional implications and applications of sociohistorical psychology.* Cambridge, MA: Cambridge University Press.

Pastor-Relaño, A. M. & Vásquez, O. A. (2005). *Accountability of the informal: challenges and new directions*. Unpublished manuscript.

Rogoff, B. (1994). Developing understanding of the idea of communities of learners. *Mind, Culture, and Activity: An International Journal, 1*(4), 209–229.

Saxe, G. B. (1994, Fall). Studying development in sociocultural context: The development of a practice-based approach. *Mind, Culture, and Activity: An International Journal, 1*(4), 135–157.

Springfield, S., Datnow, A., & Ross, S.M. (1998). *Scaling up school restructuring in multicultural, multilingual contexts: Early observations from Sunland County. Research Report 2.* Center for Research on Education, Diversity & Excellence. Santa Cruz, CA and Washington, DC.

Tedesco, J. C. (1998). Current trends in educational reform. In J. Delors (Ed.), *Education for the twenty-first century.* (pp. 1–5), Paris: UNESCO.

Vásquez, O. A. (1993). A look at language as resource: Lessons from *La Clase Mágica*. In B. Arias & U. Casanova (Eds.), *Bilingual education: Politics, research, and practice* (pp. 199–224). Chicago: National Society for the Study of Education.

Vásquez, O. A. (2003). *La Clase Mágica: Imagining optimal possibilities in a bilingual learning community.* New Jersey: Erlbaum.

Vásquez, O. A. (2005). Social action and the politics of collaboration. In P. Pedraza & M. Rivera (Eds.), *Educating Latino youth: An agenda for transcending myths and unveiling possibilities* (pp. 321–341). New Jersey: Laurence Erlbaum.

Vásquez, O. A., & Durán, R. (2000). *La Clase Mágica* and *El Club Proteo*: Multiple literacies in new community institutions. In M. Gallego & S. Hollingsworth (Eds.), *Challenging a single standard: Multiple perspectives on literacy* (pp. 173–189). New York: Teachers College Press.

Vygotsky, L.S. (1978). *Mind in Society: The development of higher psychological processes.* Cambridge, MA: Harvard University Press.

Wells, G. (2000). Dialogic inquiry in education: Building on the legacy of Vygotsky. In C. D. Lee & P. Smagorinsky (Eds.), *Vygotskian perspectives on literacy research: Constructing meaning through collaborative inquiry* (pp. 51–85). New York: Cambridge University Press.

Wertsch, J. V. (1985). *Social formation of mind.* Cambridge, MA: Harvard University Press.

4
Developing New Literacies among Multilingual Learners in the Elementary Grades

JILL CASTEK

University of Connecticut

DONALD J. LEU

University of Connecticut

JULIE COIRO

University of Rhode Island

MILEIDIS GORT

University of Miami

LAURIE A. HENRY

University of Kentucky

CLARISSE O. LIMA

Education Consultant, Rio de Janeiro, Brazil

This chapter explores the learning potentials that exist at the intersection between language, literacy, and the Internet for multilingual learners. We suggest that, in addition to the foundational literacy skills required within traditional book and print technologies, the Internet requires new reading, writing, and communication skills. We refer to these as new literacies and define them below. We suggest that the Internet: (1) is this generation's defining context for literacy and learning; (2) requires new skills, strategies, and dispositions to fully exploit its information and learning potential; and (3) creates special opportunities for multilingual learners in an increasingly globalized world. In this chapter, we describe our vision of these new literacies for multilingual learners and the unique potentials they hold for preparing students for their literacy and learning futures.

This chapter also seeks to provide educators, parents, and policymakers with a research-based set of principles to inform instruction in the area of new literacies. This is especially important in a world where the technologies of informational literacy are rapidly shifting from paper and book to screen, search engine, and Webpage. Specifically, we address this focal question: How might we best support the development of new literacies among elementary age learners who are simultaneously acquiring language and literacy in both English and their native language?

We believe the answer to our question is best understood by bringing together multiple perspectives. In order to both adequately represent the nature of the question, as well as begin to define appropriate solutions, we have chosen to take a multiple realities perspective (Labbo & Reinking, 1999) to frame our analysis. Using both a Multilingual Perspective (Gort, 2006) and a New Literacies Perspective (Lankshear & Knobel, 2003; Leu, Kinzer, Coiro, & Cammack, 2004), this chapter addresses issues of multiple language acquisition, literacy learning, and the important role that Internet technologies increasingly play in reading, writing, and communication. We begin by exploring principles of language and literacy development from a Multilingual Perspective. Then we explore a separate set of principles from a New Literacies Perspective. We go on to define a Globalized Perspective that integrates these two theoretical perspectives and introduces ten research-based principles that inform classroom teaching, literacy practices, and educational policies. We then use this integrated set of principles to analyze several instructional environments we viewed as exemplars for the acquisition and development of new literacies among multilingual learners in the elementary grades (see Table A4.1 in the Appendix for a comparative analysis of exemplars). This analysis permits us to consider how the principles of a Globalized Perspective can be used to support elementary age children who are simultaneously acquiring a new language and new literacies. We conclude with a discussion of the consequences of this analysis for literacy development in school settings and out-of-school contexts.

A Multilingual Perspective

With more than 176 languages spoken nationwide, the population of the United States is becoming increasingly diverse and multilingual. The number of Americans speaking a home language other than English has more than doubled since 1980 (U.S. Census Bureau, 2001). Currently, one in four school age children lives in a household where English is not the primary spoken language (Crawford, 2004). By 2030, students whose first language is not English will make up an estimated 40% of the K–12 student population (Center for Research on Education, Diversity and Excellence, 2002). These statistics only begin to describe the explosion of language diversity across the United States.

Approximately 31 million U.S. residents speak Spanish at home, an increase of almost 11 million speakers between 1990 and 2000 (U.S. Census Bureau, 2001). In 2000, Chinese replaced French as the third-most popular language spoken in the United States, nearly doubling its number of speakers within a decade. The population of Tagalog, Vietnamese, Russian, and Arabic speakers also surged in the 1990s. Of the 20 non-English languages most frequently spoken at home in the United States, the largest proportional increase was for Russian speakers, who nearly tripled in 2000. The second-largest increase was for Creole speakers, whose speakers more than doubled.

The rich learning opportunities that could exist within a multilingual educational context have yet to be realized because of perspectives that view English Language Learners as lacking in language ability. We recognize that bilingual and multilingual children possess sophisticated language skills, due to their ability to communicate flexibly in a variety of language contexts. However traditionally, the diversity that increasingly defines our society has been viewed as an obstacle.

A Multilingual Perspective views multilingualism as a powerful national asset and multilingual students as global citizens who have the potential to create global connections that will transform the future in dynamic ways. Promoting communicative and literate exchanges between and among students who use more than a single language system creates opportunities for developing expertise and knowledge in a variety of forms. Research suggests there are many positive attributes associated with being multilingual including an increase in cognitive flexibility, the ability to think more abstractly, and the ability to think independently of words (Hakuta, 1986; Peal & Lambert, 1962). Multilingual speakers demonstrate superiority in concept formation and also have advantages in metalinguistic and metacognitive awareness, including a positive transfer between languages and an increased understanding of other cultures and ways of life (Bialystok, 1988; Cenoz & Valencia, 1994; Galambos & Goldin-Meadow, 1990; Peal & Lambert, 1962). Students who speak more than one language flexibly and fluently perform better than their monolingual counterparts on tests of academic achievement (Bialystok & Hakuta, 1994). These linguistic and cognitive advantages explain the important reasons why nurturing language diversity and multilingualism among learners of all ages is a meaningful step toward providing an education that prepares students for participation in a globalized world characterized by the exchange of ideas between individuals across nations (Friedman, 2005).

Although multilingualism is the norm abroad, monolingual orientations still dominate beliefs within U.S. educational systems. Multicultural education and bilingual programs have made teachers in the United States more aware of alternative approaches to supporting language learning and cultural diversity, but we believe much more can be done to ensure that all students are provided with positive learning experiences at school and in their communities. For example, supporting multilingual students' language and literacy learning involves embracing the linguistic, cultural, and sociohistorical riches that each child brings to the classroom to achieve the benefits that diversity provides. Language diversity should not be viewed as a problem that needs to be fixed but as a respected and desired educational outcome. Gort (2006) offers the following definition of a multilingual perspective of language and literacy development.

> A multilingual perspective is based on a holistic view of the bilingual learner including validation of students' cultural and linguistic backgrounds as resources for learning, an understanding of the role of primary language (including literacy) in the acquisition of a new language, and a consideration of sociolinguistic, sociohistorical, and sociocultural factors that contribute to the child's development and experiences. (p. 330–331)

This perspective acknowledges students' entire linguistic, literate, and cultural repertoire including languages, dialects, and uses of language and literacy in many contexts.

Snow (1992) documents historical trends in language acquisition showing how, in the past, perspectives came from a linguistic or psycholinguistic philosophy and were focused on the cognitive aspects of learning languages. A more fruitful perspective, she asserts, is sociocultural, emphasizing the importance of societal attitudes and group membership in language learning. A Multilingual Perspective is informed by both sociolinguistic views and sociocultural views. Sociolinguistic views examine connections between language and societies and focus on ways languages are used for particular purposes. Sociocultural factors impact values, attitudes, beliefs, and assumptions of language and literacy learning. These factors relate to past and present relationships between cultural groups. By embracing these perspectives, we believe we can support educators in designing fruitful activities that link language, communication, and literacy together as interrelated constructs for learning.

A Multilingual Perspective identifies ten research-based principles for language learning and literacy development. These principles provide a foundation for examining learning contexts both in and out of school.

Language Is Linked to Identity Construction

Promoting students' home languages in and out of the classroom provides a foundation for building a strong sense of self (Baker, 2001). In a sociocultural sense, language teaches children how to be viable members of a cultural community, providing a context by which speakers create solidarity, express familiarity, and convey social roles. Children's ability to speak, read, and write their home language is essential to maintaining strong social and emotional ties to their parents, grandparents, extended family members, and communities. Socialization and language exchange transmits the culture of the community. As children learn their native language, they absorb the social structure of the culture. In this way, language learning becomes a means of sorting out one's identity in varying social environments.

Classroom communities can be enriched by drawing on the existing funds of knowledge in multilingual students' households (Moll, 1992). Funds of knowledge refer to historically developed bodies of knowledge and accumulated strategies (e.g., skills, abilities, ideas, practices) that are essential to a household's functioning (González et al., 1993). Students who are invited to apply their multicultural and linguistic identities within school settings are able to more easily make links between home and school and as a result, may become more invested in the culture of school.

Language and Literacy Develop Globally, not Linearly,
through Opportunities to Use Language in Meaningful Contexts
In contrast to language learning in formal instructional settings, language acquisition is optimized within everyday contexts and does not follow a prescribed scope and sequence (Krashen & Terrell, 1983). Informal learning promotes the development of language through supportive exchanges between and among speakers with meaningful communication as the goal. Vocabulary and grammar provide support for oral and written expression exchanged in ways that are mutually intelligible. Activities that promote authentic communication support language learning and involve real-world tasks (Edelsky, Altwerger, & Flores, 1991). Risk-free environments where students' background, experiences, and contributions are validated facilitate language learning (Law & Eckes, 1990).

Even though language acquisition is a natural process, the development of cognitive/academic language requires time, typically 4 to 7 years of formal instruction (Cummins, 1981, 1984, 2000; Hakuta, Butler, & Witt, 2000; Hakuta & D'Andrea, 1992). Because cognitive and academic language skills readily transfer from one language to another (Cummins, 1981), instructional techniques that draw from students' home language backgrounds support content connections across languages. Thus an important aspect of a Multilingual Perspective is the opportunity to maximize connections between both home and academic settings in order to promote the full development of one's potential.

Multilingual Learning Contexts Help Students Understand the Universals
Common to All Languages, Promoting Cognitive Flexibility
Children learn second languages in different ways depending on their native language, age, culture, motivation, individual personalities, and the context of acquisition. Learning new languages provides opportunities for increased metalinguistic awareness. Metalinguistic awareness can be seen as the ability to think about, and reflect on, the nature and functions of languages, including analyses of how languages are similar and different. Such awareness is thought to be a key factor in the development of reading in young children (Bialystok, 1997; Donaldson, 1978), suggesting that bilingual children may be ready to learn to read slightly earlier than monolingual children.

Multilingual and multicultural learning broadens students' worldview and encourages multiple lenses for thinking and problem solving. As students learn to reason, justify, and critique ideas that come from many points of view, they express their thinking in complex ways while collaborating with others. In order to formulate creative and innovative solutions, a variety of perspectives must be considered. Multilingual/multicultural teaching provides access to multiple perspectives that reflect a wide array of ideas (Gort, 2003). Bridging across cultural and linguistic contexts enables students to identify richer, more complex, and ultimately more beneficial, solutions to complex problems.

Language Competence Is Evolving and Dynamic

Each of us participates in several different speech communities that change according to time, place, and situation. Language ability involves the flexibility to operate and negotiate between settings. Affiliations and discourse patterns continuously change based on context and the comfort level of speakers. According to LePage and Tabouret-Keller (1985), individuals "create their linguistic systems so as to resemble those of the groups with which, from time to time, they wish to identify" (p. 23). For example, individuals who speak multiple languages occupy a place in multiple cultures and linguistic groups. For some, becoming English-dominant means denying the national heritage that is part of their group identity.

Multilingual individuals participate in several speech communities simultaneously and switch flexibly back and forth based on context, purpose, nature of the communication, and with whom and to whom they are speaking. Exchanges involve not only knowing how to speak a specific language, but also how to use language appropriately in a variety of social situations. Through meaningful opportunities to use languages, speakers develop a working knowledge of all the possible linguistic forms and learn to understand the reasons for choosing each one to suit their communicative purposes. As educators, we must acknowledge that individuals identify with multiple linguistic and cultural communities and that association with one does not minimize or limit membership in another. Expressions of language are constantly changing based on speakers' communicative purposes as defined by the relationships between speakers.

Multilingual Development Supports Critical Thinking

All students benefit from learning to be critical of what they read, hear, and encounter in a variety of settings, especially because perspectives embedded in reading materials and the media can be hegemonic, culturally biased, and unreliable. Literacy can serve to maintain the status quo, that is, to ensure that those in power influence what the general population reads and thinks (Edelsky, 2006). Yet, literacy can also be a liberator, or a means of opening a door to empowerment (Baker, 2001). Embracing instruction that involves the development of multiple cultural frames of reference for recognizing and responding to bias, domination, and inequality goes a long way in supporting critical thinking. Stereotypes are combated and multiple viewpoints encouraged when students and teachers interactively construct knowledge, develop consciousness, and share reflections, experiences, and reactions through critical inquiry in the classroom. Critical thinking can be enhanced through the discussion of dual language texts (e.g., The Dual Language Showcase Project http://thornwood.peelschools. org/Dual/about.htm). This multilingual program is designed to spark dialogue by examining texts in two to three languages. Exploring texts across languages facilitates collaboration in finding common themes.

*Traditional Teacher Roles and Student Roles Transform
in Language Rich Classroom Contexts*

Constructivist perspectives involve creating environments where students work together to solve problems through group-based, cooperative learning activities (Vygotsky, 1978). As students share ideas, ask questions, and exchange information, they actively construct meaning. When implemented in the classroom, communication shifts from teacher talk to student talk making the exchange of ideas between students an integral part of the learning process. According to Freire (1993) teachers "must abandon the educational goal of deposit-making and replace it with the posing of the problems of human beings in their relations with the world. Liberating education, or education as the practice of freedom, consists in acts of cognition, not transferals of information" (p. 60). Educational dialogues that incorporate exchanges between and among students are catalysts for cooperation in ways that transform the classroom and the world. Through active participation, students gain confidence and in turn become more proactive managers of their own learning (Larsen-Freeman, 1986).

*Power Relations Play a Critical Role in Social Interactions between
Language Learners and Target Language Speakers*

Bilingualism has become a fact of life in the United States as immigration has reached its highest level in U.S. history (Crawford, 2004). Many schools promote subtractive bilingualism and assimilation to the dominant language, English, with no plan for maintenance or extension of students' first language. Wong-Fillmore (1998) documented the fact that children lose their mother tongue at a far higher rate than they learn their second language. This phenomenon, she further explains, is one in which "learning a second language means losing the first one" (Wong-Fillmore, 1991, p. 341). In fact, the most recent waves of immigrants experienced substantial attrition of their native language by the second generation in the United States (Crawford, 2004).

We believe communities shortchange themselves when operating within a monolingual framework. Children and adults alike deserve the opportunity to preserve and extend their linguistic competencies. Communication that takes place on equal footing allows for respectful interchanges. Vygotsky (1978) encourages "a variety of internal developmental processes that are able to operate only when the child is interacting with people in his environment and in cooperation with his peers" (p. 90). By exercising the right to speak their language, children broaden and deepen their communicative competences.

Oral Language Can Be Used as a Tool for Developing Student Literacy

Language is used for many purposes including communication, expression of values, sharing of oral traditions, and family life. Exchanging ideas from a common cultural background facilitates language use as a powerful expression of how individuals situate themselves in relation to others. As literacy develops, students learn to connect their shared oral traditions with the language used in books. Using the spoken form of language through experiences with listening and speaking can serve as a bridge to the mastery of the more standard forms. Children need encouragement to experiment with a variety of linguistic forms in order to develop fluency across settings. Drawing on students' home background and native language demonstrates acknowledgement of the important role personal experience plays in making connections between known concepts and new ideas. Moll (1992) encourages teachers to provide "authentic literacy practices" (p. 21), to use literacy as a tool for "inquiry, communication, and thinking" (p. 21) and to extend ways for students to read and interpret information across content areas. Providing students with opportunities to think, reflect, and respond in multiple languages promotes growth in their ability to use language effectively.

Social Networks of Exchange Are Powerful Learning Agents

Communities that coalesce around common interests provide opportunities to build affiliation, deepen cultural attachments, and expand linguistic expression. Social networks are particularly powerful for elementary grade children because learning is fundamentally intertwined with friendship and socialization. Learning becomes more meaningful, engaging, and motivational when ideas can be shared among networks of individuals with whom students have an affinity. Families represent the most important social network for learning among students in elementary grades. When families become actively involved in educational experiences, learning is connected across contexts. Moll (1992, 1998) discusses the value of involving the community, including parents, as resources. Once mobilized for learning, social networks become an important intellectual resource for school.

Reading and Writing Are Literacy Processes through Which Children Create and Express Meaningful Ideas in Any Language

Literacy development draws on students' vocabulary knowledge, oral language, and a variety of strategies to promote and regulate comprehension

(Peregoy & Boyle, 1993). Prior knowledge plays a particularly important role in the development of literacy considering that individuals develop literacy skills most easily in a familiar language. Research shows the value of strong native language abilities on the development of literacy in the second language, even when languages have dissimilar writing systems (Cummins, 1991). Further, high levels of native language proficiency strongly correlate with high levels of academic achievement and linguistic proficiency in a second language (Skutnabb-Kangas & Toukomaa, 1976).

Multilingual students function in at least two cultures and languages; their success therefore requires literacy in more than one language. In order to promote the transfer of literacy skills from one language to another, learning environments should promote the examination of relationships between languages (Roberts, 1994). Providing space and freedom for students to express their ideas in the language they feel most comfortable suits several instructional purposes. These purposes include: (1) showing respect for individuality, (2) making cultural connections, and (3) promoting linguistic transfer.

Teaching Approaches Supporting Multilingual Development

A Multilingual Perspective rejects deficit views of "language as a problem" and promotes multiple language and literacy development as a personal and national resource. To extend the benefits of multilingualism, educators need to find ways to take advantage of the full range of communicative, cognitive, and cultural experiences children bring with them to school. When students who communicate in more than one language can be taught in ways that promote the sharing of language concepts and cultural nuances with their peers, a powerful learning experience that benefits all is created. Regardless of age or cultural situation, structuring learning in multilingual classrooms should incorporate events that show respect for all learners (Learning Park, 2001). Here we present three ways to begin structuring supportive learning environments both in and out of school.

First, a commitment must be made to creating an environment where each child feels safe, where risks can be taken without fear of being laughed at or made fun of. Establishing guidelines that promote a positive stress-free place to learn is of special importance in nurturing language acquisition. Second, acknowledging, inquiring about, and celebrating all students' languages and cultural backgrounds should be a priority throughout the school year. Embracing all cultures benefits the entire learning community. Third, incorporating special events that include traditions from a variety of cultures celebrates the heritage and the national backgrounds of all children. Discussing important customs of many cultures is a concrete way to show interest, as well as educate students, about different cultural practices and beliefs. Finally, frequent communication with parents and the extended family is an important way to recognize the role home cultures plays in learning. Finding ways to involve family members helps to make both learning English, and learning in general, a positive experience that unifies educators and parents. Locating a translator for conferences and sending home newsletters in students' native languages conveys respect to students and their families. When all parties cooperate toward common goals, children are supported and encouraged, building motivation and self-esteem.

A New Literacies Perspective

The Internet is today's defining technology for literacy and learning (Coiro, Knobel, Lankshear, & Leu, in press). The nature of literacy is rapidly changing as new information and communication technologies, such as the Internet, rapidly generate new literacies required to effectively exploit their potential for reading, writing, and communication (Bruce, 2003; Lankshear & Knobel, 2003; Leu, Kinzer et al., 2004). Research from diverse disciplines, such as cognitive science (Gee, 2003; Mayer, 2001), sociolinguistics (Cope & Kalantzis, 2000; Gee, 2004; Kress, 2003; Lemke, 1998), and cultural anthropology (Markham, 1998; Street, 2003; Thomas, 2007) is beginning to examine the consequences of the changes to literacy brought about by the Internet and the new social practices it permits. There is an underlying recognition across disciplines that the nature of literacy is being modified by new technologies and the new social practices they enable. New heuristics appear to inform this multidisciplinary work. A New Literacies Perspective is redefining what it means to be literate in the 21st century (Coiro et al., in press).

The construct *new literacies* is highly contested terrain; the term means many different things to many different people. However, most would agree there are at least three defining characteristics of this perspective:

1. New literacies are central to full civic, economic, and personal participation in a globalized community and, as a result, are critical to educational research and the education of all of our students.
2. New literacies are deictic—they regularly change as their defining technologies change.
3. New literacies are multifaceted—they benefit from analysis that brings multiple points of view to the discussion.

For this analysis, we follow the definition of a New Literacies Perspective used by Leu, Kinzer et al. (2004), which pays particular attention to the new literacies of the information and communication space that exist on the Internet:

The new literacies of the Internet and other information and communication technologies include the skills, strategies, and dispositions necessary to successfully use and adapt to the rapidly changing information and communication technologies and contexts that continuously emerge in our world and influence all areas of our personal and professional lives. These new literacies allow us to use the Internet and other information communication technologies (ICTs) to identify important questions, locate information, critically evaluate the usefulness of the information, synthesize information to answer those questions, and then communicate the answers to others. (p. 1572)

Engaging in the five central functions identified in this definition (identifying questions, locating information, critically evaluating information, synthesizing information, and communicating to others) provides individuals from different cultural contexts, who often speak various first languages, opportunities to connect in new and potentially powerful ways to solve important problems. Thus, the Internet extends important opportunities for increased multicultural understanding and appreciation of the linguistic diversity that defines a global society (Leu, Leu, & Coiro, 2004).

In a review of research, Leu, Kinzer et al. (2004) identify ten principles as central to a New Literacies Perspective. An overview of these principles follows.

The Internet and Other ICTs Are Central Technologies for Literacy within a Global Community in an Information Age

Literacy has always been shaped by the dominant technologies of every historical period. Cuneiform tablets, papyrus scrolls, velum transcriptions, and printed paper have each demanded their own reading and writing skills to fully exploit the information potential of each technology. Today, we are moving from a period in which printed book technologies have dominated our literacy landscape to one where the Internet and other ICTs are central to literacy development in a global community. Consider, for example, just a few indications of this in workplace settings, at home, and in schools.

During 2005, 93% of workers in U.S. companies with more than 100 employees reported using the Internet and other online information resources in the workplace (Harris Interactive, Inc., 2005). Earlier survey data from the United States indicated that in just one year (August 2000 to September 2001) use of the Internet at work among all employed adults 25 years of age and older increased nearly 60% from 26.1% of the workforce to 41.7% (U.S. Department of Commerce, 2002). If this rate of increase continues, nearly everyone in the workforce will be using the Internet at work within just a few years.

Statistics on Internet usage at home in the United States parallel these changes in the workplace. Nearly 75% of all households reported that they had Internet access in 2004 (Nielson/Net Ratings, 2004). In 2005, 87% of all students between the ages of 12 and 17 in the United States reported using the Internet; nearly 11,000,000 did so daily (Pew Internet and American Life Project, 2005). Interestingly, Internet users report decreasing time spent viewing television while increasing time spent online (Lebo, 2003). Moreover, the percentage of U.S. households with broadband Internet access doubled each year from 1998 to 2001, an adoption rate in households exceeding that of any previous technology including telephones, color televisions, videocassette recorders, cellular phones, and pagers (U.S. Department of Commerce, 2002).

The Internet is also appearing in school classrooms in the United States and other countries at a rate that parallels its appearance in the workplace and at home. In only ten years (1994–2004), the percentage of classrooms in the United States possessing at least one computer with Internet access went from 3% to 93% (National Center for Education Statistics, 2005). The availability of Internet access has also had a demonstrated impact on students. In 2001, 94% of children ages 12–17 who had Internet access said that they used the Internet for school-related research (Lenhart, Simon, & Graziano, 2001). Clearly, the Internet has become a central technology for information and communication.

The Internet and Other ICTs Require New Literacies to Fully Access Their Potential

New literacies skills and strategies are essential to effectively using the Internet and other ICTs. For example, reading comprehension in online environments is more complex and requires new skills and strategies (Coiro & Dobler, 2007; Coiro, 2003). Locating information with a search engine, evaluating the accuracy of information located, synthesizing key ideas from disparate information sources, participating in online discussions, and communicating with email are important new literacies to be acquired. Moreover, reading on the Internet requires new applications of inferential reasoning and self-regulated reading strategies (Coiro & Dobler, 2007). On the Internet, reading, writing, and communicating take on new forms as information is presented in more complex networks and media formats that require the development of new literacies for online reading comprehension.

New Literacies Are Deictic

The term *deixis* (dike-sis) is used by linguists and others (Fillmore, 1972; Murphy, 1986) for words whose meanings change quickly depending on the time or space in which they are used. Leu (1997, 2000) and Leu and Kinzer (2000) have argued that literacy has become a deictic term whereas the forms and functions of literacy rapidly change as technologies for information and communication change, requiring new skills and strategies for their effective use. For example, searching for information with search engines requires new kinds of reading skills to effectively examine a vast amount of information available with the click of a button. A learner may be skilled with using search engines but lack the know-how for selecting reliable information from the abundance of links these tools make available. These skills and strategies have important consequences for any discussion of literacy in the 21st century. New literacies are continuously new literacies. Increasingly, students will need to learn how to learn, not to simply master a fixed set of skills that remain static (Leu, 2000; Leu, Kinzer et al., 2004).

The Relationship between Technology and Literacy Is Transactional

New technologies transform literacy but literacy also transforms new technologies. Increasingly, this happens when educators construct new curricular resources with Internet technologies (Leu, Karchmer, & Leu, 1999). Thus, we must begin to recognize the relationship between technology and literacy as a transactional one. Because this relationship is transactional, new literacy and learning tools continually appear, providing important new resources for learners that require even newer literacies to use them effectively.

New Literacies Are Multiple in Nature

New literacies not only change on a regular basis, they are also multiple in nature. These multiliteracies (The New London Group, 2000) are open ended, flexible, and necessary to function in diverse contexts and communities. Although the notion of multiliteracies was traditionally conceived of within a more traditional framing of language, the Internet has spawned multiple technological contexts that are now a part of our everyday lives. The ability to share information globally through the Internet introduces new challenges for students expected to interact in different social and cultural contexts.

Critical Literacies Are Central to New Literacies

The Internet demands new forms of critical literacy, critical thinking, and analysis. The rapidly increasing amount of information available on the Internet, from spurious to highly reputable, presents challenges for locating appropriate information and assessing its credibility, perspectives, and appropriateness. Because open networks, such as the Internet, provide a platform for anyone to publish anything without scrutiny, it is essential that students develop critical literacy skills to determine what information is most reliable. Although schools often include some critical thinking and analytical skills in the literacy curriculum, such as lessons focused on separating fact from propaganda, a greater emphasis on critical analysis skills is needed as the Internet becomes more central to classroom learning. A New Literacies Perspective draws from the work of the critical literacy and media literacy communities. It argues that sophisticated higher-level and critical thinking skills are required in the changing literacy contexts that define the Internet.

New Forms of Strategic Knowledge Are Central to New Literacies

In order for new technologies to be used effectively, new skills and strategies are required. Each technology presents different contexts and resources to construct meaning and requires different strategies to do this successfully

(Mayer, 1997). New literacies are defined by the strategic knowledge that is central to the use of information in rich, elaborately networked environments. The types of strategic knowledge important to new literacies include the ability to locate, evaluate, and effectively use the resources available on the Internet. The number of online resources is growing exponentially, therefore new forms of strategic knowledge will continue to be central to developing new literacies.

Speed Counts in Important Ways within the New Literacies

Because of the vast amount of information available through the Internet, new literacies will be defined by the rate at which one can read, write, and communicate. Additionally, the rate at which one is able to acquire, evaluate, and use information to solve problems is central to success. Thus the acquisition of these skills is an important instructional issue to consider. Speed is central to developing new literacies skills and strategies, both in relation to Internet connections as well as the ability to quickly locate and share information. The gap between highly literate and literacy challenged students is also an issue that needs to be addressed to prevent a widening gap of inequity. Students who have difficulty with reading tasks and read haltingly will be left further and further behind compared to their peers who have the ability to quickly skim Web pages and sift through large amounts of information in a short time. Substantial resources need to be devoted to addressing this issue to prevent an ever-widening gap among same-age learners.

Learning Is Often Socially Constructed within New Literacies

Two aspects of social learning strategies are important to recognize in a New Literacies Perspective. First, social learning plays an important role in exchanging new skills and strategies needed to successfully interact with new technologies. Many of today's students possess new literacies skills that their teachers have not yet acquired. Therefore, when it comes to Internet instruction, the traditional teacher–student model may not be ideal. It is nearly impossible for one individual to possess all the new literacies needed for learning with the Internet and other ICTs. However, each individual will know something unique, distinct, and useful to others that can be easily shared in a social learning context. Secondly, social learning is not only important for how information is learned but also for how information is constructed. Much of the information on the Internet is constructed through social knowledge shared among various individuals. For example, telecollaborative projects and threaded discussions are collections of information provided by multiple participants from diverse backgrounds. Therefore, the new technologies of literacy provide opportunities for collaboratively constructed solutions to important problems drawn from many different contributors.

Thus technology provides an opportunity for increased collaboration across learning contexts and has the ability to draw us closer to others from different cultures.

Teachers Become More Important, Though Their Role
Changes, within New Literacy Classrooms

Teachers will be challenged to orchestrate learning experiences and guide students' learning within the complex environments of the Internet and other ICTs. It will be important for them to provide increasingly richer and more complex opportunities for themselves and their students as technologies continue to change and new literacies continue to emerge. Instead of acting as dispensers of literacy skills, because at times their students will possess skills that they have not yet acquired, teachers will need to orchestrate more complex contexts for literacy learning and development. At times, roles between student and teacher may become reversed as students who possess new literacies become the experts in the classroom and share their expertise with others, including the teacher. Students who have teachers that understand the complexities of a New Literacies Perspective will be advantaged over those who do not. Teacher education and professional development needs to provide more opportunities to explore the complexities of new literacies in literacy instruction.

A New Literacies Perspective argues that new technologies create new literacies that are increasingly important to our lives in a global information age. Specifically, the nature of reading, writing, and communicating is being transformed in fundamental ways through the use of the Internet and other ICTs. Families, schools, and society need to begin to understand these changes if we seek to prepare our children for the world they deserve.

Teaching Approaches Supporting the Development of New Literacies

There is a variety of teaching techniques compatible with Internet integration, literacy learning, and language acquisition. In this section we describe three approaches that support the development of new literacies. These suggestions engage children in the full range of evolving Internet activities that include: 1) using the Internet as an information resource for learning about a wide range of topics and 2) using the Internet as a communication context where ideas are shared and exchanged dynamically with others around the world. These teaching approaches create meaningful learning contexts and build knowledge of how to adapt to the ever-changing nature of Internet events.

Collaborative writing projects that promote sharing perspectives across contexts invite students to apply writing and communication strategies while involving children in authentic learning activities. Discussion boards facilitate the exchange of ideas using an interactive format (see ePALS Student Talk http://www.epals.com/tools/forum/forum.e?bo=69&at=db). On the ePALS discussion board, students from all over the world communicate to a wide audience about the ideas that are important to them including culture, global issues, and current events. These exchanges yield rich opportunities for literacy development, social interaction, and cross-cultural understanding. Participation encourages students to formulate new perspectives and share ideas with clarity. Revision, reorganization, and reworking ideas become more purposeful because communication is the goal. Sending messages around the world, both in English as well as in students' home languages, helps develop reading, writing, and communication skills that are an important part of students' daily lives. Such communication also enriches linguistic and cultural understanding by teaching students to appreciate diverse points of view and means of expression.

Involving students in interpersonal exchange projects that extend reading, writing, and communication is motivating and inspiring. Think.com (www.think.com), Oracle Education Foundation's collaboration site, extends interactive learning tools to thousands of schools around the world in eight languages reaching more than 275,000 students in 26 countries. The free tools available on this site make it possible for teachers to facilitate student collaboration providing schools with new options for managing student interaction. Collaboration applications encourage students to collect, organize, and share information while making connections with others. Students can use email tools available on this site to share ideas and pose questions to others around the world. In the process, learners are able to participate in cross-cultural literacy exchanges in multiple languages.

Participation in Internet projects provides opportunities for young people to engage in collaborative activities that transform the world around us (U.S. Department of Education, 2006). For example, the United Nations has organized a Cyberschool Bus project (http://cyberschoolbus.un.org/) as a means of exposing students to issues of global concern. This multilingual portal offers curriculum resources for social action projects in six languages. A social action-oriented project such as Schools Demining Schools (http://www.un.org/cyberschoolbus/banmines/index.asp) provides students with resources to learn about current international issues that plague our world. Classes can read current reports about what schools have been doing in support of landmine clearance or hear the latest reports from the field. Students are also invited to reflect on solutions using this site's online space to discuss and publish their ideas. By supporting students' engagement in collaborative activities, educators capitalize on the appeal and motivation of the Internet in ways that enhance learning and collaboration. Through these efforts, children assess situations, take global trends into consideration, and ultimately participate in the formulation of solutions that may impact the realities of tomorrow.

A Globalized Perspective for Language and Literacy

Change defines literacy in our increasingly globalized and multilingual world and is both the result *and* the cause of increasingly powerful ICTs that, themselves, rapidly change, prompting continuously newer literacies (Leu, 2000; The New London Group, 2000). Any consideration of how to support students with literacy and learning must take advantage of this essential truth. Moreover, we must begin to acknowledge a second essential truth: our nation is no longer a monolingual society. Instead, despite regular resistance to the contrary, our nation is increasingly multilingual and multicultural.

Central to both a Multilingual Perspective and a New Literacies Perspective is the idea of change. Fundamental changes must take place in our conceptualization of education, both at home and at school, if we hope to prepare all children for their futures in an increasingly globalized world where one's ability to effectively use information within diverse linguistic, cultural, and technological contexts is essential to fully realizing each individual's potential. Schools, for example, often continue to assume that only one language is possible in classrooms. Moreover, they privilege books and other traditional print materials as information sources. Neither assumption is consistent with the realities of today's world. Unfortunately, our mindset, in both society as a whole and in schools in particular, continues to reflect assumptions of a static system, more typical of a monolingual and industrial era.

For the first time in our history, many students now are more literate than their teachers. When it comes to navigating the Internet, reading and posting to blogs, utilizing search engines to collect information resources, sharing Instant Messages and text messages, editing and compiling information from Wikipedia, and effectively utilizing new technologies for information and communication, today's students are the experts. Meanwhile, strategies for learning with the Internet and exchanging ideas online remain unfamiliar to many classroom teachers. Therefore, we see instruction involving the Internet as empowering to both educators and young people, inviting opportunities for dialogue and demonstration of strategies for effective use.

We see a Globalized Perspective as informing some of the important opportunities for systemic change that are essential to educational systems today. We must begin to conceptualize how best to prepare our students for the 21st century by drawing on their experiences in both language and technology as a stepping-stone to a successful future in a global society. The following sections provide an overview of ten principles of a Globalized Perspective that integrate both a Multilingual and New Literacies Perspective.

New Realities, Inherent in the Rapidly Changing Nature of Life
in the 21st Century, Must Be Recognized as We Consider Any Issue
in Education but Especially Issues of Language and Literacy

It is fruitless to consider any issue in education today without grasping the essential nature of the rapid changes taking place in our world. The two most important changes that drive these new realities consist of the rapidly globalizing nature of our world and the rapid changes taking place to information and communication technologies. Each affects the other, increasing the speed with which both changes are taking place.

Globalization places each of us in closer and closer proximity, both physically and intellectually, and results in schools having to confront the realities of the global and multilingual society in which we all live. Each day, it is less possible for schools, in any society, to maintain the fiction that only a single language exists for literacy and learning.

It is also less and less possible to maintain the fiction that only book technologies, and the traditional print literacies they require, provide essential information for teaching and learning. Manguel (1996) notes that the function of literacy has never been static; it continually changes in different historical, cultural, and technological contexts. In our earliest societies, literacy was a way to record sheep, crops, and taxes. Among many religions, it was a way to enforce a common dogma. In a postreformation world, Luther and his Protestant followers viewed literacy as the means to individual salvation. In a Jeffersonian democracy, literacy was seen as essential to the survival of the civic enterprise as informed citizens made reasoned decisions at the ballot box. In an industrial world, literacy was seen as a means to accurately transmit production information from top to bottom in a hierarchically organized company. In the information age in which we live, literacy is essential to enable individuals, groups, and societies access to the best information in the shortest time, to identify and solve the most important problems, and to communicate this information to others.

Problem solving, information acquisition, and communication are essential to success in the information age in which we live. This has prompted a rapid revolution in the technologies of information and communication, generating new ICTs, such as the Internet, that require new literacies to fully exploit their potential. The Internet now requires new reading comprehension skills. These include knowing how to effectively use a search engine to locate information, reading search engine results to navigate to the most reliable information resource in the shortest time, critically evaluating the accuracy of information in a context where anyone may publish anything, and communicating using new technologies (Leu, Kinzer et al., 2004). Online communication tools such as blog technologies, Instant Messaging platforms, email interfaces, wikis, presentation software, and Web editors also demand new writing skills. Reading and writing are mutually interdependent processes on the Internet; as readers and writers exchange information, they are simultaneously composing and comprehending as their online conversations unfold.

In short, globalization and the rapid spread of newer and newer ICTs means that education systems must confront the new realities posed by increasingly multilingual societies as well as the new literacies that new ICTs require.

New Realities Provide New Opportunities to Increase the Potential of Every Student

In spite of the fact that some view the coming confrontation between schools and the new realities of both multilingualism and new literacies as a challenge that must be overcome, we prefer to see these as important new opportunities to increase the learning potential of students. Becoming proficient in more than a single language provides multiple avenues for conceptualizing and solving a problem. Even more importantly, being sensitive to the value of multiple languages means that one is more capable of communicating effectively with others who come from a variety of linguistic and cultural traditions. Finally, recognizing the reality of the multiplicity of different languages in today's world means that one can take full advantage of the potentials for problem solving that become manifest with different ways of looking at the global issues that confront us.

Conflicts around the world, based largely on the inability of different cultural and religious groups to respect and understand one another, help us to better appreciate the importance of respecting and understanding diverse cultural traditions. New literacies and new technologies provide new opportunities to help us achieve this goal. One aspect of the Internet's educational potential is the opportunity it provides to increase multicultural understanding and take full advantage of the diversity that defines our lives. Recognizing how to take full advantage of different points of view to solve the increasingly complex problems that define our world will become central to the preparation of students. Understanding others and the cultural context from which they come is an increasingly important goal as we build a global village with the aid of new technologies.

It is quickly becoming clear that the Internet provides special opportunities to help everyone better understand the importance of appreciating the unique qualities in each of our cultural traditions. No other instructional resource available to classrooms is as rich in its potential for developing an understanding of the diverse nature of our global society and for helping each of our students take advantage of the opportunities that diversity provides. Utilizing diverse linguistic forms provides important opportunities for classrooms to solve global challenges.

Linguistic Capital and Background Knowledge that Students Bring with Them to Learning Contexts Are Essential Resources for Their Development

Central to seeing the changes to language and literacy as opportunities is recognizing the inherent potential existing in the linguistic capital and background knowledge that students bring with them to learning contexts. The linguistic capital students possess about their own languages may provide powerful resources for communication with others around the world as students work to identify and solve common problems. The background knowledge students possess about new literacies may be used to teach others these new skills; increasingly these "others" include teachers. Much as Moll's funds of knowledge demonstrated an inextricable link between home and school cultures and the need for teachers to value what students bring to school from home (González et al., 1993), educators would benefit greatly from taking time to learn about students' technology experiences. By acknowledging, celebrating, and drawing on the new literacies expertise students bring to the classroom, we acknowledge young people as valuable contributors to learning. This recognition transforms the learning environment, increasing educational engagement and investment in classroom learning.

Historically, our society has tended to force all students into a single language and a single literacy assuming that students had little to bring to the learning process. Continuing on this path will increasingly deny important opportunities for literacy and learning. Constructions of both in-school and out-of-school learning need to be based on the understanding that students bring both linguistic capital and background knowledge about new literacies to learning contexts.

Students Become Important Contributors to Literacy Development

Increasing numbers of students come to school with primary languages other than English. In addition to new languages, students come to classrooms with new literacies, often developed outside of the classroom (Chandler-Olcott & Mahar, 2003). For example, young people are capitalizing on the global reach of the Internet by building worldwide affinity groups that cross social, cultural, and linguistic boundaries (Lam, 2004). In the process, multilingual learners foster cultural and linguistic participation among those who reside both inside and outside the United States. In many cases, English is used as the medium of communication, in addition to the native languages shared by the population. Topics discussed are wide ranging in nature and include the appreciation of Japanese animé, discussion of popular fiction, and debates about current events.

Recognizing that students possess important strategies for using the Internet, and that those strategies can be exchanged in ways that benefit others, means that new ways of organizing contexts for literacy and learning need to be constructed (Gee, 2004; Lankshear & Knobel, 2003). Increasingly, the information and skills that students' possess are gradually finding their way into literacy and learning contexts in new teaching and learning formats. Book Clubs, for example, are forums where students exchange their individual ideas about texts in shared forums where all opinions are valued and accepted (Raphael, Florio-Ruane, & George, 2001). Inquiry approaches (Lee & Smagorinsky, 2000) where children's interests and curiosity drive the learning process also represent this trend. Telecollaborative projects (Harris & Jones, 1999; U.S. Department of Education, 2006) where children are invited to exchange information, solve common problems, and share ideas about world issues are also empowering learners to collaborate in new ways. These approaches place students in control of their own learning and have prompted out-of-school technology integration models such as KidProj, DUSTY, and 5th Dimension (see Durán, this volume). These efforts are especially important in contexts where schools fail to take full advantage of the contributions that students make to their own learning.

Language and Literacy Are Socially Constructed Processes

The issue of whether language and literacy are cognitive or social processes has a long and complex history (Piaget & Inhelder, 1969, 1973; Vygotsky, 1962, 1978). The rapid changes to literacy brought about by continually changing ICTs and globalization inevitably shift the calculus of this issue to one that is far more socially constructed than ever before. This has important consequences for how we view the acquisition of both oral language and new literacies.

It is vitally important to recognize the social aspects of language learning. Learners bring important linguistic capital to the classroom using what they know to further their own understanding and make personal connections. The same is true for new literacies. The technologies of literacy change too quickly and are too extensive for us to be literate in them all. Each of us, however, will know something useful. Reading an instructional manual for a new technology, for example, is often less efficient than simply asking another student who is familiar with the software. Social learning strategies, such as knowing who knows what type of information and how to quickly exchange it either in person, in an email, instant message, or on a bulletin board, become essential when literacy technologies rapidly change.

Social learning strategies also become important because networked technologies for literacy permit us to communicate much more extensively with people around the world. Much of the new information that becomes available on the Internet resides in the people who inhabit it, not in isolated texts. In order to access this type of information, we must develop new social components to our literacy skills. Engaging in collaborative projects with others around the world prepares learners in important ways for what their futures will entail as they network using new and continually evolving ICTs.

New Forms of Literacy and Language Will Regularly Appear
in Both Out-of-school and In-school Contexts

We have seen how change increasingly defines the nature of literacy in an information age. Literacy rapidly and continuously changes as new technologies for information and communication repeatedly appear and new envisionments for exploiting these technologies are continuously crafted by users. Most importantly, these new technologies for information and communication, because they are increasingly networked technologies, permit the immediate exchange of even newer technologies and envisionments for their use. This speeds up the already rapid pace of change in the forms and functions of literacy, increasing the opportunities that become available to prepare students for their literacy futures. Today, continuous, rapid change regularly redefines the nature of literacy.

Globalization also prompts the appearance of new language forms in school classrooms, whether it is prompted by new students from new cultures, or by technologies that put us immediately in touch with other students and classrooms from around the world. The rapid spread of new words and symbols appearing on Instant Messaging technologies is just the beginning of these new language forms, whether in the workplace (Isaacs, Walendowski, Whittaker, Schiano, & Kamm, 2002) or in less formal settings (Gross, Juvonen, & Gable, 2002).

Critical Literacies Become Essential in Globalized Learning Contexts

Earlier we discussed how the Internet and other ICTs increase the need for new critical literacies while reading and communicating on the Internet. We framed that discussion around the need for these new literacies because online, anyone can publish anything. It becomes increasingly important that students learn how to distinguish more accurate from less accurate information. Both the nature and the need for new critical literacies expand with the globalization of both language and literacy. New critical literacies will be required that enable an understanding of how to read between the lines of information that arrives with different cultural assumptions about the world will be required. Because each of us brings our own cultural perspectives to the information we share, we need to become increasingly aware of how to identify these cultural assumptions in messages we receive from individuals who have a different primary language from ours, even if the message appears in our own primary language. Evaluations of information will need to incorporate new and broader configurations.

Home and School Connections Become Even More Important within Globalized Learning Contexts, Though This Relationship Changes in Important Ways

Connections between school and home have always been important. They have, however, been largely unidirectional, from school to home. Schools have provided information to families about how students best learn and communicated the policies that schools institute to promote these views (Epstein & Sheldon, 2002). In ethnically and linguistically diverse homes, the picture is further complicated by the mismatch, or disconnect, between the culture of the school (mainstream) and the culture of the home (other). In globalized classrooms, the nature of this relationship is more fully equalized. Homes are viewed as important repositories of cultural and linguistic knowledge as well as sources where new literacies often emerge when students are reading and writing online. This makes home and school connections even more important and requires us to look at new ways of framing sources of information and authority around this issue.

We recognize that school is an important context for learning, but we cannot make the assumption that formal learning takes place only at school. A report of After-School Programs and Activities in 2005, published by the National Center for Education Statistics, reports the number of kindergarten through eighth grade (K–8) children who participation in after-school activities and programs in the United States. In 2005, 40% of students in K–8 grade were enrolled in after-school care that occurred at least once each week. Of the 16,005 students who participated, 18% came from families where no parent spoke English at home. All 18% of these students participated in programs that focused on computer activities (Carver & Iruka, 2006). It is clear that out-of-school activities play a substantial role in developing children's linguistic competence and technology skills even outside of formal learning settings.

Though Narrative Experiences Provide Imporant Foundations
for Language and Literacy, Information and Communication
Are Essential Elements for Globalized Learning Contexts

Narratives provide young children entry into the world of story, whether in oral language contexts or in written contexts (Anderson, Hiebert, Scott, & Wilkinson, 1985, Applebee, 1978). They are also a traditional means for carrying important cultural lessons from one generation to another through oral language traditions (Rosenblatt, 1938/1976). In a globalized learning context, narratives are also important because they may be used to share important cultural lessons between individuals from different cultural traditions. Ultimately, however, the genre of informational texts become central to language and learning in globalized learning contexts because these information sources are essential to acquiring content area knowledge. Although this trend is changing, the vast majority of texts found in classrooms today remain narrative in nature (Duke, 2000). With the integration of the Internet, a greater number of informational texts are available on a variety of topics. These online texts often include embedded animations and graphic supports that help the content become more accessible to all learners. In some cases, exposure to these high-interest texts may improve concept knowledge and overall academic achievement.

Language and New Literacies Learning Need to be Integrated
into Authentic Social Action Projects on a Global Level

Informational experiences should not simply be used to acquire knowledge. To do so would waste important opportunities to improve the world we inhabit and limit the potential of any learning experience in important ways. In a world that is quickly shrinking, we need to prepare students with an orientation and a commitment to using information to improve our global community. Thus social action projects between classrooms from different cultural contexts appear to be a promising means by which we might take full advantage of students' multilingual potential. They contain the power inherent to simultaneously promote learning and the new literacies that will increasingly define our students' future. The Internet can be used to extend cooperative problem-solving activities around the world and can serve as a context for social action-oriented telecollaboration projects that have the potential to shape young people toward thinking globally. These projects empower the future leaders of our planet: our children. For example, Kidlink (http://www.kidlink.org), a free educational program that helps teachers worldwide relate local curriculum guidelines to students' personal interests and goals, facilitates dialogue around social action. Kidlink invites students to participate in discussions about global issues of critical importance to our world. On this site, learners have shared ideas for how to work for peaceful solutions to global conflicts, brainstormed ideas about how to address the starvation in Somalia, and discussed ideas for how to improve the condition of our global environment. These discussion forums provide a place where students can speak with a global voice by writing in their own language that is translated into multiple languages for all to read. The Internet provides the platform to communicate for real purposes, making it possible to connect children in dialogue for the purpose of exchanging perspectives.

A Globalized Perspective on Language and Literacy: A Summary

A Globalized Perspective suggests that there are special potentials inherent in the multilingual nature of our world that are being realized for children who are acquiring language and literacy in both English and their native language. This perspective suggests that these children bring special abilities to a globalized learning context involving new literacies and the Internet. It is essential that both in-school and out-of-school literacy and learning experiences begin to exploit these special affordances. And to do so, we must begin to fashion a new vision of what is possible, a vision based on new possibilities not old limitations. New literacies provide unique opportunities for students who speak a language other than English to become privileged in learning contexts, because the Internet is a space where many different languages and cultural contexts appear.

Learning takes place increasingly in both in-school and out-of-school contexts. Most importantly, however, we need to begin to view two new sources of knowledge as important strengths. Increasing numbers of students are bringing new knowledge to learning contexts: (1) cultural and linguistic capital and (2) new literacies of the Internet and other ICTs. Both will be essential to their future. The impact of these twin realities for language and learning issues will increasingly be felt by every nation but especially in the United States, given our increasingly diverse population and the rapid appearance of the Internet here.

The achievement gap between students of diverse backgrounds and their mainstream peers remains substantial and troubling (Cummins, this volume). School classrooms, although traditionally resistant to change (Cuban, 2001), are coming under new pressures to respond to these changes (Leu & Kinzer, 2000; Leu, Kinzer, et al., 2004). Alternative contexts are also appearing outside of school to foster the important language and learning needs of students, when these are not being met in schools. A Globalized Perspective helps us to understand these changes. Most importantly, a Globalized Perspective allows us to evaluate both in-school and out-of-school technology use and learning contexts in order to evaluate their utility and to draw implications for schools, homes, and public policy initiatives.

Instructional Exemplars: Developing New Literacies among Multilingual Learners in the Elementary Grades

How might we best support the development of new literacies among elementary age children who are simultaneously acquiring language and literacy in both English and their native language? This is the question we seek to answer. Having established a useful theoretical perspective that integrates elements of both a Multilingual Perspective and a New Literacies Perspective, we can now apply the principles of this Globalized Perspective to analyze examples of learning projects from out-of-school settings, in-school settings, and combined settings. This analysis will allow us to consider how the principles of a Globalized Perspective might be used to support elementary age children who are simultaneously acquiring a new language and new literacies. It will provide useful direction for those interested in planning literacy and learning programs using technology to support multilingual learners. We will analyze three different sets of projects:

1. Out-of-school technology projects (Fifth Dimension, La Clase Mágica, and DUSTY);
2. Online international projects often used in schools (project registry sites, Water Quality, and International Schools Cyberfair); and
3. Combined projects that may be used in school or out of school (Kidlink: KIDPROJ and Kidlink: KIDFORUM).

A summary of our analysis appears in the Appendix in Table A4.1. We recognize that the purpose of this framework and analysis is not definitional. It serves, however, as a useful heuristic to begin to understand emerging uses of new technologies for literacy and learning. We also recognize that our analysis, by necessity, is framed from an etic rather than an emic (Pike, 1967) perspective. Being outsiders imposes some limitations on our analysis because we were not involved in the inception of these projects or programs. Inferences made about their aims, goals, and outcomes were based exclusively on the research literature available. Finally, we recognize that each exemplar succeeds because it regularly adapts to new conditions. Consequently, our analysis may not be based on the most recent changes. It was driven largely by published work, which is always a bit behind the most recent iteration of any exemplar.

Out-of-School Technology Projects

University–Community Links Fifth Dimension Project

The Fifth Dimension distributed literacy consortium was designed to promote elementary children's cognitive development and improve their computer and print literacy. Students from a number of nations around the world, from Boys and Girls Clubs, YMCAs, YWCAs, and recreation centers, worked with university students who served as their learning guides. By mixing play and education in a fantasy world setting, children were challenged to work through various game-based activities that required decision-making to solve complex problems (see http://129.171.53.1/blantonw/5dClhse/clearingh1.html for a more complete description). Participants learned communication skills along with new technologies as they participated in semi-structured after-school activities. The Fifth Dimension consortium encouraged unique ways for kids to use computers. These activities, in turn, brought to light new and different ways of thinking about intellectual challenges, new and different ways for children to play together, and purposeful ways for adults and children to interact with each other (Blanton, Greene, & Cole, 1999).

In addition to playing traditional board games and strategy-rich computer-based games, the children interacted with an electronic figurehead (wizard/wizardess, Maga, or Golem) who lives in the Internet. In the mythology of the Fifth Dimension, the wizard/ess acted as the participants' magic imaginary friend, who provided games and other materials, settled arguments, shared value lessons, and helped with computer problems. This fantasy being wrote email and chat messages to the entire learning collective on a regular basis to encourage children in their endeavors. Messages often introduced challenges that required participants to locate information using either the Internet or book-based resources. These messages encouraged interactions with both narrative and information texts. Resources and information were pooled collectively among the children to promote a sense of accomplishment and positive self-concept. Students were encouraged to explore their cultural traditions throughout these tasks which were designed to explore historic and religious traditions. The Fifth Dimension invited expressions of personal identity and celebrated cultural diversity through guided learning opportunities (Blanton et al., 1999).

A key design feature of the Fifth Dimension was networked access among participating sites. Organizers recognized collaboration as a tool to encourage language and literacy development and provided communication resources via the Internet that allowed for the distribution of information to the collective easily and quickly. Wide distribution made it possible for organizers to support interests of participants at any level of the system. Some sites cultivated active relationships with one another, while others focused more on activity and communication among participants through the use of community resources (Blanton, Simmons, & Warner, 2001).

The Fifth Dimension's educational activities linked university and community institutions around a common goal of improving student achievement. Children were empowered to think, act, reflect, and develop new skills as they worked in partnerships with others. University students served as learning guides who motivated and supported children to set and achieve goals. Partnerships built on the background knowledge and linguistic capital each student brought to the learning context, using personal interests to guide learning aims. These facilitators coordinated learning within and across contexts, cultures, and languages to help children seek, interpret, and integrate new knowledge as they engaged in problem solving. Partnerships set in motion a new approach to learning that had powerful social implications for redefining teaching and learning (Blanton, Moorman, Hayes, & Warner, 1997).

La Clase Mágica

La Clase Mágica is a Fifth Dimension and University–Community Links project-based learning model developed as a multisystem collaboration between the University of San Diego, the Latino community, and local families. This project was one of the longest-running, well-documented efforts to use technology to promote the academic achievement and self-esteem of students from diverse backgrounds. A longitudinal study was designed to follow participants between Fall 1989 and Spring 1996 to determine how many students went on to enroll in college (Vásquez, 2003). The program examined the long-term impact on learning using a cross-cultural educational approach called collaborative critical inquiry (Cummins & Sayers, 1995). The goal was to develop a multifaceted, multicultural curriculum to promote social change.

La Clase Mágica shares characteristics with the Fifth Dimension model in that it also promotes cognitive development, literacy learning, and higher-level thinking for meaningful purposes in a motivating context for elementary students (Vásquez & Durán, 2000). This after-school club implemented semistructured computer-mediated activities and provided a university mentor to each participating student. The project was designed around a computer game during which students attempted to complete a maze using reading, writing, and strategic thinking to solve problems introduced in each new room. Students communicated online with a wizard (La Maga) to get help in solving problems. Cultural communities were used to build affinity among participants as identity concepts were explored. Learning partners supported student-centered pedagogy geared toward meeting individual needs. Educators promoted the idea that relevant pedagogy must adapt flexibly to the unique needs of each child (Vásquez, 2003).

Originally, the project failed to attract Mexican–American students, even though it was located in the community where the students lived. Several changes were implemented to meet this challenge, including relocating the project to a church attended by Mexican–American families, changing the language used from English to Spanish, and redesigning activities so that they became culturally relevant to participants. Additionally, bilingual community members were invited to participate in the project's decision-making process and eventually took on the major responsibility for running the project.

Teaching and learning concepts embedded in this model transcend conventional notions of teaching and learning. University mentors and participating students co-constructed knowledge as they learned together. Shared knowledge often took the form of strategic thinking that extended the limits of the physical context and expertise of the educators. As a result, participation in La Clase Mágica redefined the relationship between teacher and student (Vásquez, 1994). Students' self-concept as bilingual individuals improved as a result of working closely with their University mentors .

Interconnectedness between the local and the global was nourished through participation in this multilingual/multicultural learning exchange. The learning activities had cultural relevance because they addressed the local sociolinguistic context from which the participating students came (Vásquez, 1994). As a member of a cultural and linguistic group created within the learning setting, students' experiences and languages were valued and promoted. Participants were invited to celebrate and analyze cultural literature, traditions, and values and, in turn, made a significant contribution to society.

DUSTY

Digital Underground Story Telling for Youth (DUSTY) is a partnership between the University of California and the Prescott Joseph Community Center in West Oakland. It is also affiliated with the University–Community Links program. The project aimed to support youth ages 7–18 in acquiring computer-related literacy skills through the use of information and communication technologies (Hull & Zacher, 2004). DUSTY's after-school programs encourage participants to think in new ways about self-expression, identity, and community. Participants learn the art of digital composition by creating their own original works. During sessions lasting 12–14 weeks, students developed 3–5 minute multimedia compositions consisting of an author-recorded text reading, photographs, images, videos, drawings, and music. Digital storytelling offered participants flexibility in self-expression using new textual practices that juxtapose narratives with images (Hull, 2003). These personal narratives transformed poetry, short stories, and essays into multimedia compositions that celebrated family, community, and culture.

DUSTY's programs made technology resources accessible to youths who did not have access in their homes or communities (Hull & Zacher, 2004). Sessions took place one to two times each week and were facilitated by a trained educator. Organizers took advantage of the role social construction and collaboration plays in learning activities by pairing each student with a university undergraduate who acted as a tutor/mentor. Structured group lessons supported students through the composition process by utilizing a writer's workshop format. Group members provided feedback and revision suggestions to improve the overall tone and quality of each work. Organizers supported the acquisition of Internet searching strategies as students located images for use in their stories. The primary interface for multimedia composition, Adobe Premiere, was taught in several stages over the course of the program. In addition, one hour of each session was dedicated to homework completion (Hull & Zacher, 2004).

Participants included youth from a variety of backgrounds and nationalities and reflected the diversity of the surrounding community. Although most projects were composed in English, students were welcome to communicate in the language of their choice. DUSTY made use of multimedia composing as an artistic expression of identity and affinity. Literacy activities, such as digital storytelling, offered youth the opportunity to communicate via multiple modalities and provided students tangible ways to develop their own definitions of who they are and who they would like to become (Hull, 2003). DUSTY encouraged appreciation of diversity by promoting social practices geared toward celebrating self-expression. Public showings invited community members and families to appreciate the works. The community thus played an important role in supporting student learning.

Online International Projects Often Used in Schools

Project Registry Sites

Internet projects are designed and produced by numerous organizations and individuals around the world. These projects were created for students from different locations to complete together online. They focused on developing collaborative partnerships between students, classrooms, and schools to promote learning in various topic areas. Internet project registry Web sites were created to help organize and coordinate projects for classroom teachers. Three such sites are Global School Network (http://www.gsn.org/gsh/pr/index.cfm), OzProjects (http://ozprojects.edna.edu.au/), and iEARN (http://www.iearn.org/projects/index.html). Teachers can join existing projects or develop one of their own and invite participants.

Global School Network is a virtual clearinghouse for collaborative projects from across the globe. The Global SchoolNet Foundation and other reputable organizations hosted all projects within the registry. This site provided outstanding partner projects conducted by teachers worldwide. Projects focused on providing global online collaborative learning opportunities for students in K–12 classrooms.

OzProjects is a registry site from Australia that listed and described a wide variety of online curriculum projects that offered unique learning opportunities. The site assisted teachers in locating suitable online curriculum projects and provided access to a host of resources to support classroom involvement. This site also provided access to online tools including links to software, teaching tools, and assessment options. In addition, the latest project news and updates were posted as well as a calendar of upcoming events. The objectives set forth by the OzProjects site highlighted the value of online curriculum projects, the use of changing technologies, and promoted national and international collaboration among students. OzProjects is an initiative of the Education Network Australia (EdNA) Schools Project supported by the EdNA School Advisory Group. Its development was funded by the Commonwealth of Australia and the South Australian Department of Education, Training and Employment division.

Projects within iEARN were designed and facilitated by participants to fit curriculum guidelines and classroom schedules. The iEARN network was open to all teachers and students, with resources available across age levels and disciplines. iEARN featured a Learning Circle, which contained highly interactive, project-based partnerships among small numbers of schools located throughout the world. All iEARN projects involved the creation of a final product or exhibition of the learning that took place as part of the collaboration. These products included magazines, creative writing anthologies, Web sites, letter-writing campaigns, reports to government officials, arts exhibits, workshops, performances, charity fundraising, and many more. These projects provided examples of youth taking pride in and ownership in their own learning.

Bucket Buddies

Bucket Buddies (http://www.k12science.org/curriculum/bucketproj/index. html) is a curriculum-based inquiry project for elementary-level students. In this project, students teamed up with others from around the globe to test fresh water samples in their community. Students collected samples from local ponds to determine whether organisms found in pond water were the same all over the world. Participating classes collected samples from ponds near their schools and used a variety of resources to identify the macroinvertebrates (animals lacking a backbone and visible without the aid of a microscope) they found. The students then shared their identifications with other project participants. The collected data were used to determine whether fresh water sources around the world contained the same organisms. Finally, the students published their conclusions in a report posted to the project Web site.

International Schools Cyberfair

International Schools Cyberfair (http://www.globalschoolnet.org/gsh/cf/) is an international learning program that encourages youth to connect knowledge with real-world applications. The program averaged about 200 submissions each year and has brought together more than one million students across 100 countries. It was designed as a way for students, schools, and communities to use the Internet to share resources, establish partnerships, and work together to accomplish common goals. Students collaboratively researched and showcased online what was special about their local community. Local and international collaboration through the use of ICTs was a key aspect of the program. Students were encouraged to serve as "ambassadors," sharing what they had learned in a way that contributed to their local communities. Through their participation in the project, students from many cultures were united as they learned to (a) collaborate with fellow students and their community; (b) conduct original research; (c) create a web project; (d) evaluate their work and the work of others; and (e) act as ambassadors to showcase their work.

As part of the learning process, each student was asked to evaluate up to six other project submissions. An international panel of adults judged the top 40 projects based on the peer reviews. Winners were announced at an annual global event that took place "virtually." Recognition was given to the best projects in each of eight categories: local leaders, businesses, community organizations, historical landmarks, environment, music, art, and local specialties. Award-winning projects showcased people and programs that actively provided solutions for solving problems. All projects and their accompanying narrative descriptions were either written in English or translated. A few projects were shared in students' native languages. Winning projects for 2004 can be viewed at http://www.globalschoolnet.org/gsh/cf/winners/winners2004.html.

Online International Projects Used Both in School and out of School

Kidlink

Kidlink (http://www.kidlink.org) is an international, volunteer organization that seeks to promote a global dialogue among students from around the world. Since its creation in 1990, students from 162 countries have participated in Kidlink's activities in more than 20 languages, either as individuals or within their classrooms. The organization offered a translation service that was run by volunteers. Although there are several elements to Kidlink, we have chosen to focus on two: KidProj and KidForum.

KidProj

KidProj is the area in Kidlink that provides opportunities to plan, design, and implement collaborative, Internet projects. KidProj creates opportunities for students to become more aware and engaged global citizens. A belief in, and encouragement, of multiculturalism is central to KidProj. Diversity in languages, perspectives, beliefs, knowledge, and practices was highly valued by the participants. Common problems faced globally were discussed along with strategies to solve them. These discussions empowered students to take ownership of their own learning, encouraged inquiry and discovery, and improved literacy and analytical skills. Participants also developed positive attitudes toward technology, using a variety of media and formats to effectively communicate information and interact with peers, experts, and other audiences. Students not only shared experiences and perspectives, they also made lasting friendships.

KidProj's activities encouraged expressive communication. Students used the activities in ways that transcended language barriers, building bridges among the cultures. Through the creation of drawings, pictures, collages, photographs, sound and video, participants developed a global community by telling the stories of their own everyday lives. And, as they worked together with other students, they recognized and celebrated their cultural diversity.

KidForum

KidForum (http://www.kidlink.org/KIDFORUM/) is Kidlink's discussion forum. It offered students an online location for student discussion. A variety of discussion topics were scheduled in advance. These forums were designed for students from all over the world to discuss matters of importance to them. Most often, entire classes participated in KidForum discussion topics; however, individual children could also participate. Using KidForum, teachers worked together to develop better understandings of the world around them. Discussions emphasized ideas for international collaboration aimed at solving global issues such as war, poverty, and pollution.

Patterns in this Brief Analysis of Exemplars

What can we learn from this brief review of exemplary projects that moves us closer to greater recognition of the fundamental changes that lie ahead for both multilingualism and new literacies? We offer overall conclusions as well as conclusions about the different contexts in which these efforts appear: in school, out of school, or both in and out of school.

First, several overall conclusions emerged from the analysis of these projects. A summary of these conclusions appears in Table A 4.1. Most obvious is that we are beginning to see the initial stages of language and literacy practices that recognize the globalization of our learning space. Some, like La Clase Mágica and DUSTY, are just beginning to recognize the global nature of these new learning spaces whereas others, like KidProj, KidForum, Project Registry sites, and CyberFair, have been quicker to see the potential in globalized learning spaces with new technologies, new literacies, and the potential benefits that multiple linguistic contexts provide for learning. In all cases, though, learning contexts are beginning to provide us with important insights about how best to build a global learning community around a globalized perspective that recognizes both multilingualism and new literacies.

Second, we see that technology projects seem to work best when they present students of diverse backgrounds with challenging, generative tasks that require them to read, write, and think in new and demanding ways. The time, energy, and thought students devote to participating effectively in these projects suggests that they are readily able to take advantage of constructivist forms of instruction that introduce the knowledge and strategies needed to engage with new forms of literacy and electronic media (Lankshear & Knobel, 2003).

Table A4.1 illustrates that none of these exemplars we have chosen to examine explicitly recognize that changes to literacy are likely to be a regular feature in our future because new technologies will continuously appear (Principle #6 in Table A4.1). Educators must come to recognize that we are in a period of continuous change in the nature of literacy; however, not a single exemplar has consciously recognized the deictic nature of literacy (Leu, 2000). As new technologies emerge, learners need to develop new literacies in order to take full advantage of them. There may even be a tendency to resist new technologies, because they create significant challenges. Change is never easy to accommodate once a learning space has been defined and a structure has been established. Yet, students need to be prepared for a landscape in which technologies and literacies continuously change. Central to this concept of literacy as deixis is cognitive flexibility. Students will increasingly need to be prepared to "learn how to learn" from continuously changing technologies, rather than to simply master a fixed set of literacies. Learning how to learn will generalize far better to a landscape of continuous change in technologies and the literacies required to effectively use them.

We recognize there are obvious patterns related to the location of a project. For example, *La Clase Mágica* recognized early on that changes were necessary in order to attract local Mexican–American students. Housing the project in the community where these students lived was not enough; if the project was to be accessible to students, it needed to be moved to a centralized location that Latino families frequented, in this case a community church. Further, engaging the local community in the project and including bilingual individuals who share a common cultural background with the students, become crucial components of successful projects. Thus, for English language learners, technology projects must be rooted in the cultures and communities of the students being served.

We also see that out-of-school projects less frequently engage students in social action projects on a global level (Principle #10 in Table A4.1). University–community partnerships are an example of social action projects designed to address inequities in communities of need. Providing opportunities for students to engage in meaningful online activities is just one of their aims. Although they aid in literacy development and help improve oral English skills, they do not take advantage of the full range of activities the Internet makes widely available including information gathering, multilingual communication, and idea exchanges. This may be due to the fact that many of these projects have yet to fully connect their work with the work of other educators around the world, a potential more fully realized in combined and in-school projects. This is not to say, of course, that all classrooms engage in this, only that the potential is there for classrooms to do so through combined efforts like KidProj and KidForum as well as in-school projects like the project registry sites and specific projects such as Bucket Buddies and International Schools CyberFair.

On the other hand, the out-of-school projects that we analyzed appear more often to recognize the importance of various languages students bring with them to learning spaces as well as their background knowledge about new literacies (Principle #3 in Table A4.1). In-school projects do not always do this, though the potential does exist. Moreover, recent English-only initiatives in California, Arizona, and Massachusetts severely limit the ability of schools to use languages other than English for instructing English language learners.

It is clear that we still have much to accomplish in this area. Many of the online experiences we examined do not yet fully take advantage of the opportunities inherent in online connections between learners around the world. More often, learning contexts focus on narrative experiences, identity construction, and engagement in learning activities. Less often, they take advantage of online possibilities for using information to solve problems that are important within a global context, supporting students in their ability to work with others who speak a different language, who bring different cultural perspectives to an issue, and who develop new literacies as they engage in important collaborative work.

Implications for Educators, Schools, Community Organizations, and Policymakers

We conclude this chapter with a discussion of the consequences of this analysis for literacy development around both in-school and out-of-school contexts. We begin with what may be most obvious: new visions are emerging for supporting the development of new literacies among elementary age children who are simultaneously acquiring language and literacy in both English and their native language and maximizing the potential for academic achievement on the part of all students.

Prompted by the powerful, reciprocal forces of globalization and information technology growth, the natures of language and literacy are rapidly changing. As a result, we need to reconceptualize our traditional, normative conceptions of a monolingual, book-based classroom, as the primary context for learning among school-aged students. How might we best support the development of new literacies among elementary age children who are simultaneously acquiring language and literacy in both English and their native language? The answer to this question is not an easy one due to the widespread systemic reforms that are called for. It will require change at all levels of the educational system, including access issues, professional development, school leadership, classroom instruction, and assessment. New visions of what is possible will need to be crafted. We have tried to assist this process by carefully defining the major components of a Globalized Perspective so that others may also see the new potentials in new literacies and new technologies for multilingual students. This type of vision will be required to spark change at all levels of the complex educational system we have in this nation.

Access, of course, will be a central issue. Families of students of diverse backgrounds often lack the resources to make technology available at home. Unlike their mainstream peers, whose homes often have computers and Internet access, students of diverse backgrounds usually rely on schools and other institutions for opportunities to engage in productive uses of technology. This means that, for students of diverse backgrounds in particular, schools, homes, and after-school gathering locations will need to have full access to the important technologies of the Internet and other ICTs. This is essential for all students to engage in the types of literacy experiences we envision where students use the Internet to identify important problems, search for information related to those problems, critically evaluate the resources they find online, synthesize the most relevant information to solve the problem, and communicate solutions to others.

Professional development will also be a central issue. Teachers, as well as instructional leaders in out-of-school settings, will need to be literate in the Internet and other ICTs if they hope to pass on these literacies to students and build on the new literacies that children are acquiring as they use new technologies in their out-of-school lives. Currently, schools only provide 20% of the recommended level of professional development in this area (Leu, Leu, & Coiro, 2004). Clearly, more will be required if we are serious about meeting all students' needs. In addition, teacher education programs will need to integrate new literacies and recognize the promise of multilingual students in their preparation programs.

School leadership will also be called for given that few changes take place in school settings without a leader who possesses a vision of change. Superintendents, curriculum directors, and principals will all need to embrace the learning potential of the Internet, new literacies, and multilingual learners before they can provide the support required in the classroom. In view of the fact that so much of instruction is currently driven by state standards and because these seldom include standards for acquiring new literacies in reading and language arts, change will have to take place at this level as well. State departments of education will need to rethink their recently completed definitions of what it means to be a reader and a writer in the 21st century.

More importantly, state assessments will need to change to include new literacies such as searching for information, reading and comprehending search engine results, critically evaluating information resources, and communicating with various tools such as instant messaging, email, blogs, wikis and other new technologies. This will not be easy to accomplish. New literacies, such as reading on the Internet or within other ICTs, are not included on any state assessments, and most states have no immediate plans to include these within literacy assessments (Leu & Ataya, 2002). Moreover, most states have seen the assessment of new literacies, such as comprehending text on the Internet, composing email messages, or writing with a word processor, as a technology assessment issue, not a reading or writing assessment issue. This continues to occur even though the ability to locate, read, and evaluate information on the Internet is increasingly a part of our daily lives (Lebo, 2003).

One cannot be especially optimistic about changing state assessments. Consider, for example, that one of the most obvious changes, enabling any student who wishes to use a word processor instead of a pencil on state writing assessments, has yet to occur in any state. This traditional format continues despite evidence that the most important writing done by all individuals is now done with the aid of a word processor. In fact, nearly 20% more students are able to pass the Massachusetts state writing assessment when permitted to use word processors (Russell & Plati, 2000).

And, of course, even more profound shifts will need to occur in the manner in which we approach students who are acquiring English along with their native language. We must begin to value the linguistic and cultural capital these students bring to the classroom. We must begin to forge strong and honest connections between home and school, respecting the cultural traditions embodied in each of our students. And, we must begin to support children in using their native language skills for the important communication opportunities that exist on the Internet so that all students in their class may benefit from their expertise.

Perhaps just as important is the well-documented tendency for schools to provide students of diverse backgrounds with literacy instruction that centers on lower-level skills rather than higher-level thinking. For example, Fitzgerald (1995) concluded that English language learners tended to receive instruction heavily oriented toward lower-level skills, such as phonics and pronunciation. Studies of elementary schools indicate that students of diverse backgrounds are frequently placed in the lowest reading group within the classroom or sent to remedial reading classes (Bartoli, 1995). Instruction in these situations focuses on lower-level skills of decoding with little attention to comprehension and higher-level thinking observed in reading instruction for other students (Allington, 1983). Research in secondary schools reveals the same pattern. Oakes and Guiton (1995) studied a large urban high school and found that a disproportionate number of Latino students were placed in the vocational track, where teachers did not have high expectations for their academic performance and did not provide them with challenging content. This tendency prevents students of diverse backgrounds from gaining experiences with technology and from developing the cognitive strategies required to engage successfully in new forms of literacy.

Equally profound shifts will be required as we consider out-of-school literacy and learning experiences. The tendency is to think in terms of providing software solutions to learning English at home. Even though this thinking will undoubtedly be helpful, far more powerful language and literacy experiences may be made available by more collaborative environments in after-school centers and clubs, similar to those pioneered by University–Community Links Fifth Dimension programs such as La Clase Mágica and DUSTY. This may be accomplished if these programs turn their attention to the greater collaboration possible with students in other nations over the Internet and if these collaborations focus on important global issues that may be improved with joint action around the world.

If we are able to bring greater understanding about the potentials that lie in our students who speak a native language other than English and in the new literacies of the Internet, there is little we cannot accomplish. We can shift our perception of multilingual students from a problem to be solved to an opportunity to deepen and extend learning; we can shift our perception of the Internet as simply a technology to viewing it as a new and very powerful context for literacy learning; and we can begin to bring our common intelligence to bear on important cultural, environmental, social, and religious conflicts that abound across our planet.

References

Allington, R. L. (1983). The reading instruction provided readers of differing abilities. *Elementary School Journal, 83*(5), 548–559.

Anderson, R.C., Hiebert, E.H., Scott, J.A., & Wilkinson, I.A.G. (1985). *Becoming a nation of readers: The report of the Commission on Reading.* Washington, DC: The National Institute of Education.

Applebee, A.N. (1978). *The child's concept of story: Ages two to seventeen.* Chicago: University of Chicago Press.

Baker, C. (2001). *Foundations of bilingual education and bilingualism (3rd edition).* Clevedon: Multilingual Matters.

Bartoli, J. S. (1995). *Unequal opportunity: Learning to read in the U.S.A.* New York: Teachers College Press.

Bialystok, E. (1988). Levels of bilingualism and levels of linguistic awareness. *Developmental Psychology, 24,* 560–567.

Bialystok, E. (1997). Effects of bilingualism and biliteracy on children's emerging concepts of print. *Developmental Psychology, 33,* 429–440.

Bialystok, E., & Hakuta, K. (1994). *In other words: The science and psychology of second language acquisition.* New York: Basic Books.

Blanton, W. E., Greene, M. W., & Cole, M. (1999). Computer mediation for learning and play. *Journal of Adolescent and Adult Literacy, 43*(3), 272–278.

Blanton, W.E., Moorman, G.B., Hayes, B.A., & Warner, M.L. (1997). Effects of participation in the Fifth Dimension on far transfer. *Journal of Educational Computing Research, 16*(4), 1–8.

Blanton, W. E., Simmons, E., & Warner, M. W. (2001). The Fifth Dimension: Application of cultural-historical activity theory, inquiry-based learning, computers, and telecommunications to change prospective teachers' preconceptions. *The Journal of Educational Computing Research, 2,* 214–225.

Bruce, B. C. (Ed.). (2003). *Literacy in the information age: Inquiries into meaning-making with new technologies.* Newark, DE: International Reading Association.

Carver, P. R., & Iruka, I.U. (2006). After-school programs and activities: 2005. Retrieved July 17, 2006 from the National Center for Educational Statistics Web site http://nces.ed.gov/pubs2006/2006076.pdf.

Cenoz, J., & Valencia, J. F. (1994). Additive trilingualism: Evidence from the Basque Country. *Applied Psycholinguistics, 15,* 195–201.

Center for Research on Education, Diversity and Excellence. (2002). *National Study of School Effectiveness for Language Minority Students' Long-Term Academic Achievement Final Report.* Retrieved June 22, 2004, from: http://www.crede.ucsc.edu/research/llaa/1.1_final.html.

Chandler-Olcott, K., & Mahar, D. (2003). "Tech-savviness" meets multiliteracies: Exploring adolescent girls' technology-mediated literacy practices. *Reading Research Quarterly, 38,* 356–385.

Coiro, J. (2003). Reading comprehension on the Internet: Expanding our understanding of reading comprehension to encompass new literacies. *The Reading Teacher, 56,* 458–464.

Coiro, J. & Dobler, E. (2007). Exploring the online reading comprehension strategies used by sixth-grade skilled readers to search for and locate information on the Internet. *Reading Research Quarterly, 42,* 214–257.

Coiro, J., Knobel, M., Lankshear, C., & Leu, D.J. (Eds.) (in press). Central issues in new literacies and new literacies research. In J. Coiro, M. Knobel, C. Lankshear, & D. Leu (Eds.), *Handbook of research on new literacies.* Lawrence Erlbaum, Mahwaw, NJ.

Cope, B. & Kalantzis, M. (Eds.). (2000). *Multiliteracies: Literacy learning and the design of social futures.* London: Routledge.

Crawford, J. (2004). *Educating English learners: Language diversity in the classroom (5th edition).* Bilingual Educational Services, Inc.: Los Angeles.

Cuban, L. (2001). *Oversold & underused: Computers in the classroom.* Cambridge, MA: Harvard University Press.

Cummins, J. (1981). The role of primary language development in promoting educational success for language minority students. In California State Department of Education (Ed.), *Schooling and language minority students. A theoretical framework* (pp. 3–49). Los Angeles, CA: Evaluation, Dissemination and Assessment Center, CSULA.

Cummins, J. (1984). Wanted: A theoretical framework for relating language proficiency to academic achievement among bilingual students. In C. Rivera (Ed.), *Language proficiency and academic achievement* (pp. 2–19). Avon, England: Multilingual Matters.

Cummins, J. (1991). Interdependence of first- and second-language proficiency in bilingual children. In E. Bialystok (Ed.), *Language processing in bilingual children* (pp. 70–89). New York: Cambridge University Press.

Cummins, J. (2000). Putting language proficiency in its place: Responding to critiques of the conversational/academic language distinction. In J. Cenoz & U. Jessner (Eds.), *English in Europe: The acquisition of a third language.* Clevedon: Multilingual Matters.

Cummins, J., & Sayers, D. (1995). *Brave new schools: Challenging cultural illiteracy through global learning networks.* New York: St. Martin's Press.

Donaldson, M. (1978). *Children's minds.* Glasgow: Fontana/Collins.

Duke, N. K. (2000). 3.6 minutes per day: The scarcity of informational texts in first grade. *Reading Research Quarterly, 35,* 202–224.

Edelsky, C, (2006). *With literacy and justice for all: Rethinking the social in language education.* Mahwah, NJ: Erlbaum.

Edelsky, C., Altwerger, B., & Flores, B. (1991). *Whole language: What's the difference?* Portsmouth, NH: Heinemann.

Epstein, J. L., & Sheldon, S. B. (2002). Present and accounted for: Improving student attendance through family and community involvement. *Journal of Educational Research, 95,* 308–318.

Fillmore, C. J. (1972). How to know whether you're coming or going. In K. Huldgaard-Jensen (Ed.), *Linquistik. 1971* (pp. 369–379). Amsterdam: Athemaiim.

Fitzgerald, J. (1995). English as a second language reading instruction in the United States: A research review. *Journal of Reading Behavior, 27,* 115–152.

Freire, P. (1993). *Pedagogy of the oppressed.* New York, NY: The Continuum Publishing Company.

Friedman, T. L. (2005). *The world is flat: A brief history of the twenty-first century.* New York: Farrar, Straus & Giroux.

Galambos, S. J., & Goldin-Meadow, S. (1990). The effects of learning two languages on levels of metalinguistic awareness. *Cognition,* 1–56.

Gee, J. (2003). *What video games have to teach us about learning and literacy.* New York, NY: Palgrave MacMillan.

Gee, J. (2004). *Situated language and learning: A critique of traditional schooling.* New York, NY: Routledge.

González, N., Moll, L.C., Floyd-Tenery, M., Rivera, A., Rendón, P., Gonzales, R., et al. (1993). *Teacher Research on Funds of Knowledge: Learning from Households.* Retrieved July 12, 2006 from http://repositories.cdlib.org/crede/ncrcdslleducational/EPR06/.

Gort, M. (2003). Transdisciplinary approaches in the education of English language learners. In D. Kaufman, D. M. Moss, & T. A. Osborn (Eds.), *Beyond the boundaries: A transdisciplinary approach to learning and teaching* (pp. 117–130). Westport, CT: Bergin & Garvey.

Gort, M. (2006). Strategic codeswitching, interliteracy, and other phenomena of bilingual writing: Lessons learned from classroom-based research. *Journal of Early Childhood Literacy, 6,* 327–358.

Gross, E., Juvonen, J., & Gable, S. (2002). Internet use and well-being in adolescence. *Journal of Social Issues,* 58, 75–90.

Hakuta, K. (1986). *Mirror of Language: The debate on bilingualism.* New York: Basic Books.

Hakuta, K., Butler, Y. G., & Witt, D. (2000). *How long does it take English learners to attain proficiency?* Retrieved July 18, 2006, from http://faculty.ucmerced.edu/ khakuta/research/publications.html.

Hakuta, K., & D'Andrea, D. (1992). Some properties of bilingual maintenance and loss in Mexican background high-school students. *Applied Linguistics,* 13, 72–99.

Harris Interactive, Inc. (2005). Web@work survey 2005. Retrieved March 13, 2005, from http://www.websense.com/company/news/research/webatwork2005.pdf.

Harris, J. B., & Jones, J. G. (1999). A descriptive study of telementoring among students, subject matter experts, and teachers: Message flow and function patterns. *Journal of Research on Computing in Education,* 32, 36–53.

Hull, G. (2003). At last, youth culture and digital medial: New literacies for new times. *Research in the Teaching of English,* 38, Retrieved August 30, 2004, from http:// www.ncte.org/library/files/Publications/Journals/rte/0382-nov03/RT0382Last. pdf.

Hull, G., & Zacher, J. (2004). What is after-school worth? Developing literacy and identity out of school. *Voices in Urban Education,* 3. Retrieved August 26, 2004, from http://www.annenberginstitute.org/VUE/spring04/Hull.html.

Isaacs, E., Walendowski, A., Whittaker, S., Schiano, D., & Kamm, C. (2002). The character, functions, and styles of instant messaging in the workplace. In *Proceedings of the ACM Conference on Computer Supported Cooperative Work* (pp. 11–20). New York: ACM Press.

Krashen, S.D., & Terrell, T.D. (1983). *The natural approach: Language acquisition in the classroom.* London: Prentice Hall.

Kress, G. (2003). *Literacy in the new media age.* London, UK: Routledge.

Labbo, L.D., & Reinking, D. (1999). Multiple realities of technology in literacy research and instruction. *Reading Research Quarterly,* 34, 478–492.

Lam, W. S. E. (2004). Second language socialization in a bilingual chatroom: Global and local considerations. *Language Learning and Technology,* 8, 44–65.

Lankshear, C., & Knobel, M. (2003). *New literacies: Changing knowledge and classroom learning.* Maidenhead, UK: Open University Press.

Larsen-Freeman, D. (1986). *Techniques and principles in language teaching.* Oxford, UK: Oxford University Press.

Law, B., & Eckes, M. (1990). *More than just surviving: ESL for every classroom teacher.* Winnigpeg, Manitoba: Peguis Press.

Learning Park (2001). *Multilingual teaching and learning.* Retrieved July 12, 2006 from http://archive.tpt.org/learningpark/topics/TGuide_12.pdf.

Lebo, H. (2003). *The UCLA Internet report: Surveying the digital future, year three.* Los Angeles: UCLA Center for Communication Policy. Retrieved January 4, 2005, from http://www.ccp.ucla.edu/pdf/UCLA-Internet-Report-Year-Three.pdf.

Lee, C. D., & Smagorinsky, P. (Eds.). (2000). *Vygotskian perspectives on literacy research: Constructing meaning through collaborative inquiry.* New York: Cambridge University Press.

Lemke, J. L. (1998). Metamedia literacy: Transforming meanings and media. In D. Reinking, M. C. McKenna, L. D. Labbo, & R. D. Kieffer (Eds.), *Handbook of literacy and technology: Transformations in a post-typographic world* (pp. 283–301). Mahwah, NJ: Erlbaum.

Lenhart, A., Simon, M., & Graziano, M. (2001). *The Internet and education: Findings of the Pew Internet & American Life Project.* Retrieved July 12, 2006 from http://www.pewinternet.org/reports/toc.asp?Report=39.

LePage, R., & Tabouret-Keller, A (1985). *Acts of identity.* Chicago: Chicago University Press.

Leu, D. J., Jr. (1997). Caity's question: Literacy as deixis on the Internet. *The Reading Teacher, 51,* 62–67.

Leu, D. J., Jr. (2000). Literacy and technology: Deictic consequences for literacy education in an information age. In M.L. Kamil, P.B. Mosenthal, P.S. Pearson, & R. Barr (Eds.), *Handbook of reading research* (Vol. 3; pp. 743–770). Mahwah, NJ: Erlbaum.

Leu, D. J., Jr., & Ataya, R. (2002, December). *Assessing assessment strategies among the 50 states: Evaluating the literacies of our past or the literacies of our future?* Paper presented at the annual meeting of the National Reading Conference, Miami, FL.

Leu, D. J., Jr., & Karchmer, R., & Leu, D. D. (1999). The Miss Rumphius effect: Envisionments for literacy and learning that transform the Internet. *The Reading Teacher, 52,* 636–642.

Leu, D. J., Jr., & Kinzer, C. K. (2000). The convergence of literacy instruction and networked technologies for information and communication. *Reading Research Quarterly, 35,* 108–127.

Leu, D. J., Jr., Kinzer, C. K., Coiro, J., & Cammack, D. (2004). Toward a theory of new literacies emerging from the Internet and other information and communication technologies. In R. B. Ruddell & N. Unrau (Eds.), *Theoretical models and processes of reading, fifth edition* (1568–1611). Newark, DE: International Reading Association.

Leu, D. J., Jr., Leu, D. D., & Coiro, J. (2004). *Teaching with the Internet K–12: New literacies for new times* (fourth edition). Norwood, MA: Christopher Gordon.

Manguel, A. (1996). *A history of reading.* Pittsburgh, PA: Penguin.

Markham, A. (1998). *Life online.* Walnut Creek, CA: AltaMira Press.

Mayer, R.E. (1997). Multimedia learning: Are we asking the right questions? *Educational Psychologist, 32,* 1–19.

Mayer, R.E. (2001). *Multimedia learning.* Cambridge, UK: Cambridge University Press.

Moll, L. C. (1992). Bilingual classroom studies and community analysis: Some recent trends. *Educational Researcher, 21,* 20–24.

Moll, L. C. (1998). Turning to the World: Bilingual Schooling, Literacy, and the Cultural Mediation of Thinking. *National Reading Conference Yearbook, 47,* 59–75.

Murphy, S. M. (1986). Children's comprehension of deictic categories in oral and written language. *Reading Research Quarterly, 21,* 118–131.

National Center for Education Statistics. (2005). *Internet access in public schools and classrooms: 1994–2003.* Retrieved July 18, 2006, from http://nces.ed.gov/surveys/frss/publications/2005015/.

New London Group, The. (2000). A pedagogy of multiliteracies: Designing social futures. In B. Cope & M. Kalantzis (Eds.), *Multiliteracies: Literacy learning and the design of social futures* (pp. 9–38). London: Routledge.

Nielsen/NetRatings (2004). Three out of four Americans have access to the Internet, according to Nielsen/NetRatings. Retrieved on March 18, 2004, from http://www.nielsen-netratings.com/pr/pr_040318.pdf.

Oakes, J., & Guiton, G. (1995). Matchmaking: The dynamics of high school tracking decisions. *American Educational Research Journal, 32,* 3–33.

Peal, E., & Lambert, W. E. (1962). The relationship of bilingualism to intelligence. *Psychological Monographs, 76,* 1–23.

Peregoy, S., & Boyle, O. (1993). *Reading, writing, and learning in ESL: A resource book for teachers*. White Plains, NY: Longman.

Pew Internet and American Life Project (2005). Internet Evolution. Retrieved July 18, 2006 from http://www.pewinternet.org/.

Piaget, J., & Inhelder, B. (1969). *The Psychology of the Child*. NY: Basic Books.

Piaget, J., & Inhelder, B. (1973). *Memory and intelligence*. NY: Basic Books.

Pike, K. L. (1967). *Language in relation to a unified theory of the structure of human behavior* (2nd edition). Berlin: Mouton De Gruyter.

Raphael, T. E., Florio-Ruane, S., & George, M. (2001). Book club *plus*: A conceptual framework to organize literacy instruction. *Language Arts*, 79, 159–168.

Roberts, C. (1994). Transferring literacy skills from L1 to L2: From theory to practice, *The Journal of Educational Issues of Language Minority Students*, 13, 209–221.

Rosenblatt, L. (1938/1976). *Literature as exploration*. New York: Modern Language Association.

Russell, M., & Plati, T. (2000). *Mode of Administration Effects on MCAS Composition Performance for Grades Four, Eight and Ten. A report submitted to the Massachusetts Department of Education by the National Board on Educational Testing and Public Policy*. Retrieved December 12, 2003, from http://www.nbetpp.bc.edu/statements/ws052200.pdf.

Skutnabb-Kangas, T., & Toukomaa, P. (1976). *Teaching migrant children's mother tongue and learning the language of the host country in the context of the sociocultural situation of the migrant family*. Helsinki: The Finnish National Commission for UNESCO.

Snow, C. (1992). Perspectives on second-language development: Implications for bilingual education. *Educational Researcher*, 21, 16–19.

Street, B. (2003). What's new in new literacy studies. *Current issues in comparative education*, 5, 1–14.

Thomas, A. (2007). *Youth Online: Identity and Literacy in the Digital Age*. New York, NY: Peter Lang.

U.S. Census Bureau. (2001). *Ability to Speak English for U.S. Residents Ages 5–17, 2000*. Retrieved September 4, 2006, from http://factfinder.census.gov/home/saff/main.html?_lang=en.

U.S. Department of Commerce: National Telecommunications and Information Administration. (2002). *A nation online: How Americans are expanding their use of the Internet*. Washington, DC: Author.

U.S. Department of Education. (2006). *Teachers guide to international collaboration on the Internet*. Retrieved July 12, 2006 from http://www.ed.gov/teachers/how/tech/international/index.html.

Vásquez, O. A. (1994). The magic of *la Clase Mágica*: Enhancing the learning potential of bilingual children. *The Australian Journal of Language and Literacy*, 17, 120–128.

Vásquez, O. A. (2003). *La Clase Mágica: Imagining optimal possibilities in a bilingual community of learners*. Mahwah, NJ: Erlbaum.

Vásquez, O. A., & Durán, R. (2000) *La Clase Mágica* and Club Proteo: Multiple literacies in new community institutions. In M. Gallego and S. Hollingsworth (Eds.), *What counts as literacy: Challenging the school standard* (pp. 173–189). New York: Teachers College Press.

Vygotsky, L. S. (1962). *Thought and language*. Cambridge, MA: MIT Press.

Vygotsky, L.S. (1978). *Mind in society*. Cambridge, MA: Harvard University Press.

Wong-Fillmore, L. (1991). When learning a second language means losing the first. *Early Childhood Research Quarterly, 6*, 323–346.

Wong-Fillmore, L. (1998, October). *Keeping pedagogy in and politics out of our ESL classrooms.* Paper presented at the meeting of Indiana Teachers of English to Speakers of Other Languages, Indianapolis, IN.

APPENDIX: ANALYSIS OF EXEMPLARS

Table A4.1. Analysis of Exemplars

Principles of a Globalized Perspective	Out-of-school				In-school		Combined	
	Fifth Dimension	La Clase Mágica	DUSTY	Project Registry Sites	Bucket Buddies	International Schools CyberFair	Kidlink KidProj	Kidlink KidForum
1. Acknowledges new realities of rapid globalization and rapid change in ICT	✓	✓	✓	✓	✓	✓	✓	✓
2. New realities and new opportunities are used to increase the potential of each student	✓	✓	✓	✓	✓	✓	✓	✓
3. Recognizes the inherent potential of the linguistic capital and background knowledge about new literacies each student brings to learning contexts	✓	✓	✓			✓	✓	✓
4. Encourages both students and teachers to contribute to literacy development	✓	✓		✓	✓	✓	✓	✓
5. Recognizes the crucial role of social construction and collaboration in language and literacy development	✓	✓		✓	✓	✓	✓	✓
6. Recognizes that new forms of literacy and language will regularly emerge								
7. Promotes an awareness and application of critical literacies (e.g. evaluation of assumptions inherent in the information accessed and exchanged)		✓				✓	✓	
8. Recognizes the important relationship between home and school environments	✓	✓	✓					
9. Promotes extensive experiences with information texts instead of only narratives	✓	✓		✓		✓	✓	✓
10. Integrates language and literacy learning into authentic social action projects on a global level		✓		✓		✓	✓	✓

REFLECTION

Integrating Language, Culture, and Technology to Achieve New Literacies for All

BRIDGET DALTON

Vanderbilt University

Castek and colleagues (this volume) present a hopeful view of multilingual students' literacy futures that is situated within a globalized perspective integrating their new literacies framework (Leu, Kinzer, Coiro, & Commack, 2004) with Gort's (2006) multilingual perspective. Two core principles ground a globalized perspective: (1) multilingualism is an asset, conveying positive benefits for both the individual and the larger global community; and (2) the Internet and other information communication technologies (ICTs) require new literacies that by their very nature are evolving in a transactional relationship with rapid technology innovation. Castek and her colleagues make a compelling case for the need to shift from the prevailing view in U.S. education that privileges English monolingualism and the technology of the printed book, to a globalized perspective that reflects the new realities of multiculturalism and ICTs. A globalized perspective not only integrates two important perspectives—multilingual and new literacies—it potentially brings together diverse communities in service of the overarching goal of preparing all students for their literacy futures (Leu, 1999), and thus a more productive and hopeful future for us all.

As I read this important and provocative piece, I naturally sought points of connection and divergence with the work I have been involved in over the last several years in collaboration with colleagues Patrick Proctor, Annemarie Palincsar, Peggy Coyne, and others developing and studying digital literacy environments and tools for diverse learners (for an overview, see Dalton & Proctor, 2007; Palincsar & Dalton, 2005). Whether students are reading a hypertext version of a book originally designed for print or a Web site replete with multimedia and options for user interaction, we are taking advantage of the inherent flexibility of digital text, tools and media to create scaffolded learning environments where supports can be adjusted in relation to students' needs and preferences, including students for whom English is their second language. As students' competence develops, the scaffolds can be reduced to optimize the balance of challenge and support for each student. The overarching goals of this work are to develop students who are able to read, view, and communicate across a range of digital and print contexts, who are strategic in their approach to varied tasks, literacy mediums, and potential support systems, and who are engaged and efficacious learners.

In this reflection, I focus on three of Castek and colleagues' ten principles of a globalized perspective in relation to the role that technology can play in supporting students' literacy development, and specifically, the development of bilingual students' literacy (beyond providing the context for literacy). I follow this discussion with recommendations for classroom practice and suggestions for accelerating the research and development in this area.

Three of the ten globalized perspective principles:

- New realities provide new opportunities to increase the potential of every student (Principle 2). For students learning in a multicultural digital world, there is an increased need and benefit attached to bilingualism and new literacies competence. Students will be able to bring multiple perspectives and experience with language, culture, and new literacies to understanding complex issues, collaboratively solving problems, and communicating with a diverse audience.
- Linguistic capital and background knowledge that students bring with them to learning contexts are essential resources for their development (Principle 3). To realize the benefits of multilingualism and new literacies, classrooms must change so that students' knowledge and background become part of the learning content, resources, and ways of learning. Importantly, shifting the nature of the learning community should contribute to success for the group, as well as the individual, and for the teacher, as well as the student.
- Language and literacy are socially constructed processes (Principle 5). The opportunity to take advantage of the linguistic and cultural capital that students bring to the classroom expands with ICTs that connect students to people, resources, and information from around the world. Strategies for social learning and collaboration are increasingly important and should reflect both multilingual and new literacies perspectives (Castek et al., this volume).

Castek and colleagues highlight the increasing match between the needs of a globalized society that is technology-based and the talents, perspectives, and skills of multicultural, multilingual individuals. Expanded opportunity to realize human potential in the unbounded space represented by the Internet and other ICTs suggests that not only is literacy undergoing a transformation, but who is considered to be highly literate may also be changing. Communication is no longer primarily a verbal medium, whether in written or oral form.

Kress (2003) makes an eloquent case that we are all designers, calling for a literacy that is based on an ability to read, view, and communicate with integrated media. Many assume that a highly skilled reader and writer of books and print materials will easily make the transition to being a highly skilled reader and composer in a digital context. However, that notion is challenged when one considers the complex nature of dynamically evolving new literacies, and the repositioning of written verbal language within a larger communicative text where oral language, media skills, critical literacy and social intelligence play a more prominent role.

Highly skilled literacy performances are demonstrated by struggling learners in new literacies contexts such as digital storytelling (DUSTY, 2006; Hull & Zacher, 2004), video games (Gee, 2003), blogging (Lankshear & Knobel, 2006), and Internet commerce (Lankshear & Knobel, 2003). Unlike print text, where one size fits all, these digital contexts offer students multiple pathways for learning, engagement and success, an approach that is more likely to realize bilingual students' potential. To take one example, bilingual students do not have to choose between one language or another to communicate in a digital storytelling environment. Instead, they can mix languages or offer a translation via captioning or a dual sound track. They may also extend their communication palette with graphics, sound, and video. Students may access Web-based resources available in their first language during the planning and research phase, and then reconstruct and communicate their understanding in their second language. Bilingual students also have cultural knowledge resources that can be shared with their audience, again using multiple languages and mediums of expression.

It is essential to study and understand literacies as they evolve in naturally occurring contexts in and out of school while simultaneously developing digital learning environments that reflect our current knowledge base and that can be applied now in schools, recognizing that they will be replaced as new innovations occur and the knowledge base advances. In our work at the Center for Applied Special Technology (CAST, www.cast.org), we are developing digital literacy environments and tools to support both traditional print literacies and new literacies. Our instructional design is guided by three universal design for learning principles: (1) provide multiple means of representation, (2) provide multiple means of expression and skill development within a cognitive apprenticeship framework, and (3) provide multiple means of engagement (Rose & Dalton, 2002; Rose & Meyer, 2002). Drawing on the universal design concept in architecture (Mace, 1998), universal design for learning advocates that the needs of the broadest possible range of users be considered at the design stage, rather than adapting after the fact for a particular group of learners, such as students who are English language learners (ELLs), students who are struggling readers, and students who are gifted and talented. The assumption is that the end result will contribute to improved outcomes for all learners, not just the immediate group with the pressing need (e.g., consider the widespread use of curb cuts, TV captioning, and audio-books by the general populace). Universal design for learning and a global literacies perspective share a social justice orientation and valuing of diversity.

Building on previous research on universally designed digital literacy environments with embedded strategy instruction and access supports (Dalton & Proctor, 2007; Dalton, Pisha, Eagleton, Coyne, & Deysher, 2002), my colleague Patrick Proctor and I enhanced universal learning editions of several folktales and informational texts to include specific supports for bilingual students, such as a bilingual agent coach who offers think-alouds and models in either Spanish or English, cognate alerts to encourage Spanish-speaking students to apply their knowledge of Spanish vocabulary to the learning of English vocabulary, and Spanish translations of directions and instructional content (Proctor, Dalton, & Grisham, 2007). With funding from the Institute of Education Sciences, we are collaborating with Catherine Snow of Harvard University on the Improving Comprehension Online Project (ICON) to develop and study the role of digital texts with interactive vocabulary and embedded strategy support on fifth-grade bilingual and monolingual English students' reading achievement (Dalton et al., 2006).

The ICON team is especially interested in understanding the relationship between learner characteristics such as bilingual students' first and second language skills and reading achievement, students' use of the various instructional supports, and learning and engagement outcomes. Are there some supports that are generally helpful to students, such as embedded strategy instruction, whereas others are useful to particular individuals or groups of students? For example, we are finding it useful to analyze bilingual Spanish-speaking fifth-grade students' vocabulary learning in relation to Spanish and English language and literacy skills, based on differences we are seeing between "functional bilinguals" who demonstrate average English and Spanish reading and listening skills and "struggling bilinguals" who demonstrate low to low-average skills in both languages, but are somewhat stronger in English (Uccelli, Proctor, & Dalton, 2006). The mode of response is proving to be an interesting mediating factor, with struggling bilinguals tending to produce higher quality captions for graphics illustrating a core vocabulary word when they chose to record their responses, because their oral English skills were more developed than their written English skills.

A defining characteristic of new literacies environments is the integration of media. Speaking and listening, although always part of the language arts curriculum, play an expanded role in digital environments, and as just suggested, may be especially important in supporting students who are English language learners because they may facilitate first language transfer to second language learning and the bridging of first and second languages. The ICON digital hypertext offers students the option of listening to text via text-to-speech functionality, and allows students to respond to prompts and activities by writing or audio-recording. A further example of the power of opening up response options is illustrated by Anita, a fifth-grade Spanish-speaking girl who describes herself as "nice, but not very smart" (Dalton et al., 2006). Her teacher confirmed this view, stating that Anita was failing all of her subjects and that "she is the kind of kid who wants to disappear and not be noticed." After reading the ICON folktale, Anita created a multimedia retelling using a five-scene PowerPoint template that we had created. Anita revealed her storytelling talent as she audio-recorded her retelling, dramatically expressing the story in English. She proudly presented her retelling, taking a bow to classroom applause. Anita's teacher was surprised and pleased to see Anita in a successful learning context. Her view that Anita was a failing student with low learning aptitude was no longer valid. From a globalized perspective, there is a greater chance of improving academic achievement and realizing potential because digital technologies offer a far more flexible and varied medium in which to work and learn.

Accelerating Research and Development as We Rethink What Works

The answer to the question "Does this work, for whom, and under what conditions?" matters in a different way than it has in the past. Previously, we have relied on what works "on average" to guide instructional design and to make decisions about effective instructional methods and materials. We knew that some children would not thrive under these conditions and that consequently we would need to develop supplementary and intervention programs to address their needs. This reflects a deficit view of individual differences, one where the child who does not succeed is viewed as the problem to be fixed, a problem that will require more resources and time.

We now have the technical knowledge and capacity to create literacy environments that can be responsive to individual differences, and that can adapt to changing goals, contexts, and increasing levels of language and literacy competence. We can also develop tools to support students in open-ended contexts such as the Internet. We are constrained, however, by the lack of knowledge about how diverse students learn in digital environments, even those designed with an educational purpose in mind. Am I suggesting we invest in a rigorous research and development program in this area? Most emphatically, yes. Am I suggesting that we wait until there is a strong research foundation before developing and implementing technology-based tools, texts, and approaches? Most emphatically, no.

First, consistent with Castek et al.'s global perspective principles, we should look to bilingual students and students who are using new literacies in multiple contexts outside of school to contribute to the development of supported digital tools, texts, and applications. Second, given that information communication technologies represent a moving horizon, it is no longer productive to employ our traditional research criteria to determine "what works" (Palincsar & Dalton, 2005). For example, to carry out multiple experiments with a particular application that has a short shelf life is a waste of precious resources. So, how do we move forward in a way that will make a difference in students' lives, and the lives of their teachers, who report that they are woefully unprepared to address issues of multilingualism, multiculturalism, and digital literacies?

It may be that we need to make a fundamental shift in how we support educational research and innovation. The "What Works Clearing House" (http://www.whatworks.ed.gov) recently expanded its offerings to include methods and programs demonstrating "promise." This makes particular sense when evaluating technology-based approaches and new literacies, and should advance adoption of innovation in schools. It also makes sense to expect that schools will need to evaluate these promising innovations in relation to their particular context, considering community, school, class, teacher, and student factors that mediate technology integration.

In addition to a more open acceptance of promising research (with the caveat that ongoing evaluation and a critical consumer perspective would be important accompaniments to this increased flexibility), there needs to be an acceleration in our research and development program. Of course, this would require an infusion of funds and resources at a level commensurate with the importance of our educational goals.

Another viable option for advancing research and development is to use digital technologies to support collaboration and data sharing amongst researchers. Although researchers within teams rely on technology for communication and other research purposes, conferences and publications remain the primary venue for dissemination, with restricted sharing of data. The Bill and Melinda Gates Foundation recently announced that its HIV projects program would not fund AIDS researchers unless they pooled data, with the hope that increased data sharing and collaboration would lead more quickly to solutions (Chase, 2006). To accelerate development in literacy and technology research, the federal government could set aside a portion of educational research funding for researchers who agree to share data and results on an ongoing basis. And, given the paucity of research on bilingual students, they could set a priority on research that included underrepresented groups. It would make sense to target researchers in the field of technology and literacy because of their high level of technology expertise and access to technology resources and technical support. They might be considered the low-hanging fruit, individuals more willing to gamble on a different model of conducting research and development. Collaboration with researchers in the field of bilingualism and biliteracy should be a requirement, as well. And finally, mechanisms for involving students and teachers as developers of new literacies could lead to more effective outcomes for all.

Making a Difference in Classrooms: Five Suggestions for Improving Bilingual Elementary School Students' Literacy and Learning Outcomes

A globalized perspective and universal design for learning share a common goal (realizing human potential), an appreciation of diversity (an asset to the individual and to society), and an emphasis on ICTs and new literacies. From a universal design perspective, it is useful to frame the question, "How do we use technology to support bilingual students' literacy development?" within the broader question, "How do we teach the full range of students who are present in today's classrooms?" Although there are specific technology-based tools and instructional approaches that will be especially helpful to bilingual students, there are also technology-based tools and approaches that are likely to be suitable for both bilingual and monolingual students. Benefits will vary in relation to degrees of oral and written language skills in first and second languages (as well as other cognitive and affective characteristics). All students bring resources to the learning table; bilingual students' resources are especially important in a digital globalized world. A challenge for educators is to fully realize the power of these resources to achieve diverse students' potential and to contribute to the larger common good. The teaching suggestions that follow are intended to provide a basic foundation for moving forward to achieve these important goals.

1. *Take advantage of students' oral language and listening comprehension in English to develop reading skills and motivation.* Many digital storybooks and online texts offer read aloud options so that students may listen to selected words, sentences, or text passages as they follow along reading the printed text. For some students, the read aloud will provide a model of English word pronunciation and expression. For others, it will help students link words that they have heard, but do not yet recognize, to the printed words. And for still others, the read aloud will allow them to process text more quickly. Many of these texts also provide links to glossaries and background knowledge. Students can learn to use their listening skills in flexible ways to bootstrap their reading skills. In turn, increased access and development of competence is likely to motivate students to read more, and to view themselves as successful readers.

2. *Use text-to-speech (TTS) tools in English and the child's first language for instructional and assessment purposes.* Any text that is in digital format, including Internet content, assessments, teacher-developed materials, and students' own writing, can be read aloud using a text-to-speech tool. Importantly, these tools work in a variety of languages, allowing students to move flexibly between first and second languages as they further develop bilingual/biliteracy skills. TTS is

also an important assessment option for separating the evaluation of students' content knowledge from assessment of second language reading (Dolan, Hall, Banerjee, Chun, & Strangman, 2005). For example, some bilingual students will be better able to demonstrate their understanding of math content with a digital math test that allows them to listen to the directions and word problems in English, or in their first language, depending on their English level. In addition to commercial TTS programs, there are also free programs available online (for more information about TTS tools and instructional applications, see CAST, 2001).

3. *Involve students in both creating and reading/viewing multimedia texts and presentations.* Multimedia composing tools, such as PowerPoint, KidPix, and the iLife series make it easier than ever before to communicate across media and across languages. PowerPoint can be used with young children to create language experience texts that combine text, graphics, color, and video (Labbo, Eakle, & Montero, 2002) whereas older students may compose a variety of narrative and informational multimedia texts. Very young children or students who are just learning English may orally record in their first language, with their teacher writing one version in the first language and then a second version in English. Older students may partner with peers to compose bilingual texts, podcasts, and videos that can be shared with a broader audience, including posting to a class blog, school Web site, or other publishing venues increasingly available to educators on the Internet.

4. *Engage bilingual students in collaborative Internet projects that connect them with classrooms and experts from around the world.* There are numerous collaborative Internet projects available for K–5 students, ranging from international book clubs, to data collection projects, to social action projects (Leu, Leu, & Coiro, 2004). These projects put students in highly motivating contexts for learning with, through, and about language and culture as they tackle important problems, or simply enjoy sharing their interest in Harry Potter. There are also opportunities to develop relationships with a sister class that extends beyond a specific project, allowing for an ongoing exchange that promotes multilingual, multicultural perspectives and collaboration.

5. *When purchasing technology-based tools, texts, and programs, consider the needs and talents of bilingual students in a rapidly-evolving digital world.* From a universal design perspective, ask "To what extent does the tool or product provide all students, and especially bilingual students, multiple means of representation, multiple means of expression, and multiple means of engagement?" From a globalized perspective, ask "How does the tool or product leverage and advance bilingual students' language, culture, and new literacies skills and interests?"

Final Thoughts

Learning How to Learn

There is promising research on enhancements to digital text to support reading achievement and engagement (for reviews, see Dalton & Strangman, 2006; Strangman & Dalton, 2005). I agree with Castek and colleagues (this volume) that a priority should be to teach students to "learn how to learn" on the Internet. Just as we scaffold a hypertext, there are opportunities to scaffold the new literacies of ICTs so that students are not only successful with particular tasks, and in particular environments, but that they are developing the knowledge, skills, strategies, and dispositions of mind that will make them flexible and strategic in their approach to any digital environment. Strategic students will ask "How can I use the system of supports to advance my literacy and learning goals?"

Partnerships with Educational Print and Internet Publishers

There is an urgent need to influence educational publishers, software designers and Web-site designers as they rapidly move forward in developing digital versions/extensions of traditional print materials, designing new ICT literacy environments, and inventing new technologies for learning, communication, and community building. This acceleration is fueled in the educational arena by the reauthorization of the Individuals with Disabilities Education Act (IDEA, 1997, 2006) and the establishment of the National Instructional Materials Accessibility Standards (NIMAS) for the development and distribution of accessible digital versions of textbooks and other instructional materials to students with print disabilities (http://nimas.cast.org). Although the standards are targeted to students with disabilities, publishers and developers are already considering implications for a broader range of students, including bilingual students, and are moving forward with development plans.

In closing, I return to Castek and colleagues' hopeful vision for developing new literacies among multicultural learners. I share their hopefulness and believe the vision is achievable for all learners. The new NIMAS regulations and development of digital learning environments, tools and texts present a window of opportunity to influence the future direction of ICTs, and thereby influence the potential for success for multilingual students, as well as their monolingual peers.

References

CAST. (2001). *Using text-to-speech technology resource guide*. Waltham, MA: CAST, Inc. Retrieved October 22, 2006, at http://www.cast.org/system/galleries/download/pdResources/tts.doc.

Chase, M. (2006, July 20). Gates won't fund AIDS researchers unless they pool data. *The Wall Street Journal, MarketPlace* (p. B1). NY: Dow Jones & Co.

Dalton, B., Pisha, B., Eagleton, M., Coyne, P, & Deysher, S. (2002, December). *Developing strategic readers: A comparison of computer-supported versus traditional strategy instruction on struggling readers' comprehension of quality children's literature.* Final Report to the US Office of Education.

Dalton, B., & Proctor, C. P. (2007). Reading as thinking: Integrating strategy instruction in a universally designed digital literacy environment. In D.S. McNamara (Ed.), *Reading comprehension strategies: Theories, interventions, and technologies* (pp. 423–442). Mahweh, NJ: Erlbaum.

Dalton, B., Proctor, P., Snow, C., Uccelli, P., Mo, E., Robinson, K., et al. (2006). *Improving reading comprehension for struggling readers: Understanding the roles of vocabulary development, guided strategy use, and Spanish language supports in a digital reading environment.* Annual report to the US Department of Education, Institute of Education Sciences.

Dalton, B., & Strangman, N. (2006). Improving struggling readers' comprehension through scaffolded hypertexts and other computer-based literacy programs. In M.C. McKenna, L. D. Labbo, R.D. Keiffer, & D. Reinking (Eds.), *International Handbook of Literacy and Technology, Volume II* (pp. 75–92). Mahwah, NJ: Erlbaum.

Digital Underground Storytelling for Youth [DUSTY]. Project website. http://oaklanddusty.org/.

Dolan, R. P., Hall, T. E., Banerjee, M., Chun, E., & Strangman, N. (2005). Applying principles of universal design to test delivery: The effect of computer-based read-aloud on test performance of high school students with learning disabilities. *Journal of Technology, Learning, and Assessment, 3*(7).

Gee, J.P. (2003). *What video games have to teach us about learning and literacy.* NY: Palgrave Macmillan.

Gort, M. (2006). Strategic codeswitching, interliteracy, and other phenomena of bilingual writing: Lessons learned from classroom-based research. *Journal of Early Childhood Literacy, 6*, 327–358.

Hull, G., & Zacher, J. (2004). What is after-school worth? Developing literacy and identity out of school. *Voices in Urban Education*, 3. Retrieved August 26, 2004, from http://www.annenberginstitute.org/VUE/spring04/Hull.html.

Individuals with Disabilities Education Act (IDEA) Amendments. (1997, 2006). PL 105-17, 20 U.S.C. § 1400 et seq.

Kress, G. (2003). *Literacy in the new media age.* London: Routledge.

Labbo, L.D., Eakle, A.J., & Montero, M.K. (2002, May). Digital Language Experience Approach: Using digital photographs and software as a Language Experience Approach innovation. *Reading Online, 5*(8). Available: http://www.readingonline.org/electronic/elec_index.asp?HREF=labbo2/index.html, retrieved August 12, 2006.

Lankshear, C., & Knobel, M. (2003). *New literacies: Changing knowledge and classroom learning.* Philadelphia, PA: Open University Press.

Lankshear, C., & Knobel, M. (2006, April). *Blogging as participation: The active sociality of a new literacy.* Paper presented at the Annual Meeting of the American Educational Research Association, San Francisco, CA.

Leu, D.J., Jr. (1999). Caity's Question: Literacy as Deixis on the Internet. *Reading Online.* Retrieved October 22, 2006 at http://www.readingonline.org/electronic/RT/caity.html.

Leu, D.J., Jr., Kinzer, C.K., Coiro, J., & Cammack, D. (2004). Towards a theory of new literacies emerging from the Internet and other ICT. In R.B. Ruddell & N. Unrau (Eds.), *Theoretical models and processes of reading*, 5th Edition (pp. 1568–1611). Newark, DE: International Reading Association.

Leu, D. J., Jr., Leu, D. D., & Coiro, J. (2004). *Teaching with the Internet: New literacies for new times (4th ed.)*. Norwood, MA: Christopher-Gordon. Full text available at http://www.sp.uconn.edu/~djleu/fourth.html.

Mace, R. L. (1998). Universal design in housing. *Assistive Technology*, 10(1), 21–28.

National Instructional Materials Standards (NIMAS). Development and Technical Assistance Centers Website at http://nimas.cast.org/. Retrieved August 30, 2006.

Palincsar, A., & Dalton, B. (2005). Speaking literacy and learning to technology; Speaking technology to literacy and learning. In B. Maloch, J. Hoffman, D. Schallert, C. Fairbanks, & J. Worthy (Eds.), *54th Yearbook of the National Reading Conference* (pp. 83–102). Oak Creek, WI: National Reading Conference, Inc.

Proctor, P., Dalton, B., & Grisham, D. (2007). Scaffolding English language learners and struggling readers in a digital environment with embedded strategy instruction and vocabulary support. *Journal of Literacy Research*, 39(1), 71–93.

Rose, D., & Dalton, B. (2002). Using technology to individualize reading instruction. In C.C. Block, L.B. Gambrell & M. Pressley (Eds.), *Improving comprehension instruction: Rethinking research, theory, and classroom practice* (pp. 257–274). San Francisco, CA: Jossey Bass.

Rose, D., & Meyer, A. (2002). *Teaching every student in the digital age: Universal design for learning*. Alexandria, VA: ASCD.

Strangman, N., & Dalton, B. (2005). Technology for struggling readers: A review of the research. In D. Edyburn, K. Higgins, & R. Boone (Eds.), *The handbook of special education technology research and practice* (pp. 545–569). Whitefish Bay, WI: Knowledge by Design, Inc.

Uccelli, P., Proctor, C.P., & Dalton, B. (2006). *"Caption-it": Teaching and assessing depth of vocabulary knowledge in fifth-grade bilingual Spanish-speaking students*. Poster session presented at the Annual Research Conference of the Institute for Education Sciences, U.S. Department of Education, Washington, DC.

5

Technology and Second Language Learning
Promises and Problems

YONG ZHAO AND CHUN LAI
Michigan State University

This chapter provides an overview of the capacities of a broad range of technologies for second language learning and discusses how technology can be better designed to support second language learning in both formal and informal settings. This chapter is divided into two sections. Following a general framework that specifies the conditions for effective language learning, the first section discusses the promises of technologies in terms of their functions for creating an optimal language learning environment with specific examples drawn from previous empirical research. Specifically, this section analyzes technology on four dimensions: technology that enhances language input/exposure, technology that improves exercise and feedback, technology that facilitates authentic communication, and technology that sustains motivation. The second section discusses design, development, and deployment issues related to technology and second language education that need to be addressed to realize the promises. The chapter concludes with specific recommendations for policy, development, research, and second language teaching and learning in and out of school settings.

To What Problem Is This a Solution:
Finding the Right Interpretation Framework

Technology, especially modern information and communication technology, holds great potential for significantly improving second language learning (Chapelle, 2001; Egbert, Chao, & Hanson-Smith, 1999; Levy, 1997; Pennington, 1996; Salaberry, 2001; Zhao, 2003a). However the potential does not automatically lead to learning gains because most of the technologies that second language educators believe to have the potential to significantly improve second language learning were not necessarily invented for this purpose and thus there are no explicit straightforward directions about how each technology should be used. Nor is there any compelling internal logic to connect technology and second language learning. Hence when faced with a technology (such as the radio), second language educators need to interpret its technological capacity in the terms of second language learning. In other words, educators must work out how this technology can be used to help enhance second language learning. This "figuring out" process is essentially a reinventing process that translates the capacities of a technology into a solution to a problem in the second language learning process (Zhao, 2003b).

How a technology is used is the direct result of this translation process, which is affected by the translator's (educator's) understanding of the capacities of technology, which is inevitably constrained by the real functions of the technology, and her view of the educational goals and process, which is in turn influenced and limited by the context in which the learning occurs. Thus depending on the framework that is used to guide the interpretation, the same technology can have many qualitatively different uses. The computer, for instance, when viewed as a tool for teachers, is used to address problems teachers face: communicating with their peers, students, and parents, record keeping, or preparing for classes. When viewed as a tool for the learner, the computer is then used to solve problems of the learner: accessing learning materials, completing homework, or obtaining feedback.

Therefore the power or capacity of technology can only be discussed in relation to the problem it is used to address. That is, the power of technology only lies in its uses. And because the uses are the result of the user's interpretation guided by their knowledge of technological capacities, identification of problems, and thinking about the internal connection between the capacity and the problem, how the uses of each technology are conceptualized becomes one of the determining factors affecting the ultimate impact of technology.

Traditional conceptualization of technology uses in second language learning has a number of problems that have limited the impact of technology on second language acquisition. First, it tends to focus on the potential uses of individual technologies instead of the combined potential of all technologies. Thus we see a large amount of individual software or hardware for language education but seldom see a comprehensive environment that integrates the capacities of multiple technologies to support language learning. For example, currently most language learning software is developed for the computer and thus can only be used when a computer is available, making it impossible for the learner to access the learning materials when he or she does not have access to a computer or is unable to use a computer. This is especially problematic for children from low-income or minority families. Although the overall home ownership of computers in the United States has been increasing dramatically and in the year 2000, about 50% of families in the United States owned a computer, the distribution is uneven. Although 88% of family households with incomes of $75,000 or more owned at least one computer in 2000, only 28% of households with incomes of $25,000 or less had a computer (U.S.

Census Bureau, 2001). This means more than 70% of low-income families are not able to take advantage of computer-based learning materials at home. Additionally, it is impractical and pedagogically inappropriate to expect that children spend all their time on a computer learning a second language. Language learning can occur in cars, on the playground, and other places where children spend their time without access to a computer.

Second, traditional conceptualization of technology uses in second language learning tends to focus on individual language learning issues instead of the learning process as a whole. Thus, we see numerous individual tools and experiments that help with grammar, vocabulary, reading, or writing but rarely see a comprehensive design that coherently uses technology to help the learner with all aspects of learning. This is particularly true of uses of technology in formal language instruction. A comprehensive review of the literature suggests that the majority of journal publications about technology uses in second language learning reported uses of individual tools and experiments (Zhao, 2003a).

Third, it tends to focus on newer technologies while ignoring older technologies. Thus, we see repeated abandonment of promising uses of older technologies for newer technologies. Over the past century or so, we have seen multiple waves of attempts to use technology to support language learning: motion pictures, radios, televisions, mainframe computer systems, laser discs, CD-ROMs, Hypermedia, and now the Internet. Each time a new technology emerged, it quickly replaced older technologies. Today, only a minority of language learning materials is available on and delivered with technologies other than the computer, with the exception of print-based technologies, which are, of course, rarely considered as technology any longer. The replacement of traditional audiovisual language labs with newer computer-based networked language learning centers is a telling example. It should be noted that some language learning materials are still available on audio cassette tapes, but the trend is certainly moving toward more digital technologies.

Lastly, existing research on technology for language learning tends to have focused on adult language learners. Thus we see much more research and development efforts for technology for adult language learners in instructional settings than for younger learners in the home environments. After an extensive review of the research literature of computer-assisted language learning, Zhao (2003a) concludes that: (a) the settings of instruction where the studies were conducted were limited to higher education and adult learners, (b) the languages studied were limited to common foreign languages and English as a foreign or second language, and (c) the experiments were often short term and about one or two aspects of language learning (e.g., vocabulary or grammar).

Thus, we need a new, more fruitful conceptualization of how to use technology to enhance second language learning. This conceptualization should aim to develop an effective language learning environment through a combination of technologies instead of merely developing effective uses to support one aspect of language learning or making use of one type of technology. Furthermore, this conceptualization should be grounded in second language acquisition research and focus on supporting the whole language learning process with all available technologies. The following paragraphs outline such a conceptual framework. This framework focuses on the essential elements of effective language learning environments.

Defining the Framework:
Conditions for Effective Language Learning

Many language educators and researchers have been seeking ways to improve the quality of foreign/second language education. While there exists tremendous amount of disagreement about the specifics of an optimal language learning environment, research and practice seem to suggest that successful language learning can only occur when four conditions are met: (1) high-quality input; (2) ample opportunities for practice; (3) high-quality feedback, and (4) individualized content.

High-quality Input

The essential role of input remains unchallenged across different perspectives to second language acquisition, be it the dominant behaviorist perspective in the 1960s or the current prevalent sociocognitive perspective. The current approaches to second language acquisition, ranging from the universal grammar position to the input-interaction perspective, all embrace input as a necessary component, although they differ in their emphases on the type and amount of input that is considered crucial to triggering learning (Gass, 1997). Simply put, a person, regardless of her age, cannot successfully learn a second or any language without sufficient exposure to authentic, diverse, comprehensible, and challenging linguistic and cultural materials of the target language.

Second language acquisition researchers have invested much effort to theorize and empirically test the quality and quantity of input that are optimal to second language acquisition. Over the years, scholars have posited and investigated several qualities of input: comprehensible input, simplified input, modified input, and enhanced input (VanPatten, 2000). The stress of early research on input was to manipulate input in certain ways to facilitate learners' comprehension of the target language, and the current foci of research have shifted towards finding ways to make input presented in manners that draw learners' attention to certain linguistic forms and help them build form-meaning connections. Krashen (1977) proposed the concept of comprehensible input, input that guarantees semantic understanding and at the same time contains the structures and vocabularies that are a little beyond one's current language level ($I + 1$), and argued that this type of input is the necessary and sufficient condition for second language development. In the effort to identify features that make input comprehensible, researchers like Larsen-Freeman and Long (1991) and Hatch (1978) discovered that in natural conversation input addressed to the learners is simplified in ways to make it easy to understand. They may be linguistic adjustments, characterized by systematic use of shorter sentences with syntactically simpler structures and a narrower range of vocabularies of high frequency, or discourse adjustments, such as reducing the speech rate. Thus came along the construct of simplified input. In his exploration of this "foreigner talk discourse," Long (1983) found that at instances of communication breakdown, learners tended to engage in negotiation of meaning, a process that made input more comprehensible to their interlocutors. He further identified some devices learners used in the negotiated interaction to modify or to elicit modification of the input: recasts, repetition, clarification requests, and confirmation checks, etc. Modified input engages learners in active participation in the communication process and thus has the potential to enhance the possibility for learners to notice certain problematic linguistic forms. According to Schmidt (1990, 2001) and many others, noticing is a necessary condition, at the minimum, for second language learning, and only when learners notice the gap in their current interlanguage[1] can they learn it. Enhanced input, in the form of text enhancement (White, 1998), input flooding (Trahey & White, 1993) and structured input (Farley, 2005; VanPatten, 1996), was put forth as a result of researchers' effort to find ways of manipulating input to draw learners' attention to certain linguistic forms, and help build form-meaning connections.

The evolution of the construct input revolved around the understanding that input, though the driving force for language acquisition, could not guarantee learning, but rather needs to be processed to become intake[2] so as to be integrated into learners' interlanguage system. Gass (1997) pointed out that selective attention is the core of this process and some important "input filters" include variables such as time available for processing the input, frequency of the input, affective factors and learners' prior knowledge, salience of forms, as well as the linguistic information of the input itself. In another word, both variables external and internal to the learners are crucial if efforts are to be made to facilitate the input-to-intake process.

Communicative Opportunities for Practice

In addition to high-quality input, language learners must have ample opportunities to practice what they have been exposed to. Thus communication has long been recognized as beneficial and essential to effective second language learning. Views of the role of communication have gone through drastic change in the past decades. For a long time communication had been acknowledged for practicing what had been previously taught, and now it is touted as not only a "medium of practice" but the "means by which learning takes place" as well (Gass, 1997).

Currently, the association between communication and learning is conceptualized and expounded in two major perspectives to second language learning: interactionist perspective and sociocultural perspective. Long (1983) in
observing the communication between native speakers (NS) and non-native
speakers (NNS) found that NS–NNS dyads would negotiate for meaning when
communication broke down, a process that helped to make input more comprehensible to their interlocutors. Based on this observation and Krashen's
Comprehensible Input Hypothesis, Long proposed the Interaction Hypothesis, in which he hypothesized that interaction is facilitative of second language learning in that it provides comprehensible input. However, the power
of communication in second language learning is largely underestimated if
we restrict it to the function of providing comprehensible input. Interactions
between NS–NNS and NNS–NNS also expose learners to negative evidence,
which helps learners to recognize the inadequacy in their interlanguage system
(Long et al., 1998; Mackey et al., 2000; White, 1987, 1991). Thus, communication also provides learners the opportunities to produce output and pushes
them to modify their incomprehensible output, a process that can help learners
to notice the "hole" in their interlanguage (Schmidt, 1990), test their hypotheses about the target language and engage in metatalk (Ellis & He, 1999; Swain,
1993, 1995). Realizing the limitations of his original Interaction Hypothesis,
Long (1996) suggested an updated version, in which he proposed:

> Negotiation of meaning, and especially negotiation work that triggers
> adjustments by the NS or more competent interlocutor, facilitates acqui-
> sition because it connects input, internal learner capacities, particularly
> selective attention, and output in productive ways. (Long, 1996, p. 451)

Empirical studies have been conducted since then to test the association
between interaction and L2 development (Ellis et al., 1994; Gass & Varonis, 1994;
Mackey, 1999), and so far, although no strong claims about the causal relationship can be made, we have come to the point where we can safely conclude that
negotiated interaction is facilitative of second language learning (Gass, 1997).

Sociocultural theory also makes a strong argument for the role of communication in second language learning. Sociocultural theory (Vygotsky, 1981)
argues that any higher form of mental activities are mediated by symbolic
means, language being one of the primary semiotic tools that humans used
to mediate their cognitive processes, including language acquisition (Lantolf,
1994). Language mediates both social interactions on the "interpsychological
plane" and thought on the "intrapsychological plane" (Ohta, 2000). Language
learning is a mental activity that is carried out in the joint communication
activity between experts and novices, with the former assisting the latter,
using language as a major mediating tool. In other words, it is through social
interactions, facilitated by language, that the learner or child internalizes the
external world or culture system, language being a major part of it. Social

interactions must occur in certain cultural or social contexts. Thus authentic communications or dialogs also play a significant role in facilitating the acquisition of language in context (Candlin & Mercer, 2001).

High-quality Feedback

Feedback is a classical concept in learning, whose importance is acknowledged across different learning theories. In the 60s, the heyday of behaviorism, feedback was viewed as a crucial component in the learning process (Greeno et al., 1996), and is considered as the "conditioned connection of behavior and reward" (Fischer & Mandl, 1988). Cognitivism, placing learners at the center of the learning process, values feedback more for its informative function than for its corrective-reinforcing function and takes it as a channel to provide learners with information to assist them reach their objectives by reporting their mistakes to them (Cohen, 1985). Situative theory stresses the necessity and centrality of social interaction in learning, and suggests that feedback is more often expressed in an interactive manner and serves as the core of social interaction that drives learning. Whatever perspectives on learning to adopt, it is widely accepted that feedback plays a crucial role in learning, second language learning without exception.

Research on feedback and second language learning has a long history, with early efforts focusing on predicting potential mistakes learners may make through contrastive analysis and on investigating learners' perceptions of feedback in second language learning (Macheak, 2002). More recent research in this area focused on the facilitative role of feedback in second language learning. Positive feedback, confirmation of learners' language production as being acceptable in the target language, helps learners to strengthen linguistic knowledge already registered in their interlanguage system. Whereas negative feedback, an indication that certain features in learners' language production are impossible in the target language, serves more as a catalyst for the reconstruction of learners' interlanguage grammar and it has thus attracted more research attention. Although there is still disagreement about whether negative feedback should be used in second language education because it may negatively affect the learner's motivation and discourage him from actively participating in authentic communications, it seems that most scholars agree, based on theoretical arguments (Gass, 1988; Long, 1996; White, 1987) and some empirical evidence (Trahey & White, 1993; White, 1991), that negative or corrective feedback is in some instances a necessary condition for second language acquisition (Gass, 1997). Identifying the instances under which negative feedback matters thus becomes the focus of current research, as Schachter (1991) wisely pointed out: "the kind of knowledge to be learned, the kind of evidence presented to the learner, the situation in which the learning takes place and the cognitive capabilities of the learner all play a part in the efficient or non-efficient use of negative evidence" (p. 99).

A growing body of research has examined how an interlocutor's negative feedback could promote second language learning. Long (1998) categorized negative feedback into three types: explicit negative feedback (i.e., overt correction), implicit negative feedback in the form of communication breakdown (i.e., negotiation moves) and implicit negative feedback in the form of recast. In all, literature suggests that negative feedback facilitates second language learning by helping learners to learn "information associated with individual lexical items," induce "abstract linguistic generalizations" that can be transferred to novel items and "restructure their grammars" (Carroll, 2001). Literature has it that explicit negative feedback, which either provides metalinguistic explanation or simply draws learners' attention to their problematic language productions, leads to better learning effect than implicit negative feedback (Carroll, 2001). Furthermore, the differential efficacy of different types of negative feedback varies with regard to the linguistic features in question and still remains a mystery, according to a meta-analysis of current research by Norris and Ortega (2000). In addition, research also shows that implicit negative feedback is not only available in free conversation, task-based interaction as well as in L2 classroom interaction, but also plays a role in facilitating learners' interlanguage development (Iwashita, 2003; Long et al., 1998).

What is more important are the findings on the circumstances that different negative feedback affects second language learning. Although the findings on this issue are far from being conclusive and further research is still needed, some suggestions could be drawn from current findings. In terms of the qualities of feedback: the provision of metalinguistic explanation might matter more than the degree of explicitness (Carroll & Swain, 1993), and detailed feedback, like metalinguistic feedback, may be helpful in linguistic domain that entails significant complexity but may be much less effective in other domains (Nagata, 1995). With regard to individual differences: Although their interlanguage was positively affected by negative feedback (Mackey & Oliver, 2002), both child and adult L2 learners, in their interaction with peers, showed differences in the provision of different types of negative feedback and their responses to them (Mackey et al., 2003; Oliver, 2000). For example, Mackey et al. found that although the adults provided each other more negative feedback that afforded them opportunities for modified output than children, children were more willing to respond to negative feedback and thus modified their output more often than adults. Furthermore, the proficiency level of the learners leads to differential effects of negative feedback (Iwashita, 2003; Mackey & Philp, 1998). The immediacy and saliency of the provision of negative feedback is also a threshold for its facilitative role in second language learning (Doughty & Varela, 1998; Iwashita, 2003). The length and number of changes in the negative feedback as well as the linguistic features it addresses constrain whether learners will notice and perceive it as corrective feedback (Mackey et al., 2000; Philp, 2003). Furthermore, different types of feedback might facilitate the development of different linguistic features and work differently on different learner groups (Iwashita, 2003; Nicholas et al., 2001).

In all, current research in second language acquisition confirmed the importance of the provision of feedback, negative feedback in particular, in facilitating second language learning. In addition, it suggests that a one-for-all solution or an ideal case for the provision of feedback does not exist and there is great necessity to vary the presentation of feedback to fit different learning conditions. Furthermore, it identified several important variables that need to be taken into consideration when providing feedback: the content of the feedback (specificity, length, etc.), individual differences, and the saliency of feedback.

Individualized Content

Individual differences of the learners in terms of language proficiency, cognitive development, learning objectives, and learning styles are common and significant factors that affect learners' motivation, language intake, and task performance. We know that not all language learners have the same linguistic aptitude. Some learn faster than others and some can reach a higher level of proficiency than others. In classroom situations, it is also possible that some learners may already have experiences with the target language whereas others in the same class may be absolute beginners. Furthermore, we also know that language learners differ in their purposes for learning a second language. Some learn because they want to understand and experience a foreign language. Others want to communicate and conduct business in the target language with its native speakers. Some learn the language because they hope to live and work in the target culture, whereas others simply want to be able to read scientific and technical publications in the target language. It is thus unwise to force all students to be at the same level of competence in all aspects of the language—reading, listening, writing, and speaking.

Moreover, learners also differ in their learning styles and strategies (Oxford, 1990). They have different approaches and strategies to learning grammar, vocabulary, and pronunciation. They also have different reading and listening strategies and different preferences for communicative settings. Lastly, learning occurs in different contexts. Some learners have more access to the target language at home whereas others may only have access in class. Some learners can spend more time on learning whereas others may not.

Thus an effective language learning program should be responsive to these individual differences and enable the learners to adjust the difficulty level of the content, control the pace of learning, and select content that is appropriate for their own needs. In other words, the learning should be highly individualized and customizable in order to motivate all students, meet their diverse learning goals and styles, and accommodate their individual psychological and cognitive needs. Otherwise, the learners may not be able to benefit from the environment, fall behind, lose interest, and ultimately give up learning at all.

Conditions for Optimal Second Language Learning Environments

These four conditions are generally accepted and have been articulated by other scholars, although in slightly different language. For example, Egbert, Chao, & Hanson-Smith (1999) made a similar list of conditions for optimal language learning environments:

Condition 1: Learners have opportunities to interact and negotiate meaning;

Condition 2: Learners interact in the target language with an authentic audience;

Condition 3: Learners are involved in authentic tasks;

Condition 4: Learners are exposed to and encouraged to produce varied and creative language;

Condition 5: Learners have enough time and feedback;

Condition 6: Learners are guided to attend mindfully to the learning process;

Condition 7: Learners work in an atmosphere with an ideal stress/anxiety level;

Condition 8: Learner autonomy is supported.

Translating these conditions into more specific actions, Pennington (1996) suggests that the ideal teacher or teaching system should be one that:

- Helps learners develop and elaborate their increasingly specified cognitive representation for the second language;
- Allows learners to experiment and take risks in a psychologically favorable and motivating environment;
- Offers input to both conscious and unconscious learning processes;
- Offers learners opportunities to practice and to receive feedback on performance;
- Allows learners to learn according to their own purposes and goals;
- Puts learners in touch with other learners;
- Promotes cultural and social learning;
- Promotes interactivity in learning and communication;
- Exposes the learner to appropriate contexts for learning;
- Expands the learner's "zone of proximal development";
- Builds to learner independence. (p. 7)

However many language education programs do not meet the conditions just discussed. In instructed language learning situations, such an ideal teacher or teaching system is not always readily available. This observation is resonated in other chapters. Cummins (this volume) expresses concern on the "peda-gogical divide" and about the heavy transmission orientation to pedagogy that predominates the instruction for English language learners at the elementary level. Parker also points out in her chapter that English language learners at the elementary level are facing the enormous challenge of learning both oral English skills and learning to read and write in English, and the current teaching system is not doing a satisfactory job of helping those young English language learners overcome those barriers. For instance, authentic, compre-hensible, and engaging linguistic and cultural materials, spoken or written, are not always present for many language learners. In language classrooms, teach-ers are the main source of oral linguistic and cultural input. In order to pro-vide appropriate authentic input, a teacher needs to be proficient in the target language. But such teachers are often in short supply. Even in the United States, a country with tremendous linguistic diversity, there is a severe shortage of for-eign language teachers (Branaman, Rhodes, & Rennie, 1998). The situation can get even worse when more schools start to offer foreign language programs. In other countries such as China and Japan, most English teachers are themselves not proficient in the language. The situation of written materials is not any bet-ter. Textbooks are often outdated and uninteresting to students. Lack of quality materials was cited one of the major problems facing foreign language educa-tion in the United States, in a national survey (Branaman et al., 1998).

Furthermore, in foreign language classrooms peer–to-peer communication in the target language is very limited, often mechanical and lacks authenticity, which makes it difficult for learners to sustain interest in the communication. Moreover, psychological and linguistic factors may prevent students from becoming truly engaged in real conversations in the target language (Egbert et al., 1999; Pennington, 1996). Similarly relevant and immediate feedback is not often available to language learners due to class sizes and the individual differences among students.

The Place for Technology: Creating Optimal Language Learning Environments Through Technology

Suppose our goal of using technology in second language education is to help create an optimal language learning environment. This framework identifies where technology can help with developing such an environment in and out of school language learning situations. This section discusses how technol-ogy can help enhance each condition of effective language learning and pro-vides examples from the existing literature. The examples were selected from an extensive literature review (Zhao, 2003a). Although we hoped to include studies conducted on elementary-school-aged children, it is unfortunate that very few such studies existed at the time.

Providing High-quality Input

How and What Technology Can Be Used to Provide High-Quality Input? Technology can be used to provide high-quality input in a number of ways. First, technology provides convenient access to a large variety of target language input via different media or combinations of media. Older technologies such as television, especially satellite TV, video and audio recorders/players, even films are effective means to bring authentic language and cultural materials to second language learners. It has been common practice for language teachers to use TV and radio programs, movies, and other video and audio products in their classrooms. What has not been often considered as potential technologies for enhancing language input is technology for entertainment such as video game consoles and digital versatile disc (DVD) players. Somehow there exists a gigantic perceptual gap between technology for education and technology for entertainment. In fact, DVD players and video game consoles are very powerful platforms for delivering high-quality content, and can also bring multimedia interactive content to the learner. They allow for more user control than traditional analog TVs and audio equipment. For example some of the existing video games such as Pokemon on Game Boy Advance[3], Shenmue 2 on X-Box[4], and Final Fantasy: Crystal Chronicles on Gamecube[5] can provide interactive hypertextual input in oral or written format. The multiple tracks of DVD technology can allow the learner to access input in a number of different ways: with or without captioning, in multiple languages, and with or without commentaries.

Newer technologies such as the Internet bring even more language resources. A great number of resources in different languages are available free-of-charge on the Internet, and learners can get easy access to these authentic audio and/or visual materials. Computer-mediated communication (CMC), like e-mail, online chat and video/audio conferencing, connects learners with native speakers and other learners and expands their exposure to various linguistic and cultural inputs. Hand-held digital devices, like MP3 (for MPEG audio layer 3) players and personal digital assistants (PDAs), allow learners to download audio and textual Internet materials, and have the information at their fingertips, thus enhancing the portability of these resources and freeing learners up from the physical constraints. Electronic books (e-books), with their manipulability (abilities to search and add audio conversion or short video annotation), portability and instant access, are available in a large collection of languages and offer both classical works and contemporary reading materials for a variety of ages. Their use could be further boosted by the introduction of Tablet Personal Computer (Tablet PC), which has speech recognition features and text-to-speech capabilities and recognizes learners' normal handwriting (Godwin-Jones, 2001). Moreover, electronic highlighters, like QuickLink[6] pen, allow learners to copy, clip, and store printed text, Internet links, tables and charts and then to transfer the data into their computers, PDAs or mobile phones, or to translate the text into different languages or look up its meaning from a built-in dictionary. In all, current technology not only exposes learners to an unprecedented large amount of input of great variety, but provides a lot of flexibility and convenience in the access, manipulation and organization of the information.

Second, technology lends itself to easy and quick configuration of comprehensible and enhanced input so as to increase its possibility of being processed and integrated. For one thing, text enhancement, either visual or audio, could be easily realized using technologies with highlighting functions as simple as Microsoft Word or more complicated technologies that enable interactive features. For another, technology could also simplify input through complementing it with translations, textual or visual annotations, and elaborated information through hyperlinks. Recent development in machine translation presents translation engines like GO Translator (http://translator.go.com) and Babelfish (http://babelfish.altavista.com/translate.dyn) that present free translation of web pages into different languages. Some stand-alone handheld devices, for example, the pen-like device, Quicktionary (http://www.quick-pen.com/), allow users to easily scan a word and view its translation or definition on its own liquid crystal display (LCD) screen. Furthermore, technologies such as Enounce[7] (http://www.enounce.net/) and SoundEditor (http://vitotechnology.com/en/products/soundeditor.html) enable learners to adjust the speech rate of listening materials to assist their comprehension, and present spectrum of speech waves and visual depictions of mouth and tongue movement to ease the learning of pronunciation.

In addition to the functions of enhancing the text and simplifying/enriching input, technologies hold great capacity to realize input flooding as well. Concordancer[8] (http://www.geocities.com/Athens/Olympus/4631/textanal.htm) is one such technology that generates lists of any given word/phrase used in various contexts for learners to explore the different meanings and usages of specific linguistic items (see review and discussion by Godwin-Jones, 2001; Reppen, 2001). Moreover, some concordance software even allows cross-language comparison (e.g., ParaConc (http://www.paraconct.com/) allows up to four languages to be analyzed in parallel) and others provide corpus of language in a certain genre (e.g., the Corpus of Spoken Professional American English[9] (http://www.athel.com/cspa.html) provides transcripts of American spoken English in professional settings such as committee meetings, faculty meetings, and White House press conference).

Third, the advantage of technology in appealing to different learning styles and proffering individualized input could accommodate to internal variables that are crucial to the input-to-intake process. Multimedia software as well as most online materials delivered via a combination of different media can meet the needs of learners with different cognitive styles. Technology also helps to lower affective filters: input provided in the form of games or simulations fulfills the fun component of learning; hypertext allows self-selected path of navigation and makes input more individualized and personally meaningful. The flexibility and learner control offered by technology enable learners to choose linguistic input that is more appropriate to their learning needs which would, to a great extent, enhance the possibility of the incorporation of input into their interlanguage system. For instance, Chengo[10] (http://www.elanguage.cn), a web-based language learning project co-developed by the U.S. Department of Education and the Chinese Ministry of Education, employs multiple technologies to deliver English and Chinese learning in a game and simulation format for learners of English and Chinese.

Evidence of Effectiveness: Research Findings on Technology and High-quality Input Empirical studies have provided preliminary and limited evidence that technology can be used to effectively enhance language learning through the provision of high-quality input. Specifically, it has been suggested that technology can be used to enhance the quality of input in the following ways:

Enhancing Access Efficiency through Digital Multimedia Technologies. Digital multimedia technologies make access to learning materials more efficiently than print media or audio recorders because (a) multimedia (visual, audio, and text) presentations can create stronger memory links than a single medium alone and (b) digital technology allows instant and accurate playbacks, which helps the learner to access specific segments much more easily without spending time to locate them, which can be tedious and a waste of time (Hanson-Smith, 1999; Thorton & Dudley, 1996). Shea (2000) compared the time college students needed to complete their language learning tasks using captioned video versus interactive video disc (IVD) and found that the students using IVD completed the tasks significantly faster ($p < .05$). Labrie (2000) found that although students spent more time learning a set of French words on paper than those who studied on computer where they could hear a word pronounced and see a picture about the word, they did not learn more words. In another study, Nutta (1998) found that after spending the same amount of time (one hour per day for seven days) learning verb tenses in English in two conditions: attending a regular class and receiving instruction from the teacher as compared with using a multimedia (audio, video, recording capabilities, etc.) computer program, the ESL students using the computer program performed as well as or significantly better (on 3 out of 6 measures, $p < .10$) than their counterparts attending the class.

Enhancing Authenticity Using Video and the Internet. Video materials can bring natural and context-rich linguistic and cultural materials to the learner whereas the Internet enables the learner to access authentic news and literature in the target language, which can reflect current cultural changes more effectively than printed sources and is also more motivating (Bacon & Finnemann, 1990; Hanson-Smith, 1999; Herron, Cole, Corrie, & Dubreil, 1999; Herron, Dubreil, Cole, & Corrie, 2000; Kitajima & Lyman-Hager, 1998; Lafford & Lafford, 1997; Lee, 1998; Weyers, 1999). Weyers (1999) studied the effectiveness of authentic video on college Spanish students. He had one class of students watch a Mexican television show as part of a second semester Spanish class that met 60 minutes daily for a total of 8 weeks while the other class followed the regular curriculum without the video. He found that the video group's performance on both listening comprehension and oral production were significantly better than the regular group ($p < 0.01$). The video group also outperformed their counterparts on other measures of communicative competence. Herron et al. (2000) found that video also helped their first year college French learners develop significantly better understanding of the target culture. In another study, Green and Youngs (2000) substituted regular classroom instruction with web activities one class period per week for beginning college French and German students. After a semester, they found that "the substitution of one class day for directed, pedagogically sound Web activities seems to have allowed the treatment groups to continue to progress toward their personal and professional goals and allowed them to learn language at a rate similar to that of their peers in the control groups. It also appears, in general, that the students had a positive experience using the Web ... " (p. 108).

Enhancing Comprehensibility through Learner Control and Multimedia Annotations. Comprehensible input is necessary for language learning but useful learning materials must also contain enough unfamiliar materials (Krashen, 1985). For language learners, especially beginning and intermediate ones, authentic materials are often beyond their language proficiency and may become incomprehensible without help. To enhance comprehensibility of spoken materials, full caption, keyword caption, or reducing the speech rate have been found to be effective (Shea, 2000; Zhao, 1997). Zhao (1997) found that the college ESL students who had the flexibility to slow down or speed up the speech rate had significantly better listening comprehension than those who did not ($p < 0.05$). For reading materials, glossing or multimedia annotations have been effective means to enhance comprehension (Al-Seghayer, 2001; Chun & Plass, 1997; Johnson, 1999; Lyman-Hager, 2000). Al-Seghayer (2001) compared adult ESL students' vocabulary learning in different annotation conditions and found that "a video clip in combination with a text definition is more effective in teaching unknown vocabulary than a picture in combination with a text definition . . . The variety of modality cues can reinforce each other and are linked together in meaningful ways to provide an in-depth experience." ($p < 0.001$; p. 225).

Providing Meaningful and Authentic Communication Opportunities

How and What Technology Can Be Used to Provide Communication Opportunities? Engaging in authentic communication in the target language is another essential condition for successful language learning; however, such opportunities do not exist for most learners. Technology can be used in many different ways to create opportunities for language learners to communicate in the target language (see Hanson-Smith, 1999; Kelm, 1998; Muyskens, 1998; Warschauer & Kern, 2000).

Currently, the most prevalent use of technology in this regard is computer mediated communication (CMC). CMC technologies engage learners in social interaction with their language partners, either NSs or NNSs, via e-mail, listserv, discussion board, online chat, and audio/video conferencing. CMC has been theorized as a crucial means to realize interactivity in online teaching and learning environments and promote a 'learner-centered interactive approach,' and to raise learners' awareness of the sociocultural nature of the target language and enhance the development of situated cognition (Romiszowski & Mason, 1996; Salaberry, 1996).

Existing CMC software or systems can be classified into two major categories: synchronous systems and asynchronous systems. Synchronous CMC includes text-based conferencing systems (e.g., English clubchat; ICQ), audio-based conferencing systems (Netscape CoolTalk; StudyCom), video-based conferencing systems, and combinations thereof (MSN messenger; iVisit; PalTalk, etc.). Most current synchronous CMC systems provide all the three modalities, with varying degrees of anonymity and user control (see Cziko & Park, 2003 for a review of several free and widely used synchronous CMC systems). In addition, there are also some three-dimensional virtual worlds available, such as Second Life that allow learners to choose their own avatars, move about freely in the virtual worlds, and create their own virtual spaces and activities such as playing online games, shopping, and making friends with people.

Different from synchronous CMC, asynchronous CMC provides communications free of time constraints. The majority of asynchronous CMC are text-based and in various forms: e-mail, listserv, and threaded messages, such as discussion boards and web forums. However, audio-based asynchronous CMC is also available, such as voice mail (e.g., HandyBits VoiceMail, http://in.tech.yahoo.com/020708/94/1rqt3.html), which enables learners to send voice messages to each other using their e-mail accounts. Another emerging asynchronous CMC is in the form of weblogs. Starting in 1998 as collections of sites with similar topics or interests, weblogs are now burgeoning as short-form journals that reference each other and invite commentaries, and developing into a new and intriguing form of public conversation. In addition to creating communication environments free of time and physical constraints and fostering a special form of prose that lies in between spoken and written language, CMC, with its message archiving function, could add great convenience to research in second language acquisition, research in interactionist perspective in particular.

In recent years, the increased capacity of mobile phones and the convergence of telephone systems and the Internet, plus the decreased cost and broadened accessibility have made mobile phones a viable technology-mediated communication tool for second language learners. With easy text-messaging, multimedia interactivities, and interoperability with the Internet, mobile phones can practically be used as networked computers. Thus, many of the CMC functions can be performed with the mobile phones.

Another way technology helps to facilitate communication is through supporting learner talk around technology-based activities. Ideally any kind of technology-based activities, such as watching a sitcom on the TV, searching for information on the Internet, creating a PowerPoint presentation on a certain topic, and playing instructional software, games or simulations, could be used in manners to stimulate learner talk.

The other noteworthy application of technology in promoting learner communication is human–computer interaction, or talking with an artificial intelligence agent to be specific. This area is least explored in regard to its efficacy in second language learning due to the fact that the technology in this function is still under development and has not been widely applied yet. However, the potential of this application in second language learning is tremendous. One potential use of the technology is a chatterbot or bot, a conversation simulator based on artificial intelligence technology, programmed to conduct conversations with users on various topics (see http:// www.simonlaven.com/ for a comprehensive review of currently available chatterbots). Different kinds of chatterbots are available, with most of them being text-based (e.g., A.L.I.C.E., http://www.alicebot.org/). Some chatterbots specialize in certain topics, e.g., ALIMbot (http://faizulwahid.tripod. com/alimbot/): focuses on emotions and feelings; AMDI (http://www.over-mill.freeserve.co.uk/leon.html) is good at holding conversations about food, travel, politics and the weather); and others do enable voice function, (e.g., Cara (http://www.colorzone.co.uk/cara.html): using a selective audio stream to chat with users). Some provide transcripts of conversation (e.g., Jabberwacky, http://www.jabberwacky.com/) and others can conduct conversation in different languages (e.g., Jabberwock http://www.abenteuermedien.de/ jabberwock/index.php). The potential use of chatterbot in language learning is immense: it provides a convenient chatting environment for learners to conduct authentic conversations in the target language either by writing or by speaking, and the chat transcripts in the archives could serve as a source of the target language as well.

Speech recognition and synthesis technologies present great potential for second language learning. Applications with text-to-speech engines such as CAST's eReader (http://www.cast.org/udl/index.cfm?i= 211) and Microsoft Word enable learners to listen to the pronunciation of words while reading the text. Other applications with a speech-to-text engine such as Dragon Naturally Speaking (http://www.scansoft.com/naturallyspeaking/professional/) and IBM's ViaVoice system (http://www-306.ibm.com/software/voice/viavoice/), allow users to dictate to them in continuous speech. These applications provide a viable way to train learners' pronunciation and help them build text–sound association. Furthermore, some applications provide the possibilities for learners to interact with computers via speech input and speech output: The latest version of Apple Mac OS X (http://www.apple.com/macosx/) provides the speech recognition and text-to-speech functions, with which users can give voice commands to the computer and even hear the conversation agent speak back to them in plain English. The much-touted Microsoft Agent (http://www.microsoft.com/msagent/default.asp), when incorporating a text-to-speech engine and speech-recognition engine, is another unprecedented technology that can process voice commands from users and respond in synthesized speech, recorded audio, or text in a word balloon. This technology is used to create conversational interfaces for applications and web pages, such as reading the content of the web page, searching news on the Internet and reading them out in response to users' commands, etc. Speech-enabled systems have already been used in customer services. For instance, one can talk to United Airlines' speech agent to check flight information, employee ticket reservations, Mileage Plus, and baggage information. The speech agent can understand the spoken request and instantly responds with the most up-to-date information. These emerging technologies give learners great opportunities to engage in authentic conversation with computer agents and expand their exposure to target language. Since these new technologies are still in the developing and refining stages and not widely used yet, little research has been done on the effects of these technological applications on second language learning. However, the social and learning impacts of these applications deserve great attention in the near future.

We should also consider some common home appliances for potential uses to enhance communication and practice opportunities. For instance, the Karaoke[11] technology, a very popular entertainment device in Asia, can be used to help the learner practice the second language through role play and singing. The learner can also engage in interactive games like exercises on a DVD player. The telephone can also be used for learners to interact with artificial intelligence-driven, speech technology-enabled computer systems in the target language.

Evidence of Effectiveness: Research Findings Related to Technology for Communication Practice   Research in this area has also shown some promising results. The following section summarizes some of the recent published studies of using computers to support communication.

Interactions with the Computer.   Communicative interactions can occur in either written or spoken language or a combination of both. At the simplest level, a computer program can generate utterances either orally or in writing that require the learner to respond by selecting an answer with a mouse click or providing simple writing responses (Hanson-Smith, 1999). With the advancement of speech synthesis and recognition technologies (Ehsani & Knodt, 1998), the learner can also carry on near natural conversations with a computer program around preselected and programmed topics (Bernstein, Najmi, & Ehsani, 1999; Egan, 1999; Harless, Zier, & Duncan, 1999; LaRocca, Morgan, & Bellinger, 1999; Wachowicz & Scott, 1999). The learner can also give either a written or spoken command to a computer program in a simulation and game environment. The computer program would then perform the command (Holland, Kaplan, & Sabol, 1999; LaRocca et al., 1999). Harless et al. (1999), for example, tested the effectiveness of a virtual conversation program in Arabic at the Defense Language Institute. The program enabled the students to interview virtual characters of native speakers orally with speech recognition technology. After interacting with these virtual characters for at least eight hours per day for four days, the participants' second language reading and speaking skills increased significantly ($p < 0.05$) while their listening skill increased "convincingly." In another study, Holland and her colleagues (1999) found a speech-enabled interactive microworld program that allowed the adult learners of Arabic to construct objects by speaking to the computer-improved student motivation and oral output (1999).

Interactions with Remote Audiences through the Computer.   Computer-mediated communication and teleconferencing technologies have been used to create authentic communication opportunities for language learners since the 1980s (Beauvois, 1997; Pennington, 1996). The uses of CMC technologies, such as electronic mails, bulletin boards, and chatrooms have been found to have many benefits for language learning (Beauvois, 1997; Cahill & Catanzaro, 1997; Kelm, 1998; Salaberry, 2001; Warschauer, 1998). CMC brings the much-needed interlocutors to the language learner (Johnson, 1999). It also promotes more equal and better participation, leading to more output in the target language (Beauvois, 1997; González-Bueno, 1998). It fosters negotiation and form-focused learning (Pellettieri, 2000). CMC was also found to enhance the writing process and improve student writing (Schultz, 2000). Although CMC communication is, in most cases, conducted in writing, it has been found to improve oral proficiency as well. For instance, Beauvois (1997) found that second year college French learners who held their discussions online achieved better oral proficiency than those who discussed the texts orally in the traditional classroom setting ($p < 0.05$). Rich description about the quantity and quality of the discourse in this particular communication environment and detailed record of the social, motivational, and learning effects of CMC interaction in comparison with its face-to-face counterpart have been made available through more than a decade of research (Blake, 2000; Skinner & Austin, 1999). Research thus far has reported more balanced participation, greater syntactic complexity and lexical change in adult learners' language production, boosted motivation on using the target language and reduced anxiety over classroom participation in CMC interaction (Freiermuth, 2001; Kern, 1995; Warschauer, 1996). Moreover, it fostered development of sociolinguistic and pragmatic competence among second language learners (Abrams, 2001; Smith, 2003) and improved learners' oral communication capacity (Chun, 1994). Some evidence has also been presented in support of the role of CMC interaction in facilitating the acquisition of certain linguistic structures (Salaberry, 2001). All the theorization and empirical evidence advocated the efficacy of the use of communication technologies in promoting second language acquisition.

Interactions around the Technology. Research on communication around technology-based activities suggests that technology-based activities were effective in stimulating interactive talk and the talks were cognitively oriented. Furthermore, the studies found that different configurations of tasks, software type, program design (such as timing of feedback and scoring system) and group make-up, as well as teacher pedagogical support, had different effects on the quality of talk and collaboration (Levy & Hinckfuss, 1990; Mercer et al., 2003; Wild & Braid, 1996). Some studies investigated talk around computer and second language learning in more specific areas. For example, Choi (2001) found that dyads of fourth-graders, English-as-a-foreign-language (EFL) learners in Korea working on English learning software often repeated the utterances from the computer, which facilitated their interaction with each other and their learning of English. Moreover, both members of each pair contributed to solving problems and getting help and giving explanations to each other. Meskill (1992) examined the language produced by second language learners triggered by collaborative computer activities, and concluded that "pairing students at the computer would enhance opportunities for effective practice and motivate extended participation" (p. 8). Thus, current literature suggests that communication around computer-based activities has great potential in facilitating second language learning; however, the success of such learning environments relies to a great extent on contextual factors and the nature of the tasks. For instance, Mercer et al. (2003) summarized their previous observational research and pointed out several important conditions for the effectiveness of communication around computer-based activities, such as activities that encourage cooperation rather than competition, activities that make conversation a must of the task rather than "an incidental accompaniment," and so on (p. 82).

Providing High-quality Feedback

The capacity for technology to provide instant and individualized feedback has long been recognized by educators, including foreign language educators (Salaberry, 2001). Although early applications tended to follow the behaviorist tradition by simply assessing the learner's performance and providing simplistic feedback in a correct-or-wrong fashion, more recent applications are much more contextualized and pedagogically sound (Salaberry, 2001).

Technology holds several important advantages in terms of providing feedback to second language learners. First, technology could present feedback in ways that are difficult, if not impossible, by human beings. One such example is the provision of feedback on pronunciation. Computer technology allows for 3D animated representations of the position and coordinated movement of the tongue, lip, and teeth during the pronunciation of a given sound, which is very vivid and effective in moving learners towards the targeted pronunciation and is difficult to demonstrate with other means. Some pronunciation software, like WinPitchLTL (http://www.winpitch.com/GuideWinPich/WPLTLguide. htm), adopts speech recognition technology to provide interactive feedback that enables learners to input their pronunciation into the computer system and access the comparison of spectrograms and waveforms between their pronunciation and that of a native speaker's. Furthermore, research on cognitive psychology suggests that presenting information in multiple modalities is a way to lower the cognitive load constrained by the limited capacity of working memory (Sweller, Chandler, Tierney, & Cooper, 1990), and empirical evidence has been reported that support the advantage of dual-modality presentation in knowledge retention and transfer (Chandler & Sweller, 1999; Mayer & Moreno, 1998). Technology proffers easy and convenient ways to present feedback concurrently in multiple modes, which is difficult or inefficient to provide in oral conversation or classroom instruction. Last but not the least, technology can provide immediate and individualized feedback based on each learner's performance, which is all but impossible to achieve in classroom instruction. For instance, the Intelligent Language Tutoring System (ILTS) could keep a record of each learner's performance history and provide individualized adaptive feedback through adjusting the specificity of the feedback messages and clues, and so on (Heift, Toole, McFetridge, Popowich, & Tsiplakou, 2000).

Second, technology allows great flexibility in the provision of feedback, flexible in the sense of the great variability and options it provides. Technology could easily vary the types of feedback it provides in response to the specific linguistic items in question, and this adaptability is a plus compared with feedback via other means. Ongoing feedback could also be provided in a way, such as using pop-up windows or highlighting techniques, that minimizes the possibility of interrupting the natural flow of the language activity or learning process. Technology also can add the fun component into feedback provision, immersing learners in a great amount of feedback, implicit or explicit, through entertaining language learning activities, like games or simulations. In addition, the capability of technology in allowing the provision of feedback in multiple modes simultaneously adds greatly to its flexibility. Furthermore, different versions of feedback (e.g., feedback with different levels of specificity; feedback with various degrees of saliency, etc.) on the same linguistic item could be provided, which offers learners options to select the version that works best for them.

This flexibility of feedback provision leads to the third advantage of technology: learner control. Since technology can provide different versions of feedback on the same material, learners are able to customize the feedback system to cater to their own developmental pace, learning styles, and preferences. Learners can even have the control to enable or disable the feedback mechanism in the learning system whenever they want. On the other hand, the capacity of technology in being responsive and providing individualized feedback enables learners to have greater control over their learning process and better manage their learning progress based on the timely and detailed information provided by technology-enabled feedback systems.

The efficiency and convenience of the feedback provided by technology is another advantage. Technology makes feedback widely available just one click away: learners could easily get feedback from simple applications like Microsoft Office tools that contain spell and grammar checkers; CMC tools connect learners with native speakers and other learners, and provide them with another channel of interactive feedback, to list but a few. Moreover, technology, with its tracking capability, helps greatly in the logistics aspect of feedback provision, such as record keeping and progress tracking, and thus frees teachers from these time-consuming chores and provides teachers with valuable resources to better assist students with their language learning. By thus doing, technology-enabled feedback systems could improve the efficiency of language education at large.

Evidence of Effectiveness: Research Findings on Technology and High-quality Feedback   A number of experiments have been conducted to test the effectiveness of using simple and readily available technology for feedback. The following provides a few examples and their outcomes.

Computer-based Grammar Checkers and Spell Checkers.   Computer-based grammar checkers and spell checkers are potentially powerful ways to provide feedback to students' written output (Jacobs & Rodgers, 1999). Although the feedback provided by current grammar checkers is not always accurate, albeit immediate, due to its inability to perform semantic analysis and process deep-level structures, Burston (2001) found that advanced college students of French benefited tremendously from a French grammar checker. In this study, the students in the treatment group used a French grammar checker while writing their essays whereas the control group did not. The results suggest that "the effectiveness of the use of Antidote software in improving morpho-syntactic accuracy in assigned compositions were overwhelmingly positive" (p. 507). The treatment group's first essay scored an average of 70%, compared to 20% of the control group. The second essay showed similar results: an 85% average for the treatment group whereas a 54% average for the control.

Automatic Speech Recognition Technology. Automatic speech recognition technology holds the potential to provide feedback that would otherwise be impossible. Pronunciation is a fundamental element of language learning but to provide feedback that can be easily accessible and useful is difficult. In traditional instructional settings, feedback and modeling is only provided by an instructor who may or may not be good at judging the student pronunciation in the first place. The provision of feedback often includes either repeating the pronunciation or explaining how the sound should be pronounced in a very abstract fashion. With the advancement of speech recognition technology, the student can receive feedback in more effective ways (Dalby & Kewley-Port, 1999; Ehsani & Knodt, 1998; Eskenazi, 1999; Mostow & Aist, 2001). First, a computer program can analyze a student utterance and display the features visually, perhaps with a comparison to that of a native speaker. A computer program can also display the position and movements of the tongue when a student produces an utterance, which can also be displayed in comparison to that of native speakers. Second, computer programs can compare student pronunciation of individual words or sentences to prerecorded templates. For example, good agreement ($r = 0.81$ for high-quality speech and $r - 0.76$ for telephone-quality speech) was found between automatic and human grading of the pronunciation of English sentences produced by Japanese English learners (Bernstein, Cohen, Murveit, Rtischev, & Weintraub, 1990). More recent studies found different levels of correlation between machine and human graders: from 0.44 to 0.85 (Bernstein, 1997; Ehsani & Knodt, 1998). It was also found that such high correlation can be achieved at the discourse level (Coniam, 1998). Third, pronunciation can be evaluated against pronunciation models. In this approach, student pronunciation is not limited to preselected words because the model is a generalization of a template.

Tracking and Analyzing Student Errors and Behaviors. Tracking and analyzing student errors and behaviors is another approach language educators have experimented with so as to provide more helpful feedback. Computer programs can store student responses, which can then be analyzed either by a human instructor (Sinyor, 1997) or the computer (Nagata, 1993). The effectiveness of this approach is yet to be determined although Nagata, summarizing her study findings, suggests "traditional feedback may be as good as the intelligent feedback for helping learners to correct word-level errors (e.g., vocabulary and conjugation errors), whereas the intelligent feedback may be more helpful for understanding and correcting sentence level errors (e.g., particle errors)" (p. 337).

Realizing the Promises: Recommendations for Design, Instruction, Policy, and Research

Thus far we have discussed how technology can be used to enable the necessary conditions for effective second language learning. Within the framework of an effective language learning environment, we also analyzed the potentials of some technologies with reference to currently published studies on the effectiveness of technology for second language learning. Again, it is apparent that today we have available a large set of technologies with tremendous capacities for significantly improving second language learning. However, these potentials cannot be actualized unless we reconsider how we conceptualize, design, develop, and deploy technologies in support of second language teaching and learning. To translate these promises into learning outcomes, a number of changes need to take place in how we think about technology and how we apply it. In this section, we first suggest a few general conceptual changes that should apply to policymakers, researchers, technology designers, as well as teachers. We then recommend a set of specific actions for each group of individuals.

Rethinking Technology for Second Language Education: Conceptual Changes

From Individual Applications to Comprehensive Language Environments. First, we need to change from designing and developing individual technology uses to designing and developing comprehensive second language programs enhanced by technology. Individual, isolated pieces of software or gadgets are unlikely to be adopted or have significant impact on the learning outcomes. Moreover, we cannot, and should not, expect any one piece of technology to deliver the high-quality language learning experiences we desire. Thus, we need to consider designing and developing whole language learning programs that support all aspects and all stages of language learning. We need to have language learning tools and content for the learner in the classroom as well as develop tools and content for learners outside the classroom. At present, it is rare to find a quality technology-enhanced comprehensive program that fulfills such purposes.

As discussed in this chapter, an effective language learning environment should provide high-quality input, ample opportunities for communication and practice, high-quality feedback, and customizable content to maximize motivation. Thus we first need to consider all sorts of technologies for enhancing input—use video, audio, speech technology, and other multimedia technology to bring authentic language and cultural materials to students, use speech rate control technologies to enable the users to manipulate the speed of audio/video input, use digital video technology to focus the learner's attention on desired content, use hyperlink tools to enable the learner to access graphical, audio, visual, and text annotations, use speech technology to enable the learner to control the mode of input by converting written input into oral input and vice and versa, use concordance tools to identify and modify input, and use database technology to allow the learners to access individualized content.

We need also to consider a variety of technologies that can create opportunities for communication and practice. As we have seen in the examples reviewed in the chapter, learners can engage in communications with, through, and around the technology. Simulated conversation agents on the computer, with assistance of speech technologies, can directly communicate with the learner in simulated explorations or tasks. Simpler reading and writing technologies such as the LeapPads[12] and AlphaSmart[13] tools can provide basic interactive functions between the technology and the learner. Computer-mediated-communication technologies, telephones, PDAs, and videoconferencing systems, and other network-enabled devices provide the capacity for learners to communicate with each other and others across distance and time. Technologies also provide the opportunities for learners to communicate in the target language around the content or activity enabled by the technology (for instance, students as a group can gather around to discuss a video clip, a radio story, or an electronic book).

We should also expand our view of technology that can be used to provide high-quality feedback because at different stages of language development and for different users, feedback should take different forms and be delivered in different ways. Speech and sound technologies can give visual feedback on pronunciation and intonation; combined with gaming technologies, speech technology can also provide more engaging feedback in the form of actions and social consequences (e.g., a character can provide further information or perform certain actions on correct or incorrect input from the learner); multimedia technologies can also be used to provide feedback in audio, video, or other interesting formats; database technologies can be employed to provide more relevant and individualized feedback to the learners after analysis of cumulative performances of the learner.

From Classroom to the Whole Learning Process. Second language education does not only occur in the classroom and should not stop after the learner leaves the school. Language learning in classroom situations is restricted by both time and physical constraints, and thus is quite limited in the amount of input, the opportunities for communicative practices, and the feedback that can be made available to the language learners. As Parker points out in her chapter, children may need assistance developing academic English skills outside the school day in order to keep up with their native English speaking peers. Language learning that extends beyond the classroom could not only enrich the amount and quality of the crucial language learning conditions elaborated on previously, but also can help learners to relate their language learning to their personal life and thus perceive more meaning in language learning. Thus an effective language learning program should always include components for uses in and out of the classroom. It should have tools and resources to support instructional and learning activities in the classroom as well as student learning out of the classroom. In other words, technological tools and materials should be designed to be used by students, teachers, and parents/caregivers. And the tools and materials to support learning at school and learning at home should be coherently connected so that the learners could perceive the various components of their language learning experience as meaningful and supportive of each other.

From Technology to a Combination of Technology and Human Instructors. Furthermore, we must consider how human instructors interact with the technology system. We need to think about the different yet complementary roles of technology and human beings. We should not expect that technology alone will deliver effective language learning. With the recognition that technology can significantly enhance the language learning experience, we need to also consider how the human adults (teachers and parents) can work together with the technology to provide effective language education to children. However, we should be mindful of the different contributions technology and human beings can make. As a general suggestion, we should let the technology do things that human beings are unable or unwilling to do or while human beings are able and willing to do, but less efficiently or less effectively. For instance, in the case of foreign language learning where learners have little access to native speakers and have little chance to use the language in authentic contexts, computer-mediated communication and simulation could easily create such language learning experience that would otherwise be difficult, if not impossible, to realize.

From New and Expensive to All Technologies. We need to consider the capacities of all technologies, especially existing and inexpensive ones, instead of only cutting-edge ones, such as the computer and the Internet. Many existing technologies possess tremendous potential for language education due to their portability and availability, and more importantly, familiarity to the learner.

For example, the television can be a simple and effective platform for delivering authentic language and cultural materials. It is an existing platform and simple to operate. What is, however, needed is to develop engaging and educational content. The content needs to be linguistically, culturally, and developmentally appropriate. But it should not be simple dry lectures. Good language education content can come in the formats of TV shows for children (e.g., *Sesame Street*, *Sagwa*, and *Dragon Tale*). Other home entertainment technologies, such as compact disc (CD) and DVD players should also be considered as language technologies that can be used to deliver high-quality input.

What is especially worth pursuing is videogame consoles. An estimate of 70% of American households own at least one game console but very often these powerful machines are used to deliver entertainment rather than educational content. These machines are perfect for creating powerful language learning materials to learners who may already be familiar with the system.

It is also worth special noting that a new line of very affordable educational/entertainment or edutainment technologies have emerged recently. One example is the LeadPad by LeapFrog. At a market price of about $40, these devices can achieve most of the functions of the popular Living Books—a CD-ROM-based product line that allows the user to listen and read a book and to interact with the content and texts. Many similar products have been developed by others (e.g., Fisher Price's PowerTouch, http://www.fisher-price.com/us/powertouch/default_flash.asp).

From Instructional Technology to Learning Technology. Moreover, we need to reconsider the pedagogy of technology-enhanced language learning. Traditionally much effort has been focused on developing and using technology to assist instruction or as instruction, but what is important is to consider technology as providing language and cultural experiences as well as tools to learn from these experiences for the learner. What has gradually emerged as a viable and promising educational approach in this regard in recent years for technology-enhanced language education is gaming and simulation. For example, the U.S.–China Elanguage project has taken a gaming approach toward second language education. Designed as an adventure game, the software employs a multitude of technologies to help the students learn Chinese or English as a second language.

Recommendations for Policy, Research, and Practice

A number of actions can be taken at multiple levels to reflect these recommended conceptual changes. First, policymakers at public and private funding agencies should consider investing in a limited number of large-scale research and development programs that focus on designing and evaluating comprehensive language learning programs enhanced by technology. Traditional development in this field has been fragmented, resulting in many low-level repetition of development. Funding agencies (government and foundations) have often invested in individual projects that result in individual pieces of software or content, but history has proven that these fragmented, scattered development efforts cannot amount to significant changes in second language education.

Second, policymakers should consider supporting language education initiatives undertaken by coalitions of institutions, including traditional broadcasting agencies such as public television and radio stations for their broad reach, traditional textbook publishers for their content expertise and presence in schools, traditional language software companies for their experiences with multimedia technologies, and schools for their role in delivering language education.

Third, online education should be considered a viable way to deliver effective language education. Today technology has developed to such a level of sophistication that high-quality language learning can be provided virtually through computer networks. Online language courses can also have the potential to integrate multiple technologies and reach learners who may otherwise not have the opportunity to learn a foreign or second language. However, some may still remain doubtful of the effectiveness of online language courses. Thus it is important for policies that recognize the capacity of technology for delivering quality language programs online.

Fourth, research on technology and language education should orient itself toward a set of new issues brought about by the conceptual changes discussed earlier. How different technologies interact with and complement each other to create effective language learning environments, for example, has become an important issue but has rarely been explored. Due to the differences in function, cost, and demand of user abilities, different technologies should play different roles in supporting language learning. It is hence important to understand how these different technologies work together and how they may be combined to achieve most learning at minimal cost. Another important issue is how learners interact with different technologies. As we know, due to differences in proficiency level, age, learning styles, familiarity with technology, and access to technology, different learners can benefit from different technologies or different combination of technologies. In order to maximize the effects of technology, we need to know what technologies or combination thereof help what types of learners for what language goals. A final example of emerging issues is the relationship between teachers and technology. As technology becomes more prominent in providing language learning, the role of the teacher changes but this does not mean human teachers will or should disappear. Instead, we need to understand what new skills and abilities teachers need to teach in a technology environment where the human instructor serves more of the role of coordinating and designing than instructing and how teachers learn to shift their roles.

Lastly, teachers need to consider themselves as designers rather than adopters of technology. Traditionally teachers have been cast as either the gatekeepers or the adopters of new technologies. In other words, teachers are only there to passively accept or reject technological innovations. Today several changes in technology make it possible for teachers to become active designers of the learning environment instead of making the simple decision of adopting or rejecting. Technology has become increasingly available, many at low or no cost, thus teachers can pick and choose what technology to use without worrying too much about cost and access. Technology has also become simpler to use and less mysterious to ordinary teachers and in the meantime teachers' overall technology proficiency has improved, hence they are capable of making more informed decisions without relying on technology experts. These changes have made it possible for teachers to become designers of a language learning environment. Teachers therefore should take advantage of these changes and start designing language learning programs that suit their own contexts.

Conclusion: An Example of Ideal Technology-Supported Language Learning System

We believe we have developed sufficient knowledge about what makes an effective language learning environment and what technologies may be useful for language education, we have also learned enough from past experience that coherent programs that connect school and home are most effective for learning. It is time that we moved to create a comprehensive, coherent language learning environment that reflects our best knowledge of language acquisition, education, child development, and technology.

While there are many possible conceptualizations of such an ideal system, based on what we have discussed so far in this chapter, we think such a system should have the following elements:

A TV show to expose children to language and culture in context. The TV show would have a well-designed curriculum presented in an entertaining and engaging format to children.

DVD/CD products of the TV content and additional learning materials, including participatory activities such as family-style Karaoke activities, simple language, and cultural games.

Video games based on the TV show to engage students in language exercises.

Books and other print materials to expand and extend the TV content for students to use at home and in classes.

Teaching materials and tools for teachers to use in class with students.

Books and materials delivered with sound and activities on inexpensive reading devices such as PowerTouch and LeapPads.

Computer software for individual learner uses and teacher uses.
Toys and other objects that are based on the TV show content and characters for students to play with language.

Although we have not seen such a comprehensive language education program, the *Magic School Bus* series for science education comes closest to what we are proposing. It was a TV show on PBS, accompanied by books, a magazine, and activities materials, as well as computer games. In the comprehensive language education program just proposed, the materials that could be potentially used and elaborated in the classroom under the guidance of the instructor, such as related books and print materials, teaching materials, computer software, etc., and those that could be used and enjoyed out of class together with other peers and parents, such as related games, Karaoke activities, toys, etc., form a coherent language learning ecology around the anchor TV shows. Learning activities at school and at home reinforce each other and elaborate on each other, making the whole language learning experience rich and engaging.

Such comprehensive language learning programs rely on pedagogically sound selection and combination of individual technologies. The success of this type of comprehensive language learning environment needs to build on research findings that guide the pedagogical interpretations of the capacity of individual technologies and be informed by research that examines how different technologies may work together and explores ways of combining different technologies effectively and efficiently.

Notes

1. *Interlanguage* is a commonly used term in the second language acquisition literature. It is used to refer to the systematic knowledge of a second language which is independent of both the learner's first language and the target language (Selinker, 1972). Interlanguage "is composed of numerous elements, not the least of which are elements from the NL (native language) and the TL (target language). There are also elements in the IL (interlanguage) that do not have their origin in either the NL or the TL" (Gass & Selinker, 2001, p. 12).
2. *Intake* is a term used to refer the input that is internalized by the learner. This term was coined to distinguish between language input (exposure to a language) and actual learning, or in simpler words, between what the learner is exposed to and what the learner takes in.
3. A handheld video game player manufactured by Nintendo.
4. X-Box is a video game player developed by Microsoft.
5. A videogame player manufactured by Nintendo.
6. QuickLink pen is a series of hand-held, pen-like devices that can scan and process text and, depending on the specific product, can translate the scanned text into different languages, or read out the scanned text. More information can be found at: http://www.wizcomtech.com/.

7. Enounce and SoundEditor are software programs that enable the user to manipulate the speed of digitalized language, making the speech faster or slower.

8. A concordance is an alphabetical index of all the words in a text or corpus of texts, showing every contextual occurrence of a word. Concordances can be very useful for language teaching in a number of ways: (a) allow students to see how words or phrases are used in different contexts; (b) allow teachers to select authentic examples of language uses; and (c) allow teachers to develop better instructional materials. Computer technology can be used to create concordances more efficiently. There are now many computer programs that can be used to create concordances. Concordancer and ParaConc are just two examples.

9. Corpus of Spoken Professional American-English is developed by Athelstan. It selects from existing transcripts of interaction in professional settings, such as faculty council meetings, committee meetings, and White House press conferences and so on, and contains around two million words.

10. Chengo is an ongoing project sponsored by the U.S. Department of Education and the Chinese Ministry of Education that aims to provide second language instruction to middle school students in China and the United States via the Internet. The U.S. Department of Education is responsible for developing content for English learners in China and the Chinese Ministry of Education Chinese content for Chinese learners in the United States. It uses animation and simulation extensively to engage students in a videogame fashion. The original plan was to produce 36 episodes that would help learners with zero proficiency to lower intermediate level proficiency in the target language. The program has passed and is still under development. A few episodes have been piloted in a very limited number of focus-group sessions.

11. Originated in Japan, Karaoke is a technology now widely used in many countries for entertainment. The word "karaoke" comes from "kara," empty (as in karate–empty hand) and "oke" (short for okesutora), orchestra. Rather than including both vocals and music, karaoke tracks only have the music. The vocals are provided by a live person (not a professional) who holds a microphone and sings while following the words displayed on a screen or in a book. This can be used by language learners to practice speaking.

12. LeapPad is a series of devices developed by LeapFrog (http://www.leapfrog.com) that enables the user to use a "magic pen" to retrieve stored sound files by touching an area of the book placed on a platform. As such, the content of the stored files and books can be different. Over the past few years, LeapPad has evolved into different lines of products for different age groups. The device is inexpensive (about $40 U.S.), simple to operate, and holds great potentials for language learning, especially for young children. Fisher Price has developed a similar line of products called PowerTouch.

13. AlphaSmart was first developed as a storage device with simple word processing capacities that would allow the user to write down ideas and upload to a computer. Over the years, it has added more powerful and wireless networking capabilities and other functions such as e-mail. It can be used as a low-cost, portable language learning device, especially for teaching writing. More information can be found at: http://www1.alphasmart.com/.

References

Abams, Z. I. (2001). Computer-mediated communication and group journals: Expanding the repertoire of participant roles. *System, 29,* 489–503.

Al-Seghayer, K. (2001). The effect of multimedia annotation modes on L2 vocabulary acquisition: A comparative study. *Language Learning and Technology,* 5, 1, 202–232.

Bacon, S. & Finnemann, M. (1990). A study of the attitudes, motives, and strategies of university foreign language students and their disposition to authentic oral and written input. *Modern Language Journal, 74,* 459–473.

Beauvois, M. H. (1997). Computer-mediated communication: Technology for improving speaking and writing. In M. D. Bush (Ed.), *Technology enhanced language learning* (pp. 165–184). Lincolnwood, IL: National Textbook Company.

Bernstein, J. (1997). *Automatic spoken language assessment by telephone* (Tech. Rep. No. 5–97). Menlo Park, CA: Entropic, Inc.

Bernstein, J., Cohen, M., Murveit, H., Rtischev, D., & Weintraub, M. (1990). Automatic evaluation and training in English pronunciation. Paper presented at the *International Conference on Spoken Language Processing (ICSLP),* Kobe, Japan. November 18–22.

Bernstein, J., Najmi, A., & Ehsani, F. (1999). Subarashii: Encounters in Japanese spoken language education. *CALICO Journal,* 16(3), 361–384.

Blake, R. (2000). Computer mediated communication: A window on L2 Spanish interlanguage. *Language Learning & Technology,* 4, 120–136.

Branaman, L., Rhodes, N., & Rennie, J. (1998). A national survey of K–12 foreign language education. *ERIC Review,* 6(1), 13.

Brown, A. (1992). Design experiments: Theoretical and methodological challenges in creating complex interventions in classroom settings. *The Journal of the Learning Sciences,* 2(2), 141–178.

Burston, J. (2001). Exploiting the potential of a computer-based grammar checker in conjunction with self-monitoring strategies with advanced level students of French. *CALICO Journal,* 18(3), 499–515.

Cahill, D., & Catanzaro, D. (1997). Teaching first-year Spanish online. *CALICO Journal,* 14(2), 97–114.

Candlin, C. N., & Mercer, N. (2001). *English language teaching in its social context: A reader.* London and New York: Routledge.

Carroll, S. E. (2001). *Input and evidence: The raw material of second language acquisition.* Philadelphia: John Benjamins.

Carroll, S. E., & Swain, M. (1993). Explicit and implicit negative feedback: An empirical study of the learning of linguistic generalisations. *Studies in Second Language Acquisition,* 15(2), 357–386.

Celce-Murcia, M. (2001). Language teaching approach: An overview. In M. Celce-Murcia (Ed.), *Teaching English as a second or foreign language* (pp. 1–3). Boston: Heinle & Heinle.

Chandler, P., & Sweller, J. (1996). Cognitive load while learning to use a computer program. *Applied Cognitive Psychology,* 10(2), 151–170.

Chapelle, C. A. (2001). *Computer applications in second language acquisition: Foundations for teaching, testing, and research.* Cambridge, MA: Cambridge University Press.

Choi, H. (2001). *Peer interaction at the computer: Korean primary school children working with software for learning English.* Unpublished doctoral dissertation, Columbia University, Teachers College.

Chun, D. M. (1994). Using computer networking to facilitate the acquisition of interactive competence. *System,* 22(1), 17–31.

Chun, D. M., & Plass, J. L. (1997). Research on text comprehension in multimedia environments. *Language Learning and Technology,* 1(1), 60–81.

Cobb, P., Confrey, J., DiSessa, A., Lehrer, R., & Schauble, L. (2003). Design experiments in educational research. *Educational Researcher,* 32(1), 9–13.

Cohen, V. B. (1985). A reexamination of feedback in computer-based instruction: Implications for instructional design. *Educational Technology, January,* 33–37.

Coniam, D. (1998). The use of speech recognition software as an English language oral assessment instrument: An Exploratory Study. *CALICO Journal,* 15(4), 7–24.

Csikszentmihalyi, M. (1991). *Flow: The psychology of optimal experience.* New York: HarperCollins.

Csikszentmihalyi, M. (1996). *Creativity: Flow and the psychology of discovery and invention.* New York: HarperCollins.

Cziko, G. A. & Park, S. J. (2003). Internet audio communication for second language learning: A comparative review of six programs. Language *Learning and Technology,* 7, 1, 15–27.

Dalby, J., and Kewley-Port, D. (1999). Explicit pronunciation training using automatic speech recognition. *CALICO Journal,* 16, 425–445.

Doughty, C., & Varela, E. (1998). Communicative focus on form. In C. Doughty & J. Williams (Eds.), *Focus on form in classroom second language acquisition* (pp. 114–138). New York: Cambridge University Press.

Doughty, C., & Williams, J. (1998). *Focus on form in classroom second language acquisition.* NY: Cambridge University Press.

Egan, K. B. (1999). Speaking: A critical skill and a challenge. *CALICO Journal,* 16(3), 277–293.

Egbert, J., Chao, C.-c., & Hanson-Smith, E. (1999). Computer-enhanced language learning environment: An overview. In J. Egbert & E. Hanson-Smith (Eds.), *CALL environments: Research, practice and critical issues* (pp. 1–16). Alexandria, VA: TESOL.

Egbert, J,. & Hanson-Smith, E. (1999). *CALL environments: Research, practice, and critical issues.* Virginia: TESOL Publications.

Ehsani, F., & Knodt, E. (1998). Speech technology in computer-aided language learning: Strengths and limitations of a new CALL paradigm. *Language Learning and Technology,* 2(1), 45–60.

Ellis, R., Tanaka, Y. & Yamazaki, A. (1994). Classroom interaction, comprehension, and the acquisition of L2 word meanings. *Language Learning,* 44, 449–491.

Ellis, R., & He, X. (1999). The roles of modified input and output in the incidental acquisition of word meanings. *Studies of Second Language Acquisition,* 21, 285–301.

Ellis, R., Basturkmen, H., & Loewen, S. (2001). Preemptive focus on form in the ESL classroom. *TESOL Quarterly,* 35, 407–432.

Eskenazi, M. (1999). Using automatic speech processing for foreign language pronunciation tutoring: Some issues and a prototype. *Language Learning and Technology,* 2(2), 62–76.

Farley, A. P. (2005). *Structured input: Grammar instruction for the acquisition-oriented classroom.* Boston: McGraw-Hill.

Felix, U. (2002). The web as a vehicle for constructivist approaches in language teaching. *ReCALL,* 14, 1, 2–15.

Fischer, P. M., & Mandl, H. (1988). Knowledge acquisition by computerized audiovisual feedback. *European Journal of Psychologies of Education,* 3,(2), 217–232.

Freeman, M. A., & Capper, J. M. (1999). Exploiting the web for education: An anonymous asynchronous role simulation. *Australian Journal of Educational Technology,* 15(1), 95–116.

Freiermuth, M. (2001). Native speaker or non-native speakers: Who has the floor? Online and face-to-face interaction in culturally mixed small groups. *Computer Assisted Language Learning,* 14(2), 169–199.

García Carbonell, A., Rising, B., Montero, B., & Watts, F. (2001). Simulation/gaming and the acquisition of communicative competence in another language. *Simulation and Gaming,* 32(4), 481–491.

Gass, S. M. (1988). Integrating research areas: A framework for second language studies. *Applied Linguistics,* 9,198–217.

Gass, S. M. (1997). *Input, interaction and the second language learner.* Mahwah, NJ: Erlbaum.

Gass, S. M., & Selinker, L. (2001). *Second language acquisition: An introductory course* (2nd ed.). Mahwah, NJ: Erlbaum.

Gass, S. M., & Varonis, E. (1994). Input, interaction and second language production. *Studies in Second Language Acquisition,* 16, 283–301.

Godwin-Jones, B. (2001). Emerging technologies: E-books and the Tablet PC. *Language Learning and Technology,* 5(3), 7–12.

González-Bueno, M. (1998). The effects of electronic mail on Spanish L2 discourse. *Language Learning and Technology,* 1(2), 55–70.

Green, A., & Youngs, B. E. (2000). Using the Web in elementary French and German courses: Quantitative and qualitative study results. *CALICO Journal,* 19(1), 89–123.

Greeno, J. G., Collins, A. M., & Resnick, L. B. (1996). Cognition and learning. In D. Berliner & R. Calfee (Eds.), *Handbook of Educational Psychology* (pp. 15–41). New York: Macmillan.

Hanson-Smith, E. (1999). Classroom practice: Content area tasks in CALL environments. In J. Egbert & E. H. Smith (Eds.), *CALL Environments* (pp. 116–136). Bloomington, IL: TESOL.

Harless, W. G., Zier, M. A., & Duncan, R. C. (1999). Virtual dialogues with native speakers: The evaluation of an interactive multimedia method. *CALICO Journal,* 16(3), 313–337.

Hatch, E. (1978). Discourse analysis, speech acts and second language acquisition. In W. Ritchie (Eds.), *Second language acquisition research* (pp. 137–55). New York: Academic Press.

Healey, D. (1999). Classroom practice: Communicative skill-building tasks in CALL environments. In J. Egbert & E. Hanson-Smith (Eds.), *CALL Environments: Research, Practice, and Critical Issues* (pp. 302–314). Virginia: TESOL Publications.

Heift, T., Toole, J., McFetridge, P., Popowich, F., & Tsiplakou, S. (2000). Learning Greek with an adaptive and intelligent hypermedia system. *Interactive Multimedia Electronic Journal of Computer-Enhanced Learning,* 2, 2.

Herron, C., Cole, S. P., Corrie, C., & Dubreil, S. (1999). The effectiveness of a video-based curriculum in teaching culture. *Modern Language Journal,* 83(4), 518–533.

Herron, C., Dubreil, S., Cole, S. P., & Corrie, C. (2000). Using instructional video to teach culture to beginning foreign language students. *CALICO Journal,* 17(3), 395–430.

Holland, V. M., Kaplan, J. D., & Sabol, M. A. (1999). Preliminary tests of language learning in a speech-interactive graphics microworld. *CALICO Journal,* 16(3), 339–359.

Iwashita, N. (2003). Negative feedback and positive evidence in task-based interaction: Differential effects on L2 development. *Studies in Second Language Acquisition,* 25, 1–36.

Jacobs, G., & Rodgers, C. (1999). Treacherous allies: Foreign language grammar checkers. *CALICO Journal,* 16(4), 509–530.

Johnson, B. (1999). Theory and research: classroom atmosphere. In J. Egbert & E. Hanson-Smith (Eds.), *CALL environments: Research, practice, and critical issues.* Virginia: TESOL Publications.

Kalyuga, S., Chandler, P., & Sweller, J. (1999). Managing split-attention and redundancy in multimedia instruction. *Applied Cognitive Psychology,* 13, 351–371.

Kelm, O. R. (1998). The use of electronic mail in foreign language classes. In K. Arens (Ed.), *Language Learning Online* (pp. 141–154). Austin TX: The Daedalus Group Inc.

Kern, R. G. (1995). Restructuring classroom interaction with networked computers: Effects on quantity and characteristics of language production. *Modern Language Journal,* 79(4), 457–476.

Kern, R., & Warschauer, M. (2000). Introduction: Theory and practice of network-based language teaching. In M. Warschauer & R. Kern (Eds.), *Network-Based Language Teaching: Concepts and Practice* (pp. 1–19). NY: Cambridge University Press.

Kitajima, R., & Lyman-Hager, M. A. (1998). Theory-driven use of digital video in foreign language instruction. *CALICO Journal,* 16(1), 37–48.

Krashen, S. (1985). *The input hypothesis: Issues and implications.* London: Longman Press.

Krashen, S. (1977) The monitor model for adult second language performance. In M. Burt, H. Dulay, & M. Finocchiaro (Eds.) *Viewpoints in English as a second language* (pp. 152–161). New York: Regents.

Labrie, G. (2000). A French vocabulary tutor for the web. *CALICO Journal,* 17(3), 475–499.

Lafford, P. A., & Lafford, B. A. (1997). Learning language and culture with the Internet. In R. M. Terry (Ed.), *Technology-Enhanced Language Learning* (pp. 215–262). Lincolnwood, IL: The National Textbook Company.

Lantolf, J. P. (1994). Sociocultural theory and second language learning: Introduction to the special issue. *Modern Language Journal,* 78, 418–420.

LaRocca, S. A., Morgan, J. J., & Bellinger, S. M. (1999). On the path to 2X learning: Exploring the possibilities of advanced speech recognition. *CALICO Journal,* 16(3), 295–309.

Larsen-Freeman, D., & Long, M. H. (1991). *An introduction to second language acquisition research.* New York: Longman.

Lee, L. (1998). Going beyond classroom learning: Acquiring cultural knowledge via online newspapers and intercultural exchanges via online chatrooms. *CALICO Journal,* 16(2), 101–120.

Levy, M. (1997). *Computer-assisted language learning: Context and conceptualization.* Oxford, UK: Oxford University Press.

Levy, M., & Hinckfuss, J. (1990). Program design and student talk at computers. *CAELL Journal,* 1, 4, 21–26.

Long, M. H. (1983). Linguistic and conversational adjustments to non-native speakers. *Studies of Second Language Acquisition,* 5, 177–193.

Long, M. H. (1996). The role of the linguistic environment in second language acquisition. In W. C. Ritchie, & T. K. Bhatia (Eds.), *Handbook of second language acquisition* (pp. 413–454). London: Academic Press, Inc.

Long, M. H. (1998). *Task-based language teaching.* Oxford, UK: Blackwell.

Long, M. H., Inagaki, S., & Ortega, L. (1998). The role of implicit negative feedback in SLA: Models and recasts in Japanese and Spanish. *Modern Language Journal, 82*, 357–371.

Lyman-Hager, M. A. (2000). Bridging the language-literature gap: Introducing literature electronically to the undergraduate language student. *CALICO Journal, 17,* 3, 431–452.

Macheak, T. (2002). *Learner vs. instructor correction in adult second language acquisition: Effects of oral feedback type on the learning of French grammar.* Unpublished doctoral dissertation, Purdue University.

MacIntyre, P. D., Clement, R., Dornyei, Z., & Noels, K. A. (1998). Conceptualizing willingness to communicate in a L2: A situational model of L2 confidence and affiliation. *Modern Language Journal, 82*, 545–562.

Mackey, A. (1999). Input, interaction, and second language development–an empirical study of question formation in ESL. *Studies in Second Language Acquisition, 21,* 557–587.

Mackey, A., Gass, S., & McDonough, K. (2000). Learners' perceptions about feedback. *Studies in Second Language Acquisition, 22,* 471–497.

Mackey, A., & Oliver, R. (2002). Interactional feedback and children's L2 development. *System, 30*(4), 460–477.

Mackey, A., Oliver, R., & Leeman, J. (2003). Interactional input and the incorporation of feedback: An exploration of NS–NNS and NNS–NNS adult and child dyads. *Language Learning, 53*(1), 35–66.

Mackey, A., & Philp, J. (1998). Conversational interaction and second language development: Recasts, responses, and red herrings? *Modern Language Journal, 82,* 338–356.

Mayer, R. E., & Moreno, R. (1998). A split-attention effect in multimedia learning: Evidence for dual processing systems in working memory. *Journal of Educational Psychology, 90,* 312–320.

Mercer, N., Fernandez, M., Dawes, L., Wegerif, R., & Sams, C. (2003). Talk about texts at the computer: Using ICT to develop children's oral and literate abilities. *Reading Literacy and Language,* July, 81–89.

Meskill, C. (1992). Off-screen talk and CALL: Role of the machine/participant. *CAELL Journal, 3*(1), 2–9.

Mostow, J., Aist, G. (2001) Evaluating tutors that listen: An overview of project LISTEN. In K. Forbus and P. Feltovich (Eds.) *Smart machines in education: The coming revolution in educational technology* (pp. 169–234). Menlo Park, CA: MIT/AAAI Press.

Muyskens, J. A. (1998). *New ways of learning and teaching: Focus on technology and foreign language education.* Boston: Heinle & Heinle.

Nagata, N. (1993). Intelligent computer feedback for second language acquisition. *The Modern Language Journal, 77,* 330–339.

Nagata, N. (1995). An effective application of natural language processing in second language instruction. *CALICO Journal, 13,* 1, 47–67.

Nicholas, H., Lightbown, P. M., & Spada, N. (2001). Recasts as feedback to language learners. *Language Learning*, 51, 4, 719–758.

Norris, J. M., & Ortega, L. (2000). Effectiveness of L2 instruction: A research synthesis and quantitative meta-analysis. *Language Learning*, 50(3), 417–528.

Nutta, J. (1998). Is computer-based grammar instruction as effective as teacher-directed grammar instruction for teaching L2 structures? *CALICO Journal*, 16(1), 49–61.

Ohta, A. S. (2000). Rethinking interaction in SLA: Developmentally appropriate assistance in the zone of proximal development and the acquisition of L2 grammar. In J. P. Lantolf (Ed.). *Sociocultural theory and second language learning* (pp. 51–78). Oxford, MA: Oxford University Press.

Oliver, R. (2000). Age differences in negotiation and feedback in classroom and pairwork. *Language Learning*, 50, 119–151.

Oxford, R. L. (1990). *Language learning strategies: What every teacher should know*. New York: Newbury House.

Pellettieri, J. (2000). Negotiation in cyberspace: The role of chatting in the development of grammatical competence. In M. Warschauer & R. Kern (Eds.), *Network-based language teaching: Concepts and practices* (pp. 59–86). Cambridge, UK: Cambridge University Press.

Pennington, M. C. (1996). The power of the computer in language education. In M. C. Pennington (Ed.), *The power of CALL* (pp. 1–14). Houston, TX: Athelstan.

Philp, J. (2003). Constraints on "noticing the gap": Nonnative speakers' noticing of recasts in NS–NNS interaction. *Studies of Second Language Acquisition*, 25, 99–126.

Pica, T., Lincoln-Porter, F., Paninos, D., & Linnell, J. (1996). Language learners' interaction: How does it address the input, output, and feedback needs of L2 learners? *TESOL Quarterly*, 30, 1, 59–84.

Reppen, R. (2001). Review of Monoconc Pro and Wordsmith tools. *Language Learning and Technology*, 5(3), 32–36.

Romiszowski, A. J., & Mason, R. (1996). Computer-mediated communication. In D. H. Jonassen (Ed.), *The handbook of research for educational communications and technology* (pp. 438–456). New York: Simon & Schuster Macmillan.

Salaberry, M. R. (1996). A theoretical foundation for the development of pedagogical tasks in computer mediated communication. *CALICO Journal*, 14(1), 5–34.

Salaberry, M. R. (2001). The use of technology for second language learning and teaching: A retrospective. *The Modern Language Journal*, 85(1), 39–56.

Sauvignon, S. (2001). Communicative language teaching for the twenty-first century. In M. Celce-Murcia (Ed.), *Teaching English as a second or foreign language*. (pp. 3–13). Boston: Heinle & Heinle.

Schachter, J. (1991). Corrective feedback in historical perspective. *Second Language Research*, 7, 89–102.

Schmidt, R. W. (1990). The role of consciousness in second language learning. *Applied Linguistics*, 11, 129–158.

Schmidt, R. W. (2001). Attention. In P. Robinson (Ed.), *Cognition and second language instruction* (pp. 3–32). New York: Cambridge University Press.

Schultz, J. (2000). Computers and collaborative writing in the foreign language curriculum. In M. Warschauer & R. Kern (Eds.), *Network-based language teaching: Concepts and practice*. (pp. 121–150). New York: Cambridge University Press.

Selinker, L. (1972). Interlanguage. *International Review of Applied Linguistics* (10), 209–231.

Shea, P. (2000). Leveling the playing field: A study of captioned interactive video for second language learning. *Journal of Educational Computing Research,* 22(3), 243–263.

Sinyor, R. (1997). An analysis of student behavior and error sources in an Italian CALL context. *CALICO Journal,* 14(2–4), 35–50.

Skehan, P. (1998). *A cognitive approach to language learning.* Oxford, UK: Oxford University Press.

Skinner, B., & Austin, R. (1999). Computer conferencing–Does it motivate EFL students? *ELT Journal,* 53, 270–277.

Smith, B. (2003). Computer-mediated negotiated interaction: An expanded model. *Modern Language Journal,* 87(1), 38–57.

Surry, D. W., & Ensminger, D. (2001). What's wrong with media comparison studies? *Educational Technology,* July–August, 32–35.

Swain, M. (1993). The output hypothesis: just speaking and writing aren't enough. *The Canadian Modern Language Review,* 50, 158–164.

Swain, M. (1995). Three functions of output in second language learning. In G. Cook & B. Seidlhofer (Eds.), *Principle and practice in applied linguistics: studies in honour of H. G. Widdowson* (pp. 125–144). Oxford, UK: Oxford University Press.

Sweller, J., Chandler, P., Tierney, P., & Cooper, M. (1990). Cognitive load as a factor in the structuring of technical material. *Journal of Experimental Psychology: General,* 119(2), 176–192.

Taylor, M. (1990). Simulations and adventure games in CALL. *Simulation and Gaming,* 21(4), 461–466.

Thorton, P., & Dudley, A. (1996). The CALL environment: An alternative to the language lab. *CAELL Journal,* 7(4), 29–34.

Trahey, M., & White, L. (1993). Positive evidence and preemption in the second language classroom. *Studies of Second Language Acquisition,* 15, 2, 181–204.

U.S. Census Bureau. (2001). *Home computer and internet uses in the United States: August 2000.* Washington DC: Author.

VanPatten, B. (1996). *Input processing and grammar instruction.* Norwood, NJ: Ablex.

VanPatten, B. (2000). Thirty years of input. In B. Swierzbin, F. Morris, M. E. Anderson, C. A. Klee, & E. Tarone (Eds.) *Social and cognitive factors in second language acquisition: Selected proceedings of the 1999 Second Language Research Forum* (pp. 287–311). Somerville, MA: Cascadilla.

Vygotsky, L. S. (1981). The genesis of higher mental functions. In J. V. Wertsch (Ed.), *The concept of activity in soviet psychology.* (pp. 144–188). Armonk, NY: M. E. Sharpe.

Wachowicz, K. A. & Scott, B. (1999). Software that listens: It's not a question of whether, it's a question of how. *CALICO Journal,* 16(3), 253–276.

Warschauer, M. (1996). Computer-assisted language learning: An introduction. In S. Fotos (Ed.), *Multimedia Language Teaching* (pp. 3–20). Tokyo: Logos International.

Warschauer, M. (1998). Researching technology in TESOL: Determinist, instrumental and critical approaches. *TESOL Quarterly,* 32(4), 757–761.

Warschauer, M., & Kern, R. (2000). *Network-based language teaching.* Cambridge, UK: Cambridge University Press.

Weyers, J. R. (1999). The effects of authentic video on communicative competence. *Modern Language Journal, 83*(3), 339–349.

White, L. (1987). Against comprehensible input: The input hypothesis and the development of second language competence. *Applied Linguistics, 8,* 95–110.

White, L. (1991). Adverb placement in second language acquisition: Some effects of positive and negative evidence in the classroom. *Second Language Research, 7*(2), 133–161.

White, L. (1998, October). Universal grammar in second language acquisition: The nature of interlanguage representation. Paper presented at the UG Access In L2 Acquisition: Reassessing The Question. Second Language Research Forum, University of Hawai'i at Manoa, 15–18 October, 1998.

Wild, M., & Braid, P. (1996). Children's talk in cooperative groups. *Journal of Computer-Assisted Learning, 12*(4), 216–231.

Zhao, Y. (1997). The effects of listener's control of speech rate on second language comprehension. *Applied Linguistics, 18*(1), 49–68.

Zhao, Y. (2003a). Recent developments in technology and language learning: A literature review and meta-analysis. *CALICO Journal, 21*(1), 7–27.

Zhao, Y. (2003b). *What should teachers know about technology: Perspectives and practices.* Greenwich, CT: Information Age Publishing.

REFLECTION

Technology and Second Language Learning
Current Resources, Tools and Techniques

GARY A. CZIKO

University of Illinois at Urbana–Champaign

Firmly based on what current theory and research tell us about the conditions for efficient and successful language learning, Zhao and Lai's chapter provides an excellent point of departure for both teachers who are beginning to use technology for language teaching and language instructors looking for ways to expand the role of technology in their teaching.

The purpose of this reflection is to expand on certain themes raised by Zhao and Lai and describe a number of resources, tools and techniques that teachers may find especially useful in motivating young learners of English to improve their language abilities throughout their school years and beyond. This is done from a perspective that recognizes young English learners as purposeful learners who develop skills and knowledge that are appropriate to their own interests and goals. Also presented is a means (namely the ATALL Wikibook, http://en.wikibooks.org/wiki/ATALL) by which language teachers and learners can keep abreast of the latest developments in the use of technology for language learning and contribute their own knowledge and experiences to the language teaching community.

Language Learning: Purposeful and Goal-Directed

I wish to emphasize at the outset my belief that learning is best understood as a purposeful, goal-directed activity. Although incidental learning can occur (for example, learning with no clear intent to do so the words to a catchy jingle played in a TV commercial), whenever considerable new knowledge or a complex new skill is learned, it is learned for a reason or purpose. The motivation for learning may be "extrinsic" such as getting a good grade in a high school French class or more "intrinsic" such as a desire to know more about a favorite sports team, athlete or entertainer or to communicate with a friend. Although not dealing specifically with language learning, Powers (1973, 1998) provides a useful and well-supported framework for understanding how human behavior is motivated by an attempt to control some aspect of one's environment.

In the case of language learning, it is important to understand that language is the primary tool used by our species for the acquisition of new knowledge and skills, social interaction and bonding, and control of one's social and physical environment. Although certain individuals may develop a deep interest in a language and endeavor to learn all they can about it, for most individuals language is "simply" a tool that allows them to learn about their social and physical environment, interact with it, and control certain aspects of it.

Seen from this perspective, a powerful approach to motivating a young student's language learning is for the teacher to attempt to see the world from the student's perspective in order to discover the student's interests and goals and to subsequently show to the student how language can be used (and the prerequisite knowledge and skills developed) to support these interests and attain these goals. Thus the importance that Zhao and Lai attribute to the individualization of instruction to meet the abilities, interests and goals of language learners. The wide availability of computer technology, in particular the diverse multimedia resources of the Internet, allows for the individualization of language learning on an unprecedented scale. Indeed, the case could be made that all language learners should learn how to find and use the technological tools and resources that will allow them to control and individualize their own language learning as autonomous learners. Let us now take a look at some of these resources.

Input

There is widespread agreement among language acquisition researchers today that extensive and appropriate exposure to a language (i.e., language input in aural and/or written form) is needed for language acquisition to take place. Fortunately, today's multimedia Internet provides an amazing variety of language input in text, audio and video formats. And sophisticated search engines such as Google (http://www.google.com) and directories such as Yahoo (http://www.yahoo.com) provide a quick and easy way to find language input on just about any topic imaginable. Showing students how to locate information on the Internet appropriate to their own interests and language abilities is perhaps the single most important skill that today's language teacher can provide his or her students. For age-appropriate web surfing, Yahoo's Yahooligans directory (http://kids.yahoo.com) provides links to sites that have been checked to be appropriate for children aged 7 to 12 years old and Google's SafeSearch Filtering (under "Preferences") allows filtering out explicitly sexual text and images from search results.

Perhaps the best place to start for English text input for young English learners is the American Library Association's Great Web Sites for Kids (http://www.ala.org/greatsites). This directory lists Web sites that are classified into age-appropriate groups: prekindergarten, elementary, middle school and parents/teachers/caregivers.

For students interested in news and current affairs, Google News (http://news.google.com) provides a convenient way to access articles targeted to over 30 countries in over a dozen languages. In addition, Google News allows the user to create a personalized front page of their virtual newspaper, creating sections of articles related to chosen topics (e.g., science, sports or entertainment) or content words (e.g., soccer, football, World Cup) in languages of their choice.

For general reference, the Wikipedia (http://www.wikipedia.org/) is arguably the most encompassing and useful resource of the Internet. With versions in over 100 languages and over 1.8 million articles in English alone, the Wikipedia has become one of the most-used references on the Web. Of particular interest to English learners is the Wikipedia in Simple English (http://simple.wikipedia.org) that uses "easy words and shorter sentences so people who speak little English may easily read them" (from Web site). Other Wikimedia projects (including Wikibooks and Wikinews) can be found at http://wikimedia.org.

Because almost all of the text found on the Internet is written for native speakers of the language, language learners, especially young ones, may have difficulty understanding some vocabulary of Internet texts. Fortunately, the WordTranslator tool of the Google Toolbar (http://toolbar.google.com) provides users of the two most popular web browsers, Internet Explorer and Mozilla Firefox, quick translations of English words into Chinese, French, German, Italian, Japanese, Korean or Spanish. The translations pop up in a small window automatically whenever the cursor is placed on a word, which is certainly much easier and faster than consulting a bilingual dictionary, even one online. Although non-English to English-language translations are not (yet?) provided by Google's WordTranslator, similar pop-up translations from other languages to English are provided by Wordchamps' free web reader (http://wordchamp.com).

A very different type of language input, and one of particular interest to young learners, is provided by comic strips and comic books available via the web and sometimes referred to as "webcomics." Including both comics available only online as well as web versions of printed and syndicated comics, webcomics provide written language input within an attention-getting graphic context that has much to offer young language learners. One of the world's most well known and respected authorities on second language acquisition, Stephen Krashen, has long promoted the reading of comic books as an excellent way to develop literacy skills in a first or second/foreign language (Krashen, 2004). An extensive list of English-language webcomics can be found in the Wikipedia at http://en.wikipedia.org/wiki/List_of_webcomics (and see http://en.wikibooks.org/wiki/ATALL/Input and search for "comics" for additional sources of webcomics in English and other languages).

The Internet is also a repository of a great variety of spoken language in many different languages. The most convenient format of audio programs is a podcast (see http://en.wikipedia.org/wiki/Podcast) to which learners can subscribe (via software such as iTunes) to automatically download new versions of the program as they become available (do a Google search for "podcast directory"). The learner can then play these programs when desired (no Internet connection required) either on a computer or on a portable digital media player such as an iPod or audio-capable PDA. If the speed of the audio is too fast for a language learner, it is possible to use Windows Media Player (for Windows) or QuickTime Player (for Mac or Windows) to slow the speed of playback without affecting the pitch of the audio (see http://en.wikibooks.org/wiki/ATALL/Input#Speed_Control_.28Variable-Speed_Playback.29 for details).

Video in many languages, but especially in English, in the form of live and archived TV programs, video podcasts and short films are also available on the Internet. Perhaps the best source for short (and free) English-language films for learners can be found at Atom Films (http://atomfilms.com), although many of these are not suitable for younger learners and unfortunately do not provide captions to augment the audio with text. Lingualnet (http://www.lingual.net) provides subtitles for its English movies and Yabla (a fee-based service) provides videos in English, French and Spanish with subtitles. Joost (http://www.joost.com) has recently begun to provide high-quality, full-screen TV programs, pointing the way to the future of TV delivered via the Internet.

The current availability of relatively inexpensive video cameras and free and low-cost video editing software also makes it possible now for language learners to create their own videos or narrated slide shows, providing a potentially powerful motivator and context for improving their language skills. (For additional up-to-date information about using technology to provide input to language learners see the ATALL Wikibook's module on Input at http://en.wikibooks.org/wiki/ATALL/Input.)

Interaction and Feedback

Zhao and Lai provide a useful overview of many types of computer-mediated communication (CMC) and how they can be used for interactive language activities to motivate and foster language learning. One useful technology not mentioned by them is the wiki (see http://en.wikipedia.org/wiki/Wiki), an interactive Web site that allows users to edit and add information easily. The Wikipedia was mentioned earlier as a valuable resource reference in many languages, but because it is a wiki it is possible for any user with a web browser to edit almost any Wikipedia article (or begin a new one) and have the changes instantly appear for all to see. So in addition to finding information on a topic of interest in a language being learned, learners can also add to this information and share it with the world. As all versions of a wiki are usually archived and easily restored and compared with other versions, wikis have great potential for interactive writing projects involving groups of students and their teachers, either on a local restricted wiki, or on a public wiki such as the Wikipedia or Wikibooks. Cooperative writing projects involving students learning each others' languages could also be implemented for cross-cultural communication and interaction. Wikis can be public (as is the Wikipedia) or private. Anyone can set up a public wiki for free at BluWiki (http://bluwiki.org) or Wikia (http://wikia.com). For a private wiki that a teacher wants to restrict to a language class, PBwiki (http://pbwiki.com/tour/1.html) can be used. Other wiki possibilities can be found at http://en.wikipedia.org/wiki/Comparison_of_wiki_farms.

Blogs (see http://en.wikipedia.org/wiki/Blog) are another interactive form of text in which a writer or group or writers provide regular entries on a particular topic and readers can often leave comments. Although most blogs are primarily text with some images, many include audio as well and some even video. Blogs can be created for free using a service such as Blogger (http://www.blogger.com).

Perhaps the most exciting and motivating form of interaction provided by the Internet is synchronous communication among two or more individuals using some combination of text, audio and/or video. Zhao and Lai mention many programs that provide synchronous communication over the Internet, but the one that has now become the most popular (with over 170 million registered users and up to seven million users logged in at any one time) is Skype (http://www.skype.com). Skype provides free text, audio and video conferencing for Windows, Macintosh and Linux computers (no video yet for Linux). It is possible to search for language learning partners using Skype's own directory (where users in particular countries and speaking particular languages can be found). However, separate directories for Skype users specifically wanting to find language exchange partners may be more useful, such as xLingo (http://www.xlingo.com). A similar directory for language learners communicating primarily via text chat is SharedTalk (http://www.sharedtalk.com). For young learners, however, ePALS (http://www.epals.com) may be a better way to find classroom exchange partners. ePALS provides a paid "SchoolMail" service, a secure e-mail environment with built-in language translation. (For more information on using the Internet for interactive language activities, see http://en.wikibooks.org/wiki/ATALL/Interaction.)

Promoting Language Learning and Learner Autonomy

Language is an indispensable tool for learning, social interaction and development for young learners eager to learn more about the world around them and interact with their peers and other members of their local and worldwide communities (the latter made increasingly accessible by the Internet). Digital technologies, including the Internet, provide other tools for education, interaction and entertainment that can motivate, promote and facilitate the development of language skills by young learners. By making these technological tools available to their students, language teachers can help promote autonomous learners who will know how to use technology and who will develop the language skills necessary to accomplish their goals as learners and social beings.

But many challenges remain, especially for young learners of English in the United States and their teachers. The so-called "digital divide" between wealthier students and their schools and less well-off students such as those of immigrant families and their schools is one obvious challenge, although there are ways of dramatically reducing the cost of educational technology using inexpensive and recycled computers, thin-client hardware and open-source software such as Linux (see, for example, the Ndiyo Project at http://ndiyo.org and the OLPC Project at http://laptop.org/). Providing a safe computing environment is also a concern for all young users of the Internet as the same tools that allow students to explore the world via the Web make it possible for them discover Web sites and come into contact with individuals that may be detrimental to their development and security. Two Web sites with useful information for safe Internet use are SafeKids.com (http://www.safekids.com) and NetSmartz Kids (http://www.netsmartzkids.org).

But despite these concerns and dangers, the Internet provides an enticing environment in which young learners of English and other languages can be motivated to use and improve their listening, speaking, reading and writing skills in addition to becoming familiar with the technology that they will no doubt need to use in their continuing education and careers. And the ATALL Wikibook (http://en.wikibooks.org/wiki/ATALL), unlike Zhao and Lai's chapter and this reflection, provides a continually updated resource for how technology can be used to motivate and facilitate language learning of all language learners, including young learners of English.

References

Krashen, S. D. (2004). *The power of reading: Insights from the research* (2nd ed.). Englewood, CO.: Libraries Unlimited.

Powers, W. T. (1973). *Behavior: The control of perception*. Chicago: Aldine de Gruyter.

Powers, W. T. (1998). *Making sense of behavior: The meaning of control*. New Canaan, CT: Benchmark Publications.

6

Technology in Support of Young English Learners in and out of School

L. LEANN PARKER

University of California, Berkeley

With the rapidly increasing population of limited or non-English speaking children in U.S. schools, especially in the southwestern states, and the demands on schools to meet state and federally mandated achievement levels for all children, educators are pressed to provide the kinds of learning experiences that will help children do well in school. The challenge for many young English learners[1] is to learn the content and academic skills that their native English-speaking peers are learning, while at the same time trying to learn their new language.

English learners in the elementary school grades need to acquire basic English vocabulary, grammar, and functional language skills, foundational reading and math skills, and the communication skills for conversing with English speakers and for participating in classroom instruction. Around the third and fifth grades, English learners, like all children, need to be able to deal with more complex demands of English—academic English—in order to participate in instructional activities, to comprehend informational texts, to learn content, and to solve problems (e.g., see Cummins, 2001). Although learning academic English is not the only factor in school achievement, it is a crucial one. Because learning this kind of English takes several years, learners may need additional support beyond regular school instruction to develop the rich academic English skills needed to succeed in school (Hakuta, Butler, & Witt, 2000).

For several decades now, educators have increasingly turned to electronic technologies for support in teaching new languages. Indeed, there is a wealth of electronic tools, such as portable electronic translators and foreign language teaching software, for enhancing second language skills both in and out of school. However, much of the research on technology has tended to focus on older learners at the secondary school and college levels who are learning a foreign language. The question for this chapter is whether technology can make a difference for English learners at the elementary grades. Thus it is useful to consider the kinds of technological support systems available to help jumpstart and enrich young learners' second language skills and the factors that make those systems useful. Synthesizing findings of existing research reviews, reports, and other sources, this chapter surveys some of the technologies, design features, and issues surrounding the use of technology for second language and reading development for children, with a focus on factors likely to promote English-as-a-second-language development in and out of school.

Two general questions guide this discussion: What kinds of technologies and technology-based language learning programs are currently available for young children? And what factors need to be considered that would be helpful in using or designing new technologies or technology-mediated activities for young English learners? To address these questions, this chapter first surveys various technologies and their potential to assist young second language learners. The second section focuses on characteristics and effectiveness of language development software and games for developing oral second language and reading skills. The third section focuses on sociocultural factors that influence the capacity of new technologies to assist young English learners. The final section turns to implications for the classroom, out-of-school settings, design and development, and research. Before launching into those discussions, it is useful to take a look at the process of second language development and the nature of technology.

Second Language Development   Although a full discussion of second language and literacy development is beyond the scope of this chapter, it is important to highlight the process that learning a new language entails. Learning a first or a second language involves cognitively mastering the forms of the language: the syntactic (structural) forms; idioms, vocabulary, meanings (including connotations and appropriate uses of lexical items), and the sounds and intonational patterns of the language. It involves developing oral skills such as pronunciation and listening comprehension. It involves the ability to communicate fluently and appropriately with native speakers in different settings (the grocery store, school, the doctor's office) and social situations (e.g., to adults as well as to other children). It involves understanding the language spoken by others and making oneself understood (Lightbown & Spada, 1993). There is always a tension between the ability to make oneself understood in the new language and the ability to use linguistic forms appropriate to the situation (Crookall, 2002; Kramsch, 1993). Learning the linguistic forms and the ways to use them for oral and written communication can be considered part of the same task for the second language learner (Kramsch, 1993). Recent analyses from a sociocultural theoretical perspective emphasize that second language development is grounded in social interaction, and suggest the importance of the complex inter-relationship among the learner, the activity, the context, and the nature of communication, rather than learning discrete forms of the language (for discussions see Lantolf, 2000; Zuengler & Miller, 2006; for more information on the nature of second language development, see Lightbown & Spada, 1993; Peregoy & Boyle, 2005).

Literacy—reading and writing—is another crucial set of skills that learners need to develop. There is evidence that first language literacy supports the development of literacy in the second language, that there is a relationship between oral proficiency and literacy, and that instruction in English reading skills can foster oral as well as literacy development (August, 2003). However, these foundational reading skills are necessary but not sufficient for comprehension (August & Shanahan, 2006). Second language fluency develops as learners become more adept in their ability to comprehend oral language and written text and to communicate through speaking and writing appropriately for various settings (for more information on literacy development, see August & Shanahan, 2006; National Institute of Child Health and Human Development [NICHHD], 2006b; Snow, Burns, & Griffin, 1998).

Second language learning specialists tend to agree on several key conditions that are necessary for supporting the development of language skills. Zhao and Lai (this volume) have condensed them to four: (1) *high-quality input*—the access to realistic (authentic), comprehensible yet demanding language and cultural materials, (2) *ample opportunities for practice*—the practice of linguistic forms and communication in naturalistic settings, (3) *high-quality feedback*—the reactions and corrections to the learner's language and focusing the learner's attention on aspects of the language that need to be refined, and (4) *individualized content*—the content to meet the language learning needs and learning styles of the student. As discussed later in this chapter, a number of sociocultural factors are also at play in second language acquisition.

Technology   In recent years, technology has come to refer almost exclusively to electronic technologies that provide information or entertainment. Yet, the term has multiple meanings and can be used in multiple ways. For example, a sociocultural view of technology holds that tools are used to mediate or affect human activities (see Lantolf, 2000). Thus, from an educational perspective, classroom technologies could also include otherwise traditional items such as chalkboards, chalk, pen, paper, and textbooks, as well as computers and other electronic tools that help children learn. Kern (2006) lists three kinds of electronic technologies based on function: *tutors* that provide instruction and feedback, *tools* that provide access to second language materials and references, and *medium* that includes sites for communication and distance learning. Throughout this chapter, *technology* will be used broadly, but will in general refer to electronic software and hardware devices. The term will be used to refer to older electronic delivery systems such as audio/video tapes and recorders and television; to newer systems such as computers and the Internet, game consoles, MP3 players (such as iPods) and cell phones; and to an array of digital tools such as speech recognition, digital audio and video, animation, and artificial intelligence. In addition, the term will refer to electronic instructional products and activities that employ one or more of these technologies to promote second language and/or literacy development.

The Potential of Second Language Learning Tools for Children

Although much of the research on technology for second language learning has focused on adults, this section will examine the potential of specific tools for children. The discussion focuses on (a) audio and video technologies, such as audiocassettes and television; (b) computers; (c) the Internet; (d) game and simulation technologies; (e) small mobile computers and electronic books (e-books); (f) MP3 players, cell phones, and other new technologies; and (g) specialized electronic tools.

Audio- and Video-based Technologies

For decades, audio technologies such as radio broadcasts and audio cassettes have been a major contribution to language learning technologies because of their ability to provide learners good audio models of the spoken forms of the language (see Rhodes & Pufahl, 2004, and Salaberry, 2001, for discussions). However, audio programs have always had the inability to anticipate student responses, which limits the effectiveness of this kind of technology compared to interaction with a teacher (Salaberry, 2001). When television came along, language educators were able to add a visual component with audio. Television and videotaped programs are still widely used for foreign language teaching (Rhodes & Pufahl, 2004). There are a growing number of television programs for young Spanish heritage preschool English learners. For example, *Dora the Explorer* on the Nickelodeon cable channel, is a show in which the animated characters speak both English and Spanish (originally as a way to teach Spanish to non-Spanish speakers; Texeira, 2006); the channel has related games for parents to play with their children on its Web site, http://www.nickjr.com/. Although there appear to be relatively few analyses of television on children's second language learning, the Center for Children and Technology (2004) has found that the appropriateness of content and the level of difficulty, along with audio features, not only help keep young viewers' attention, but may also be significant in promoting literacy skills. Moreover, some television programs may have a positive effect on children's academic achievement and motivation to read, their knowledge of content subjects, and cultural awareness (Center for Children and Technology, 2004).

Other research suggests features of the technology environment that may be relevant for language learners of all ages. For example, Salaberry (2001) points out that production quality of the sound and video, the appropriateness of the content for the learner, and the expertise of instructors in helping learners take advantage of audio/video technologies are crucial to determining how successful these technologies can be. Videos can support comprehension of texts in the target language that learners later read, especially when accompanied by preliminary oral or written discussion of the topic. Subtitles, captions, and interactive technology help learners connect oral and written forms of target language vocabulary.

Audio and video learning environments have been very popular for the past several decades, especially for elementary schools which do not have certified foreign language teachers. A study by Rhodes and Pufahl (2004) of five highly regarded video-based Spanish-as-a-second-language instruction programs indicated that elementary-school children learned basic Spanish and developed positive attitudes about the language and Spanish cultures. Teachers and parents offered some important insights into features that were effective. Among the more useful features identified were repetition, sole use of the target language, clear pronunciation, use of gestures to convey meaning, songs, pictures, and videos to reinforce concepts, cartoon characters, engaging story lines that motivate students, and humor. Survey respondents emphasized the importance of, and preference for, a real foreign language teacher in each classroom. The responses also indicated that content needs to be engaging, motivating, and appropriate to learners (to maintain their interest); to focus heavily on target language rather than translate; to build on prior learning; and to address cultural information better. Respondents also identified a number of limitations. Among those cited were the lack of other multimedia technologies, immediate feedback mechanisms for learners, and opportunities for authentic communication with native speakers. Respondents also complained about the narrow content of the programs, which had no flexibility for children to learn additional vocabulary or use it in new contexts. Although interactive video technologies helped overcome these issues, the cost of production and equipment was seen as a major barrier to its use. It was noted that children who do well in these narrowly focused video-based programs sometimes cause educators (especially those who do not speak the target language) to believe that the children have learned more than they actually have. This study underscores the importance of features like content flexibility, focused individualized feedback, and well-trained teachers for promoting language learning.

Computer-based Technologies

Personal computers, especially after they became widely available in the 1980s, added a new dimension to language instruction (Chapelle, 2001; Warschauer, 1996). Computer-based technologies were used to teach foreign languages through text-based instruction and practice exercises with instant feedback. As computer technology advanced, processing became faster and storage capacity increased exponentially, enabling the storage of large complex programs and resources such as dictionaries and audio and video files. Computers are now powerful enough to provide the array of audio, video, and text needed for robust second language support to satisfy many of the conditions needed for second language acquisition such as those described by Egbert, Chao, and Hanson-Smith (1999) and Zhao (2003). Such technologies provide language that the learner can understand (comprehensible input) and help learners figure out meaning (see Zhao & Lai, this volume, for more discussion). Computers can tutor specific linguistic forms, support learners' comprehension of electronic text (including electronic books) through features such as hyperlinks to other information such as audio (reading a word or a passage to the reader) or graphics and video to show relevant images to support meaning, and help develop written language skills with word processors and grammar checkers that focus learners' attention on grammatical constructions making it easier for learners to write longer passages and write better than without these tools (Chapelle, 2001; Holum & Gahala, 2001; Sherman, Kleiman, & Kirsten, 2004).[2]

A key issue with respect to second language learning with computers is the nature of the educational approach in language teaching software and games. This issue is taken up in a subsequent section.

Internet-based Support Systems

The Internet offers a dazzling array of language learning resources for learners of all ages. Although some have argued that the Web and its collaboration possibilities may be deleterious to children (e.g., see Monke, 2005), the Internet provides access to a rich and varied collection of Web sites, authentic resources in the target language (e.g., newspapers), online courses, and opportunities for collaboration and communication (e.g., through e-mail, chatrooms, and social networking Web sites) (see Cziko, this volume; Felix, 2003; Warschauer, 1996; Warschauer & Kern, 2000; for more information). Although some Web sites, such as *Dave's ESL Café* (http://www.eslcafe.com/) and *Randall's Cyber Listening Lab* (http://esl-lab.com/index.htm), are aimed primarily at older English learners and their teachers, others can serve as the basis for English language development for children. For example, *Roy the Zebra* (http://www.roythezebra.com) has some free interactive reading activities, and zoo Web sites can be used to assist young second language learners (LeLoup & Ponterio, 2005). Some portals to language learning and teaching resources for instructors and students are aimed at elementary school classrooms and are primarily for teachers (Krajka, 2002); these include *FLES Web* (http://www.public.iastate.edu/~egarcia/fles.html) for foreign language learners, and *Jardín mundial* (http://www.geocities.com/Athens/Acropolis/4616/content/directory.htm), a teacher-developed Web site of Spanish-English resources. Cziko (this volume) describes a variety of Internet-based resources that might be useful for elementary and secondary school aged students.

The Internet also enables learners to engage in collaborative activities with native speakers of the target language through e-mail, bulletin boards, blogs, chatrooms, and realtime video or audio conferencing. Although these collaborative technologies may not result in specific feedback on the accuracy of linguistic forms, their collaborative nature provides opportunities for participants to negotiate meaning, which may help second language learners improve their knowledge of the language. Pen pal programs managed by teachers, such as *De Orilla a Orilla,* (http://www.orillas.org/), offer another kind of opportunity for educators and their students to communicate and work with peers in other parts of the world, thus providing language learners with authentic cultural information and opportunities to use the new language with native speakers (Cummins & Sayers, 1995; French, 2001–2002; also see other chapters in this volume for more discussion).

Game and Simulation Technologies

Videogames came to prominence as an entertainment form in the 1970s and spread rapidly through floppy disks, CDs, and the Internet, to arcade games, and to game console platforms (e.g., Gameboy, PlayStation, and Xbox). Some educators have been intrigued about the possibility of using these ubiquitous devices and software platforms for educational purposes, especially for developing and improving literacy skills (Gee, 2003). Their popularity and characteristics also make these technologies attractive for second language development (Zhao & Lai, this volume). As with computers, the potential of electronic games and simulations lies in the content and educational approach. This issue is discussed in more detail later.

Small Mobile Computers and E-books

Handheld Computers and Personal Digital Assistants (PDAs)   PDAs are small, relatively inexpensive, mobile computers, often with wireless capabilities. Since the first Apple Newton came out in 1993, PDAs have been touted as important technology for learning.[3] (In fact, Apple made a version of the Newton specifically for schools in 1997, called the Emate 300; however, it was not successful as an educational tool [for more information, see http://en.wikipedia.org/wiki/Apple_Newton].) In short, these devices can do much of what desktop computers are used for, and they have the advantage of being portable, but there is also a lack of good educational software that makes the most of the device (Savill-Smith & Kent, 2003). There have been adaptations for second language acquisition, primarily for older learners, in the form of electronic dictionaries and phrase books.[4]

Inkpen (1999) found that children like the size and portability of these small computers; the ability to print; the ability to put in their own information; the possibilities for surfing the Internet, playing games, using the calculator, keeping a diary, and e-mailing friends, and would like them to have special functions like speech and drawing. Handhelds have been used in schools to support children's activities such as collecting data for science projects and literacy development. For example, PDAs have been used in K–5 classrooms to promote thinking about texts, exposure to different genres, word games, writing facilitated by keyboards, and oral reading using the built-in recording and playback capabilities (Baumbach, Christopher, Fasimpaur, & Oliver, 2004). Educators are also beginning to investigate the potential of PDAs. One ESL middle-school teacher in the Washington, DC area considered using them to help English learners access the Internet for quick translations of vocabulary or for summaries of content material in their native language (Shapira, 2003).

A drawback of small mobile technology for younger learners is that the devices may currently be too fragile for use in a lively school environment, especially for very young children. Also, small devices may be difficult for younger children to operate because they do not have fully developed fine hand movement control, and the screen size may present difficulties for beginning readers (Chinnery, 2006). Changes in the form factor (physical dimensions) for children's use and improvements in speech recognition and oral text reading technologies may make these kinds of devices more useful to children in the future. Beyond these factors, some children may find this format quite conducive for English language development if appealing software were available. However, whether and how children would use small mobile devices, especially outside of school, is unclear.[5]

E-Readers and E-Books   Now that PDA technology is more advanced (e.g., color and backlit screens), it can make reading on a small mobile device more enjoyable. An electronic book, or e-book or e-reader, is a small mobile device that holds texts, such as books, and sometimes related software such as glossaries; e-books are also the digital format of books. E-books can provide access to a wide range of reading materials, and up-to-date content materials along with tools such as special dictionaries, talking word processors and text readers, and larger buttons suitable for younger audiences. However, there are several drawbacks to using e-books such as the lack of a standard format (which currently makes it necessary to use proprietary software to download and read the books). These factors may result in little motivation for readers to purchase this technology and in copyright issues (Savill-Smith & Kent 2003), which may in turn limit this tool's usefulness to promote extensive reading.

Nonetheless, the reading products and platforms designed to develop beginning reading skills may be helpful to young native speakers as well as second language learners. For example, *LeapFrog* (http://www.leapfrog.com)

has developed interactive books for its LeapPad platform. Their *Language First* books for beginning readers focus on building a rich vocabulary in English, with an option of native language support in six languages (LeapFrog School House, 2004). These interactive books allow children to hear a storybook as they read along supported with text enhancements that focus children's attention on the written words. The design philosophy includes combining interesting stories (to encourage children to reread them) with engaging multicultural characters that children can identify with. It also emphasizes the importance of practicing skills with feedback, learning words in context, as well as opportunities to answer questions (i.e., interact with the materials) to demonstrate comprehension. A recent study of the LeapPad device by Romig, Yan, and Zhao (2006) found that many of the target at-risk first graders in their study scored higher than a control group in phonics, oral reading fluency, and retelling. The researchers concluded that the machine was helpful in some but not all domains of early reading skills.

MP3 Players, Cell Phones, and Other New Technologies

A number of technologies such as MP3 players (like iPods) and cell phones are being used to support second language development directly or indirectly, even though they were not originally developed for that purpose (Chinnery, 2006; Godwin-Jones, 2005). Cell phones are being used to teach vocabulary and talk to tutors, although the audio quality and tiny screens sometimes limit the usefulness to learners (Chinnery, 2006).[6] It is questionable, however, whether the small form factor and the cost of instant messaging would make cell phones a feasible device for some children and whether this format would be useful for developing their second language skills. Originally developed for transferring and listening to music, Apple iPods and other MP3 players, which can be synchronized with computers, are also being used for language learning. For the most part, these technologies have been used for second language learning at the high school or university level, especially to assist with pronunciation and new vocabulary (Godwin-Jones, 2005). Because of their ubiquity and popularity among students, there may be new possibilities for some elementary school-aged English learners who have access to these technologies.

Specialized Electronic Tools

A number of other tools may offer special supports to language learners. It is difficult to trace all of the work being done in this arena. However, the following is a sample of a few of the new technologies that may hold promise for use with children (see Zhao & Lai, this volume, for additional discussion).

Speech Recognition, Speech Synthesis, and Chatterbots Technologies that analyze the learner's speech and respond to the learner appropriately (speech recognition) and that generate an oral version of written text (speech synthesis) have been used to support authentic communication skills through interactions with a computer. However, speech technology has not yet been developed sufficiently to be a useful aid to second language learning (Cole, 2003; Ehsani & Knodt, 1998). For example, speech recognition software may have problems understanding children as well as non-native speech forms such as accented speech (Li & Topolewski, 2002; Selinker & Mascia, 2001; T. Shulz, personal communication, January 28, 2005). Chatterbots (also called chatbot, chatterbox) are tools designed to simulate communication with a person on specific topics (see http://en.wikipedia.org/wiki/Chatterbot).[7] Although their ability to converse is generally limited, chatterbots may eventually have potential for second language learning support for children and adults; however, they have been little used for that purpose so far and their effectiveness is not well known.

Text Readers   Text readers use synthesized voices to read text aloud to learners who are reading a book. Anecdotal evidence suggests it may be useful for young English learners. For example, *Kurzweil 3000* (http://www.envisiontechnology.org), which was developed for people with learning difficulties, scans and reads text aloud. It was voted by educators as a useful tool for English language learners ("Readers Choice Awards," 2004). Another text reader, *ReadingBar2 for Internet Explorer* (http://www.readplease.com/), produced by AT&T Natural Voices, reads Web pages aloud, highlights words, magnifies pages, translates Web pages into four languages, and provides dictionary lookup function. Text readers in interactive books for children (such as those in the Leap Frog series) suggest potential for assisting young English learners.

Intelligent Tutors   Sophisticated artificial intelligence (AI) tools combine a variety of features such as animation, speech recognition, and conversation to promote reading skills or speech and communication. Within the parameters that are programmed, electronic tutors using AI are able to diagnose errors, provide feedback, analyze the learner's weaknesses and strengths, and make suggestions for future activity based on that analysis (American Association for Artificial Intelligence, 2004). An example of an intelligent tutor is the *Colorado Literacy Tutor* (http://cslr.colorado.edu/beginweb/reading/reading.html), which has been used in several K–12 classrooms. It includes animated characters with realistic gestures and facial movements that ask guiding questions and make suggestions to learners as they read interactive books. In this program, the software assesses children's weaknesses and provides appropriate tutoring to teach or reinforce the skills. Related technology promotes reading comprehension by encouraging children to write summaries of what they read, and then assesses the summaries and provides feedback to the learners (Cole, van Vuuren, Pellom, Hacioglu, Ma, Movellan, et al., 2003). Another example is *Baldi*, the name of an animated talking head and body, which uses realistic facial speech and emotion with synthesized or natural speech and appropriate gestures (Cohen, Massaro, & Clark, 2002; Massaro, Ouni, Cohen, & Clark, 2005). Baldi can serve as both a language tutor and a reading tutor and can support communication over the Internet as well as in multiperson games. With English and Spanish versions, it has been used in the United States and Chile to help deaf children learn to speak.

Reading Comprehension Support Tools   Other tools have been developed to support English learners ability to read academic texts. For example, the *Thinking Reader* developed by the Center for Assistive Technologies (CAST, http://www. cast.org/products/ereader/index.html) and the *e-Lective Language Learning Program* developed by Chascas and Cummins (see Cummins, this volume) enrich learners' knowledge of written English. *Thinking Reader* works with texts provided by its developer, and *e-Lective* works with any text that can be scanned into a computer or accessed over the Internet. Features of such tools include digitized speech that reads text aloud, monolingual and bilingual dictionaries, exercises to help children practice new words and comprehension, immediate feedback, vocabulary assessments, activities to encourage critical thinking about text, and opportunities to respond to text in writing. These particular tools were designed specifically to scaffold the literacy development of elementary-age and older children; the e-Lective system was designed especially for second language learners.

Digital Storytelling Tools   Multimedia authoring tools combined with word processing and other tools such as digital cameras, scanners, and audio and video editing software, can help children develop their oral and literacy skills by creating individual or collaborative stories and presenting them in a coherent digital format. Practice using different kinds of audio and video technologies and equipment is a side benefit for the children. Digital storytelling has been used successfully to promote literacy of struggling readers, including English learners (Underwood, Welsh, Emmons, Lerner, & Sturak, 2002; also see Durán's and Castek et al.'s chapters in this volume).

Special tools such as those described in this section hold much promise for assisting younger English learners to cope with texts, expand their comprehension of English, and enhance their ability to communicate comprehensibly in English. Studies of these technologies with English learners and children will be important to determine how best to employ these technologies.

Educational Software and Games

Educational software contains the packages of digital tools, pedagogical approaches, and activities that support learning. This section will consider some of the issues related to software products and electronic games formats for young second language learners.

Language Teaching Software

Because the content of educational software is at the crux of how computer and Internet-based technologies can support second language learning, it is important to examine general characteristics of software for young second language learners. These products provide self-contained, learning environments in which children are involved primarily with the activities in the virtual world created for the software. The rapid proliferation of digital multimedia technologies over the past two decades has resulted in a wide variety of educational software products developed by commercial and nonprofit educational organizations that are aimed at advancing the academic skills of pre-kindergarten-through-twelfth (pre-K–12) grade learners. These products are offered primarily for computers via CDs and DVDs and increasingly over the Internet. More recently, educators are looking at gaming technologies, MP3 players, and cell phones for conveying these virtual learning environments. The sheer numbers of such educational software products are astonishing. As one indicator, the *Children's Technology Review* (formerly *Children's Software Revue;* http://www.childrenssoftware.com) has reviewed over 7800 CDs, Web sites, videogames, and smart toys since it began in 1993.

It is difficult to get a good picture of what language learning software for children does to support learning a new language and how well, since there is no comprehensive database of all available educational software products developed by commercial vendors and by nonprofit or educational institutions (S. Burdick, personal communication, November 30, 2004). However, it is possible to get a sense of the characteristics, quality, and best practices by examining professional reviews of software products.

In 2004, I surveyed reviews of children's language learning products found in *Children's Technology Review* (CTR), focusing on products designated as appropriate for grades K–5 or ages 5–11 and rated at 4.0 (fair) or better (Parker, 2004). The CTR is a good choice for this kind of survey.[8] It has a large searchable online database of product reviews for CDs with educational programs, videogames, smart toys, and Web sites for which it provides fairly systematic reviews and numerical ratings of quality based on a set of evaluation criteria. Its search feature also enables relatively straightforward counts of products according to several criteria, such as title, publisher, rating, copyright date, issue in which the review appeared, grade, platform, and keywords.

The goal was to survey the kinds of second language software available and what reviewers judged as key features. At that time, the CTR software product database yielded some 70 products for elementary-school-aged children that were tagged as related to English as a second language (ESL) or foreign language development. Over half of these products (41) were focused specifically on teaching a foreign language (FL) other than English. About one fifth (15) were tagged as foreign language and included English teaching (FL/ESL).

About one fourth (19) were tagged specifically as ESL. The survey did not include reviews of products that were actually bundles of other developers' software or similar products but for different languages (e.g., Topic Entertainment's *Instant Immersion 102 Language,* http://www.topics-ent.com/). The following description is based on these reviews.

Language of Focus The products predominantly focused on teaching European languages such as French, Spanish, and German, although some included lessons for languages such as Japanese and Mandarin, while a few taught English as a foreign language. Another set of products focused on teaching English as a second language, that were either directly or indirectly developed for English learners in U.S. schools. Others were designated as teaching reading (for English speakers), or for special education. The majority of products focused on foreign language teaching. Although that may have been an artifact of what the reviewers chose to review, it may also indicate that there are fewer products aimed at young English learners.

Quality CTR reviewers rate products on a scale of 1.0 to 5.0, with the higher numbers indicating excellent and successively lower numbers indicating good, fair, poor, and "duds." Somewhat more than fourth (28.6%) of the ESL products were rated as good to excellent, somewhat less than half (42.2%) of the FL products, and somewhat less than one third (30.8%) of the FL/ESL products were rated as good to excellent. These percentages suggest that a substantial number of products may not be very strong, and lead one to question the relative effectiveness of language learning software products. The reviews themselves hold clues to the features that affect what is likely to work for children.

Target Audiences Although this project searched for products for elementary-school-aged children, the reviews indicated that publishers had designated the products as appropriate for multiple ages or grade levels (most likely to appeal to as large a market as possible. A few products centered on a narrow age or grade range such as primary school. For example, some were designated as appropriate for children in preschool through first grade; others were targeted at grades 1–5; and others were aimed for a wide range of ages (e.g., from grades 4 or 5 through high school). Although one may be able to argue that the content is appropriate for multiple grades, it is questionable whether some of the features, such as pictures of adult learners or non-age-specific exercises, would be motivating or effective for child learners.

Technologies The majority of reviewed products in this survey were on CDs; two were Web-based, and one was for the LeapPad platform. Some software required users to have their own microphones and headsets, whereas other products contained them in the package. There appeared to be a trend for developers to provide additional activities and support on product Web sites. Multimedia for interactive activities, glossaries, and colorful animations and graphics were among the most mentioned tools in product reviews. Video was mentioned less often, although clearly some reviewers felt that live video and photographs were more desirable than animations and graphics for illustrating concepts and how native speakers speak. A few reviewers mentioned intelligent software that adjusts the difficulty of content or could adjust a test to the learner's performance (e.g., the intelligent tutor in DynEd's *First English* (http://dyned.com/education/). However, it was not clear from the reviews how prevalent such technologies are in available products.

A number of products also employed special audio features, such as digital recordings of native speakers, or the ability for the learner to speak into a microphone. Although not specified by reviewers, one might surmise that many of the audio models of native speech are digitized recordings rather than synthesized speech. Another fairly common audio component involved recording and playback capacity, so that learners can record, hear, and compare their own voices to recordings of native speakers. Speech recognition was noted as a feature of a few products, such as Auralog's *Tell Me More Kids: Inglés* (http://www.auralog.com/us/individuals_tellmemorekids.htm), but was restricted to a limited set of vocabulary and phrases programmed into the software. Reviewers rarely described speech recognition in much detail, but a few commented that it is still too primitive to be a useful tool for young language learners.

Ease of navigation was a key issue according to reviewers. They often noted when navigation interrupted learning and tended to give lower ratings to products with such problems. A reviewer commented that child testers of one product for grades K–4 (ages 5–9) liked the activities but were put off by bugs in the program, a difficult installation, freezing, jerky speech quality, and slow transitions from one activity to another.

Content Focus   The reviewers indicated that the kind of content offered varies by the instructional scope of each product. However, a prominent emphasis, especially for products for elementary grades, is on developing basic vocabulary, common sentence structures such as questions, some reading skills (often word recognition, particularly in the earlier grades), and pronunciation and listening comprehension skills. LeapFrog's *Fiesta in the House* (http://www.leapfrog.com), a product aimed at Grades 1–6 (ages 6–10), for example, is principally focused on a small range of vocabulary items (e.g., colors, numbers, clothing items, body parts, and musical instruments). CTR reviews leave the impression that many, if not most, of the products focus on learners who are at the beginning level of learning the new language. More work would need to be done to find out what educational software is available for children at intermediate or advanced levels of second language learning.

Products for slightly older children tended to have a broader content focus. One of the most sophisticated (based on the description in the CTR reviews) is DynEd's *English for Success* (http://dyned.com/education/), which is aimed at students in Grades 5–12 (ages 11–17). Although this program also focuses on vocabulary and phrases, it puts them in the context of school tasks, such as discussing class assignments with teachers and subject matter learning, with basic vocabulary for a few subject areas such as science, as a way to help these students prepare for high school. Products also varied in the quantity and nature of the content. For example, some products offered a small number of vocabulary items and syntactical forms, even though others offered substantially more. Some reviewers noted that the language used throughout the various products was so tightly controlled that learners had little access to challenging language beyond the linguistic forms provided in the products. This observation raises questions about the extent to which any individual product can provide learners with access to a sufficiently broad range of authentic language forms and communication skills that will support their use of English outside of school and in the classroom.

Instructional Approaches and Design   Several instructional approaches were mentioned by reviewers. Some commented that some products used an immersion approach, that is, used only the new language throughout activities, but made it as comprehensible as possible through visuals and a highly focused but restricted set of interactive activities. A frequently mentioned instructional approach involved providing reinforcement and practice through simple games and activities (e.g., electronic flashcards) with immediate positive reinforcement for learners based on their performance. Another common approach was an engaging story line that involved interactive activities.

It appears that many software developers try to offer comprehensible input by controlling the range of language forms. In addition, products often included special support systems in the form of multimedia and/or first language instructions, glossaries, and help information to assist learners when they got stuck and motivate them to continue with the activities. An issue for some reviewers was whether the exercises and activities would be sufficiently interesting and engaging to children, based on the logic that a child who does not enjoy the program is not likely to use it or learn from it.

One kind of instructional approach is exemplified by *Fiesta in the House* (http://www.leapfrog.com), a Spanish–English bilingual book. Learners can select the primary language for instructions and explore the software as they please in a nonlinear fashion. One of the activities involves building a robot that speaks two languages and helping it learn the new language as it progresses through various activities. In another example, *First English* (http://dyned.com/education/), a program for upper elementary students according to the review, makes heavy use of practice and repetition. This program also records learner performance and includes assessments and an Intelligent Tutor tool that adjusts content difficulty for the learner. Geared to the classroom, this product encourages teachers to take an active role in assessing students, placing them at the appropriate level of the activity, and monitoring students' progress.

Virtual Language Learning Environments   CTR professional product reviews suggest that many virtual language learning environments focus on mastery of discrete linguistic forms (e.g., vocabulary, phonetic patterns or sounds, and grammatical patterns), albeit usually in playful, engaging ways that may even adjust to a learner's level of proficiency to some extent. However, such products do not duplicate naturalistic language learning, in part because speech technology is not sufficiently advanced to enable a context in which the learner can communicate with characters in the software in the same way they would with native speakers in face-to-face environments. Nonetheless, some products try to help learners get a sense of the way native speakers use the language with strategies such as sole use of the new language for both instructions and activities or video/audio clips of native speakers speaking the language fluently and appropriately for the depicted social situation.

Effectiveness   Although there is a great deal of literature on technology (particularly about computers) and second language learning, there appears to be little in the way of well-designed experimental long-term research (Liu, Moore, Graham, & Lee, 2002; Zhao, 2003; Zhao & Lai, this volume). Further, there have been relatively few studies of effectiveness on technologies used for young learners, and even fewer for English learners from different language backgrounds. Thus, it is difficult to arrive at definite conclusions about the effectiveness of language learning software for children. However, there is a growing literature that suggests that computers and other technology can play a role in supporting language development of all children. Research suggests that computers indirectly foster more complex speech and language fluency, that children are likely to narrate as they draw and move images around on the computer screen, and that when collaborating on computer activities, children use much more complex language and communication skills than with more traditional activities such as assembling puzzles (Mayer Schustack, & Blanton, 1999; Van Scoter, Ellis, & Railsback, 2001).

Wood (2001) took on the issue of the learning environment created within 16 highly recommended software products designed to teach vocabulary to children in grades 3–5. By examining both explicit and implicit teaching strategies for their consistency with what literacy experts recommend for teaching vocabulary, as well as the media employed, she sought to find out how multimedia strategies contributed to instruction. She found that products that involved more indirect than direct approaches were aligned with current accepted literacy practice. All of the products employed only a few vocabulary learning strategies, such as relating the new word to known information and associations through multiple exposures. Wood concluded from her analysis that technology provides strong advantages for vocabulary learning. For example, animations can engage children's attention. Video clips can help children comprehend complex concepts by providing support for vocabulary learning. Hyperlinks can help children learn vocabulary by linking to information that triggers prior knowledge or that expands "semantic webs" of meaning between words. However, Wood was generally critical of the instructional approach and scope in these products. She found that the words taught in products covered a wide range of difficulty levels (one product's content covered 15 grade levels). She also found little in the products that required deep thinking. Her concern was that this might hamper young English learners who need more help with learning high-frequency words. She noted that, in products using an indirect approach, many of the target words were not included in accepted published word lists for this age level, perhaps because of efforts to provide thematic vocabulary. By contrast, products using a direct approach tended to focus on general vocabulary aligned with the developmental levels of the target grades.

An important question this author raises is whether children are deeply and cognitively involved in learning, even if engaged in the activity. Among the improvements Wood suggested are providing activities to encourage children to use the new words in authentic ways, providing activities that involve writing, promoting independent reading (e.g., through online bibliographies or texts), exploiting technologies that address different learning styles and needs (e.g., recording and playback, narrating slide shows that the individual has created, access to different font sizes), and addressing discourse patterns, cultural values, and interactional styles of learners from various linguistic and cultural backgrounds. Concluding that children may not learn vocabulary best through computer-based products alone, she argued that teachers are important in helping students comprehend and extend their knowledge and familiarity with new words.

Literacy Software, Academic Achievement, and the Learning Environment

Educators are still debating the effectiveness of technologies for promoting reading and academic achievement, even for English speakers (see Sherman et al., 2004, for discussion of research, and Cummins, this volume). Some analysts conclude that technology is helpful in tutoring young English learners in beginning reading skills, supporting vocabulary development, and facilitating comprehension. However the findings about the overall effect of technology on reading are not definitive (National Institute of Child Health and Human Development [NICHHD], 2000a; Sherman et al., 2004). Other analysts such as Parr (2003) and Kulik (2003, cited in Sherman et al., 2004) suggest that there is little evidence of gains in reading and subject matter learning with computer-assisted instruction. Still other analysts have reported stronger relationships between the use of reading software and the development of academic literacy skills among English learners. For example, in their review of literature on the use of computer-based technologies with young English learners in classroom settings, Svedkauskaite and Reza-Hernandez (2003) suggest that software and interaction with computers can be a positive influence on English language learning and development of concepts in subjects such as science. The authors also cite the successes (based on improved scores on state tests) of the El Paso, Texas, school district, which has a high number of Latino English learners, in integrating technology and challenging content into instruction to support learning across the curriculum for all students.

Because there is no definitive answer as to the impact of reading and oral English language development software on the academic achievement of young English learners, the issue could benefit from additional research. Two conclusions stand out from the analyses. One is that well-prepared teachers are essential for making sure that technologies support the needs of English learners in their classes (e.g., see Sherman et al., 2004; Wood, 2001). The other is that effectiveness depends on how the technologies are being used (Kern, 2006).

The Potential of Electronic Games and Simulations

Owing to increased attention to the educational use of electronic games (e.g., see Gee, 2003) and the fact that they have great appeal for some youth, it is appropriate to consider their potential for young second language learners. The format of electronic games varies from those with a simple focus for individual players (such as traditional games put into electronic form, like *Hangman* or *Solitaire*), to more elaborate and sophisticated games requiring skill for individual attainment, to complex multiplayer competitive games in a simulation format played over the Internet (for a discussion of the types of electronic games, see Mitchell & Savill-Smith, 2004).

Findings of studies about the relation between playing educational games and academic performance are mixed. Mitchell and Savill-Smith (2004) argue that this technology has been found effective for teaching subjects that have specific learning objectives, especially math and language arts (including spelling and reading comprehension) to children even as early as kindergarten, but that differences in academic performance depended on the subject matters in which games were used. Especially impressive is their ability to motivate young learners. Students often find game formats, especially electronic games, more interesting and fun than more traditional instructional activities, because of their ease of use, speed, variety, complexity, need for skill, quality graphics, and humor (Mitchell & Savill-Smith, 2004). However, there are significant challenges in using games for instruction. Drawbacks, for example, include learners' difficulties using pointers, virtual keyboards, slow processing speeds, and limitations with the font and image sizes of computer screens and other devices (Chinnery, 2006). Research also suggests that educators need to find game contexts that are likely to interest both genders (American Association of University Women, 2000; Ito, 1997; Wartella, Lee, & Caplovitz, 2002), and to address behavioral issues such as children who play unethically or focus on competition over what they are supposed to be learning from the game (Halleck, 2002; Ito, 1997).

Second language educators have been particularly interested in games, simulations, role-playing, and other game formats for all age levels even before there were electronic games (Crookall & Oxford, 1990). Electronic simulations are of particular interest because they provide virtual worlds in which learners need to use the new language in relatively realistic or authentic situations. Simulations and games can be useful as language learning tools, owing to their ability to promote practice of skills, motivate and engage learners, and enable learners to control what they learn (also see Zhao & Lai, this volume). However, in addition to having to address the behavioral issues associated with gaming, second language educators and software designers have other challenges. Crookall (2002), for example, has observed that there is a fine line between promoting both fluency and accuracy through a simulation if the goal is to foster communication skills. He notes that simulation designers may opt for fluency over accuracy to keep the game going and motivation of learners high, and suggests that teachers can play an important role in getting students to recognize their motivations with respect to the games and in helping them address issues of accuracy of linguistic forms.

An example of an electronic simulation developed specifically for young English learners is *Zip and Terry* (Li & Topolewski, 2002), a product marketed in China and intended to provide education through entertainment. It provides meaningful situations in which children learn English vocabulary and basic phrases to converse and follow directions by interacting with animated characters in a simulated world. The automatic speech recognition feature helps learners adapt their pronunciation to standard English pronunciation. Of concern to the developers, however, is whether it is more important to keep the activities moving along by having the speech recognition adapt to the learners' imperfect pronunciation or whether to have it correct learners' speech and thereby slow down the activity and (and perhaps affect the players' interest). In other cases, language teachers have used simulation games, like The Learning Company's *Oregon Trail* (http://thelearningcompany.com), to encourage learners to develop their second language skills, such as giving directions or discussing what they are planning with others in class (see Butler-Pascoe & Wiburg, 2003; Godwin-Jones, 2005).

Although a number of games for second language learning have been developed for computers, there are few such games for game consoles. Some of these devices can ostensibly run standard PC programs with minor modifications (for more information, see the *Active Box* Web site at http://www.activewin. com/faq/x-box.shtml). Because these gaming platforms are very popular and widely available to children, they could provide a means for assisting English learning, especially for consoles like the Microsoft Xbox, which is actually a modified IBM compatible personal computer. Moreover, it is quite likely that families with low incomes have access to them more than computers and high-speed Internet connectivity. However, it appears that little is known about how well games on game consoles might support English language acquisition for elementary school-aged children from different linguistic and cultural backgrounds.

Thus, the effectiveness of game and simulation technology for young second language learners remains an open question and in need of additional research. Moreover, research also needs to examine how the improvements can enhance learning and be incorporated into instruction (Squire, 2003). When considering electronic games and simulations, educators will need to keep in mind which second language skills the games foster, the extent to which they create conditions for second language acquisition and meet diverse learner needs (e.g., paying attention to gender preferences and ethnicity and providing options for learners who do not like or have trouble interfacing with the games), and the importance of children collaborating on games that foster use of the new language.

Factors That Affect Technology for Young English Learners

Whether new technologies can live up to their potential to help children from diverse backgrounds develop strong oral English and reading skills depends heavily on historical and local contexts, interaction among participants, activities, and learners' personal goals and perspectives (Lantolf, 2000). An in-depth examination of these issues is outside the scope of this chapter (for discussions of sociocultural theoretical perspectives, see the summary in chapter 1 of this volume, in addition to more in-depth discussions by Lantolf, 2000; Schultz & Hull, 2002; and Zuengler & Miller, 2006). However, several sociocultural factors—the context of technology-mediated language environments, cultural relevance, access, and learner perspectives—are discussed here to demonstrate why they are essential to understanding what may or may not work for diverse English learners.

Technology-mediated Language Learning Environments

The context in which technology is used and how it is used are crucial factors in how well it may support English learners (Anderson-Inman & Horney, 1998; Greenleaf, 1994; Kern, 2006; Labbo & Reinking, 1999). Teachers (whether classroom teachers or informal teachers in after-school programs) can utilize a variety of educational software to give children extra practice on particular skills, to enrich content knowledge, and to motivate children to develop their English and reading skills. A number of authors have provided extensive suggestions for teachers on how to integrate educational software (whether on CDs, DVDs, or the Internet) into instructional activities that enhance English language and reading skills (e.g., see Butler-Pascoe & Wiburg, 2003; Meskill, 2002; Warschauer, Shetzer, & Meloni, 2000; Willis, Stephens, & Matthew, 1996).

Technology-mediated learning environments have been found to support English development if crafted well by the teacher, as case studies by Meskill, Mossop, and Bates (1999) illustrate. They studied the effectiveness of educational software products integrated into classroom instruction for supporting English learning. Through discourse analysis of childrens' and teachers' talk around the use of electronic texts in classrooms, these researchers show how technology can support young English learners' focus on both linguistic forms and meaning of content. Their case studies investigated and described the specific features of electronic texts (e-texts) that appear to support English language and literacy development of elementary school students in small groups or dyads based on 20 videotaped classroom sessions, videotaped recalls and interviews with the teachers, and interviews with district personnel. These researchers showed how the communication was grounded in, and motivated by, children's authentic needs to use English—whether in discussions about the unreliability of the technology or in solving the problems posed by the software products. In addition, the authors noted that this kind of talk begins to acquaint young English learners with genres they might not otherwise have access to, such as talk about computers. The success of these sessions was achieved by creative and skillful teachers who, with the support of district administrators, had figured out how to craft or translate computer-based activities into language learning opportunities that scaffolded the learners' attention to linguistic forms and meaning.

When software is carefully designed and children have been coached to discuss the topic, oral language development ensues, as Mercer, Fernández, Dawes, Wegerif, and Sams (2003) and Wegerif (2004) have shown for small groups of monolingual English-speaking children. They found that the software needs to be designed to present choices clearly to learners, use interesting storylines that involve choices, present compelling problems that benefit the children by discussing them, and provide options to learners. When coached to explore their reasoning and to collaborate on decision-making in response to software activities, the children exhibited more complex language and reasoning than when the group left decision-making up to the child who had the mouse (as they found occasionally happened). Further, in a study of 119 9- and 10-year-olds using selected math and science software designed to elicit such conversations, this research team found that children in the intervention activities showed evidence of learning about the content (Wegerif, 2004).

These findings may have important implications for second language learners. One might hypothesize that such coaching may help learners interact with English-speaking peers and at the same time may help them develop the English needed for explanations and reasoning. Such research also suggests that it is important for teachers to be aware of how educational software products support thinking and language and to be able to coach native English speakers and English learners alike in ways to think and talk about the content being taught.

Other researchers have suggested that, when children are encouraged to collaborate and to communicate with other children and/or adults with technology, they are likely to develop their oral second language and literacy skills (Meskill et al., 1999; also see chapters by Castek et al., Cummins, and Durán in this volume). Although not specifically designed to teach English as a second language, projects such as the *University–Community Links* program (http://www.uclinks.org), the *iEARN* project (http://www.iearn.org), the *Orillas* project (http://www.orillas.org), and *WebQuest* (http://webquest.sdsu.edu/), can indirectly support it through uses of technology for distance communication. For example, the WebQuest Web site provides a number of examples of how teachers have organized Internet-based projects (such as planning a virtual trip to South America) to motivate secondary English learners to use English to communicate with each other or to read and write English in gathering, and presenting Web-based information.

Communication among participants may be more important than the latest and greatest technologies for good language development environments. The University–Community (UC) Links program shows instances of how both newer and older technologies can be used informally in after-school programs to foster reading skills of at risk children. Some of the UC Links sites use older computers and software; others use more current computers and the Internet; still others use a variety of technologies such as digital video cameras, story authoring tools, audio/music, and other tools to enable children to create their own stories.

The point is that second language development can be supported by groups of children working on computer-based activities, and may be especially helpful when educators have prepared children on what to talk about, and how. The challenge for teachers is to balance the focus on accuracy and appropriateness of linguistic forms with the ability to produce comprehensible, fluent communication about ideas and subjects. However, more applied research will be needed to find ways to structure such activities for English learners from different cultural and linguistic groups.

Cultural Relevance

An unanswered question is the extent to which the cultural relevancy of content in software can help young learners from different cultural backgrounds

(Lee, 2003). Pinkard's (1999) work, for example, suggests that building on children's home background knowledge presents an effective scaffold to support reading skills. Her study focused on African–American elementary school students' use of popular commercial reading software and culturally relevant African–American oral traditions and familiar activities that she developed. The students preferred the culturally relevant products over the more general commercial products and also improved their vocabulary, leading Pinkard to suggest that cultural relevance may be a factor in the effectiveness of software programs for enhancing reading skills. It would be important to know whether (or in what circumstances) educational software that includes cultural traditions and characteristics of the target learners would be helpful to young English learners. There are some indications from the literature. For example, in studying the impact of social science simulations on high school students, Squire and Jenkins (2003) found that cultural issues were significant in encouraging some students to play the games. Some students were reluctant to play *Civilization III* until realizing they could win the game with a civilization representing their own culture. Research by Orellana (2004) on Latino elementary school children's needs for English outside of school (e.g., translating for their parents in conversations with doctors and social service workers or reading teachers' notes to parents) raises the possibility that educational software to help children with such tasks might be useful. These examples raise interesting questions about the kinds of digital activities that might be most useful to young English learners.

Access

The discussion heretofore has been premised on the assumption that young English learners have access to the technology—the equipment and the software—and that they use it productively for learning. The digital divide—the availability of technology to low-income households—may play a significant role in whether young students have access to the necessary technology-based learning tools. These digital divide factors are especially significant for many young English learners from low-income families (see, e.g., the Benton Foundation, 2004; Warschauer, 2002).

Access at Home   Families from non-English language and cultural backgrounds usually have televisions and VCRs, and often have game consoles or lower-end computers, but their access to more sophisticated computer- and Internet-based technologies and quality English language teaching activities is uneven (Ba, Tally, & Tsikalas, 2002; Knobel, Stone, & Warschauer, 2002). Although indicators suggest that home access is growing, it is probable that this type of learning tool is not as commonly found in these homes as in more affluent communities (Fairlie, 2003; Tornatzky, Macias, & Jones, 2002; Wartella et al., 2002; also see Durán, this volume). Tornatzky and his colleagues

(2002) noted that access to computers and the Internet varies across the United States, but is higher in urban areas. Using Department of Commerce data, the authors reported that 40.0% of Latinos in 2001 had computers in their homes compared to 60.6% of non-Hispanic Whites and that 32.0% of Latinos had Internet connectivity at home compared to 55.4% of Whites. Fairlie (2003) has reported that Latino and African-American families indicate cost as the primary reason for lack of computers and connectivity to the Internet, and he notes that children may have less access than adults in the home. Although some homes may have computers, the technology may be old and, if Internet connections are available at all, they may be the slower dial-up rather than high-speed broadband because of the cost (Ba, Culp, Green, Henríquez, & Honey, 2001; Ba et al., 2002).

Research suggests that patterns of use also vary in the home by factors such as age (generation) and access to technical support (Knobel et al., 2002; Durán, this volume). Additionally, because much of Internet information is in English and may be difficult for limited-English speaking parents to read (Fairlie, 2003; Lazarus, Lipper, Roberts, Fireman, & Rose, 2003), some parents and other caregivers may not see a need to invest in Internet connectivity or computers, or not know how to select appropriate oral language and reading software for their children. Moreover, families may have only one computer located in a public room of the house such as the living room for the whole family to use. This physical setting may limit younger children's access when competing with other family members for computer time and may make it difficult for children to concentrate on educational software or Internet activities due to distractions (Ba et al., 2002).

Another issue in access is what is commercially accessible to families. Walking down the aisle of retail stores that sell software products, one is overwhelmed by the huge number of software programs available for children. However, the educational software available often varies from one store to another. This suggests that parents of English learners may not be able to find highly rated educational software, even if they know what to look for (Parker, 2004). Also, parents may not know how to locate quality online language and reading activities for their children.

Access at School   Schools have made great strides in making computers and Internet access available to children at all grade levels. In fact, one might conclude that schools still provide the best access to computer and Internet technology for at-risk children. However, not only do schools across the nation vary in the type, amount, and quality of computer and Internet connectivity, they also vary in the level of access they allow children before and after school, according to national surveys of schools and student opinions (Education Evolving, 2005; Knobel et al., 2002; Tetreault, 2003). For example, although most schools in California are connected to the Internet, there are

10.49 children for every multimedia computer in schools with high proportions of children on the free and reduced price lunch program (an indicator of low-income status), compared to 8.84 children in schools with children from more affluent families (Tetreault, 2003).

Real access in school is not simply an issue of availability. It is also a function of the amount of equipment and software available and the access to technical support to fix problems (e.g., see Knobel et al. 2002), which are all significant barriers.

Real access at school also depends on well-prepared teachers. There is a great need for teacher preparation and professional development regarding the use of computers and technology (M. Calderon, personal correspondence; also see Chapelle, 2001; Greenleaf, 1994; Knobel et al., 2002; Meskill et al., 1999; NICHHD, 2000a). It is important for teachers to understand how to utilize technologies, how to find and select appropriate software and Internet activities and make them work well for building oral English as well as reading skills. It is important that teachers help children learn how to use computer and Internet tools. However, it is also important that children learn to use them productively. Knobel and her team (2002) observed in their study of several low-performing high schools with large groups of English learners from low-income families that it was fairly common to see learners who were mechanically doing research on the Internet by cutting and pasting their way through sites brought up by their search strategy, but that it was questionable whether the children were developing the conceptual understanding of the information they had located, or were just plagiarizing online information.

Any number of guides for educators (e.g., Bishop, 2001; Boswood, 1997; Butler-Pascoe & Wiburg, 2003; Egbert, Chao, & Hanson-Smith, 1999; Meskill, 2002; Valmont, 2003, Valmont & Wepner, 2000; Van Scoter et al., 2001; Willis et al., 1996) attest to the need for teacher professional development at all grade levels for integrating technology into instruction for all children and especially for English learners. The issues around teacher professional development related to technology are much too complex for this chapter to explore. Suffice it to say here that children will not have real access to the potential of technology for language and literacy development until teachers are able to incorporate it effectively into learning activities, and until schools can provide regular technical support and keep equipment in good working order.

Access in After-school Programs   Another setting for children to find access to computers and the Internet is in public libraries and community centers such as community technology centers, especially in urban areas. However, there, too, access varies considerably. For example, public libraries may put restrictions on hours of availability or on the amount of time children can spend on a computer (Gordon, Moore, Gordon, & Heuertz, 2003; J. Mimms, personal communication, February 5, 2005). Similarly, access varies in after-school programs, which may have limited access to newer computers (or at least to consistently functioning ones), the Internet, technical support, and a variety of educational software (Underwood et al., 2002). Thus although the potential exists, technology in after-school settings may be, in reality, of limited availability to young English learners.

The Learner

The perspective of the individual English learner is crucial to how effective technology can be to support their oral English and literacy development. Attitudes toward the new language, its native speakers and culture, and to reading, as well as personal needs for oral English and reading skills has been found to affect how well learners learn the language (see chapters by Cummins, Durán, and García in this volume). Learners' levels of oral English and reading skills also affect whether educational software will make a difference. The design of software may also affect learners: even the best-designed software for kindergarten children may turn off slightly older learners, even if the level of English used is appropriate for them (Parker, 2004).

Similarly, learners' attitudes and familiarity with technology also play a role in what they are likely to learn from using technology (Wartella et al., 2002). Anderson-Inman and Horney (1998), for example, found that at-risk middle school students' reading of electronic texts was as good or better than with regular print textbooks. Students who enjoyed real books did not use the digital support tools (e.g., multimedia glossaries) in the electronic texts but could still follow the main points, whereas students who were "studiers" used and enjoyed the tools and were able to recall details. By contrast "resource junkies" tended to focus on the tools they preferred (e.g., oral pronunciation tools), but were unable to understand the texts very well or recall details. These researchers suggest that it is important for educators and software designers to understand the needs of students with different learning challenges and to encourage students to use digital support resources while reading.

Another issue is how technologies promote children's vision of themselves as English speakers, and encourage them to communicate with native English speakers in classrooms and outside of school (see Cummins, this volume). Case studies by researchers such as Lam (2004; 2006) and Black (2005) illustrate how adolescent English learners can develop their identity and confidence as English speakers outside of school by participating in chatrooms with peers from their home country and by writing stories such as *anime* and *fanfiction* on their own Web sites. More research would be required to show to what extent either primary or upper elementary grade children use such tools, and how that influences their English language and literacy skills. However, educators may want to recognize the potential of these avenues for language development in both classroom and after-school activities.

It is also important for educators and developers to consider the tools and educational software that may appeal to elementary school-aged English. For example, many children, especially boys, may like to play video games. However, even if educational software is available, what will the children learn from game technologies? What technologies will appeal to elementary school-aged English learners with different interests? What features and situations will cognitively engage them in learning?

As this section has emphasized, availability and access are essential but not sufficient for technology to support educational development of any kind. Children need to know how to use it, have access to appealing and high-quality instructional content, and need to be cognitively engaged in the instructional aspects for it to make a difference. Teachers and well-informed adult guides are also essential to helping make technology work as language learning tools (Anderson-Inman & Horney, 1998; Labbo & Reinking, 1999; Wood, 2001). Further, much still needs to be learned about the extent to which young English learners are able to take advantage of electronic technologies.

Implications and Concluding Thoughts

This chapter has surveyed the potential of new technologies used in and out of school to strengthen English skills for children learning to speak and read English as a new language in their critical elementary school years and discussed some of the social and personal factors that influence the use and effectiveness of technology to support these learners. In this section, the focus is on what it implies for the classroom, for out-of-school uses of learning technology, for instructional product design (whether provided via CDs, Web sites, game devices, or other technologies), and for research. Because space precludes an in-depth discussion of these topics, only a few implications will be highlighted.

Classroom Implications

The bounty of activities for young second language learners on the Internet and in educational software products is tantalizing (see, e.g., Cummins and Sayers, 1995; Labbo & Reinking, 1999; LeLoup & Ponterio, 2003; Sherman et al., 2004). One of the repeated findings across the literature is that teachers make a difference for children when electronic technologies are in the picture. The challenges for teachers, however, are many. Integrating technology into instruction involves being knowledgeable about and locating relevant technology, software, or online activities, and being creative enough to integrate them productively into instruction. Yet there are relatively few finding aids to make this easy for these busy professionals.

In order for technology to bridge issues of access, engagement for entertainment and motivation, and cognitive engagement for learning, it needs to be appropriate for learners' level of familiarity and skills, or lack thereof

(Anderson-Inman & Horney, 1998; Butler-Pascoe & Wiburg, 2003; Knobel et al., 2002; Wartella et al. 2002; Wood, 2001). In addition to learning how to use the technology, children—both native English speakers and English learners—may need help learning how to talk, read, and write to each other about what they are learning via the technology, both to strengthen content knowledge and to develop English skills (Mercer et al., 2003; Wegerif, 2004; Wegerif, Mercer, & Dawes, 1998). The kinds of English skills that children bring will influence the kinds of software or Web sites teachers recommend for developing and enhancing oral English and reading skills. English learners will need to learn how to move between the writing they do for instant messaging and talking on cell phones, and the appropriate forms of oral and written English for the classroom. Moreover, because most of the information on the Internet is in English and requires critical thinking skills to use the information effectively, it is imperative that children learn the new literacies associated with the Internet well (Leu, Kinzer, Coiro, & Cammack, 2004). As technology changes, and in the process changes literacy and communication (see Castek et al., this volume, and Kern, 2006), teachers will have to be ready to address these issues.

With such a daunting array of challenges, there is a clear need for teacher professional development to assist teachers in using technologies in instruction. Teachers need other kinds of support, too. For example, they need easy-to-use resources to locate free and/or inexpensive technology, software and Web sites that would benefit the particular children they teach. School administrators also need to recognize the importance of not simply making computers and the Internet accessible; they must also include equipment refreshment and readily available technical support in their planning and budget process.

Implications for Non-school Settings

Activities after school constitute important language development opportunities for young English learners, whether at home or in after-school programs at schools, community centers, or libraries. Electronic technologies afford many English learning possibilities outside of school, through television, computers, MP3 players (like iPods), and game console devices. However we know little about which technologies children from diverse non-English background communities have and use, or what kinds of technology and supplemental resources might help them and their families. Some parents may benefit from suggestions about software, useful Web sites, and how to plan for technology that will support their children's efforts to learn English.

Because after-school programs may not have an explicit goal to foster English language development, adult guides may also need help finding out about and accessing sound, but affordable, content resources and may benefit from assistance in turning some of their usual technology-based activities into language and reading development activities. Although many after-school programs make good use of whatever technologies they have available, they face the challenges of dealing with a lack of technical support, outdated equipment, and difficulties finding useful software and Web sites. Additional funding for after-school programs is one answer. Assistance finding information and technology resources to develop children's English skills might also be useful.

Implications for Design and Development

Despite the creative and appealing virtual learning environments that product designers have developed to support second language learning and reading skills, we know relatively little about how effective these efforts are with young English learners. The question is what kind of bridges between the design of technology and best educational practices will enable us to achieve our goals.

As we have seen, a number of common themes can be found across the literature about what makes software or other technology-based activities successful for second language learners. Among these themes are the need to use the new language in multiple meaningful contexts, including frequent repetition and multimedia support to reinforce learning, and to provide opportunities for meaningful communication and interaction in the language and feedback mechanisms (see, e.g., discussions of video-based second language teaching courses in Rhodes & Pufahl, 2004; about vocabulary teaching software in Wood, 2001; educational games in Mitchell & Savill-Smith, 2004; and second language teaching software reported in this chapter). These features are consistent with the fundamental conditions for good second language learning environments that Zhao & Lai (this volume) have discussed, and they can be used in developing software and Web sites for young English learners.

However, there are issues specific to young English learners in low-income areas that designers and product developers need to consider. These include the types of technology delivery systems, interfaces, and tools that may be affordable and appealing to elementary school-aged English learners. Game consoles and televisions, for example, are likely to be found in many households of economically challenged areas; so utilizing existing platforms could be cost efficient. Also, new technologies, such as text readers, and natural speech recognition and synthesis, might help children develop both their English literacy and their oral English skills if such tools were built into more products. We are on the verge of technology that might also permit a video of a native speaker to ask a question of a language learner and the learner responds orally in the new language. Such software might recognize the learner's speech and provide feedback on accuracy or might use a character to respond as a native speaker might, so that the learner can literally hold a conversation with his/her technology device. Designers and product developers could explore developing English support instructional resources for new multimedia-capable technologies such as MP3 players and cell phones.

There is a need for more authentic and culturally relevant communication activities that address some of the interests or goals of young learners. As one example, English language development activities based around communication with doctors, banks, and other daily activities might be helpful and appealing to both children and their parents, and could expand their oral skills. Moreover, designers need to take into consideration the kinds of English skills that children have and figure out even more sophisticated ways for software/Web site activities to adjust what is taught to the learners' language ability. These are just a few of many possibilities for design and development.

Research Implications

As has been discussed, many issues might benefit from further research. However, several areas deserve special mention. One area is the need for research on the communities of English learners from different language backgrounds—their access to various kinds of technologies, the relevance of cultural factors in instructional design of virtual learning environments, and the perspectives of the learners themselves. We also need to understand better the potential of newer technologies such as game consoles and hand-held computers to support second language and literacy development. For example, handheld computers with touch screens may offer children a better solution, in many ways, than desktop computers (because of portability and intuitive ease of use)—and so might television and VCRs. Moreover, given the attraction of games to many children and the excitement of doing collaborative projects for an authentic purpose, it is important to investigate the kinds of games and activities that work well for diverse groups of children. A third area involves applied research to help teachers incorporate technology as a language learning tool into regular classroom instruction.

In any case, it will be important for research to find ways to address the issue of changing technologies. It is not only difficult to generalize findings from studies using a specific set of technologies; it may be impossible (Leu, 2000). Rather than focusing on specific technologies, it may be more productive to investigate the role of tools as one part of the context of language learning environments. Addressing the challenges of technology in learning may also require addressing difficult theoretical and methodological questions in the process.

Some Concluding Thoughts

Learning a new language is complex and grounded in social and cultural contexts. As noted at the beginning of this chapter, technologies—like language learning—are also influenced by the social milieu (Labbo & Reinking, 1999;

Lantolf, 2000). The nature and contexts of the activities, access, and learner perspectives must be factored into questions of whether technology can adequately support second language learning. No one set of technologies or one software program or set of Internet-based activities, no matter how brilliantly designed, will likely be the answer. So, the challenge becomes one of figuring out what mix of technologies, infrastructure, language learning products (on CDs, the Internet, audiotapes, videotapes, and so on), design features, and learning environments will provide the best balance of content and motivating activity for young second language learners. *How* these technologies are used, rather than the technologies themselves, is likely to be the crucial factor in supporting English language development.

Acknowledgments

The author is grateful to Vince de'Armond, information technologies consultant, for advice on new technologies, and for suggestions from Carla Meskill and an anonymous reviewer on an earlier version of this chapter.

Notes

1. For this chapter, I use the term *English learner* to refer to children from diverse language and cultural backgrounds in U.S. schools who are learning English as another language. Other authors in the book use terms such as English language learners, ELLs, or bilingual children. I use the term *second language learner* to refer both to learners of other or foreign languages as well as to English learners.

2. One aspect that is sometimes overlooked in discussions of computers and learning is the interface itself, which may have implications for children. In addition to the ubiquitous keyboard and mouse, new computer-interface technologies, such as touchscreens, are being developed (for examples of interfaces, see Chinnery, 2006; for discussions of universal designs for learning, see http://www.cast.org). It will be important to understand how these innovations affect young second language learners.

3. In their review of literature about uses of small mobile computers for young disaffected adults, Savill-Smith and Kent (2003) argue that these devices can motivate learning, foster organization, support both independent and collaborative inquiry, access reference tools and electronic books, be used for assessment, support the learning of information and communications literacy skills, and provide entertainment (e.g., in the form of games).

4. For example, *PocketLingo* (http://www.pocketlingo.com) has added a special reference tool for intermediate and advanced adult English learners called *PocketLingo ESL.* It provides access to *The American Heritage Dictionary for Learners of English,* a database of sentences and phrases, study cards, adjustable font sizes, an auto-suggest feature, and a fast search feature.

5. Certain devices, such as the Nintendo DS and the Sony PSP, which are basically handheld gaming devices that use cartridges, have become very popular with both children and adults. Thus, the form factor may work for children, but there may be other issues that influence children's use of small devices as

educational tools. For example, cultural differences among learners may be a factor. Anecdotal evidence from an after-school program for middle school students in Oakland, California, suggests that some of the Vietnamese English learners use electronic dictionaries but that the Latino children do not use them or have access to them. Ethnographic research could increase our understanding of such situations.

6. MP3 players and cell phones are not as powerful as PDAs and other handheld computers, but have the advantage of being less expensive and much more popular than computers among students (presumably older students). Godwin-Jones (2005) notes that some teachers have incorporated the use of instant messaging (IM) and blogs into instruction to motivate students to read and write, and that some educators, primarily in Europe, are using short messaging services (SMS) along with radio broadcasts and cell phones to support English instruction for non-European countries.

7. Most chatterbots attempt to pick up cue words or phrases from the person that will allow them to use pre-prepared or pre-calculated responses to continue the conversation in an meaningful way without requiring the bot to know what it is talking about. An exception to this approach is *Jabberwacky* (http://www.jabberwacky.com), which attempts to replicate the way humans learn new information and language.

8. In addition to *Children's Technology Review* (CTR, http://www.childrenssoftware.com), there are a number of other respected educational software review groups, such as *Reviewcorner.com* (http://www.reviewcorner.com), *SuperKids* (http://www.superkids.com), *the Educational Software Preview Guide* (http://www-ed.fnal.gov/espg/what.htm, also available at http://www.iste.org), the *California Learning Resources Network* (CLRN, http://www.clrn.org) and *TEEM* (a British teacher-based organization that reviews software, http://www.teem.org.uk). However, they vary on what features can be searched. CTR had the best combination of features for the purposes of the study discussed here.

References

American Association for Artificial Intelligence. (2004, 2006). *Intelligent tutoring systems*. Retrieved December 5, 2004, from http://www.aaai.org/AITopics//html/tutor.html.

American Association of University Women [AAUW]. (2000). *Tech-savvy: Educating girls in the new computer age*. Washington, DC: American Association of University Women Foundation. Retrieved June 10, 2006, from http://www.aauw.org/research/girls_education/techsavvy.cfm.

Anderson-Inman, L., & Horney, M. A. (1998). Transforming text for at-risk readers. In D. Reinking, M. C. McKenna, L. D. Labbo, & R. D. Kieffer (Eds.), *Handbook of technology and literacy: Transformations in a post-typographic world* (pp. 15–44). Mahwah, NJ: Erlbaum.

August, D. (2003). *Supporting the development of English literacy in English language learners: Key issues and promising practices* (No. 61). Baltimore, MD: Center for Research on the Education of Students Placed At Risk (CRESPAR)/Johns Hopkins University.

August, D., & Shanahan, T. (2006). Executive summary. In D. August & T. Shanahan (Eds.), *Developing literacy in second-language learners: Report of the National Literacy Panel on Language-Minority Children and Youth*. Mahwah, NJ: Erlbaum. Retrieved May 22, 2006, from http://www.cal.org/natl-lit-panel/reports/Executive_Summary.pdf.

Ba, H., Culp, K. M., Green, L., Henríquez, A., & Honey, M. (2001). *Effective technology use in low-income communities: Research review for the America connects consortium*. Newton, MA: America Connects Consortium. Retrieved March 1, 2004, from http://www.americaconnects.net/research/litreview.pdf.

Ba, H., Tally, B., & Tsikalas, K. (2002). *Children's emerging digital literacies: Investigating home computing in low- and middle-income families*. New York: Education Department, Center for Children & Technology, Corporation for Public Broadcasting. Retrieved July 23, 2007, from http://cct.edc.org/.

Baumbach, D., Christopher, T., Fasimpaur, K., & Oliver, K. (2004). Personal literacy assistants. *Learning & Leading with Technology, 32*(2), 16–20.

Benton Foundation. (2004). *Digital divide network [Website]*. Retrieved July 23, 2007, from http://www.digitaldivdenetwork.org.

Bishop, A. (2001, April). An expert's guide to products for the multilingual classroom. *Technology and Learning, 21*(9), 39ff. Retrieved March 1, from http://www.ncela.gwu.edu/resabout/technology/3_instruction.html.

Black, R. W. (2005). Access and affiliation: The literacy and composition practices of English-language learners in an online fanfiction community. *Journal of Adolescent & Adult Literacy, 49*(2), 118–128.

Boswood, T. (Ed.). (1997). *New ways of using computers in language teaching*. Alexandria, VA: Teachers of English to Speakers of Other Languages, Inc.

Butler-Pascoe, M. E., & Wiburg, K. M. (2003). *Technology and teaching English language learners*. Boston: Allyn-Bacon.

Center for Children and Technology. (2004). *Television goes to school: The impact of video on student learning in formal education*. New York: Corporation for Public Broadcasting. Retrieved July 23, 2007, from http://cct.edc.org.

Chapelle, C. A. (2001). *Computer applications in second language acquisition: Foundations for teaching, testing, and research*. Cambridge, UK: Cambridge University Press.

Chinnery, G. M. (2006). Emerging technologies: Going to the MALL: Mobile assisted language learning. *Language Learning & Technology, 10*(1), 9–16. Retrieved June 12, 2006, from http://llt.msu.edu/vol10num1/emerging/default.html.

Cohen, M. M., Massaro, D. W., & Clark, R. (2002). *Training a talking head*. Paper presented at the Proceedings of the IEEE Fourth International Conference on Multimodal Interfaces, Pittsburgh, PA. Retrieved July 22, 2006, from http://mambo.ucsc.edu/psl/dwm.

Cole, R. (2003, September). *Roadmaps, journeys and destinations: Speculations on the future of speech technology research. Panel Presentation*. Paper presented at the INTERSPEECH-2003/Eurospeech-2003, Geneva, Switzerland. Retrieved July 10, 2004, from the Center for Spoken Language Research's website at http://cslr.colorado.edu/beginweb/whats_new/ron%20cole%20eurospeech%204.pdf.

Cole, R., van Vuuren, S., Pellom, B., Hacioglu, K., Ma, J., Movellan, J., et al. (2003, August). *Perceptive animated interfaces: First steps toward a new paradigm for human computer interaction*. Proceedings of the IEEE: Special issue on Multimodal Human Computer Interface. Retrieved July 22, 2006, from the University of Colorado's Center for Spoken Language Research Web site at http://cslr.colorado.edu/beginweb/reading/reading.html.

Crookall, D. (2002). Editorial: Simulation in language learning. *Simulation & Gaming,* 33(3), 273–274.

Crookall, D., & Oxford, R. L. (1990). Linking language learning and simulation/gaming. In D. Crookall & R. L. Oxford (Eds.), *Simulation, gaming, and language learning* (pp. 3–24). New York: Newbury House.

Cummins, J. (2001, September/October). Magic bullets and the fourth grade slump: Solutions from technology? *NABE News,* 25, 4–6.

Cummins, J., & Sayers, D. (1995). *Brave new schools: Challenging cultural illiteracy through global learning networks.* New York, NY: St. Martin's Press.

Education Evolving. (2005). *Listening to student voices on technology: Today's tech-savvy students are stuck in text-dominated schools.* St. Paul, Minnesota: Center for Policy Studies and Hamline University. Retrieved March 21, 2006, from http://www.educationevolving.org/studentvoices.

Egbert, J., Chao, C., & Hanson-Smith, E. (1999). Computer-enhanced language learning environments: An overview. In J. Egbert & E. Hanson-Smith (Eds.), *CALL environments: Research, practice, and critical issues* (pp. 1–13). Alexandria, VA: Teachers of English to Speakers of Other Languages.

Ehsani, F., & Knodt, E. (1998). Speech technology in computer-aided language learning: Strengths and limitations of a new CALL paradigm. *Language Learning & Technology,* 2(1), 45–60. Retrieved December 5, 2004, from http://llt.msu.edu/vol2num1/article3/index.html.

Fairlie, R. (2003). *Is there a digital divide? Ethnic and racial differences in access to technology and possible explanations: Final report to the University of California Latino Policy Institute and California Policy Research Center.* Santa Cruz: University of California. Retrieved October 5, 2004, from http://cjtc.ucsc.edu/docs/r_techreport5.pdf.

Felix, U. (2003). An orchestrated vision of language learning online. In U. Felix (Ed.), *Language learning online: Towards best practice* (pp. 7–20). Lisse, The Netherlands: Swets & Zeitlinger.

French, K. (2001–2002). Opening doors to the world. *Learning & Leading with Technology,* 29(4), 42–48.

Gee, J. (2003). *What video games have to teach us about learning and literacy.* New York: Palgrave MacMillan.

Godwin-Jones, B. (2005). Emerging technologies: Messaging, gaming, peer-to-peer sharing: Language learning strategies & tools for the millennial generation. *Language Learning & Technology,* 9(1), 17–22. Retrieved May 31, 2006, from http://llt.msu.edu/vol9num1/emerging/default.html.

Gordon, M. T., Moore, E. J., Gordon, A., & Heuertz, L. (2003). Kids have access, enjoy computers: Libraries key for many, especially the disadvantaged (A report to the Bill & Melinda Gates Foundation U.S. Library Program on a survey of youth ages 12–18). Seattle, WA: University of Washington Public-Access Computing Project. Retrieved July 15, 2007, from http://www.gatesfoundation.org/NR/Downloads/libraries/eval_docs/pdf/Kids_have_access_10-03.pdf.

Greenleaf, C. (1994). Technological indeterminacy: The role of classroom writing practices and pedagogy in shaping student use of the computer. *Written Communication,* 11(1), 185–230.

Hakuta, K., Butler, Y., & Witt, D. (2000). How long does it take English learners to attain proficiency? *University of California Linguistic Minority Research Institute Policy Report 2000–1.* Also available from http://lmri.ucsb.edu/publications/policyreports.php#00_hakuta.

Halleck, G. (2002). Guest editorial: Simulation in language learning. *Simulation & Gaming, 33*(4), 276–279.

Holum, A., & Gahala, J. (2001). *Critical issue: Using technology to enhance literacy instruction.* Naperville, IL: North Central Regional Educational Laboratory. Retrieved March 3, 2003, from http://www.ncrel.org/sdrs/areas/issues/content/ cntareas/reading/li300.htm.

Inkpen, K. M. (1999). Designing handheld technologies for kids. *Personal Technologies, 3*(1–2), 881–889.

Ito, M. (1997, October). *Kids and simulation games: Subject formation through human–machine interaction.* Paper presented at the Annual Meeting of the Society for the Social Studies of Science. Retrieved December 7, 2005, from http://www. itofisher.com/mito/publications/.

Kern, R. (2006). Perspectives on technology in learning and teaching languages. *TESOL Quarterly, 40*(1), 183–210.

Knobel, M., Stone, L., & Warschauer, M. (2002). *Technology and academic preparation: A comparative study.* Irvine, CA: University of California. Also available at http://www.gse.uci.edu/faculty/markw/research.html.

Krajka, J. (2002). EFL/ESL portal sites — An attempt at a comparison. *TESL-EJ, 6*(2). Retrieved July 10, 2004, from http://www-writing.berkeley.edu/TESL-EJ/ej22/ m1.html.

Kramsch, C. (1993). *Context and culture in language teaching.* Oxford, UK: Oxford University Press.

Labbo, L. D., & Reinking, D. (1999). Negotiating the multiple realities of technology in literacy research and instruction. *Reading Research Quarterly, 34*(4), 478–492.

Lam, W. S. E. (2004). Second language socialization in a bilingual chat room: Global and local considerations. *Language Learning & Technology, 8*(3), 44–65. Retrieved May 31, 2006, from http://llt.msu.edu/vol8num3/lam/default.html.

Lam, W. S. E. (2006). Re-envisioning language, literacy, and the immigrant subject in new mediascapes. *Pedagogies.* Retrieved May 31, 2006, from http://www.sesp. northwestern.edu/profile/?p=492&/EvaLam/.

Lantolf, J. P. (2000). Introducing sociocultural theory. In J. P. Lantoff (Ed.), *Sociocultural theory and second language learning* (pp. 1–26). Oxford, UK: Oxford University Press.

Lazarus, W., Lipper, L., Roberts, K., Fireman, R., & Rose, M. (2003). *The search for high-quality online content for low-income and underserved communities: Evaluating and producing what's needed.* The Children's Partnership. Retrieved July 10, 2004, from http://www.childrenspartnership.org.

LeapFrog SchoolHouse. (2004). *Language First! English language development program Phoenix K–2 study, 2003–2004.* Retrieved October 10, 2004, from http:// www.leapfrogschoolhouse.com.

Lee, C. D. (2003). Toward a framework for culturally responsive design in multimedia computer environments: Cultural modeling as a case. *Mind, Culture, and Activity, 10*(1), 42–61.

LeLoup, J. W., & Ponterio, R. (2003, December). *Second language acquisition and technology: A review of the research [Digest].* Retrieved September 23, 2004, from http://www.cal.org/resources/digest/0311leloup.html.

LeLoup, J. W., & Ponterio, R. (2005). On the net: Let's go to the zoo! Sites for young language learners. *Language Learning & Technology, 9*(1), 4–16. Retrieved July 10, 2006 from http://llt.msu.edu/vol9num1/pdf/net.pdf.

Leu, D. J. (2000). Literacy and technology: Deictic consequences for literacy education in an information age. In M. L. Kamil, P. B. Mosenthal, P. D. Pearson, & R. Barr (Eds.), *Handbook of Reading Research: Vol. III* (pp. 743–770). Mahwah, NJ: Erlbaum.

Leu, D. J., Kinzer, C. K., Coiro, J., & Cammack, D. (2004). Toward a theory of new literacies emerging from the Internet and other information and communication technologies. In R. B. Ruddell & N. Unrau (Eds.), *Theoretical models and processes of reading* (5th ed., pp. 1568–1611). Newark, DE: International Reading Association.

Li, R.-C., & Topolewski, D. (2002). ZIP & TERRY: A new attempt at designing language learning simulation. *Simulation & Gaming, 33*(2), 181–186.

Lightbown, P. M., & Spada, N. (1993). *How languages are learned.* Oxford, UK: Oxford University Press.

Liu, M., Moore, Z., Graham, L., & Lee, S. (2002). A look at the research on computer-based technology use in second language learning: Review of literature from 1990–2000. *Journal of Research on Technology in Education, 34*(3), 250–273.

Massaro, D. W., Ouni, S., Cohen, M. M., & Clark, R. (2005, July). *A multilingual embodied conversational agent.* Paper presented at the IEEE Proceedings of the 38th Annual Hawaii International Conference on System Sciences, Los Alamitos, CA. Retrieved July 22, 2006, from http://mambo.ucsc.edu/psl/dwm/.

Mayer, R. E., Schustack, M., & Blanton, W. (1999). What do children learn from using computers in an informal collaborative setting? *Educational Technology, 9,* 27–31. Retrieved July 31, 2006, from the Fifth Dimension Clearinghouse at http://129.171.53.1/blantonw/5dClhse/publications/tech/tech.html.

Mercer, N., Fernández, M., Dawes, L., Wegerif, R., & Sams, C. (2003). Talk about texts at the computer: Using ICT to develop children's oral and literate abilities. *Literacy, 37*(2), 81–89.

Meskill, C. (2002). *Teaching and learning in real time: Media, technologies and language acquisition.* Houston, TX: Athelstan.

Meskill, C., Mossop, J., & Bates, R. (1999). *Electronic text and English as a second language environments.* (No. 12012). National Research Center for English Learning and Achievement. Retrieved April 19, 2004, from http://cela.albany.edu.

Mitchell, A., & Savill-Smith, C. (2004). *The use of computer and video games for learning.* London: Learning and Skills Development Agency. Retrieved December 8, 2004, from http://www.lsda.org.uk/files/PDF/1529.pdf.

Monke, L. (2005). Charlotte's webpage: Why children shouldn't have the world at their fingertips. *Orion Magazine.* Retrieved July 23, 2007, from http://www.orionmagazine.org/index.php/articles/article/159/.

National Institute of Child Health and Human Development [NICHHD]. (2000a). Chapter 5: Computer technology and reading. In *Report of the National Reading Panel. Teaching children to read: An evidence-based assessment of the scientific research literature on reading and its implications for reading instruction: Reports of the subgroups.* Washington, DC: U.S. Government Printing Office. Retrieved May 22, 2006, from http://www.nichd.nih.gov/publications/nrp/report.cfm.

National Institute of Child Health and Human Development [NICHHD]. (2000b). *Report of the National Reading Panel. Teaching children to read: An evidence-based assessment of the scientific research literature on reading and its implications for reading instruction.* Washington, DC: U.S. Government Printing Office. Retrieved May 22, 2006, from http://www.nichd.nih.gov/publications/nrp/smallbook.cfm.

Orellana, M. F. (2004). *Latino children as family translators: Links to literacy.* Retrieved June 4, 2004, from http://www.gseis.ucla.edu/faculty/orellana/Translations.html.

Parker, L. L. (2004). *Characteristics of second language software for children.* Unpublished data.

Parr, J. (2003). *A review of the literature on computer-assisted learning, particularly integrated learning systems, and outcomes with respect to literacy and numeracy: Report to the Ministry of Education.* Auckland, New Zealand: Ministry of Education. Retrieved October 10, 2004, from http://www.minedu.govt.nz/index.cfm?layout=document&documentid=5499&data=l.

Peregoy, S. F., & Boyle, O. (2005). *Reading, writing, and learning in ESL: A resource book for K–12 teachers* (4th ed.). Boston: Pearson Education.

Pinkard, N. (1999). *Learning to read in culturally responsive computer environments*: Center for the Improvement of Early Reading Achievement. Retrieved October 23, 2003, from http://www.ciera.org/library/reports/inquiry-1/1-004/1-004.html.

Readers' Choice Awards: School reading software. (2004, November/December). *eSchool News,* pp. 33–35. Retrieved November 5, 2004, from http://www.eschoolnews.org.

Rhodes, N. C., & Pufahl, I. (2004). *Language by video: An overview of foreign language instructional videos for children.* Washington, DC: Center for Applied Linguistics.

Romig, N., Yan, B., & Zhao, Y. (2006, June). *The effects of inexpensive, portable, interactive learning systems on emergent reading.* Paper presented at the American Educational Research Association meetings. San Francisco, CA.

Salaberry, M. R. (2001). The use of technology for second language learning and teaching: A retrospective. *Modern Language Journal,* 85(1), 30–56.

Savill-Smith, C., & Kent, P. (2003). *The use of palmtop computers for learning: A review of the literature* (literature review for the m-learning project,). London: Learning and Skills Development Agency. Retrieved December 8, 2004, from http://www.m-learning.org/docs/the_use_of_palmtop_computers_for_learning_sept03.pdf.

Schultz, K., & Hull, G. (2002). Locating literacy theory in out-of-school contexts. In G. Hull & K. Schultz (Eds.), *School's out! Bridging out-of-school literacies with classroom practice* (pp. 11–31). New York: Teachers College Press.

Selinker, L., & Mascia, R. (2001). Interlanguage speech recognition by computer: Implications for SLA and computational machines. *Applied Language Studies,* 1(1), 19–55. Retrieved December 5, 2004, from http://www.solki.jyu.fi/apples/010101/ISPRC.htm.

Shapira, I. (2003, August 24). ESL students may get hand-held computers. *Washington Post,* p. LZ03.

Sherman, D., Kleiman, G., & Kirsten, P. (2004). *Technology and teaching children to read.* Boston: Education Development Center. Retrieved July 23, 2007, from https://secure.edc.org/publications/prodView.asp?1640.

Snow, C. E., Burns, M. S., & Griffin, P. (Eds.). (1998). *Preventing reading difficulties in young children.* Washington, DC: National Academy Press.

Squire, K. (2003). Video games in education. *International Journal of Intelligent Simulations and Gaming,* 2(1). Retrieved July 22, 2006, from http://website.education.wisc.edu/kdsquire/research.html.

Squire, K., & Jenkins, H. (2003). Harnessing the power of games in education. *Insight,* 3(1), 5–33. Retrieved July 22, 2006, from http://website.education.wisc.edu/kdsquire/manuscripts/insight.pdf.

Svedkauskaite, A., & Reza-Hernandez, L. (2003). *Critical issue: Using technology to support limited English-proficient (LEP) students' learning experiences*: North Central Regional Educational Laboratory (NCREL). Retrieved March 8, 2004, from http://www.ncrel.org/sdrs/areas/issues/methods/technlgy/te900.htm.

Tetreault, D. (2003). *Summary of year 2003 school technology survey findings: California statewide report*. Sacramento, CA: California Department of Education. Retrieved October 10, 2005, from http://www.cde.ca.gov/ls/et/rs/documents/castsreport03.pdf.

Texeira, E. (2006). Latino characters, Spanish dialogue commonplace in kids' shows. *Oakland Tribune*, p. 3.

Tornatzky, L., Macias, E., & Jones, S. (2002). *Latinos and information technology: The promise and the challenge*. Claremont, CA: Tomas Rivera Policy Institute. Retrieved January 20, 2005, from http://www.trpi.org/PDFs/LatinosandIT.pdf.

Underwood, C., Welsh, M., Emmons, C., Lerner, D., & Sturak, T. (2002). *University–Community Links to higher learning: Annual report for 2001–2002*. Oakland, CA: University of California Office of the President.

Valmont, W. J., & Wepner, S. B. (2000). Using technology to support literacy learning. In S. B. Wepner, W. J. Valmont & R. Thurlow (Eds.), *Linking literacy and technology: A guide for K–8 educators* (pp. 2–18). Newark, DE: International Reading Association.

Van Scoter, J., Ellis, D., & Railsback, J. (2001). *Technology in early childhood education: Finding the balance*. Portland, OR: Northwest Regional Educational Laboratory. Retrieved March 29, 2004, from http://www.nwrel.org/request.

Warschauer, M. (1996). Computer-assisted language learning: An introduction. In S. Fotos (Ed.), *Multimedia language teaching* (pp. 3–20). Tokyo, Japan: Logos International. Retrieved December 17, 2004, from http://www.ict4lt.org/en/warschauer.htm.

Warschauer, M. (2002). Reconceptualizing the digital divide. *First Monday, 7*(7). Retrieved May 9, 2005, from http://www.firstmonday.dk/issues/issue7_7/warschauer/.

Warschauer, M., & Kern, R. (Eds.). (2000). *Network-based language teaching: Concepts and practice*. Cambridge, UK: Cambridge University Press.

Warschauer, M., Shetzer, H., & Meloni, C. (Eds.). (2000). *Internet for English teaching*. Alexandria, VA: Teachers of English to Speakers of Other Languages, Inc.

Wartella, E., Lee, J. H., & Caplovitz, A. G. (2002). *Children and interactive media: An updated research compendium*: Markle Foundation. Retrieved May 17, 2004, from http://www.digital-kids.net/modules/downloads/file_archive/final_compendium_ac.pdf.

Wegerif, R. (2004). The role of educational software in teaching and learning conversations. *Computers and Education, 43*(2), 179–191.

Wegerif, R., Mercer, N., & Dawes, L. (1998). Software design to support discussion in the primary classroom. *Journal of Computer Assisted Learning, 14*(3), 199–211.

Willis, J. W., Stephens, E. C., & Matthew, K. I. (1996). *Technology, reading, and language arts*. Boston: Allyn and Bacon.

Wood, J. (2001). Can software support children's vocabulary development? *Language Learning & Technology, 5*(1), 166–201. Retrieved February 5, 2003, from http://llt.msu.edu/vol5num1/wood/default.html.

Zhao, Y. (2003). Recent developments in technology and language learning: A literature review and meta-analysis. *CALICO Journal, 21*(1), 7–27.

Zuengler, J., & Miller, E. R. (2006). Cognitive and sociocultural perspectives: Two parallel SLA worlds? *TESOL Quarterly, 40*(1), 35–58.

REFLECTION

ELLs and Technology
Transforming Teaching and Learning

CARLA MESKILL

University at Albany, State University of New York

If you have ever witnessed a talented, experienced teacher integrating computer uses into her teaching, you know well the potential of technology to support and enhance teaching and learning processes. If you have ever witnessed computers applied poorly in teaching and learning—for example, children sitting alone in front of screens clicking away with no one guiding, instructing, and supporting; with no one to share, consult, or converse with—you might scratch your head and ask, "All this money for *this*?" Much of both go on in U.S. classrooms every day with English language learners (ELLs). What distinguishes the two scenarios is a matter of affluence; not affluence of dollars, machines, wires, or bandwidth, but affluence of mind: the engaged, generative minds of teachers and learners conversing, and thereby learning, using readily accessible software tools, instructional games and simulations, and online resources.

Here I first discuss the complex of factors that leads to the development of young English language learners' language and literacy proficiency, the goal of teaching English to Speakers of Other Languages (ESOL). In following, I outline the elements that make up a successful ELL and technology ecology and specific uses of instructional technology in the service of this language and literacy development. The constitution of the truly excellent teaching that shapes these ecologies will then be taken up. I conclude by noting the contributions of ELLs and technology to the reshaping of contemporary schooling and the affluence of mind that makes for excellent instruction.

Learning a Second Language and School Literacy

The ultimate goal of ELL instruction is for non-native English speaking children to make and understand meaning as does a native speaker. This goal has been struggled for and achieved by immigrants to the United States for the entire history of the nation. What marks this particular time in history is that expectations have changed. All English language learners in U.S. schools are to achieve not only a social/functional level of language proficiency, but an academic one on par with their native-English speaking peers. With the widespread abandonment of bilingual education, the measured academic achievement of ELLs is now almost wholly dependent on the English language proficiency required to succeed on yearly tests, with the amount of native language assistance provided children on content area tests varying from state to state. In her chapter, Parker establishes that attaining such academic proficiency in a second language takes a very long time and requires a good deal of instructional support. Indeed, consider that for native monolingual speakers of U.S. English it is difficult to imagine learning a foreign language to a level of proficiency to succeed in, say, a middle school in China. That would be considered a very gifted or talented individual from a U.S. perspective; mastering the academic language and concepts of science, mathematics, Chinese art, history, and literature to the level of a native Chinese speaker! This is precisely what we expect of our hundreds of thousands of ELL children every day, often with very little in the way of support.

Central to understanding the teaching and learning of ELL children is that, unlike adolescent and older language learners, young children do not need to, indeed should not be required to employ the metacognitive and metalinguistic skills we require of older language learners. That is, young children will not benefit from the explicit teaching of grammatical rules or the dictionary definitions of words or explanations of the phonological system of the target language—aspects of learning foreign languages that are employed with older learners due to their capacity to think and reason at such a level of abstraction. Young children have the capacity to learn language naturalistically as they learned their native language through productive, pleasurable interaction with their environment and those communicating within it. They are also intellectually well equipped, like their native-speaker counterparts, to learn age-appropriate academic content if that content is sequenced in terms of linguistic complexity and rendered comprehensible to them through various supports: native language supports and/or the many forms of visual and verbal scaffolding inherent in Sheltered English approaches (Short, 2002).

Another important factor that Parker highlights is that in the United States standard ways of doing school—thinking, talking, and understanding academically—are similar to ways of thinking, talking, and understanding enacted in White middle- and upper-class homes (Gee, 1990; Heath, 1983). Children from such homes thereby have little trouble assimilating to the language and ways of thinking and doing school. In the homes of many ethnic groups, however, "talking school" is as foreign as speaking and understanding an exotic language and culture. This is certainly the case with many Hispanic households where interpersonal communication is markedly different from the academic-like speech of the White middle and upper classes. This is one reason why learners whose home language/culture does not mesh with that of their schools have special challenges on top of learning the language; they must simultaneously learn the language of doing school (Meskill, 2005a).

These are tremendous challenges for which ESOL instruction and support from mainstream teachers are essential.

What constitutes optimal contexts for such language and literacy learning? Chang-Wells and Wells (1993) construct the claim that sociocultural learning—learning the language and cultural complexity of others through generative interaction with those others, by apprenticing to the target so as to assimilate to their world—is indeed language learning. Language competence—the ability to say the right thing, at the right time, in the right context, with the desired effect—cannot be learned in a vacuum but must be learned by guided immersion within the linguistic and cultural practices of the target population. When that guided immersion includes authentic, content-rich materials—the materials of school—and engaged, literate talk about and around those materials, optimal contexts for children's second language and literacy learning are realizable. In our longitudinal study of technology uses with ELLs, for example, we witnessed (1) how computer and English language learner ecologies can be ripe and potent venues for language and literacy learning; (2) how the mindset and attitudes of district and local administrators, staff, indeed all school personnel contributed to the success of the intellectually affluent learning ecologies we observed; and (3) how the key factor was teachers actively teaching by making use of what literacy/content material appeared on the computer screen. Indeed, enlightened stances toward both the English language learners and optimal uses of instructional technology prevailed throughout our observations and interviews. We witnessed continuous pride and accomplishment through active social academic learning (Meskill, Mossop, & Bates, 1999; see also Vásquez, 2003).

ELL and Technology Ecologies

An effective ELL and technology ecology is an "ecosocial system" (Lemke, 1998, p. 296) whereby complex forms of judgment are continuous and verbally acted on; this as opposed to learners being led passively through linear information. Children are indeed in front of computer screens, but the impetus, models, and guidance for their decision making lie not on the screen, but in the language and literacy community that surrounds them. Larger instructional goals are made clear prior, during and after computer use, with supporting literacy activities like reading reference texts, planning strategies on paper, and the like happening prior to, during and in conjunction with navigating what is on the computer screen; indeed, the computer itself is one of many literacy tools the community taps to further and enhance the language, literacy, and content area learning that is going on. The essence of such an ecology is *negotiated interaction* (Long, 1996) whereby the object of study is less concerned with straight language and comprehension and more concerned about authentic communication. This includes making things happen on the computer screen that make sense.

This type of talk is widely considered the key locus of initiation into discourse communities and for second language acquisition per se (Ellis, 2005; Lindfors, 1989; Mackey, Gass, & McDonough, 2000; Pica, 2005). Learners advance their language and literacy skills through engaging in the social and literate practices of the institution, the discipline(s) being studied, and of the immediate academic community as "insiders" (Gee, 2003). They engage in the kinds of textwork in which literate individuals engage as part and parcel of scholarship. Indeed, in productive learning environments with textwork as a focus, in order to compute and contribute, learners "build situated worlds of experiences in [their] minds" (p. 26). Situated experiences might be considered those where language and literacy practices are wholly engaged and, thus experienced. Learners thus come to know firsthand how things get talked about, represented, and comprehended via participating in contexts of inquiry and collaboration.

What's on the Screen?

Unlike linear print, electronic texts (what appears on the computer screen) offer multiple entry points. This encourages perspective-taking, questioning, and critical engagement while stimulating thinking and talking in thoughtful, informed, and referenced (what's on the computer screen) ways. However, what appears on the computer screen is only really important insofar as it has potential to be used as fodder and stimulus for active, social content learning, academic language learning, academic literacy learning, and literate thinking. Where much has been made of the motivational factors of computer-supported learning—visual novelty does indeed excite the senses—excitation is, however, only the bare beginnings. The excitation must be carefully, expertly cultivated into engaging processes that work to develop language and literacy mastery.

What appears on the computer screen also matters in that we are well into the era of the digital. Indeed, with the widespread integration of digital forms in our everyday and academic literacies, it can be said that we are "in a new phase of representation" (Funge, 1998). Incorporating malleable visual and aural elements can augment learning processes and products, can amplify the meaning-making involved now that the associativeness between semiotic elements is commonly a part of our everyday digital literacy practices. Building digital, multimodal representations is easily accomplished by using common computer publishing and productivity tools in conjunction with Internet resources. ELLs can understand and generate such products while enjoying the supportive and enriching joint meaning-making enterprise of a learning community. They are, at the same time, generating tangible, observable evidence of their learning. Students become digital authors, their products and their processes of creation providing ongoing evidence of their language and literacy learning.

How Teachers Shape and Exploit These Ecologies[1]

Parker raises the critical question of the effectiveness of including computers as part of language education. Based on observations of young ELL children in U.S. schools and an after-school computer camp, I outline some of the ecological elements that we have observed that determine effectiveness in intact technology and ELL environments. I then describe how these elements conjoin in contexts where powerful language and literacy learning takes place by English language learners using software designed not for this purpose but as productivity tools that native speakers of English use to write, to read, and to engage content area curricula through games and simulations. Precisely how experienced teachers make use of the "repurposed" software and resources in their orchestration of language and literacy instruction will then be discussed.

Teaching around and with computers represents powerful opportunities for modeling and engaging academic thinking, curiosity, questioning what one knows and does not, and extending invitations to think out loud. In short, the kinds of literate practices we undertake with texts. In the ELL and technology classrooms we observed, we continually witnessed teachers doing what Jerome Bruner has long advocated: modeled wondering versus fixed knowing (Bruner, 1996). The language of thinking, problem solving, and task persistence was modeled by teachers and quickly appropriated by English language learners as they too engaged the problems presented by the information on the screen and their immediate goals be it changing the amount of rainfall for their SIM city, or inserting a comma in a document that would be published on the class home page. Teacher scaffolding, guidance, indeed their oral language and literacy practices were enacted to nurture just the kinds of thinking and speaking that young children are so well equipped to emulate, to learn. Not surprisingly, learners quickly became teachers using the same types of supportive linguistic moves that had been modeled for them as they assisted their peers with taking considered actions on the screen.

All discourse is essentially multimodal (Scollon & Levine, 2004) with words and the tangible things they refer to being intertwined throughout expressive and interpretative communication. When the tangibles are on a computer screen, they are public (open to public viewing, referring, and comment), malleable (subject to manipulation, change), unstable (vulnerable to invisible programming effects), and anarchic (anyone can control them at any time). We found, given these features, excellent teachers, and supportive schools, language and literacy learning potential par excellence (Meskill et al., 1999). We also found that these elementary and middle school ELLs had particularly quick and ready agility with computers through which they could demonstrate their intelligence and life experiences (Meskill, Mossop, & Bates, 2000). Orchestration of these elements consistently generated engaged, winning language and literacy learning as evidenced in student talk, writing, and the products they constructed along the way. In short, expert ELL teachers capitalize on the here and now aspects of authentic communication. They orchestrate conversations that urge mutual, yet shifting perspectives as what is on the computer screen shifts. They use what is on computer screens to encourage "interthinking," the thinking that we do together through the medium of language (Mercer, 2000).

What exactly constitutes the affluence of mind behind such powerful, enlightened practices? Interviews, video talk-back sessions, and observations with experienced, expert ELL and technology professionals revealed:

1. solid foundations in both the theoretical and practical issues involved in language and literacy learning;
2. a deep, abiding respect for learners and their families and what they contribute to otherwise monolingual and monocultural institutions;
3. a facility with recognizing the potential of elements in the environment that they could make use of authentically in their teaching;
4. an attitude towards technology that was as nonchalant as towards a book or pencil;
5. a commitment to teaching language and literacy and ways of doing school through authentic content and contexts;
6. a quick, ready ability to assess teachable moments and fully exploit these; and, finally
7. passion for their craft and a high degree of professional engagement.

This list invites additions by ELL teaching professionals. Here it serves merely to underscore the complex, critical alchemy that makes up the affluence of mind required for the language and literacy challenges of ELLs in U.S. schools.

How ELLS and Technology Are Transforming Teaching and Learning

Many aspects of both instructional technologies and English language learners are contributing to the evolution of teaching and learning in U.S. schools. First, technologies in education can teach us that learning can indeed be a pleasurable experience. Second, working with ELL children teaches us that teaching those from other cultures can likewise be a pleasurable, enriching experience. Educators around the country are being affected by both.

In terms of technology's contributions, the Internet itself supports many voices. No longer are we restricted in our knowing to information that is predigested and reshaped by a few with vested interests. We can explore just about any phenomenon from a variety of positions and perspectives from around the globe to form our own opinions and ideas. Likewise, working with ELLs continually broadens our worldview and ways of knowing the world.

Technology is an excellent tool and catalyst for ongoing teacher professional dialogue and development, from learning about the home languages and cultures of their ELL students, to discussing current theory and practice with their colleagues from around the world, the days of monolingualism and monoculturalism may indeed be numbered if not completely over for most U.S. teaching professionals (Meskill & Light, 1996). Technology has played and plays an important role in broadening perceptions of our ever-changing world and one's ever-changing place within it. Broadened and enriched discourses on teaching and learning, and of the critical roles of language and culture in the enterprise can only lead to positive growth in educator professionalism and, consequently, quality education.

Teaching English language learners also calls our attention to the fundamental role of language as our primary instructional tool. We often take for granted that being an excellent teacher requires excellent language skills. Indeed, teachers of all disciplines need not only to be excellent users of language, but also understand how language works (Snow & Wong-Fillmore, 2002). Being a good student, moreover, means speaking and understanding in ways that are socially/institutionally appropriate, something that does not come naturally for all, especially those whose lives out of school do not include school's ways of thinking, speaking, and being. What ELLs have done for teaching in this regard is open up the conversation from the monologic (teacher imparting to student), to being more dialogic, authentic, conversational. Language is simultaneously the medium and the object of study and interactive discourse with learners and teachers as equal opportunity participants. The cultural and perspectival contributions of ELLs render these conversations rich, multidimensional and rewarding. Teachers are increasing their metacultural and metalinguistic awareness as a result of their increased contact with and developing understandings of ELLs. In a digital world where information seeking, using, and understanding require sophisticated metacultural and metalinguistic skills, this can only be positive. In short, in working with ELLs and technology, teachers develop an appreciation for different ways of understanding the world.

Conclusion

Instructional technology, in spite of its bumpy beginnings where it was sorely constrained by limited and limiting theories of learning, has never been about what button to press any more than writing has been about the width of one's pencil. From the past four decades of experimentation with learning technologies we have learned that instruction is wholly a human endeavor, especially when the goal is mastery of language in all of its social and academic complexity. It is clear that computers can be called into the service of these affluent endeavors in positive, contributing ways. As Parker points out, what ultimately contributes to the development of this affluence of mind and practice are well trained, well supported language teaching professionals who are given the time and resources to plan and orchestrate these language and literacy learning events (Meskill et al., 2006), and mainstream classroom teachers and other school personnel who are well educated about the needs and contributions of ELLs (Meskill, 2005b). Acknowledgement and valuing of the assets that ELLs and their families represent in the community also contribute to an atmosphere of trust and respect that is supportive of English language and literacy mastery.

Note

1. Sample videoclips from such ELL and technology ecologies are available at: http://www.albany.edu/faculty/meskill/TALL/resource/resource_video.htm.

References

Bruner, J. (1996). *The culture of education.* Cambridge, MA: Harvard University Press.

Chang-Wells, G., & Wells, G. (1993). Dynamics of discourse: Literacy and the construction of knowledge. In E. Forman, No. Minick, & C. Stone (Eds.), *Contexts for learning: Sociocultural dynamics in children's development.* (pp. 58–90). New York: Oxford University Press.

Ellis, R. (2005). Principles of instructed language learning. *System, 33,2, 209–224.*

Funge, E. (1998). Rethinking representation: Media studies and the postmodern teenager. *English and Media Magazine, 39, 33–36.*

Gee, J. (1990). *Social linguistics and literacies: Ideology in discourses.* New York: Falmer Press.

Gee, J. (2003). *What video games have to teach us about learning and literacy.* New York: Palgrave.

Heath, S. (1983). *Ways with words. Language, life and work in communities and classrooms.* New York: Cambridge University Press.

Lemke, J. (1998). Metamedia literacy: Transforming meanings and media. In D. Reinking, M. McKenna, L. Labbo, & R. Kieffer (Eds.), *Handbook of literacy and technology* (pp. 283–301). Mahwah, NJ: Erlbaum.

Lindfors, J. (1989). The classroom: A good environment for language learning. In P. Rigg & V. Allen (Eds.), *When they don't all speak English: Integrating the ESL student into the regular classroom* (pp. 39–54). Urbana, IL: National Council of Teachers of English.

Long, M. (1996). The role of the linguistic environment in second language acquisition. In W. C. Ritchie & T. K. Bhatia (Eds.), *Handbook of language acquisition Vol. 2. Second language acquisition* (pp. 413–468). New York: Academic Press.

Mackey, A., Gass, S. M., & McDonough, K. (2000). How do learners perceive interactional feedback? *Studies in Second Language Acquisition, 22, 471–497.*

Mercer, N. (2000). *Words and minds: How we use language to think together.* New York: Routledge.

Meskill, C. (2005a) Triadic scaffolds: Tools for teaching English language learners with computers. *Language Learning Technology, 8(4).*

Meskill, C. (2005b) Infusing English Language Learner Issues Throughout Professional Educator Curricula: The Training All Teachers Project. *Teachers College Record. 107(4), 739–756.*

Meskill, C., Anthony, N., Hilliker, S., Tseng, C., & You, J. (2006). CALL: A survey of K–12 ESOL teacher uses and preferences. *TESOL Quarterly, 40, 2, 439–451.*

Meskill, C., & Light, R. (1996). *Technology as Catalyst for Child Advocacy in ESL Teacher Training*. Working paper at the University at Albany, SUNY. Retrieved from http://albany.edu/lap/Papers/Catalyst.html.

Meskill, C., Mossop, J., & Bates, R. (1999) *Electronic Texts and English as a Second Language Environments*. Albany, NY: National Research Center on English Learning and Achievement. Retrieved March 21, 2006, from http://cela.albany.edu/reports/meskill/meskillelectronic12012.pdf.

Meskill, C., Mossop, J., & Bates, R. (2000) Bilingualism, cognitive flexibility, and electronic texts. *Bilingual Research Journal*, 23, 2, 3.

Pica, T. (2005) Classroom learning, teaching and research: A task-based perspective. *The Modern Language Journal*, 89, 3, 339–352.

Scollon, R., & Levine, P. (2004). Multimodal discourse analysis as the confluence of discourse and technology. In R. Scollon & P. Levine (Eds.), *Discourse and technology* (pp. 1–6). Washington, DC: Georgetown University Press.

Short, D. (2002). Language learning in sheltered social studies classes. *TESOL Journal*, 11, 18–24.

Snow, C., & Wong-Fillmore, L. (2002). *What teachers need to know about language*. Washington, DC: Center for Applied Linguistics.

Vásquez, O. (2003). *La Clase Mágica*. Mahwah, NJ: Erlbaum.

7
Technology Opening Opportunities for ELL Students
Attending to the Linguistic Character of These Students

EUGENE E. GARCÍA

Arizona State University

As others in this volume have discussed, the United States continues to diversify ethnically and racially. This diversification is especially pronounced amongst school-age children (García, 2005). With this growing diversity, promoting educational equity in our classrooms has become a critical challenge and goal for teachers, administrators, and policymakers (NRC, 1999). Many linguistically diverse students have unsuccessful schooling experiences in which their strengths and needs are not adequately addressed (García, 2001b). Uses of technology, which are traditionally considered "culture-free," actually often foster inhospitable and intractable environments for diverse learners in classrooms (Lee & Fradd, 1998). In short, there are no culture-free classrooms or related learning environments. Technology that is foreign, intrusive, and misunderstood by students who have not encountered it can move from the realm of beneficial to the realm of harmful.

English Language Learners (ELLs) cannot afford to be absent from technological advances related to learning, broadly, to academic subject matter in English, and to opportunities to communicate in a globalized world as the chapter by Castek and his colleagues suggests. Not only must students pursue appropriate grade-level content for its own sake, but supporting language learning through content such as science and math, has also been shown the most effective means of building academic language proficiency (Chamot & O'Malley, 1986; Cohen, De Avila, & Intili, 1981; Cummins, 1984; De Avila & Duncan, 1984; Echevarría, Vogt, & Short, 2000; Mohan, 1979; Short, 1999). Multiple utilizations of technological advances—some directly addressed in this volume—with multiple opportunities for hands-on and visual interaction with the academic concepts provide rich contexts supporting academic language development. Chapters by Zhao and Lai and by Parker in this volume, for example, provide an overview of various electronic delivery systems, such as TV, DVD, software, the Internet, and portable technologies that can assist young second language learners. Cummins foregrounds the centrality of pedagogical issues related to technology within three broad pedagogical orientations—*transmission, social constructivist,* and *transformative*—that have significant consequences for how computers and other new technologies will be used to support learning a second language. Durán reminds us literacy must be examined in a fuller manner, attentive to the range of meaning-making capabilities of humans and the many symbol systems that humans have devised to make sense of the world and that guide their interactions with others and the environment. In the contributions to this volume, all would agree that academic language proficiency is critical to students' future success throughout the schooling process.

In designing any learning environments it is important to understand literacy to include not only reading and writing but also critical thinking and problem-solving—the ability to use language as a tool for understanding and learning. For example, in the science learning process, students also need to be supported in learning the discourse of science and inquiry (Ballenger, 2004; Lemke, 1990; Rosebery, Warren, & Conant, 1992; Warren & Rosebery, 1995). Argumentation is an important aspect of the science inquiry discourse (Driver, Newton, & Osbourne, 2000; Kuhn, 1993; Lemke 1990; Siegel, 1995; Toulmin, 1958) and much of science involves dialectical and rhetorical argumentation (Latour & Woolgar, 1986; Longino, 1994). In this vein, several researchers have shown that students' participation in discourse paralleling that by scientific communities is key to successful science education (e.g., Lemke, 1990; Rosebery, Warren, & Conant, 1992; Schauble, Glaser, Duschl, Schulze, & John, 1995). As others in this volume have argued, we want language learners to actually engage and participate in these communities while also engaging with the academic language that is at the heart of these and many other academic communities. However, somewhat more explicit in this chapter is the role of the second language learner's primary language in supporting the development of academic varieties of English. Although the focus is on acquiring English as a second language in the content are of science, the key issue forwarded is that technology affords us instructional flexibilities that can more facilely bridge first language expertise to second language learning.

Theoretical Background

To consider guidelines for technological environments it is important to understand the intersection among (a) the role of language in learning and teaching, (b) cognition and language for bilingual students, (c) primary language instruction, comprehensible input, and the acquisition of English, (d) computer-supported collaborative science learning environments, and (e) the broader cognition and learning research.

In this section, I summarize findings from these areas. In the following section, I attempt to synthesize a set of design guidelines for technology-based learning environments specifically to support English language learners in learning environments based on what we know "works" for ELL students.

The Role of Language in Learning and Teaching

Learning, from a constructivist perspective, involves students building upon and reorganizing prior knowledge in interaction with new ideas and experiences. Clearly a student's first language represents a critical component of the student's prior understanding (Cole & Cole, 2001; García, 2001; Tharp & Gallimore, 1988). The monolithic culture transmitted through the traditional pedagogy of U.S. schools, however, tends to (a) exclude systematically the histories, languages, and experiences of diverse students from the curriculum, (b) impose a "tracking system" that restricts access to higher order curricula, and (c) limit access to developmentally appropriate learning configurations (García, 2001; García & Lee, in press).

Although mainstream curricular configurations tend to ignore the linguistic resources of diverse students, studies indicate important advantages of considering students' home language. Such curricula provide important cognitive and social foundations for students' success in the second language (García, Bravo, Dickey, Chun, & Sun-Iminger, 2004). Incorporation of the students' linguistic resources has also been shown to make a positive academic difference (August & Shanahan, 2006; August & Hakuta, 1997) and to promote participation and positive relationships in the classroom (Au & Kawakimi, 1994; Trueba & Wright, 1992). Furthermore, by leveraging students' linguistic knowledge, educators can greatly assist students in accessing the school curriculum (Cummins, 2000; Valenzuela, 1999). Ultimately, more comprehensive incorporation of the students' home language facilitates greater potential for academic success.

August and Shanahan (2006), in a review of optimal learning conditions to serve linguistically diverse students, make several recommendations relevant to learning environment design including (a) provision of a customized learning environment, (b) use of native language in instruction, (c) a balanced curriculum focusing on both higher order and basic skills, (d) opportunities for practice, (e) systematic student assessment, and (f) staff and parent involvement. Other studies support these findings regarding the importance of incorporating linguistic components into the curriculum (Ovando, Collier & Combs, 2003) as well as the importance of active, discovery, and cognitively complex learning. Roseberry, Warren, and Conant also support these findings and place strong emphasis on the importance of authentic activities to induct students into the discourse of science (1992). García and Lee (in press) similarly suggest focusing on (a) bilingual/bicultural skills and awareness, (b) high expectation of diverse students, (c) treatment of diversity as an asset,

(d) attention to and integration of home cultures/practices, (e) maximizing student interactions across categories of English proficiency, (f) student and teacher input in lesson planning and design, (g) a thematic approach to learning activities with the integration of various skills, and (h) language development though meaningful interactions and communications.

Metalinguistic Advantages of Bilingual Students

Leopold (1939), in one of the first investigations of bilingual acquisition, reported a general cognitive plasticity for his young bilingual daughter. He suggested that linguistic flexibility (in the form of bilingualism) be related to a number of nonlinguistic, cognitive tasks such as categorization, verbal signal discrimination, and creativity. Peal and Lambert (1962), in a summary of their work with French/English bilinguals and English monolinguals suggested that the intellectual experience of acquiring two languages contributed to advantageous mental flexibility, superior concept formation, and a generally diversified set of mental abilities. Goncz and Kodzepeljic (1991) and Swain and Lapkin (1991) provide excellent overviews of international work in this arena.

U.S.-related research with Chicano bilingual children reported by Kessler and Quinn (1985, 1987) supplies empirical support for the emerging understanding that, all things being equal, bilingual children outperform monolingual children on specific measures of cognitive and metalinguistic awareness. Kessler and Quinn (1987) had bilingual and monolingual children engage in a variety of symbolic categorization tasks that required their attention to abstract, verbal features of concrete objects. Spanish/English, Chicano bilingual children from low socioeconomic status (SES) backgrounds outperformed low SES English monolinguals and high SES English monolinguals on these tasks. Such findings are particularly significant given the criticism by MacNab (1997) that many bilingual "cognitive advantage" studies have used only high SES subjects of non-U.S. minority backgrounds. (It is important to note that findings of metalinguistic advantages have been reported for low SES Puerto Rican students as well [Galambos & Hakuta, 1988]). A common finding of these "cognitive flexibility" studies is that bilingual children have mastered the ability to strategically use one language or another or both to acquire new academic material (García, 2001). The direct use of Spanish/English cognates in science instruction is an example. Because many scientific terms have Latin roots, the formal Spanish and English vocabulary in the sciences is very similar—a student knowing this metalinguistic root relationship can be advantaged in moving from Spanish to English in this instruction venue. This metalinguistic ability could prove highly advantageous in a technology-driven learning environment that can facilitate the access to both languages during the teaching event.

**Primary Language Instruction, Comprehensible
Input, and the Acquisition of English**

A number of studies have found that instructional time spent in the native language of English learners is positively related to academic achievement measures in English. For example, using a large national sample, Ramírez and colleagues (1991) studied children in English-only, late exit, and early exit bilingual programs, and found that children could be "provided with substantial amounts of primary language instruction without impeding their acquisition of English language and reading skills," and that doing so allowed them to catch up to their English-speaking peers in English language arts, reading and math. Meta-analyses (Greene, 1998; Willig, 1985) and two research reviews conducted by the National Research Council (August & Hakuta, 1997; Meyer & Fienberg, 1992) have reached similar conclusions.

A limitation of using academic achievement measures to evaluate programs for English learners, as is commonly done in the program comparison literature, is that such measures are generally not constructed in relation to a theory of language ability (Thompson, DiCerbo, Mahoney, & MacSwan, 2002), leaving us with limited understanding of the independent impact of bilingual instructional programs on the separate constructs of academic achievement and English language development. For instance, learners' test scores may increase due to improved language ability but reflect little actual growth in the academic content areas. Conversely, increases in test scores may reflect greater mastery of content but only minimal second language proficiency, sufficient to improve comprehension of test items but not reflective of substantive gains in English language ability. Furthermore, although program evaluation research is helpful in setting initial hypotheses, it does not in itself help us understand the specific mechanisms responsible for the observed outcomes. For that, a specific learning theory must be constructed and evaluated.

One possibility is to base such a theory on a well-known hypothesis that predicts gains in second language ability for children in native language instructional environments known as the Comprehensible Input Hypothesis (Krashen, 1985, 1996). The central component of a theory of second language learning, the Comprehensible Input Hypothesis proposed that second language learners acquire a new language by understanding messages. Hence, Krashen theorized that native language instruction provides a conceptual framework for English language learners, which in turn gives them a conceptual and analytical framework to make English-medium messages comprehensible. Creating second language messages that are comprehensible to learners, according to Krashen, results in acquisition of both vocabulary and grammatical structure because learners' knowledge of the underlying semantic message permits them to analyze the grammatical structure at a subconscious level. Although this suggestion has not previously been tested empirically, theoretical work in first language acquisition, similarly aimed at explaining gaps between language input and learner output, has also proposed that children use "semantic bootstrapping" to decode messages and make complex inferences about underlying linguistic structure. For instance, Grimshaw (1981) and Pinker (1984) provide evidence suggesting that children's knowledge of word meaning is used to infer syntactic properties of lexical items. Expanding on these concepts regarding optimal second language learning opportunities, Zhao and Lai in this volume suggest that the type of overall engagement and feedback are critical.

The following discussion is intended to enhance our understanding of the effects of native language instruction on academic achievement and language growth by evaluating these constructs separately in the specific context of science education. Furthermore, we can evaluate the prediction of the Comprehensible Input Hypothesis that increased use of the native language in an instructional setting results in increases in knowledge of English vocabulary and grammar, as suggested by Krashen. If the prediction is false, then an alternative theory of second language learning in academic settings will be pursued. If the prediction is correct, then the finding will increase confidence in the value of native language instruction and in the particular theory of second language acquisition proposed by Krashen.

Research on Technology-Based Collaborative Learning Environments to Support Learning

The value and strength of technology-based learning environments as a medium for this pedagogy focuses on the versatility of the technology. In theory, once design guidelines are created to incorporate metalinguistic supports for one group of linguistically diverse learners, the guidelines can be implemented for other groups into the same environment simultaneously so that all learners can access linguistically appropriate supports. As an example, I will focus on how this might work in designing technology-based learning environments. Technology has already been harnessed to create structured environments to support science inquiry learning (e.g., Edelson, Gordon, & Pea, 1999; Linn & Hsi, 2000). Within the realm of science learning environments, collaborative Internet-based learning environments reflecting the emerging computer-supported collaborative learning (CSCL) paradigm (Koschmann, 1996) offer great potential for language learners. CSCL reflects social constructivism (Bauersfeld, 1995; Cobb, 1994), Russian sociocultural theory (Cole & Engestrom, 1993; Vygotsky, 1978), and situated cognition (Brown, Collins, & Duguid, 1989; Greeno, 1989; Lave, 1988). CSCL-based collaborative online learning environments tend to involve content resources or materials, activities or assignments, assessments, collaboration tools (e.g., e-mail, discussion board, calendar, chat room, videoconferencing), information about participants (e.g., bios, web pages), representation tools (e.g., simulation tools, modeling tools, shared whiteboards, shared virtual workspace), help features (e.g., systems-based or human tutor/instructor), and search tools. Examples of these collaborative online learning environments include MUNICS (Troendle et al., 1999), Knowledge Forum (Scardamalia & Bereiter, 1996), Knowledge Master (Erlach, Hausmann, Mandl, & Trillitzsch, 2000; Erlach, Reinmann-Rothmeier, Neubauer, & Mandl, 2001; Winkler & Mandl, 2002), and the Web-Based Inquiry Science Environment (Linn, Clark, & Slotta, in press). These environments not only provide rich visualizations and contexts but also provide powerful opportunities for social supports and discourse that sheltered instruction researchers consider critical in scaffolding academic language development (Johnson, Johnson, Holubec, & Roy, 1984; Kagan, 1986).

Text-based CSCL online environments, reinforced with the representations and capabilities that online environments provide, offer great potential for language learners studying science. Text-based CSCL offers the possibility to structure the learners' discourse (Baker & Lund, 1997; Jonassen & Remídez, 2002; King, 1998; Scardamalia & Bereiter, 1996) to guide students through a trajectory of activities. This structuring through the use of content-based and interaction-oriented scripts and prompts offers a direct way to influence the quality of discourse by scaffolding students through the process of inquiry and argumentation (Weinberger, Fischer, & Mandl, 2001). Because text-based environments are less constrained by time and space, and because they are modifiable by each user, text-based environments allow for universal participation by an entire class as compared with the small percentage of students who are able to participate in a face-to-face class discussion (Hsi, 1997). These text-based environments also allow students' own ideas to be represented and contrasted effectively with one another (Cuthbert, Clark, & Linn, 2002), increasing the importance of personal relevance in student discussions (Hoadley & Linn, 2000). Additionally, rather than being a challenge for the students to overcome, the availability of other students' text is in fact an excellent opportunity for new literacy learning in and of itself (i.e., it is a medium through which literacy and understanding is developed). Academic text is at the heart of literacy, and researchers are calling precisely for this type of writing within the curriculum to support literacy development. Furthermore, text-based asynchronous interactions allow learners time to compose their responses and decode the other students' contributions and so learners with varying levels of proficiency in the language of instruction can all participate with one another. Additionally, because students participate at their own pace in these discussions, educators can incorporate linguistically relevant metacognitive supports in the form of text-based hints and digital video vignettes that students can access whenever they wish. Based on these ideas, educators can also build an online discussion system geared specifically to support English language learners conducting science inquiry. These expanded activities allow for the general development of academic-related content English—the "form" of English that Cummins early in this volume seeks to advance through a variety of technology venues. These findings on language, learning, and educational technology build on the core findings from cognition and learning research about learning environment design.

Research on Cognition and Learning

In their summary and analysis of research about how people learn, Bransford, Brown, and Cocking (2000) outline some core considerations about learning environment design. Their analysis of cognition and learning research demonstrates that:

Schools and Classrooms Must Be Learner-centered

Teachers must pay close attention to the knowledge, skills, and attitudes of learners bring into the classroom. This incorporates the preconceptions regarding subject matter as well as a broader understanding of the learner in terms of cultural differences in understandings and beliefs.

Attention must be given to *what is taught, why it is taught, and what competence or mastery looks like* in order to create a knowledge-centered classroom environment. A knowledge-centered environment must provide the necessary depth of study focusing on student understanding rather than memorization of facts. Environments must also focus on teaching metacognitive strategies to facilitate future learning.

Formative Assessments Help Teachers and Students Monitor Progress

Environments must provide assessments allowing students opportunities to revise and improve their thinking, as well as help students see their own progress or the course of time. Assessments also help teachers identify problems that need to be addressed.

Learning Is Fundamentally Influenced by the Context in Which It Occurs

It is important that norms are developed within the learning environments to support learning. It is also important that the environment make connections to the outside world to support the core learning values. It is critical that classroom activities promote intellectual camaraderie amongst students. By creating a community of learners, students can support one another.

Technology and the ELL Student

As detailed in the previous sections, significant research has demonstrated the dangers of cutting students off entirely from their primary language in the classroom (García, 2005; Ovando, Collier, & Combs, 2003; Valdés, 2001). Instead, researchers have demonstrated the efficacy of allowing students to use their primary language to support their progress in gaining mastery of their second language as well as mastery of critical subject matter competence (August & Shanahan, 2006; Echevarría, Vogt, & Short, 2000; Rosebery, Warren, & Conant, 1992; Snow, Met, & Genessee, 1989; Warren & Rosebery, 1995). Therefore, it is important for technological advances to make scaffolding and content available to students in both the primary language and English so that students can switch between languages to support conceptual development. The method for delivering instruction in these languages involves some combination of the preview–review, alternate, and concurrent paradigms from bilingual and second language research (August, 2006; García, 2005; Ovando, Collier, & Combs, 2003). The ultimate goal is to harness the power of native language use for conceptual development while focusing on academic English for production of project artifacts to facilitate the academic language proficiency required to advance academically in U.S. schools.

Changing the Context

To facilitate instructional advances, specialized scaffolds within an existing Internet-based curriculum and instructional strategies that have proven to be effective with multilingual students is recommended. The international web-based availability of such opportunities is growing daily—some are clearly articulated in this volume. By leveraging the assets of the Web-based instructional resources, the development efforts especially of the tools and scaffolding needed specifically to support English language learners is immediately enhanced. This route will also ensure that the new tools and scaffolding developed by multiple efforts can be made available to all product developers and potential users almost immediately. In this way, in addition to the theoretical advances, technological advances for this population can have immediate practical value for teachers of English language learners across the country. This is in contrast to the usual mode of curriculum distribution that usually requires years from the conceptualization of new curriculum/strategies that begin with developers and find their way via "hard" copies years later.

Specialized Scaffolding

As suggested in the research review just discussed, new research should focus on supporting content and language learning by giving students metalinguistic choices in terms of language of materials and allowing them to shift back and forth as they engage in learning in an online environment. This requires using existing language switching capabilities or creating new ones, so that students can switch back and forth between their primary language and English. To facilitate students building connections as they switch between languages, it will be important to incorporate access to online glossaries, translators, and parsers. There is significant debate in the bilingual education and second language (or L2) research community about the optimal format for primary (or L1) language delivery in terms of previewing in one language and reviewing in another, alternating languages, or using both languages concurrently (Ovando, Collier, & Combs, 2003). Therefore, it is important to monitor how language switching between L1 and L2 is made available, and its effect on the development of reading comprehension, writing, and speaking skills, of English learners. The default, however, should allow students to switch whenever they choose and thereby allowing the student to access language resources that may be necessary to build either content understanding or English vocabulary. It will be important to map how and when students switch over the course of instructional engagement. The use of technological advances allows the following:

- Presenting content in English with hyperlinked Spanish definitions of terms.
- Enabling switching languages of paragraphs on a button click.
- Interlacing translation below each English line so that the students can simultaneously see both languages.

Another key innovation involves building tools that support students engaging in the academic English discourse of the content concepts. Clark (2006) has shown in a project involving ELL students and science inquiry that it is possible to build integrated/interactive refinements that:

- Scaffolds students in creating a *principle* to describe data they have collected,
- *Analyzes* the principle the students have created and uses that analysis to place students into *discussion groups* with students who have created *different principles,*
- Creates the discussions with the students' principles as the initial *seed comments,*
- Scaffolds students in the process of *critiquing* one another's ideas with the goal of helping the group learn.

This process provides linguistic, metacognitive, and content demonstrations and explanations by native speakers embedded in digital video to support students in accessing the primary project content, which should remain in English to help language learners understand the process of scientific inquiry and argumentation inherent in these activities. By supporting students in creating their own scientific understanding that they then share and critique with students who have come to different conclusions, we engage the students as scientists in the discourse of inquiry and argumentation, creating an authentic context for all students. In particular this is an authentic opportunity for language learners to participate in the production of academic language in an authentic task that is personally relevant and meaningful — exactly the engagement for which sheltered instruction researchers have been calling (Chamot & O'Malley, 1986; Cummins, 1981; De Avila & Duncan, 1984; Echevarría, Vogt, & Short, 2000). Similar activities for scaffolding academic language in other subject areas could also be developed.

Conclusion

For ELL students, research and development must address several key questions as these students engage in the technological environment related to language and content learning:

- What choices do students make in navigating between languages?
- When and how do students make those choices?
- How are these choices related to students' final understanding of the subject matter as expressed in English and the primary language?
- What does the mixed language technology "buy" us in our ability to support English language and content learning?

I would hypothesize that allowing students to move back and forth between English and the primary language will help students improve their overall academic language abilities in multiple languages. However, it is important to note that mixed language input can support student understanding of the concepts as measured in English, English vocabulary, academic English discourse structure in the content areas, and specific content discourse patterns.

Clearly, the research literature and the pressing demographic realities in our schools provide strong justification for creating a framework of design guidelines and technology-based learning environments to support English language learners. English language learners clearly need support building deep conceptual understanding of academic content while developing stronger academic language proficiency. Moreover, these goals are also clearly aligned with the funding priorities of numerous federal agencies, including the National Institute of Health and Child Development (NIHCD), the Institute of Educational Sciences (IES), the Child Development and Behavior Branch (CHDB) of the Center for Research for Mothers and Children (CRMC), the National Institutes of Health (NIH), and the National Science Foundation (NSF). For example, under the Development of English Literacy in Spanish Speaking Children (DELSS) partnership, IES and NIHCD have attempted to stimulate systematic multidisciplinary research to increase understanding of the specific cognitive, linguistic, sociocultural, and instructional factors—as well as the complex interactions among these factors—that govern the acquisition of English reading and writing abilities by Spanish-speaking children and youth. This type of research and development, well represented in this volume, holds new and enhanced teaching and learning opportunities for ELL students.

References

Au, K. H., & Kawakimi, A. J. (1994). Cultural congruence in instruction. In E. R. Hollins, J. E. King, & W. C. Hayman (Eds.), *Teaching diverse populations: Formulating a knowledge base* (pp. 5–24). Albany, NY: State University of New York Press.

August, D., & Hakuta, K. (1998). *Improving schooling for language-minority children: A research agenda.* Washington, DC: National Academy Press.

Baker, M., & Lund, K. (1997). Promoting reflective interactions in a CSCL environment. *Journal of Computer Assisted Learning, 13,* 175–193.

Ballenger, C. (2004). Social identities, moral narratives, scientific argumentation: Science talk in a bilingual classroom. *Language and Education, 31,* 2, 114–131.

Bauersfeld, H. (1995). The structuring of structures: Development and function of mathematizing as a social practice. In L. P. Steffe & J. Gale (Eds.), *Constructivism in education* (pp. 137–158). Hillsdale, NJ: Erlbaum.

Bransford, J. D., Brown, A. L., & Cocking, R. R. (2000). *How people learn: Brain, mind, experience, and school.* Washington, DC: National Academic Press.

Brown, J. S., Collins, A., & Duguid, P. (1989). Situated cognition and the culture of learning. *Educational Researcher, 18,* 32–42.

Burt, M., & Dulay, H. (1978). *Bilingual Syntax Measure II, manual, English edition.* New York: Harcourt Brace Jovanovich.

Burt, M. K., Dulay, H., Hernández-Chavez, E., & Taleporos, E. (1980). *Technical handbook. Bilingual Syntax Measure II. The Psychological Corporation.* New York: Harcourt Brace Jovanovich.

Burt, M., Dulay, H., Hernández-Chavez, E., & Taleporos, E. (1980). *Bilingual syntax measure ii, technical manual.* New York: Harcourt Brace Jovanovich.

Chamot, A. U., & O'Malley, J. M. (1986). *A cognitive academic language learning approach: An ESL content-based curriculum.* Washington, DC: National Clearinghouse for Bilingual Education.

Clark, D. B. (2006). Building hands-on labs in Internet environments: Making thinking visible through iterative refinement and design. In M. C. Linn, P. Bell, & E. A. Davis, (Eds.), *Internet environments for science education* (pp. 132–147). Mahwah, NJ: Erlbaum.

Cobb, P. (1994). Where is the mind? Constructivist and sociocultural perspectives on mathematical development. *Educational Researcher* 23(7), 13–20.

Cohen, E. G., De Avila, E., & Intili, J. A. (1981). *Executive summary: Multicultural improvement of cognitive ability.* Report to the State of California Department of Education. Sacramento, CA: California Department of Education.

Cole, M., & Cole, S. R. (2001). *The development of children* (4th ed.). New York: Worth Publishers.

Cole, M., & Engestrom, Y. (1993). A cultural-historical approach to distributed cognition. *Distributed cognition: in* G. Salomon (Ed.), *Psychological and educational considerations* (pp. 1–46). Cambridge, UK: Cambridge University Press.

Collier, V. P. (1987). Age and rate of acquisition of secondary language for academic achievement in a second language. *TESOL Quarterly, 23,* 509–531.

Collier, V. P. (1989). How long? A synthesis of research on academic achievement in second language. *TESOL Quarterly, 29,* 411–425.

Cummins, J. (1980). The construct of proficiency in bilingual education. In J. E. Alatis (Ed.), *Georgetown University Round Table on Languages and Linguistics, 1980* (pp. 12–27). Washington, DC: Georgetown University Press.

Cummins, J. (1981). Age on arrival and immigrant second language learning in Canada: A reassessment. *Applied Linguistics, 2,* 132–149.

Cummins, J. (1984*) Bilingualism and special education: Issues in assessment and pedagogy.* Clevedon, UK: Multilingual Matters.

Cummins, J. (2000). *Language, power, and pedagogy: Bilingual children in the crossfire.* Clevedon, UK: Multilingual Matters.

Curtiss, S., Schaeffer, J., Sano, T., MacSwan, J., & Masilon, T. (1996, June). *A grammatical coding and analysis system for language data from normal and brain-damaged children.* Paper presented at the Joint International Conference of the Association for Literacy and Linguistic Computing and the Association for Computers and the Humanities, University of Bergen, Norway.

Cuthbert, A. J., Clark, D. B., & Linn, M. C. (2002). WISE learning communities: Design considerations. In K. A. Renninger & W. Shumar (Eds.), *Building virtual communities: Learning and change in cyberspace* (pp. 87–101). Cambridge, UK: Cambridge University Press.

De Avila, E. A., & Duncan, S. E. (1984). *Finding out/Descubierto: Training Manual.* San Rafael, CA: Linguametrics Group.

Driver, R., Newton, P., & Osbourne, J. (2000). Establishing the norms of scientific argumentation in classrooms. *Science Education, 84*(3), 287–312.

Dulay, H. C., & Burt, M. K. (1975). Natural sequences in child second language acquisition. *Language Learning, 24*(1), 46–56.

Echevarría, J., Vogt, M., & Short, D. (2000). *Making content comprehensible to English language learners: The SIOP model.* Needham Heights, MA: Allyn & Bacon.

Edelson, D., Gordon, D., & Pea, R. (1999). Addressing the challenges of inquiry-based learning through technology and curriculum design. *The Journal of the Learning Sciences, 8*(3&4). 391–450.

Erlach, Ch., Hausmann, I., Mandl, H., & Trillitzsch, U. (2000). Knowledge Master—a collaborative learning program for knowledge management. In T. Davenport & G. Probst (Eds.), *Knowledge management case book* (pp. 179–197). Erlangen/München: Publicis MCD Verlag.

Erlach, Ch., Reinmann-Rothmeier, G., Neubauer, A., & Mandl, H. (2001). Ein virtuelles Weiterbildungsseminar zur Ausbildung zum Knowledge Master. In G. Reinmann-Rothmeier & H. Mandl (Eds.), *Virtuelle Seminare in Hoschule und Weiterbildung* (pp. 69–105). Bern: Huber.

Faltis, C. J., & Hudelson, S. J. (1998). *Bilingual education in elementary and secondary school communities: Toward understanding and caring.* Needham Heights, MA: Allyn & Bacon.

Fradd, S. H., & Lee, O. (1999). Teachers' roles in promoting science inquiry with students from diverse language backgrounds. *Educational Researcher, 28*(6), 14–20, 42.

Galambos, S. J., & Hakuta, K. (1988). Subject-specific and task-specific characteristics of metalinguistic awareness in bilingual children. *Applied Psycholinguistics, 9,* 141–162.

García, E. (1985) Review of *Bilingual Syntax Measure II.* In J. V.. Mitchell, Jr. (Ed.), *Ninth measurements yearbook* (pp. 391–392). Lincoln, NB: University of Nebraska.

García, E. (1993). Language, culture, and education. In L. Darling-Hammond (Ed.), *Review of Research in Education, Vol. 19* (pp. 51–98). Washington, DC: American Educational Research Association.

García, E. (2001) *Student cultural diversity: Understanding and meeting the challenge.* Boston, MA: Houghton Mifflin.

García, E. (2002). Bilingualism and schooling in the United States. *International Journal of the Sociology of Language, 134,* 1, 1–123.

García, E. (2005). *Teaching and learning in two languages.* New York: Teachers College Press.

García, E., Bravo, M. A., Dickey, L. M., Chun, K., & Sun-Iminger, X. (2004) Rethinking school reform in the context of cultural and linguistic diversity: Creating a responsive learning community—A case study. In L. Minaya-Rowe (Ed.), *Research in Bilingual Education* (pp. 163–179). Washington, DC: National Association of Bilingual Education.

García, E., & Lee, O. (in press). Science for all. In A. Rosebery & B. Warren (Eds.), *Teaching science to ELL students.* Washington, DC: National Science Foundation.

Glass, G., & Hopkins, K. D. (1996). *Statistical methods in education and psychology* (3rd ed.). Boston: Allyn and Bacon.

Goncz, B., & Kodzepeljic, D. (1991). Cognition and bilingualism revisited. *Journal of Multicultural Development, 12,* 137–163.

Greene, J. (1998). *A meta-analysis of the effectiveness of bilingual education.* Claremont, CA: Thomas Rivera Policy Institute.

Greeno, J. G. (1989). Situations, mental models and generative knowledge. In D. Klahr & K. Kotovksy (Eds.), *Complex information processing: The impact of Herbert A. Simon* (pp. 285–318). Hillsdale, NJ: Erlbaum.

Grimshaw, J. (1981). Form, function, and the language acquisition device. In C. L. Baker & J. J. McCarthy (Eds.), *The logical problem of language acquisition.* Cambridge, MA: The MIT Press.

Hoadley, C., & Linn, M. C. (2000). Teaching science through on-line peer discussions: SpeakEasy in the Knowledge Integration Environment. *International Journal of Science Education, 22,* 839–857.

Hsi, S. (1997). *Facilitating knowledge integration in science through electronic discussion: The Multimedia Forum Kiosk.* Unpublished doctoral dissertation, University of California, Berkeley, CA.

Johnson, D. W., Johnson, R. T., Holubec, E. J., & Roy, P. (1984). *Circles of learning: Cooperation in the classroom.* Alexandria, VA: Association for Supervision and Curriculum Development.

Jonassen, D., & Remídez, H. (2002, February). *Mapping alternative discourse structures onto computer conferences.* Paper presented at the Computer Support for Collaborative Learning: Foundations for a CSCL Community, Boulder, CO.

Kagan, S. (1986). Cooperative learning and sociocultural factors in schooling. In California Sate Department of Education (Ed.), *Beyond language, social and cultural factors in schooling language minority students* (pp. 231–298). Los Angeles: Evaluation, Dissemination, and Assessment Center, California State University.

Kessler, C., & Quinn, M. E. (1985). Positive effects of bilingualism on science problem solving abilities. In J. E. Alatis & J.J. Staczek (Eds.), *Perspectives on bilingual education* (pp. 289–296). Washington, DC; Georgetown University Press.

Kessler, C. & Quinn, M. E. (1987). Language minority children's linguistic and cognitive creativity. *Journal of Multilingual and Multicultural Development 8,* 173–185.

King, K. S. (1998). Designing 21st-century educational networlds: Structuring electronic social spaces. In C. J. Bonk & K. S. King (Eds.), *Electronic collaborators: learner-centered technologies for literacy, apprenticeship, and discourse* (pp. 365–383). Mahwah, NJ: Erlbaum.

Koschmann, T. (1996). Paradigm shifts and instructional technology: An introduction. In T. Koschmann (Ed.), *CSCL: Theory and practice of an emerging paradigm* (pp. 1–23). Mahway, NJ: Erlbaum.

Krashen, S. (1985). *The input hypothesis: Issues and implications.* London: Longman.

Krashen, S. (1996). *Under attack: The case against bilingual education.* Culver City, CA: Language Education Associates.

Kuhn, D. (1993). Science argument: Implications for teaching and learning scientific thinking. *Science Education, 77*(3), 319–337.

Latour, B., & Woolgar, S. (1986). *Laboratory life: The construction of scientific facts.* Princeton, NJ: Princeton University Press.

Lave, J. (1988). *Cognition in practice: Mind, mathematics, and culture in everyday life.* New York, Cambridge University Press.

Lave, J., & Wenger, E. (1991). *Situated learning: Legitimate peripheral participation.* New York: Cambridge University Press.

Lee, O., & Fradd, S. H. (1998). Science for all, including students from non-English language backgrounds. *Educational Researcher, 27*(4), 12–21.

Lee, O., & Fradd, S. H. (2001). Instructional congruence to promote science learning and literacy development for linguistically diverse students. In D. R. Lavoie (Ed.), *Models for science teacher preparation: Bridging the gap between research and practice* (pp. 146–160). Dordrecht, the Netherlands: Kluwer.

Lemke, J. (1990). *Talking science: Language, learning, and values.* New York: Ablex.

Leont'ev, A. N. (1932). Studies in the cultural development of the child, 3: The development of voluntary attention in the child. *Journal of Genetic Psychology, 37,* 52–81.

Leopold, W. F. (1939). *Speech development of a bilingual child: A linguist's record. Vol. I: Vocabulary growth in the first two years.* Evanston, IL: Northwestern University Press.

Linn, M. C., & Hsi, S. (2000). *Computers, teachers, peers: Science learning partners.* Mahwah, NJ: Erlbaum.

Linn, M. C., Clark, D. B., & Slotta, J. D. (in press). WISE design for knowledge integration. *Science Education.*

Long, M. 1990. The least a second language acquisition theory needs to explain. *TESOL Quarterly, 24,* 649–666.

Longino, H. (1994). The fate of knowledge in social theories of science. In F. F. Schmidt (Ed.), *Socializing epistemology: The social dimension of knowledge.* Lanham, MD: Rowman & Littlefield.

MacNab, G. (1997). Cognition and bilingualism: A re-analysis of studies. *Linguistics 17,* 231–255.

Mayer, M. (1969). *Frog, Where are you?* New York: Dial Books for Young Readers.

Meyer, M., & Fienberg, S. (1992). *Assessing evaluation studies: The case of bilingual education strategies.* Washington, DC: National Academy Press.

Mohan, B. (1979). Relating language teaching and content teaching. *TESOL Quarterly, 13,* 171–182.

National Research Council. (1996). *National science education standards.* Washington, DC: National Academy Press. http://books.nap.edu/html/nses/pdf/index.html.

National Research Council. (1999). *Improving student learning.* Washington, DC: National Academy Press.

Ovando, C. J., Collier, V. P., & Combs, M. C. (2003). *Bilingual and ESL classrooms: Teaching in multicultural contexts.* New York: McGraw-Hill Higher Education.

Peal, E., & Lambert, W. E. (1962). The relation of bilingualism to intelligence. *Psychological Monographs: General and Applied, 76*(546), 1–23.

Pinker, S. (1984). *Language learnability and language development.* Cambridge, MA: Harvard University Press.

Ramírez, D., Pasta, D., Yuen, S., Billings, D., & Ramey, D. (1991). *Final report. Longitudinal study of structured English immersion strategy, early-exit and late-exit transitional bilingual education programs for language-minority children.* (Vols. 1 & 2). San Mateo, CA: Aguirre International.

Rosebery, A. S., Warren, B., & Conant, F. R. (1992). Appropriating scientific discourse: Findings from language minority classrooms. *The Journal of the Learning Sciences, 2*(1), 61–94.

Rosebery, A., Warren, B., Conant, F. R., & Hudicourt-Barnes, J. (1992). Chèche Konnen: Scientific sense-making in bilingual education. *Hands On!, 15,* 1.

Saravia-Shore, M., &.Arvizu, S.F. (Eds.). *Cross-cultural literacy: Ethnographies of communication in multiethnic classrooms.* New York: Garland.

Saville-Troike, M. (1984). What really matters in second language learning for academic achievement? *TESOL Quarterly, 18*(2), 199–219.

Scardamalia, M., & Bereiter, C. (1996). Computer support for knowledge-building communities. In T. Koschmann (Ed.), *CSCL: Theory and practice of an emerging paradigm* (pp. 249–268). Mahwah, NJ: Erlbaum.

Schauble, L., Glaser, R., Duschl, R., Schulze, S., & John, J. (1995). Students' understanding of the objectives and procedures of experimentation in the science classroom. *Journal of the Learning Sciences, 4*(2), 131–166.

Shellenberger, S. (1985) Review of *Bilingual Syntax Measure II.* In J. V. Mitchell, Jr. (Ed.), *Ninth Measurements Yearbook.* (pp. 363–364). Lincoln, NB: University of Nebraska.

Short, D. (1999). Integrating language and content for effective sheltered instruction programs. In C. J. Faltis & P. Wolfe (Eds.), *So much to say: Adolescents, bilingualism, and ESL in the secondary school. Language and Literacy Series* (pp. 74–87). New York: Teachers College Press.

Siegel, H. (1995). Why should educators care about argumentation? *Informal Logic, 17*(2), 159–176.

Snow, M. A., Met, M., & Genessee, F. (1989). A conceptual framework for the integration of language and content in second/foreign language instruction. *TESOL Quarterly, 23,* 201–217.

Swain, M., & Lapkin, R. (1991). The influence of bilingualism on cognitive functioning. *Canadian Modern Language Review, 47,* 635–641.

Tharp, R., & Gallimore, R. (1988). *Rousing minds to life: Teaching, learning and schooling in social context.* Cambridge, UK: Cambridge University Press.

Thompson, M.S., DiCerbo, K.E., Mahoney, K., & MacSwan, J. (2002, January 25). ¿Éxito en California? A validity critique of language program evaluations and analysis of English learner test scores. *Education Policy Analysis Archives, 10*(7). Retrieved July 20, 2007, from http://epaa.asu.edu/epaa/v10n7/.

Toulmin, S. (1958). *The uses of argument.* Cambridge, UK: Cambridge University Press.

Troendle, P., Mandl, H., Fischer, F., Koch, J. H., Schlichter, J., & Teege, G. (1999). And Munics: Multimedia for problem-based learning in computer science. In S. D. Franklin & E. Strenski (Eds.), *Electronic educational environments* (pp. 38–50). London: Kluwer.

Trueba, H. T., & Wright, P. G. (1992). On ethnographic studies and multicultural education. In M. Saravia-Shore & S. Arvizu (Eds.), *Cross-cultural literacy: Ethnographies of communication in multiethnic classrooms* (pp. 299–338). New York: Garland.

Valdés, G. (2001). *Learning and not learning English.* New York: Teachers College Press.

Valenzuela, A. (1999). *Subtractive schooling.* Albany, NY: State University of New York Press.

Vygotsky, L. S. (1978). *Mind in society: The development of the higher psychological processes.* Cambridge, MA, Harvard University Press.

Warren, B., & Rosebery, A. (1995). *"This question is just too, too easy!" Perspectives from the classroom on accountability in science.* Santa Cruz California: National Center for Research on Cultural Diversity and Second Language Learning.

Weinberger, A., Fischer, F., & Mandl, H. (2001, July). *Scripts and scaffolds in text-based CSCL: Fostering participation and transfer.* Paper presented at the 8th European Conference for Research on Learning and Instruction, Fribourg (Switzerland).

Willig, A. (1985). A meta-analysis of selected studies on the effectiveness of bilingual education. *Review of Educational Research, 55,* 46–69.

Winkler, K., & Mandl, H. (2002). Knowledge Master: Wissensmanagement-Weiterbildung mit WBT. In U. Dittler (Ed.), *E-learning-Erfolgsfaktoren und Einsatzkonzepte mit interaktiven Medien* (pp. 205–215). München: Oldenburg.

AFTERWORD

Reflecting on Technology for Young English Learners

L. LEANN PARKER

University of California, Berkeley

The Introduction to this book began with the Red Queen's question to Alice, "What do you suppose is the use of a child without any meaning?" because learning a second language is about learning to communicate and make sense of the world and oneself through a new language. The central issue for this book is how electronic and digital technologies can help elementary school-age children from diverse cultures and language backgrounds develop the language and reading skills that are so crucial for negotiating one's way through school in the United States.

New technologies offer much potential, but can they fulfill their promise and, if so, in what circumstances? In order to offer some direction for our thinking about these questions, the authors of this book have analyzed key issues, considered specific technologies and programmatic examples, reviewed recent research findings, and have provided a set of rich, thoughtful and thought-provoking discussions on various aspects of these topics.

Some of the authors consider technology in relation to the characteristics, needs, goals, and linguistic and cultural resources of diverse learners; others consider its role within the larger historical and societal forces that influence academic achievement and the kinds of language, literacy, and cognitive skills needed to do well in school. Some authors examine technology from the perspective of conditions necessary to learn a second language and the possibilities of specific technologies to support those conditions. Still others focus on the research, discussing what we know about the capacity of specific technologies to support English learning for children. Some explore technology use at home and in after-school programs and the roles of classroom teachers and informal teachers in non-school settings. Others suggest specific exemplars of programs and activities, sometimes, to tease out key design principles, independently offering the same ones. Woven throughout the chapters and reflections is a focus on characteristics of technology-mediated tasks, activities, and instructional strategies that appear to make a difference for children from diverse backgrounds.

I would like to take the opportunity of this final essay to synthesize and reflect on some of the major points suggested by the authors. In so doing, I will highlight historical–cultural factors, perspectives of the learners, second language learning and technology, technology-mediated language-learning environments, and implications for research and teaching.

The Historical/Cultural Contexts of Academic Achievement and Technology

One of the themes in several chapters is the importance of understanding the larger historical context. Electronic technologies and educational software programs are not a panacea for helping children develop the English language and literacy skills that will result in school achievement. As Rueda notes in his reflection, there are multiple reasons why children from linguistically and culturally diverse groups are not doing well and are being left behind in U.S. schools. Difficulties with English are just one factor. School achievement and the learning of English are shaped by multiple historical and societal pressures and trends, such as socioeconomic conditions, low expectations for achievement, and schools with a history of low performance, societal racism, as well as linguistic and cultural differences (see Au, 1998; García, 2002; and Valdés, 1998, for discussions). Whether technology can be an asset for young English learners must be understood and evaluated with these contextual factors in mind.

That being said, it is also important to recognize the implications of technology for learning. Because technology is also part of the current historical/cultural context of life in the 21st century, it brings its own complex of imperatives to the education of children from diverse groups. Ideally, all children must be prepared to participate in the increasingly globalized world that advanced technologies are fostering. Digital technologies, especially computers and the Internet, have already had a profound impact on society. The Internet has become the major source of information and offers extensive opportunities for collaboration and communication around the world. Because much is in English, the Internet places a premium on the knowledge of English in order to access information and to communicate with others. At the same time, it has become increasingly essential for English learners, like their mainstream peers, to have an opportunity to learn how to use the Internet.

Moreover, as technologies change, they place new demands on literacy and comprehension, as several authors discuss. With the sheer amount of information available on the Internet, it is more important than ever in human history for learners to be able to analyze the quality and credibility of written, visual, and auditory information that they come across. In order to become active and successful participants in the global marketplace, all children–English language learners and native English speakers alike–will need to be able to deal with the information on the Internet, and to learn how to communicate through the Englishes that are used (sometimes from different national or cultural perspectives, because English is a major lingua franca of the Internet).

Thus, bridging the complexities of the digital divide and providing broadband access to the Internet has emerged as a major issue of equity. It is also an issue of economic competitiveness for the United States. The Internet and other advanced technologies can provide opportunities for children to understand other cultures and perspectives and to build skills in languages other than English for communicating around the world. Within this changing historical climate, it is crucial that schools help children learn to use new technologies and the Internet not only to increase their English skills but to use them productively and critically as citizens.

Learners and Technology

Another important consideration is the need to take English learners' perspectives, access, background resources, and experiences into account, avoiding a deficit model. Children's goals, interests, prior experiences, perceptions, and attitudes are powerful influences on what they learn in school, on their choices and uses of learning tools, and on the ways they interact with peers. Learners' attitudes toward school, instruction, the English language, and speakers of English, and their needs for oral English and literacy in and out of school are as important to consider as their attitudes toward and experience with various technologies.

For children who struggle with or who have been turned off by more traditional school activities, electronic technologies may stimulate their interest in learning by adding a fun factor, while at the same time giving them some control over what and how they learn and enabling them to demonstrate their learning in new ways. However, technology's potential to enhance English language skills must be kept in perspective. For example, educational software aimed at learners with limited proficiency may be inappropriate. Even if the software can adjust the difficulty level to some extent, it may not work well if learners cannot identify with its characters or content. Older learners may be turned off by software that they perceive as childish or different from what they believe their own level of knowledge, skill, or experience to be. Similarly, the utility of specific tools may be affected by learner perspectives. Although some tools such as portable electronic dictionaries may appear to be ideal for English learners, their effectiveness depends on whether children actually use them. More research could help us understand better the factors involved.

It is also important to consider the knowledge, experiences, and learning styles children bring to the learning task (Jiménez, 2003). Prior knowledge of a topic helps diverse learners make sense of often complex language in narratives with familiar themes and concepts (see Marzano, 2004, for a discussion). For instance, children interested in baseball may be more likely to comprehend a discussion about that topic in a technology-mediated activity because background knowledge has scaffolded their comprehension as much or more than the technology has. Children who like digital video games may be more likely to use technologies that foster learning through competitive game formats, especially in out of school settings. However, if they are more focused on the competitiveness factor than on the content, video games may foster little learning of English and content. Conversely, videogames may be an ineffective learning tool for children who do not like them. Thus, it is important for educators to select tools and educational software carefully and monitor how students use them in order to ensure that these technologies support English language acquisition.

Access is another important factor in assessing whether technology can serve as a useful support system for learners. Access is a complex issue involving such factors as availability of equipment at times that work for learners, technical support, and mentors to help learner use technology in productive ways. Although increasing numbers of families of young English learners own computers and are connected to the Internet (Fairlie, 2005), some children may not have the access they need for it to be a real learning tool at home if other family members also use it or if it is not connected to a high speed network (Ba, Tally, & Tsikalas, 2002). By contrast, other technologies, such as game consoles, television, and technologies already found in homes, might be useful in engaging children in English language and literacy development if appropriate educational games and other media are available.

It is also important to consider learners' perspectives about school and to recognize how difficult it can be to learn through a language one does not know well. It can be tedious, time-consuming, and disheartening to struggle with challenging concepts as well as new vocabulary and complex syntactical forms. A variety of tools to scaffold reading comprehension such as multimedia glossaries, text-to-speech software (in which the computer reads text out loud for the reader), and intelligent tutors can make the chore of slogging through texts in a second language less painful and faster if the tools are easy to use. By making reading easier and more appealing, technology may encourage reading and help children focus on comprehension in and outside of school.

In addition to their background knowledge and experiences, second language learners bring an important resource to the task of learning English: their primary language. Multilingual electronic glossaries and tools that link different languages interactively can aid comprehension. Such tools, along with Internet resources in their primary language, may have the side benefit of helping children develop academic language skills in their native language.

As Cummins notes, young English learners may also struggle with their identity and find it difficult to have a voice, especially in classroom situations that expect active oral participation by students. Technology may be able to play a supportive role in helping children see themselves as competent and knowledgeable in their culture and language of origin as well as in speaking English. For example, technologies used outside of school, such as blogs, chat groups, and fan fiction that foster personal and informal interaction with peers via the Internet, may provide new spaces for children in the upper elementary and secondary grades to develop their identities as individuals and help them develop their voice and confidence as English speakers, as some of the work by Lam (2004, 2006) and Black (2005) seems to suggest. It would be interesting to explore further the extent to which these kinds of experiences outside of school translate back into performance in school.

These examples suggest that the effectiveness of technology as a tool for second language learning depends heavily on learners' perspectives, access, personal resources, and experience. However, we need to understand better the intersection of technology and learner characteristics, preferences, and interests. Such information could help educators and developers of educational software and tools in their efforts to find productive mixes of technologies and educational approaches for particular learners from diverse backgrounds.

Second Language Learning and Technology

The nature of second language learning technologies is another theme addressed in this book. There are many technologies useful for direct instruction of a second language, for providing access to oral, written, and visual material related to the language and culture, and for providing a medium for communication and presentation of ideas (see Chapelle, 2001; Kern, 2006; Salaberry, 2001; Warschauer, 1996). For children, these technologies have frequently been used to provide practice and feedback on specific linguistic forms and reading skills, especially to develop basic or introductory levels of proficiency (although some uses appear to be little more than electronic worksheets). However, the authors in this book focused little on acquiring beginning levels of English, perhaps because English learners in the United States often pick up common vocabulary and other linguistic forms through informal conversations in and out of school, as Cummins points out. Nonetheless, the wide array and popularity of educational software for teaching beginning foreign language skills and beginning reading skills to children suggests that age and grade-level appropriate software may be helpful to introduce newcomers to English. A concern of several authors was that limiting the use of technologies to practicing initial English skills is an insufficient and ineffective use of technology. Even when fluent in some aspects of English, such as decoding written language, young English learners may not be able to translate those skills into fluent understanding of English in a textbook.

For this reason, several authors focused primarily on the acquisition of academic English. They highlighted the importance of English learners developing facility with vocabulary, the nuances, connotations, and connections between words, and the special uses of terms in different subject areas appropriate for learners' grade level. They also discussed ways that technology can be particularly helpful for vocabulary learning, such as in providing numerous instances of words in meaningful contexts (e.g., see Durán, this volume). Also emphasized was the importance of developing fluency in English along with higher order thinking skills in the context of subject matter content and authentic uses of the language rather than simply through decontextualized practice of specific skills. Multimedia explanations of complex concepts (such as animations of concepts in physics), and uses of the Internet for inquiry, gathering, and using information within a particular subject field, for example, can support the development of language with conceptual knowledge.

The authors also stressed the importance of activities that create comprehensible contexts for learning and involve technology as a tool for accomplishing tasks. Throughout the book are examples, such as computer-supported collaborative learning approaches to science learning (discussed by García), the project-based inquiry approaches (discussed by Cummins), digital storytelling and other informal technology-mediated learning activities in afterschool programs (discussed by Castek and her colleagues and by Durán), Internet-based resources and activities (such as those discussed by Cziko and Zhao and Lai), and specialized tools such as the e-Lective Language Learning tool (discussed by Cummins) and BELLA (discussed by Durán). Such activities constitute powerful technology-mediated environments that integrate contexts for learning content and for thinking, with learning through and about English. Important is that children are learning to use English in purposeful, meaningful activities through interaction and communication. A key question is how to consider language and content goals more broadly in order to design a comprehensive set of opportunities for children to develop their academic language skills.

Clearly, as several chapters emphasized, literacy in English is crucial, because in the United States much advanced learning relies on it. However, it is important to remember that classroom instruction also includes a considerable oral component that is often taken for granted once children acquire a basic level of English proficiency. Children must learn to comprehend oral explanations and complex directions and to participate orally. We need to know more about how technology can support speaking and listening skills to participate in lessons.

Learning Environments and Technology

Because context affects what is learned and how, the design of technology-mediated learning environments is a key factor in how technology can shape language and thinking skills for young English learners. As Zhao and Lai discussed, electronic technologies have become sufficiently advanced to create virtual environments that provide essential conditions needed for second language development to occur. New technologies make it easy to expose learners to nuances of the new language in a variety of meaningful ways, to enable learners to practice specific linguistic forms with immediate focused feedback on correctness, to allow learners some control or choice over how to proceed through activities, and to adjust content difficulty to the learners' level of proficiency. Educational software products employ a variety of tools to create these virtual learning environments for children. However, their usefulness in teaching the richness of language needed for school may be limited, owing to the relatively restricted number of vocabulary and grammatical patterns they teach, decontextualized from their use in different subject areas. It will be important for educators to determine when such software makes sense for individual students, but not limit English learners' experiences to those uses of technology.

Several authors also suggest readers take a broader look at the potential of using technology in rich, face-to-face learning environments, rather than focusing on specific tools or educational software products. For example, technology can be a catalyst for communication among children working on educational tasks together (Meskill, this volume; Meskill, Mossop, & Bates, 1999; Wegerif, 2004). Purposeful communicative activities that use what is on the computer screen to encourage English learners to discuss content or ideas, and activities that use email or other communication tools for learners to work together to figure out solutions are two possibilities for helping children advance their English skills. When English learners participate with fluent or native English speakers on authentic activities that require collaborative work, they are acquiring linguistic and cultural literacy—that is, they are gaining fluency in English and learning how English speakers use the language for these culturally specific tasks.

The importance of bridging learning environments in school with opportunities for learning in after-school programs and at home with older as well as newer technologies was another theme. An example is Zhao and Lai's vision of an ecology of learning that includes computer and Internet activities on a particular topic at school that are supported by related activities at home on television, videotapes, and game consoles. Another possibility involves creating informal but authentic contexts for learning (as in project-based learning) in and/or out of school that are oriented to children's particular interests and background and that create authentic situations for using English. For example, digital, or multimedia, storytelling activities enable children to explore a variety of technologies (e.g., digital cameras, video editing software and word processing) to compose personal interest stories drawing on their personal experiences and interests outside of school (see chapters by Castek et al. and Durán). Research projects, like Project FRESA in which third- and fifth-grade English learners used technology in various ways to engage in critical inquiry into their parents' work in the strawberry fields, enable children to advance oral language and literacy skills in both their languages (see Cummins, this volume).

Computer supported collaborative learning involves technologies such as animations, conceptualization and collaboration tools, and face-to-face interaction to foster content learning. This integration of technologies with content learning provides English learners with opportunities to expand their academic English skills (see García, this volume). Another strategy is to organize collaborative projects with peers in other locations; through email or interactive videoconferencing young English learners can try out their English skills with new audiences and learn to appreciate other points of view and cultures, all important understandings for the smaller globally connected, multicultural world in which we now live. Although it is too soon to tell, educators and researchers may want to explore whether simulations that provide opportunities for communication and learning, like *Second Life,* can be useful with young English learners. Whatever the context, the goal is to create technology-mediated learning environments that challenge young English learners to stretch their language and literacy skills in and out of school.

Implications for Research and Teaching

What are the implications of these discussions for designing technology-mediated learning environments? Several points stand out (Parker, 2007):

- Technology should be considered as a learning tool that is part of a coherent set of intellectually compelling learning experiences aimed at developing English language and literacy skills as well as higher order thinking skills.
- The focus of technology-mediated language learning environments should be predominantly on academic language, including the enhancement of vocabulary knowledge, the comprehension and critical analysis of written and Internet-based texts, and the speaking and listening skills needed for instruction and discussion.
- Contexts for learning in classroom activities or in educational software products should help learners figure out the meaning of the English used by others. Such conditions may include providing multilingual support and building on learners' background knowledge and culture when appropriate, as well as providing good examples of English used in context, opportunities for practice, quality feedback, and ways to individualize the content for learners.
- Activities should also be challenging, engaging, and focused in order to keep learners interested but at the same time to keep their attention on what they are learning.
- It is important to create language learning environments around technology as well as through it—technology should not be limited to drills and practice of specific skills; rather, the content on the screen can serve as a catalyst for oral and written discussions, especially among diverse groups that can strengthen English skills.
- Where possible, technology-mediated activities should build on the perspectives and on the linguistic and cultural resources of English learners. The usefulness of technology may be influenced by these

factors, just as comprehension is influenced by prior back-ground knowledge.

- Because extensive reading is an important factor in learning to read well, it is important to provide English learners with opportunities and technology tools (e.g., multilingual, multimedia glossaries) to facilitate reading of print texts as well as of Internet and hyperlinked texts.
- The growing importance of the Internet emphasizes the need for English learners to have access and opportunities to learn to use it astutely and efficiently.
- Technology needs to appeal to young learners. It needs to be as appealing and user-friendly as possible; otherwise, its potential for promoting English language and literacy skills is likely to be limited.
- Continuing to narrow the digital divide is a crucial part of this mix.

Research Issues It is also clear from the chapters and reflections, that, although we have learned a great deal about technology and second language learning, there is still much to be learned about uses of technology to support young English learners. Conducting research into related issues can help educators and educational software developers create better and more meaningful learning activities for children from diverse linguistic and cultural backgrounds. Because technologies change rapidly and can be used for multiple purposes, it is difficult for systematic research methods to examine their effectiveness (Leu, 2000). Perhaps more productive would be to investigate second language learning within technology-mediated environments, examining the interplay among the characteristics of the contexts, activities, challenges of the tasks, relationships among participants and their perceptions, and uses of available technology. Research appears to be especially limited on these issues with respect to children from diverse linguistic and cultural backgrounds. Applied and qualitative research could deepen our understanding of the role of technology in learning English as a second language regarding issues like the following:

- the impact of sociocultural variables on achievement or English development;
- ways that different technologies complement each other in language learning environments and factors that result in both higher order thinking and English literacy skills;
- comparisons among different approaches for technology-mediated interventions with respect to fostering academic achievement and English language development;
- aspects of learners' culture that are important to incorporate into educational software;
- children's preferences for tools and activities (e.g., games) and how they affect second language learning;

- uses of technology to support the full range of student abilities and language proficiencies in classrooms;
- the influence of the choices bilingual children make between their primary language and English with multimedia/multilingual software on their comprehension of content;
- credible ways to measure the effect of informal technology-mediated literacy activities outside of school on developing the kind of English needed in school;
- technologies that children from low income families already have in their homes and ways they might be marshaled to support English learning;
- ways to manage learning environments for classrooms with children at different levels of English proficiency.

These are but a few of the research issues that might be helpful in informing the design of technology-mediated language learning environments. As the discussions by Dalton and others in this volume have suggested, research methodologies will need to be flexible and strategic to enable researchers to investigate the complexities of language learning environments, rather than their specific technologies.

Implications for Teaching Teachers have a crucial role in designing and orchestrating learning environments. They will have to select appropriate technologies from those available, determine how to incorporate them into instruction, and monitor their effect on English language development as well as on other instructional goals. The key will be to organize instructional activities such that technology tools and other aspects of the learning environment can scaffold oral language and/or literacy development in meaningful ways. As Castek and her colleagues suggest, the role of the teacher is transformed from one of directing to one of guiding students in the process of learning.

There are a number of ways that teachers can incorporate technology into lessons to support literacy, such as having children use text-to-speech tools, create and view multimedia digital texts, and participate in collaborative projects over the Internet (e.g., see specific suggestions in the contributions by Dalton, Castek et al., and others in this volume). An important part of the process involves providing children with opportunities to explore new technologies in order to learn how to use them as part of their literacy development. A priority will be to teach children how to use the Internet productively. As Cziko pointed out in his reflection, there are a myriad of activities and authentic resources such as newspapers on the Internet—often free—which can support children's English development. Some of these may be incorporated into subject-matter learning activities. As discussed earlier, the growing importance of the Internet for information and communication makes it essential for teachers to teach children how to use it astutely, effectively, and ethically. Although true for all children, this priority has a special urgency for English learners, because much of the information on the Internet is presently in English and will require them (at least for the present) to have adept English abilities to retrieve and evaluate the information quickly and discerningly. It is also important for children—especially those from low-income families—to have opportunities to learn how to use other technologies such as digital cameras, PowerPoint, and authoring tools to present what they have learned. As we have seen, these opportunities can also serve as English language development activities. At the same time, activities to teach technology skills must be balanced with instructional goals. For example, assigning research on the Internet that results in mindless (or comprehension-less) cutting and pasting, or assigning PowerPoint activities that reward children's facility with that technology more than their ability to show what they have learned may achieve neither content learning nor English language development goals (although they may achieve technology literacy goals).

For the most part, teachers will need to design learning environments purposefully and strategically. They will need to be able to select technologies (including educational software), activities, and content. They will need to be able to organize participants in meaningful and engaging activities that motivate language use. As Cummins suggests, these contexts may be most productive when they provide opportunities for processing meaning at deep levels, build on children's knowledge and experiences, involve collaborative inquiry, take advantage of social aspects of learning, promote extensive reading and writing, and help children see themselves as able learners. Teachers may also want to find ways to use technology that build on and expand children's first language as well as English and to give them choices in using their languages, as García and others suggested. In addition to supporting first and second language development, such a strategy can help prepare children for interacting in the Internet-connected world.

This is a tall order. As always, teachers are on the front lines, every day, making hundreds of decisions while instructing students and have little time to add something new. Professional development—possibly embedded in technology-mediated learning environments as Meskill suggested—will be crucial. Teachers will also need clearinghouse resources to help them efficiently locate ideas for appropriate high quality activities (especially free ones). This need carries implications for the continuing collaborative connections between kindergarten–twelfth grade (K–12) and university educators.

It is also important for educators to recognize that opportunities to develop critical English language and literacy skills outside of school are important to help children keep up with their peers who have the advantage of English as a first language. Although access to technology at home is growing, it varies substantially and is still limited for many low income families. For this reason, schools and, where possible, after-school programs need access to computers and the Internet. Educators may also want to look at informal educational technology-mediated activities in non-formal educational programs outside of school for new ideas. Because after-school programs often have more flexibility than schools, they may offer insights into productive technology-mediated environments envisioned in this book and may serve as good partners with schools in this effort. Partnerships among educators, researchers, software developers, and directors of informal educational programs can continue to be helpful in making bridges among home, after-school programs, and school into a meaningful reality for young English learners.

Conclusion

Technology has advanced sufficiently in recent years to enable us to construct exciting new learning environments responsive to individual differences among learners as well as to their learning goals and the contexts in which they are learning. Further, digital technology and the explosive growth of the Internet make available a growing array of resources for language and literacy development. Although tempered with practical experience and recognition of the challenges ahead, the visions expressed throughout this book are hopeful and creative in recognizing opportunities for technology to support English language and literacy development at school as well as outside of school and in recognizing the importance of connecting these settings.

Can technology help children from diverse groups learn English and in the process help them to make sense of themselves and their world? One way to answer that question is to understand and assess technology in terms of the overall ecology of the learning environment—the complex context of interrelationships among what the learners bring to the learning experience, the participants, activities, and tools. What is powerful about technology for English learners can be seen in the vivid anecdotes about real children provided by Dalton and Vásquez and implicit in the descriptions of programs and activities described by other authors in the book. Two anecdotes bear repeating. Here is the story of Anita in Dalton's reflection (p. 159):

> …. Anita, a fifth-grade Spanish-speaking girl who describes herself as "nice, but not very smart" (Dalton et al., 2006). Her teacher confirmed this view, stating that Anita was failing all of her subjects and that "she is the kind of kid who wants to disappear and not be noticed." After reading the ICON folktale, Anita created a multimedia retelling using a 5-scene PowerPoint template that we had created. Anita revealed her storytelling talent as she audio-recorded her retelling, dramatically expressing the story in English. She proudly presented her retelling, taking a bow to classroom applause. Anita's teacher was surprised and pleased to see Anita in a successful learning context. Her view that Anita was a failing student with low learning aptitude was no longer valid.

And here are the words of Susana, now an adult, recounting her experiences as a child in the technology-mediated La Clase Mágica program, as reported by Vasquez:

> Being in La Clase Mágica helped me with reading and writing. Up to then, I had a hard time because in my classes everything was in English and I didn't understand anything. Slowly, though, I learned thanks to La Clase Mágica because I could also use Spanish there. La Clase Mágica influenced me greatly with my present interest in technology, that I now work repairing computers. I have five PCs, two laptops, and two PDAs, and everything I do is related to the world of technology. Learning to use a computer and the Internet helped me decide what I wanted to do in life. In relation to El Maga [the electronic entity], La Clase Mágica opened my eyes to a different world. I didn't know I could talk to beings in another world, which helped my imagination fly into fantasy and develop a curiosity for learning. (Martínez & Vásquez, 2006, cited by Vásquez, this volume, p.103)

These two examples show that technology can indeed help young English learners make meaning of themselves and of the new language and culture in which they came to live. Isn't that everything the Red Queen could have asked for?

Acknowledgment

The author would like to thank Charles Underwood for his insightful suggestions on an earlier version of this chapter.

References

Au, K. (1998). Social constructivism and the school literacy learning of students of diverse backgrounds. *Journal of Literacy Research, 30*(2), 297–319.

Ba, H., Tally, B., & Tsikalas, K. (2002). *Children's emerging digital literacies: Investigating home computing in low- and middle-income families.* New York: Education Department, Center for Children & Technology, Corporation for Public Broadcasting. Retrieved July 23, 2007, from http://cct.edc.org/.

Black, R. W. (2005). Access and affiliation: The literacy and composition practices of English-language learners in an online fanfiction community. *Journal of Adolescent & Adult Literacy, 49*(2), 118–128.

Chapelle, C. A. (2001). *Computer applications in second language acquisition: Foundations for teaching, testing, and research.* Cambridge: Cambridge University Press.

Fairlie, R. (2005, September). *Are we really a nation online? Ethnic and racial disparities in access to technology and their consequence.* Leadership Conference on Civil Rights Education Fund. Retrieved August 16, 2007, from http://www.civilrights.org/publications/reports/.

Fillmore, L. W., & Snow, C. E. (2002). What teachers need to know about language. In C. T. Adger, C. E. Snow & D. Christian (Eds.), *What teachers need to know about language* (pp. 7-54). Washington, DC: Center for Applied Linguistics.

García, E. E. (2002). Bilingualism and schooling in the United States. *International Journal of the Sociology of Language,* 155/156, 1-92.

Jiménez, R. T. (2003). The interaction of language, literacy, and identity in the lives of Latina/o students. In R. L. McCormack and J. R. Paratore (Eds.), *After early intervention, then what? Teaching struggling readers in grades 3 and beyond* (pp. 25–38). Newark, DE, International Reading Association.

Kern, R. (2006). Perspectives on technology in learning and teaching languages. *TESOL Quarterly,* 40(1), 183–210.

Lam, W. S. E. (2004). Second language socialization in a bilingual chat room: Global and local considerations. *Language Learning & Technology,* 8(3), 44–65. Retrieved May 31, 2006, from http://llt.msu.edu/vol8num3/lam/default.html.

Lam, W. S. E. (2006). Re-envisioning language, literacy, and the immigrant subject in new mediascapes. *Pedagogies* (3): 171–195. Retrieved July 23, 2007, from E. Lam's Web site at http://www.sesp.northwestern.edu/common/people/faculty/alpha/.

Leu, D. J. (2000). Literacy and technology: Deictic consequences for literacy education in an information age. In M. L. Kamil, P. B. Mosenthal, P. D. Pearson & R. Barr (Eds.), *Handbook of Reading Research: Vol. III* (pp. 743–770). Mahwah, NJ: Erlbaum.

Marzano, R. J. (2004). *Building background knowledge for academic achievement.* Alexandria, VA: Association for Supervision and curriculum Development (ASCD).

Mercer, N., Fernández, M., Dawes, L., Wegerif, R., & Sams, C. (2003). Talk about texts at the computer: using ICT to develop children's oral and literate abilities. *Literacy* 37(2), 81–89.

Meskill, C., Mossop, J., & Bates, R. (1999). *Electronic text and English as a second language environments* (no. 12012). National Research Center for English Learning and Achievement. Retrieved April 19, 2004, from http://cela.albany.edu.

Parker, L. L. (2007). *Conversations on technology in support of young English learners: A report to the William and Flora Hewlett Foundation.* Berkeley, CA: University of California, Berkeley.

Salaberry, M. R. (2001). The use of technology for second language learning and teaching: A retrospective. *Modern Language Journal,* 85(i), 30–56.

Valdés, G. (1998). The world outside and inside schools: Language and immigrant children. *Educational Researcher,* 27(6), 4–18.

Warschauer, M. (1996). Computer-assisted language learning: An introduction. In S. Fotos (Ed.), *Multimedia language teaching* (pp. 3–20). Tokyo, Japan: Logos International. Retrieved December 17, 2004 from http://www.ict4lt.org/en/warschauer.htm.

Wegerif, R. (2004). The role of educational software in teaching and learning conversations. *Computers and Education,* 43(2), 179–191.

Author and Name Index

Subject Index